Edward III [d.1377]

- **Edward the Black Prince** [d.1376]
  - Richard II [d.1400]

- **Lionel Duke of Clarence**
  - Philippa m. Edmund Mortimer 3rd Earl of March
    - Elizabeth m. Hotspur
    - Roger 4th Earl of March
      - Edmund Mortimer 5th Earl of March [heir presumptive]
      - Anne Mortimer
    - Edmund Mortimer m. Glendower's daughter

- **John of Gaunt Duke of Lancaster**
  - m. Blanche of Lancaster
    - Henry IV [Bolingbroke] [d.1413]
      - Henry V [d.1422]
        - Henry VI [d.1471] m. Margaret of Anjou
          - Edward Prince of Wales [d.1471] m. Anne Neville
  - Katharine m. Owen Tudor
    - Edmund m. Margaret Beaufort Tudor
      - Henry VII [Richmond] [d.1509] m. Elizabeth of York
        - Henry VIII [d.1547] m. Elizabeth of York
          - Edward VI [d.1553]
          - Mary [d.1558]
          - Elizabeth I [d.1603]
  - m. Katharine Swynford [orig. mistress]
    - John Beaufort Earl of Somerset
      - John Beaufort Duke of Somerset

- **Edmund of Langley Duke of York**
  - Edward Duke of York [Aumerle]
  - Richard Earl of Cambridge m. Anne Mortimer
    - Richard Plantagenet Duke of York
      - Edward IV [d.1483] m. Lady Grey
        - Edward V [d.1483]
        - Richard [d.1483]
        - Elizabeth
      - George Duke of Clarence
      - Richard III [Gloucester] [d.1485] m. Anne Neville

- **Thomas of Woodstock Duke of Gloucester**

Note: Two of Edward III's seven sons died in infancy.

Important Battles

Shrewsbury [1403] — 1 Henry IV
Agincourt [1415] — Henry V
Bosworth Field [1485] — Richard III

THE DRAMA OF POWER

The Drama of Power

Studies in Shakespeare's History Plays

MOODY E. PRIOR

NORTHWESTERN UNIVERSITY PRESS

EVANSTON, ILLINOIS　　　1973

Moody E. Prior is Professor Emeritus of English
and former Dean of the Graduate School
at Northwestern University.

Publication of this book was assisted by the
American Council of Learned Societies
under a grant from the
Andrew W. Mellon Foundation.

To C. E. P.

Contents

Preface

The English history plays of Shakespeare drew their narrative materials principally from the works of certain English historians, and the world in which their characters move and have their being is political. These two considerations determine the aim and plan of this study. Chapters II and V are intended primarily for those who are not familiar with the ideas of history and the political theory current during the sixteenth century. The other chapters relate the plays in various ways to these large areas of reference. In those essays that deal with ideas of history, the emphasis is on the possible influence of particular conceptions of history on the causal patterns of the plays. In those that are concerned with the political aspects—the greater part of the book—the various ideas about politics serve to identify the specific contemporary terms in which the conflicts are set forth in the plays and to define the choices open to the characters, and thus provide clues to the motives and compulsions which influence the conduct of political men in the world of power.

Even the most original and powerful minds are subject to the limitations of their times, but the substance of their thought and the appeal of their art remain valid and interesting for centuries. If we concern ourselves with what is of the age about their work, it is the better to discover the qualities that transcend it.

Preface

When we attempt to reconstruct the age by means of scholarship, what emerges for the most part is the common denominator, a synthesis deeply colored by the contributions of those less creative minds, the official ideologists, the popularizers, the shapers of common opinion, the propagandists, the second-rate poets, the slogan-makers, and all the other useful drudges who try to create a common intellectual environment for their age, formalize its sensibilities, and guide its conduct. Viewed thus in retrospect, the reconstructed constituent elements of an age occasionally reveal a queer cast, with traces of naïveté sometimes difficult to reconcile not merely with our own advanced knowledge but with logic and even with the realities of the life of the times that produced them. Looking back over the years we ask, Can these dead bones have lived? What this response fails to take into account is that what we have created to represent the age is a construct which, as it stands, does not reproduce any concrete reality; it does not take into account that these topical commonplaces of wisdom and piety, of political expediency and necessity, and of judgment and taste were once intimate features of a vivid life with all its excitement, exuberance, and desperation, and that they therefore gave out overtones to which a later ear must be insensitive.

Something analogous happens when, in applying our conception of the age too literally to the products of an original mind, we equate the necessarily simplified reconstructions of historical study with a still-living work of genius. Even if we were to assume that the ideas and sentiments that Shakespeare entertained were not very different from those of any ordinary contemporary, we would still have to reckon with the fact that he made use of them as a dramatic poet. They passed through his imagination and became embodied in dramatic persons who express their character through these ideas and sentiments, and sometimes fight and die in their name; they were illuminated by his intuitions and wisdom about what men are like; they acquired individuality by virtue of the uniqueness of the work of which they had become a part; and they were clothed in language which uncannily combines richness with precision. When all this has happened, the common denominator of his age has been rid of its local peculiarities and its naïveté and pedantry: it has been transmuted. To make the notions of the age the primary measure by which the plays are to be understood is not only to make the lesser the measure of the greater; it is to reverse the process of creation and to return to the plays the limited vision, the pedantry, and the commonplaceness from which the complexity of Shakespeare's forms, the richness of his art, the breadth and humanity of his understanding, and the transcendent quality of his creative powers have freed them.

From this reductive pitfall there is probably no simple or complete escape, but we can guard against the most serious distortions of the method by keeping in mind that, while we must always reckon with Shakespeare the Elizabethan, his singular achievement, to paraphrase Samuel Johnson, is that he has pleased many and pleased long. Our initial as well as our final view of Shakespeare has to be from a bias in some respects different from and even alien to that of his times. We, too, are confined by the specific attitudes, ways of thought, and nuances of feeling characteristic of our day; it is these we bring to writers of the past like Shakespeare who seem, generation after generation, to be always rewarding and hence always new; and sometimes it is the perceptions provided by our own thoughts and sensibilities that lead us to exciting discoveries in their works. The risk, however, is that we will bend a writer like Shakespeare to our will and compel him to speak our language and our thoughts through tendentious criticism and productions, or condescend to him for lacking our discrimination, like La Place who, though an admirer and translator of Shakespeare, could nevertheless write, "Le goût n'est pas de tous les siècles: plaignons Shakespeare de ne pas avoir vécu dans le notre."[1] To know more about Shakespeare the Elizabethan is to earn a measure of emancipation from our own chronological provincialism, with the expectation that the effort will lead to clarification and better understanding. The relationship between the discoveries we make in Shakespeare because of our experiences as inhabitants of our own age and those we make because of what we learn about the world he lived in is thus reciprocal. Whatever we bring to the reading and seeing of his plays in the way of knowledge, experience, and artistic sensibility is illumined and enlarged. This is one sense in which Shakespeare is not of an age but for all time. Critical study is useful to the extent that it helps us renew our appreciation of Ben Jonson's truism.

Acknowledgments

The author of a sizable work accumulates many obligations, and some of these are so considerable that it is as much a pleasure as an obligation to acknowledge them.

I owe a very special debt to Professor Erich Heller. It has been my good fortune to be able to discuss with him on numerous occasions some of the important issues which have arisen in the course of this study. Those who are familiar with his writings can appreciate how valuable and stimulating this experience has been.

The University Library of Northwestern University provided me with ideal accommodations, and the staff has been unfailingly helpful and considerate.

My thanks are also due to the staff of the Northwestern University Press, and especially to Ms. Mary O'Connell, for their interest and care in the publication of this book.

My indebtedness to the legion of Shakespeare scholars and critics is now so great that adequate acknowledgment would be embarrassing and practically difficult. The notes on a new study of Shakespeare have to be managed with restraint so that they do not become a drag on the main exposition, like barnacles on a ship. I have tried to give proper credit to those whose scholarship has provided me with the knowledge on which my argument

is built, and I have cited those whose opinions seemed significantly to support mine. I hope the notes make it clear that I am
greatly indebted to those with whom I disagree—I would not
have arrived so readily at my own views without them. Aside
from these considerations, I have tried to bear in mind the needs
of the reader, for whom the primary value of the notes is clarification, amplification, and an impression of the state of criticism
on the matters dealt with in the text.[1]

The preparation of an extended work on Shakespeare approaches a condition of infinite regress. Important studies continue to appear during the course of study and composition and
even of preparation for publication. The unusual interest which
the history plays have aroused in our times is reflected in the
number of books which have appeared recently, some comprehensive in scope and others concerned with specialized aspects.[2]
I have tried to take note of their relation to the present study
wherever it seemed appropriate and useful.

THE DRAMA OF POWER

I

Introduction

A mighty maze, but not without a plan.
— Alexander Pope, *Essay on Man*

Shakespeare wrote ten plays based on English history.[1] Of these, the eight which are the subject of these essays—*Henry VI*, Parts 1, 2, and 3, *Richard III*, *Richard II*, *Henry IV*, Parts 1 and 2, and *Henry V*—are dramatizations of episodes from the period of English history which begins with the abdication of Richard II in 1399 and ends with the death of Richard III and the accession of Henry VII in 1485. To Englishmen of Shakespeare's day this represented an important and coherent period of their past. The break with the medieval line of succession which occurred when Richard II was deposed initiated an era of political uncertainty and disorder that led to the Wars of the Roses and ended only with the establishment of a new dynasty and a new order under the first of the Tudors. The first historian to present this sequence of events as a unified narrative was Edward Hall, whose work, *The Union of the Two Noble and Illustrate Famelies of Lancastre and Yorke* (1548), was one of Shakespeare's principal

3

sources. The other of Shakespeare's main historical sources, Holinshed's *Chronicles* (1577, 1587), made extensive use of Hall and in general followed his interpretation of these events. The fascination of this era for sixteenth-century Englishmen is attested to by a popular collection of tragic verse-narratives, *A Mirror for Magistrates* (1559, final version 1587), which consists of brief accounts of the misfortunes of individual men who took part in these events, and by Samuel Daniel's *The Civil Wars* (1595), an unfinished attempt at an epic poem, beginning with Richard II and ending, in the final version of 1609, with the marriage of Edward IV to Lady Grey.

The order of composition of Shakespeare's eight histories does not follow the order of events. The first three plays constitute a trilogy dealing with the reign of Henry VI, which opens with the announcement of the death of Henry V and the succession of his infant son and ends with the victory of the Yorkist challengers and the murder of Henry VI in the Tower. The next play, *Richard III*, completes this sequence of events and ends with the triumph of Richmond, who will marry the daughter of Edward IV, uniting the rival claims to the throne, and be crowned Henry VII. On completion of this group, Shakespeare went back to the beginning of the saga, and in a series of four plays—*Richard II*, *1 Henry IV*, *2 Henry IV*, and *Henry V*—he closed the circle.

To talk about the plan of this remarkable group of plays is somewhat misleading, for "plan" implies a consciously conceived scheme which precedes the execution of its parts. We know nothing of how Shakespeare came to work on this material or why he composed the plays in the order that he followed. We can at best examine their interrelationships, in the way that a naturalist looks at the world of nature without presuming to read the mind of God. Within the plays themselves there are numerous indications of interconnection. The events which preceded the death of Henry V, dramatically announced in the opening speech of *1 Henry VI*, are twice summarized in the trilogy (Part 1, 2.4; Part 2, 2.2), with a review of the complicated genealogical claims

4

of the leading contenders for the throne in the Wars of the Roses. These accounts serve primarily as essential exposition for the plays in which they appear, but they call attention to, and so anticipate, the events dramatized in the plays that follow. Each of the first two *Henry VI* plays ends inconclusively, the closing episode leaving unresolved some issue which is taken up at the beginning of the next. The third part concludes the series with the death of Henry VI, but a play on the subject of Richard III is strongly implied. For one thing, to anyone living under the Tudors, the continuation of the story up to the destruction of Richard III and the triumph of Richmond would have appeared clearly called for. But Shakespeare had made the concluding play virtually inevitable. Richard himself appears first in *2 Henry VI* (5.1.140), and is so fully and effectively developed that he soon begins to dominate the concluding episodes of the trilogy and is already a familiar figure when he opens the following play, in which he is the central character. The subsequent plays are also tied together by the continued presence of an important character. Henry IV first appears in *Richard II* where, as Bolingbroke, he removes the king from his throne, and then continues in the two plays which bear his name. His son appears in both parts of *Henry IV* and then becomes the central character in *Henry V*, which is announced in the epilogue to *2 Henry IV*. It is a curious detail, probably a matter of chance, that the king who is the topic of the opening lines of the very first play in the cycle is the principal character in the last. There are other indications of interconnectedness among the plays in the series; the ties among them turn out, in fact, to be quite numerous.[2]

Each of these eight plays retains a sufficiently individual identity to stand performance as a single unit; nevertheless, the unmistakable signs of interrelationship have encouraged the belief that they are the product of a common inspiration, and that taken together they achieve a coherent design, often described as epic in character—in the opinion of one German critic, the only work of modern times which can be compared to the Homeric epics.[3] This Shakespearean "epic" has no single central character, but the deficiency is sometimes made up by assigning the central role to a composite character, most commonly identified as England.[4] It has also been suggested that "the central and continuous image in these plays . . . is a composite figure—that of the statesman-king, the leader and public man which Shakespeare builds up gradually through the series of the political plays from *Henry VI* to *Henry V*."[5] The idea of a composite "hero," at first glance striking, does not prove very useful as a critical device for exploring the individual plays or appreciably contributing to our understanding of them. It is chiefly interesting as a response to the impression of interrelatedness and coherence which the plays seem to convey, and as an ingenious support for the epic idea which has fascinated so many students of the plays. Regarded simply as a narrative, the plays suggest the epic in combining to tell the story of the founding and fall of a dynasty; one writer manages to include all of Shakespeare's English histories in this conception: "An exact title might be accurately stated as 'The Decline and Fall of the House of Plantagenet, with a prologue on King John and an epilogue on Henry VIII.' "[6]

In addition to being regarded as a continuous narrative of great scope, however, the histories have also been thought of as epic by virtue of conveying a central theme of appropriate magnitude, depicting the end of one national era and the emergence of a new one, or, as one writer puts it, portraying "the forces which, lying behind the rows made by vulgarly ambitious men, effect a change from one epoch to another."[7] This idea has been applied to the later plays considered separately, with the result that the second tetralogy becomes the epic of *The Henriad*: "In *The Henriad*, the action is the passage from the England of Richard II to the England of Henry V . . . the passage from the Middle Ages to the Renaissance and the modern world."[8] If the unifying idea is conceived of as primarily moral, the plays can be seen as a saga of crime and expiation, the design of the cycle a series of visitations of judgment governed by the idea of Nemesis.[9] In recent criticism, this approach has been fully developed in relation to Hall's interpretation. The events from the dethroning and murder of Richard II to the defeat of Richard III take shape in Hall's narrative as a grand moral spectacle in which the retributive justice of God moves, sometimes mysteriously but always relentlessly, to the expiation of the crime against Richard II, and God's beneficent providence provides the happy ending which relieves the English nation of further punishment and results in the founding of a new dynasty by Henry VII.[10]

The grander and more inclusive the unifying idea which the critic applies to these eight plays, the more likely it is that the individual play will lose some of its individuality and distinctiveness by being subsumed within the framework of the whole. Moreover, the most comprehensive schemes follow the historical narrative sequence, which disregards the order of composition. For these reasons, it is not uncommon to divide the eight plays into two tetralogies, a convenient arrangement which takes into consideration the order of composition and the historical chronology at the same time, and which encourages attention to changes in the two groups in consequence of developments in Shakespeare's art, and to the possibility of new patterns of interrelationships among the plays within the two groups. This arrangement, however, is not altogether free of difficulties. While it encourages distinctions between the two groups, it tends to promote an impression of general conformity within each group. One of the remarkable features of the history plays is the great variety of dramatic schemes and methods of treatment, which distinguishes the individual dramatic units from one another. *Richard II*, which opens the second tetralogy, has, in construction and in style, nothing in common with *Henry V*, which concludes it. The idea of two tetralogies locks the plays into two compartments which may have been simply an unpremeditated result of the order of composition. We have to reckon with the fact that the various formal groupings and thematic orderings which have been used to provide insights into the nature and meaning of these plays are in large measure the critics' inventions and not Shakespeare's. Like any critical scheme, therefore, they

7

may be retained so long as they prove useful in giving order to our impressions, enlarging our sensibilities, and opening the way to discoveries of our own; they may be set aside in favor of other schemes which compensate for their limitations.

Reading the plays in order of composition, one becomes aware of a radical change with *Richard III*. The most evident sign of the change is the replacement of a loosely ordered, episodic presentation of historical incidents and a broad panorama of characters with a tighter dramatic design dominated by an arresting and energetic central figure. These differences are, however, marks of an even more profound change: a whole new conception of the history play comes into being with *Richard III*, and from this point of view *Richard III* takes on importance not as the last play of the first tetralogy but as the first play in a new development in Shakespeare's dramatizations of history which determines the character of the plays that follow. The common characteristic of the five plays beginning with *Richard III* and ending with *Henry V* is that each is concerned with a particular problem of kingship in relation to legitimacy, authority, and the exercise and influence of sovereign power. Richard III gains the throne by guile, murder, and intimidation, and he identifies legitimacy with power and dissociates power from morality and public responsibility. Richard II, the king in the next play, has an unquestionably legitimate title by virtue of law and ancient tradition, but he uses his power as a personal indulgence rather than a public trust, and lacks the qualifications to make prudent and wise use of his authority. Henry IV, who succeeds him, has the personal qualifications for the administration of power and a sincere interest in exercising it for the nation's welfare, but he is a usurper and ultimately a regicide, and his tainted title handicaps him in his efforts to rule well. The first part of *Henry IV* dramatizes the immediate consequences of this anomalous position, and the second part shows how it affects Henry's reign and the son who is his successor. *Henry V* completes the series. This Henry gains the throne by succession and his title has at least a *de facto* legality supported by public approval; he has, moreover, the proper personal qualities for his high office and a proper sense of his responsibilities.

In these five plays every significant variant among the possibilities of sovereign power is represented. Taken together, they constitute a spectrum, each play one component in an exhaustive separating-out of the principal aspects of the central idea of kingship as the source of sovereign power and authority. It is possible to think even of *Henry VI*, retrospectively, as perhaps not unrelated to this scheme—a very special and unusual case, to be sure, but having some bearing on the main issue. Henry VI is a king who does not want to be a king, who has none of the personal qualifications demanded by the office, and who does not believe in the soundness of his title and therefore doubts the legitimacy of the power which he is reluctant to exercise. But Henry's is an atypical case, and the trilogy which covers his reign is significantly different in dramatic structure from the plays that follow. The three parts of *Henry VI* are the rich ore out of which the later plays are refined. In their plenitude and profusion they present many of the political problems and crises that can befall a nation, and where they do not clearly anticipate the issues which are involved in the later series, they clearly imply them. They are the great prologue, the spacious pageant which ushers in the more concentrated and specialized plays which follow. Looked at in this way, the plays reveal a pronounced political aspect, and the idea which gives a schematic character to the whole appears to be exploratory rather than doctrinaire.[11]

The founding of the Tudor dynasty gave to certain aspects of the English past an unusual prominence and placed them in a special relation to the new order. Henry VII, the founder, claimed an ancient heredity for his title on the basis of descent from King Arthur, but he won the right to wear the crown by defeating Richard III on the decisive field of Bosworth. The notion of descent from Arthur led back to the semimythical past of the Briton kings and to the body of pseudohistorical lore which celebrated its glory, while the actual means to power, the defeat of Richard III, recalled a recent turbulent period, well documented and fully narrated, which led directly to the new ruling house and the immediate present. Each of these eras was the object of patriotic and literary interest. As Edwin Greenlaw sums it up:

> With the accession of Henry VII the prophecies of Cadwallader, last of the Briton kings, were fulfilled and the realm returned to its rightful and ancient possessors. Furthermore, patriotic Englishmen were quick to see that the new dynasty marking the end of the Lancastrian-Yorkist feud, was far more significant than a mere change of monarchs. There emerged two themes. One, the tragic story of Lancaster and York, ending in the union of England, was the theme of Hall's *Chronicle* and of Shakespeare's historical plays. The other, the return to power after many centuries of the ancient Britons, was the theme of Leland and other chroniclers, of Warner and Drayton who combined chronicle with epic, and of Spenser's *Faerie Queene*.[12]

Out of each of these centers of historical interest a literary masterpiece emerged, and the form and mode selected by the poet in each case are artistically so fitting as to seem inevitably dictated by the nature of the materials and the poet's purpose. Spenser took the Renaissance epic as his model and allegory as his mode. He was mindful throughout of the political present, but he organized his poem around separate abstract virtues and alluded to the history and politics of his day through symbols. The closer we come, therefore, to relating the symbols to the persons and events shadowed in them, the more fully we realize Spenser's complex artistry, and the closer we come to understanding *The Faerie Queene*. It is otherwise with Shakespeare. The narratives of his plots are the thing itself—specific episodes involving individual persons who connived and intrigued for power, fought battles, lost and won crowns, murdered their kinsmen, and ended their lives violently or in disgrace or offered them up for the sake of their honor. The concreteness of history was sharpened and enlivened by the dramatic form into which the separate narrative episodes were translated. The individuality of each play is so marked that one gets the impression that Shakespeare had to reinvent his dramatic design for each one to make it a suitable vehicle for the particular action and its historical and political content. The history plays, though rich in meaning, are at the opposite pole from allegory. They gave a vivid, comprehensive presentation of the events out of which a new political order sprang forth, and at the same time they incorporated, in the dramatic conflicts they depicted, important political issues which had acquired a fresh significance with the coming of a new era.

One appeal which historical drama had for Elizabethan dramatists was that analogous situations from the past could be used to make oblique comments on the present, sometimes with discernible allusions to particular persons and situations, without resort to allegory. Shakespeare's plays are in one sense political because they reflected the intense political life of his times. Topical identifications at the most specific and individual level have, however, proved for the most part inconclusive, and in consequence more attention has been given to the political attitudes and ideas of the age, and to important changes and historical crises which may have left their mark on the plays.[13] Such knowledge, though interesting for its own sake, concerns the student of Shakespeare today chiefly as it provides clues to the meaning of the plays and thus to their proper appreciation. The farther away we are carried by time from Shakespeare's age, the more necessary becomes the recovery of local and topical elements as a guide to and corrective check on our own understanding, but at the same time the more remote such learning becomes in explaining our continued interest in them or our appreciation of their primary meaning. When we reflect today on the political interest of the history plays our mind is on something beyond the divine right of kings in itself or the idea of the chain of being and order as subordination. One recent writer has referred to Shakespeare's histories as "calculatedly political in very much the same way as Hobbes is in his *Leviathan*, or Burke in his *Reflections on the French Revolution*."[14] We do in fact experience in Shakespeare a breadth of perception which makes comparison with the masters of political thought seem not unreasonable. Shakespeare's genius is not, however, primarily theoretical; his insights into the ultimate nature of political thought and action reach us through his dramatic presentation of particular events and persons, and come to us clothed in their full human significance.[15]

In the eight plays which cover the period of English history from the reign of Richard II to the coming of Henry VII, Shakespeare encompassed nearly a century of turmoil, during which England lost her empire overseas but emerged with her sense of national identity heightened and her political institutions strengthened. In the record of these years Shakespeare found a wealth of exciting conflicts and dramatic situations, a variety of political crises, and a remarkable gallery of persons who walk through the pages of the history of these troubled times. In devising original dramatic forms to fit the circumstances and the theme of each new play in the series, Shakespeare was not only making a dramatic progress through a fascinating period of history; he was making a voyage of discovery. The record of the years from Richard II to Richard III became for Shakespeare what the Galapagos Islands were for Darwin. It was a well-documented story of a nation in crisis and on trial, a proving ground for institutions, theories of government, and the characters of the men whose destinies cast them in principal roles in these great affairs of state. The *Henry VI* trilogy captures the sense of the plenitude offered by this history. The five subsequent plays follow a more analytical design and take their place as distinctive parts of a comprehensive review of the nature of statecraft and the politics of power. The situation in each play is given as a kind of limiting case. The circumstances and the central character interact to define the particular problem about kingship and sovereign power in an acute form, and this pushing of the political situation to its limits contributes to the effectiveness of the works as drama at the same time as it sharpens the terms of the analysis, for it serves to maximize the opposition among the characters, with their individual inclinations and loyalties, and thus to intensify the dramatic conflict. In their totality, these eight plays present us as does no other literary work with a panoramic spectacle of political man in action.

II

Ideas of History

Historical drama begins with the historical record. What the dramatist finds in history is usually something more than narrative for his plots and the actions of men and women whom he can develop into characters; for the dramatist is subject also to the influence of the historian's political attitudes, his moral principles, and his view of history—in short, the organizing and interpretative principles which govern his selection of facts and determine the form and meaning he gives them. The principal sources for Shakespeare's history plays, Edward Hall's *The Union of the Two Noble and Illustrate Famelies of Lancastre and Yorke* (1548) and Raphael Holinshed's *Chronicles of England, Scotland, and Ireland* (1577, revised edition 1587) were in large measure guided by the providential theory of history, a Christian conception going back to Augustine and Orosius, in which the events of the past are episodes in the unfolding of God's plan, and the destinies of individual men and nations are the working of divine retributive justice. As this general view of history was applied to the English past, the political disasters and the wars of the fifteenth century were made to appear as punishments for the crimes and stupidities of certain kings and nobles and the disobedience of subjects, and the termination of these turmoils through the emergence of a strong and prudent ruling dynasty became a manifestation of God's benign plan for England. It is understandable that the Tudors should take advantage of this view of the nation's destiny and promote it in a number of ways to enhance their claims to sovereignty and obedience. The providential view of history is associated with what has come to be known as the "Tudor myth," a loose term which stands for a mixture of political theory, religious sanctions, official pronouncements on obedience, and other forms of persuasion and propaganda by which the Tudors supported their claim to the English throne and their conception of monarchy, and justified their occasional acts of absolutism.[1]

Shakespeare, it might be assumed, could scarcely avoid being influenced by this view of the English past, and an impressive body of scholarship and criticism has grown out of this assumption. Perhaps the most comprehensive and influential of such studies is that of E. M. W. Tillyard, *Shakespeare's History Plays* (1944), which relies heavily on the complex of ideas and attitudes summarized above in interpreting the form and meaning of the plays. Of the earlier group he writes: "The greatest bond uniting all four plays is the steady political theme: the theme of order and chaos, of proper political degree and civil war, of crime and punishment, of God's mercy finally tempering his justice, of the belief that such had been God's way with England."[2] The design of cause and effect in these events results from the operation of an exacting retributive justice that runs through the plays:

> What were the sins God sought to punish? There had been a number, but the preeminent one was the murder of Richard II, the shedding of the blood of God's deputy on earth. Henry IV had been punished by an uneasy reign but had not fully expiated the crime; Henry V, for his piety, had been allowed a brilliant reign. But the curse was there;

15

and first England suffers through Henry V's early death and secondly she is tried by the witchcraft of Joan.[3]

This theme, pervading all the plays, is the principal bond unifying the entire cycle: it is "the curse incurred through the murder of Woodstock, one of Edward III's seven sons, and not merely passed on but greatly intensified by the murder of Richard, that connects and animates the whole sequence of eight plays from the reign of Richard II to that of Henry VII."[4] Shakespeare would have encountered in his principal sources numerous pointed references to divine intervention and especially to retribution visited by God upon individuals, and even upon their children and their nation, for specific acts of wickedness or folly, but he would not have found fully expounded the precise providential design which Tillyard applied to the history plays on the authority of the chronicles. Moreover, fresh approaches to history were being developed during the sixteenth century, to which even Hall and Holinshed were not immune, which were, in principle, incompatible with thoroughgoing providentialism. It is reasonable to suppose that Shakespeare was not unaware of these developments and that he had in consequence some appreciation of the complexity of the historical process.[5]

The new history was written under the influence of classical, chiefly Roman, historians and of the philosophers and rhetoricians of antiquity whose praise of the uses of history was a source of inspiration; its principles and aims were repeated until they became commonplaces.[6] As such, the familiar precepts—the need for accuracy, the preservation of fame, moral instruction and consolation, and the like—might be found expressed in whole or in part by any sixteenth-century historian irrespective of his individual philosophy of history. The distinctive character of the new history came from its concern for causes construed not in terms of cosmic history and divine justice but in terms of the characters of men and the nature of polity and war, and from its bias in favor of instruction that was primarily political.[7] Some of the most celebrated of the new humanistic histories were the work of men on the Continent who had been personally involved in affairs of state during periods of stress and turmoil, and who wrote with a lively sense of the realities of politics and war and a vivid insight into the characters of the principal actors. Notable among these are Machiavelli's *Florentine History* (1532), Comines' *Memoirs* (1524), and, perhaps the most brilliant of them, Guicciardini's *History of Italy* (1561). The attitudes and methods of Continental historiography were introduced into England early in the sixteenth century, when Henry VII commissioned Polydore Vergil to write a history of England. Vergil's *Anglicae Historiae Libri XXVI*, first published in 1534, was widely used by all later English historians, even though it was unpopular because Vergil had rejected as fictitious the stories of Brute and Arthur, which had been appealed to by Henry VII in support of the Tudor succession. Thomas More's history of the reign of Richard III was written in the spirit of the new history, with its vivid characterizations, its worldly attitude toward political activity, and its virtually total lack of reference to divine providence and justice.[8] More's account was incorporated with little change in all subsequent sixteenth-century chronicles. It would have been impossible for any well-read Englishman of the times to avoid contact with the revival of the classical tradition of history, which was modifying and replacing the older Christian approach.

Although the philosophical differences between these two approaches to history are fundamental, most accounts of Renaissance historiography tend to exaggerate the polarity of the two schools as exemplified by representative historical works of the time. There is probably no example of historical writing from the sixteenth century which is purely and consistently of one school or the other. English historians usually regarded as providentialists, writing as they did during a time of intense political activity, often deal realistically and politically with individual episodes and characters. The following from Hall, isolated from its general context, has the characteristics of a historian who searches for his causes in human behavior and the ways of power:

17

> But whosoever rejoiced at this coronation [of Henry IV], or
> whosoever delighted at his high promotion, sure it is that
> Edmund Mortimer Earl of March . . . and Richard Earl
> of Cambridge . . . were with these doings neither pleased
> nor content. In so much that now the division once being
> begun, the one lineage persecuted the other, and never
> ceased till the heirs males of both the lines were by battle
> murdered or by sedition clearly extinct and destroyed.[9]

Much of Hall reads, in fact, as though he was not continuously
concerned with divine direction over the events he recounts,
and he avows several times a didactic function for history as a
guide to those who would be good governors in the hope of
acquiring fame. He begins his account of Richard III, "Loath
am I to remember but more I abhor to write," but he adds, "if I
should not declare the flagicious facts of the evil princes, as well
as I have done the notable acts of virtuous kings, I should neither
animate, nor encourage rulers of royalmes, countries, and sei-
gnories to follow the steps of their profitable progenitors, for to
attain to the type of honor and worldly fame."[10] Polydore Vergil,
generally regarded as having brought to English history the
disciplines of scholarly humanistic history, often pauses for providential commentary, and is sometimes as precise in calling attention to detailed minor examples of God's direct administration
of justice as Hall or Holinshed; for example, concerning the
death of the duke of Suffolk: "And so this William . . . received from God due deserved punishment, who, besides many
other foul facts, was reported to have practised the Duke of Gloucester's death, that by such mean thinnocent blood of thone
might be revenged with slaughter of thother."[11]

Even the acknowledged masters of the new history at times
sound like providentialists. Guicciardini, announcing his main
theme, refers to the "many years Italy suffered all those calamities
with which miserable mortals are usually afflicted, sometimes because of the just anger of God, and sometimes of the impiety and
wickedness of other men."[12] He also, though rarely, acknowledges the direct intervention of God, as, for example, in report-

ing the outcome of the debate over the form of government of Florence: "the prevailing point of view toward a limited form of government would have triumphed had not divine authority intervened in the deliberations of men through the mouth of Girolamo Savonarola of Ferrara."[13] Such sentiments sometimes appear with a disclaimer:

> but it was ordained, either by Good Fortune or the orders of some higher power (if men's imprudence and faults deserve such excuses) that a sudden remedy would intervene to remove this obstacle, since Piero de' Medici proved no more courageous or constant in adversity than he had been moderate or prudent in prosperity.[14]

This seems no different from occasional modest doubts expressed by firmly providential historians like Hall, but Guicciardini is caustic about those who attribute the devious actions of men to divine influence, as in his remarks on the election of Adrian VII as pope:

> Since this extravagance could not be explained by any sort of reason, they attributed its cause to the Holy Ghost . . . , as if the Holy Ghost, which above all loves the purest hearts and spirits, would not disdain to enter into souls full of ambition and incredible greed, and almost all dedicated to the most refined, not to say dishonest, pleasures.[15]

There is, moreover, no mistaking the fierce irony of his comment in his account of the horrors of the sack of Rome: "one could not but say that God's judgments were beclouded and concealed from mortal men, inasmuch as he allowed the renowned chastity of the Roman women to be so miserably and brutally violated."[16] It is apparent that Guicciardini despised the facile, simplistic applications of the providential view of men's affairs, and he must have felt that at times its use smacked of blasphemy, but he seems to have reserved some place for divine justice and interposition. As a student of politics at first hand, however, he does not organize his history on providential principles. Machiavelli also, on rare occasions in his historical writings, concedes the possibility of divine intervention in unexpected turns of events, and he even claims a specific instance of divine providence for his own much battered city of Florence. In reporting how on one occasion, when the enemies of Florence were poised for a destructive blow, the Turk began plundering the coast of Italy and thus created a diversion, Machiavelli comments, "But God, who always had our city under his care, caused an unhoped-for event to occur, which gave the king, the pope, and the Venetians something more important to deal with than the affairs of Tuscany."[17] When one reflects on the unrelieved succession of troubles which Machiavelli faithfully records, the only apt comment here seems to be the modern saying, With such a friend who needs enemies? Yet it is not at all certain that irony is intended.

The simultaneous presence of the two philosophies in the same work is particularly striking in Philippe de Comines, who has been called by his admirers the father of modern history. He discusses God's role in the affairs of nations in a series of three chapters, the heading of the first of which reads, "A digression, serving to demonstrate that Wars and Divisions are permitted by God for the punishment of wicked Princes and people."[18] The reason, Comines ingeniously argues, that the power of God shows itself more conspicuously against the great and mighty is that the poor and depressed are sufficiently punished for their misdeeds, but if a king violates his trust and abuses his power, "who can apply any remedy in this case but God alone?"[19] Among the examples cited by Comines are the misfortunes of the reign of Edward IV and the violent end of Richard III who for his wickedness was punished by God through Richmond:

> But his cruel reign did not last long; for being at the height of his pride, in greater pomp and authority than any King of England for a hundred years before, when he had beheaded the Duke of Buckingham, and assembled a numerous army under his command, God raised him up an enemy that destroyed him, and that was the earl of Richmond, a

person of no power, and one who had been long a prisoner in Bretagne; but he is now King of England.[20]

It is possible to suspect Comines of irony; for example, he writes of Charles VIII's expedition to Italy: "we may conclude this whole expedition, both going and coming, was conducted purely by God; for, as I said before, the wisdom of the contrivers of this scheme contributed but little."[21] Such touches of irony, if that is what they are, are incidental and do not seem to mock the serious providential statements. Comines was a sharp observer of men and events, he understood politics and statecraft, and he believed that history provides lessons helpful to rulers, but he also recognized an area in which he believed God's justice and providence could be detected. He appears to have sensed no contradiction.[22]

The strain of providentialism in these sixteenth-century historians can hardly be accounted for as an unthinking survival of traditional Christian attitudes toward history. One thing it seems to reflect is that, despite their realistic and even cynical attitude toward the political behavior of their contemporaries, they had not abandoned a prejudice in favor of a moral universe. Moreover, the providential idea offered a way of allowing for the possibility of some kind of order underlying the sometimes unpredictable and inexplicable course of human events. Summarizing the contributions of the medieval theory of history, R. G. Collingwood concludes:

> In a sense man is the agent throughout history, for everything that happens in history happens by his will; in another sense God is the sole agent, for it is only by the working of God's providence that the operation of man's will leads to *this* result and not to a different one. . . . By this new attitude toward human action history gained enormously, because the recognition that what happens in history need not happen through anyone's deliberately wishing it to happen is an indispensable precondition of understanding any historical process.[23]

The ancient idea of fortune also recognized that what happens does not always happen because it is willed and directed by man.

Fortune as an inescapable condition of life found expression throughout the Middle Ages in the emblem of the goddess with her wheel and as the theme of the *De casibus* collections of tragic narratives which recounted the fall of princes and of others whose state changed suddenly from happiness to misery. With Christianity, the idea of providence tended to absorb the idea of fortune, and the capriciousness of fortune was in this way made to seem understandable as part of a grand design not readily visible to man; but the two conceptions were never firmly fused. Guicciardini is able to say of an unexpected turn of affairs that "it was ordained, either by Good Fortune or the orders of some higher power." [24] Mowbray, in *Richard II*, says before the trial by combat, "However God or Fortune cast my lot" (1.3.85). Machiavelli devotes the twenty-fifth chapter of *The Prince* to the role of fortune in human affairs, and decides that man can exercise control over events about half the time. Certain chancy situations were notoriously unpredictable, chief of them war. Charles the Dauphin says in *1 Henry VI:*

> Mars his true moving, even as in the heavens,
> So in the earth, to this day is not known.
> Late did he shine upon the English side;
> Now we are victors, upon us he smiles. (1.2.1–4)

Guicciardini writes feelingly of these uncertainties:

> But (as everyone knows) the power of Fortune is most great in all human affairs, even more in military matters than any others, but inestimable, immense and infinite in actual warfare, where a badly understood command, or a poorly executed order, or an act of rashness, or a false rumor, sometimes coming from even the simplest soldier, will often bring victory to those who already seem defeated; and where innumerable accidents unexpectedly occur which cannot be foreseen or controlled by captains and rulers. [25]

The fickle goddess was a notorious hanger-on of armies; nevertheless, it had become practically mandatory for victorious generals to attribute their success to God and to thank him for the victory. For the serious historian the disadvantage of the concept of fortune was that it invariably suggested something wholly capricious in the surprising turn of events. It did not therefore always seem an appropriate concept to account for a favorable outcome in affairs of state for which ordinary prudence or skill seemed insufficient explanation, or for the consequence of an apparently irresistible train of events continuing over a long period of time. For such eventualities even the most sophisticated sixteenth-century historians sometimes found God's providence and justice philosophically preferable to fortune.[26]

There is, however, a considerable difference between such acknowledgments of the role of providence in history and the persistent preoccupation of historians like Hall and Holinshed with providential explanations. The difference can be illustrated by a comparison of Hall and Guicciardini in their handling of two unusual cases. The wretched career of Henry VI, a godly man, called for sensitive treatment from the providentialists. Hall summarizes two common explanations of the failure of Henry: one, that "he was a man of no great wit, such as men commonly call an innocent man, neither a fool, neither very wise, whose study was more to excel other in godly living and virtuous example than in worldly regiment or temporal dominion"; another, that of his enemies, which blamed "his coward stomach, affirming that he was a man apt to no purpose, nor meet for any enterprise were it never so small." Hall pauses—with an admonition from Solomon—to rebuke those who were unappreciative of the ideals and conduct of the king and judged them by the ordinary standards of common men:

> But whosoever despiseth or dispraiseth, that which common people allow, and marvel at, is often taken of them for a mad and indiscreet person, but notwithstanding the vulgar opinion, he that followeth, loveth, and embraceth the contrary doth prove both sad and wise (verifying Solomon's proverb) the wisdom of this world is foolishness before God.

23

Then he adds:

> Other there be that ascribe his infortunity, only to the stroke
> and punishment of God, affirming that the kingdom which
> Henry IV his grandfather wrongfully got and unjustly
> possessed against King Richard II and his heirs, could not
> by very divine justice, long continue in that injurious stock:
> And that therefore God, by his divine Providence, punished
> the offense of the grandfather in the son's son.[27]

This is the closest Hall comes to stating explicitly a grand providential design for his history, and significantly, he does not accept
full responsibility for it—"other there be." But he does not specifically reject it either, as he does the common-sense explanations
which precede, nor as he does with a few other scattered instances
of providential sentiment elsewhere. The providential explanation of Henry VI's sufferings is a touchy matter: it seems to say,
in effect, that God could not for too long leave the crime of
Bolingbroke unpunished, only just long enough to let the divine
vengeance fall on a naïve, gentle, pious, harmless man, one of
whose chief disabilities seems to have been his trust in God,
and this certainly runs counter to the simple moral pattern of
retributive justice which is the point of the usual illustrations
of providential justice. English historians made much of Henry's
great piety and goodness and called attention to his rich heavenly
rewards. Hall follows this line, extolling Henry's piety as a man
who enjoyed divine favor and whose holiness "caused God to
work miracles for him in his lifetime (as old men said)." The
disclaimer—"as old men said"—is a common trick with Hall,
perhaps an evasive tactic, for he makes much of Henry's saintli-
ness and uses it to lend authority to the providential view that
Henry's woes were at least in part a consequence of the sins
and errors of his predecessors: "this good, this gentle, this meek,
this sober, and wiseman, did declare and affirm, that those mischiefs and miseries, partly came to him for his own offense, and
partly for the heaping of sin upon sin, wretchedly by his ancestors and forefathers."[28]

The persistent concern with providential explanations of the inscrutable ways of God finds no favor with Guicciardini, and he faces the issue forthrightly in some comments on the quite opposite case of Alexander VI. He reflects on the disquieting fact that this detestable pope experienced nothing but good fortune from his youth to his death, and he uses the occasion to reject the common views of divine justice in history:

> A powerful example to confound the arrogance of those who, presuming to discern with the weakness of human eyes the depths of divine judgments, affirm that the prosperity or adversity of men proceeds from their own merits and demerits; as if one may not see every day many good men unjustly vexed and many depraved unworthily exalted; or as if interpreting it in another way, one were to derogate from the justice and power of God, whose boundless might cannot be contained within the narrow limits of the present and who—at another time and in another place—will recognize with a broad sweep, with rewards and punishments, the just from the unjust.[29]

There are phrases here which suggest a similarity with Hall, but the passage as a whole is in fact a repudiation of Hall's usual method. Guicciardini gives voice to the sense of shock to normal human sensibilities that such a monster should thrive, but he chides the pretenders to wisdom who will not face realistically the fact that merit is not always rewarded by God, and who look for a scheme of justice in which the virtuous flourish and the evil are punished here on earth. If in the face of an Alexander VI a sense of moral order is to be preserved, it can only be by a belief in God's justice meted out "at another time and in another place." Guicciardini writes of Alexander VI in the same analytical spirit which characterizes his history as a whole, but he acknowledges that in the moral sphere he confronts a mystery for which there is no satisfactory earthly answer. The whole passage is a pointed repudiation of the common practice of providentialist historians who presume to find the justice of God, for anything from an imprudent marriage (Henry VI) to a broken oath or murder, in specific cases of divine retribution, even, if necessary, in the sufferings of the nation or the guilty man's heirs. The English historians, for example, deal, on the whole favorably with Edward IV—Hall entitles that portion of his work "The prosperous reign of King Edward the iiii"—and in consequence the notorious murder of the innocent princes in the Tower is explained by Vergil, Hall, and Holinshed as God's vengeance for Edward's having broken his oath made at York and having condemned his brother Clarence to death.[30] With such precise providential accounting Guicciardini has little patience. Where the providential historians, in spite of occasional reservations and hesitations, found the meaning of history ultimately in the operation of God's providence and justice, the most thoroughly political of the new humanistic historians, like Guicciardini, though they acknowledged God's providence and for some events could find no reasonable explanation other than divine intervention, sought for the meaning of history and constructed their narratives in terms of second causes.

There is an instructive analogy in the case of the scientists and philosophers of science of the late sixteenth and seventeenth centuries, for whom Bacon's axiom, "God worketh nothing in nature but by second causes," would be accepted as setting the limits and methods for a true science of nature. Nevertheless, nearly all the leading figures in the new science occasionally expressed the conviction that behind the order which their investigations revealed there was the overriding intelligence of God, and that this order led inevitably to the Great Artificer himself and a true admiration of his works. Some even acknowledged that there were certain phenomena in nature which their methods could not account for and which could be explained only by assuming the continuous presence of the deity in nature. Such sentiments may have been inspired by piety, or deep philosophical conviction, or by prudence; but their occasional presence did not alter the primary search of the scientists for the laws of nature at a secondary level of causation. This parallel receives interesting confirmation in Francis Bacon, who was not only a philosopher of science and something of a scientist, but also a historian. Like Machiavelli and Guicciardini, he turned to the writing of history after circumstances had removed him from active participation in the affairs of his country, and he thus brought to history a lively and firsthand appreciation of what politics and statecraft were really like. Yet we find in Bacon direct references to God's concern for English affairs. One instance occurs in an account of the character of Elizabeth as a queen, "In Felicem Memoriam Elizabethae," published after his death. At one point, having reviewed all the special circumstances that preceded her success, he concludes, "All which I mention to show how Divine providence, meaning to produce an excellent Queen, passed her by way of preparation through several stages of discipline."[31] Bacon does not attribute all of Elizabeth's success to God: "Nor can so happy a fortune as I have described fall to the lot of any, but such as besides being singularly sustained and nourished by the divine favour, are also in some measure by their own virtue the makers of such fortune for themselves."[32] Bacon's *History of the Reign of King Henry the Seventh* is a modern work in method and spirit, but the first sentence is a straightforward providential pronouncement: "After that Richard, the third of that name, king in fact only, but tyrant both in title and regiment, and so reputed in all times since, was by the Divine Revenge, favouring the design of an exiled man, overthrown and slain in Bosworth Field; there succeeded in the kingdom the Earl of Richmond, thenceforth styled Henry the Seventh."[33] This may be simply the concession of a prudent, calculating man to a national myth; but we have to recall that almost without exception historians accounted for the defeat of Richard and the emergence of the obscure Richmond as an act of divine intervention, a view expounded even by Comines, a Frenchman without personal or political reasons for explaining the Tudors as God's special gift to England. Bacon might have felt, as did other serious historians of the time, that the end of civil war and the emergence of a capable ruler out of the struggle was more than could be accounted for by the ordinary laws of political causation, or as a lucky accident. That this view was encouraged by the Tudors may or may not have had weight with Bacon; but having made an initial concession to the limits of historical insight, he proceeded to write the history of Henry VII in a manner consistent with his many brilliant observations on political behavior and the principles of scientific investigation.

For the sixteenth-century English historian the providential view of history had a political usefulness which helps to account for its strong appeal and persistence. Applied to the events of the late fourteenth and fifteenth centuries, it provided strong support for the claims of the dynasty that emerged at the end of the Wars of the Roses, for if Richmond was God's appointed agent to destroy the tyrant Richard III, then Henry VII and his heirs were in a very special sense God's vicegerents. Vergil failed to provide for Henry VII a historical tie to King Arthur, but he calls attention frequently to the guiding hand of God in English affairs which led to the emergence of Henry as the national savior.[34] Hall makes the coming of the Tudors appear as a beneficent consequence of God's plan. Such readings of God's providence are unmistakably political and reflect the political preference, if not sponsorship, of the historian. A Yorkist historian would have placed a construction on God's plan different from that of Vergil, Hall, or Holinshed. In the *Historie of the Arrival of Edward IV in England and the Recovery of his Kingdome from Henry VI, A.D. M.CCCC.LXXI*, Edward IV is the hero. He is shown as a devout man to whom "God, and Saint Anne, showed a fair miracle; a good prognostic of good adventure that after should befall the king by the hand of God," and his divinely ordained task was to unseat "the usurper Henry [VI] and his complices."[35] For Sir Walter Raleigh, whose *History of the World* is explicitly providential, the sequence of divine judgments ends not with Henry VII but with James I. He judges Henry VII harshly for beheading Stanley and the young earl of Warwick, and as for Henry VIII—"If all the pictures and patterns of a merciless prince were lost in the world, they might all again be painted to the life out of the story of this king."[36] Hall and Holinshed favored the aspirations of the Tudors. Moreover, the providentialist implications of their history gave support to the politics of a strong, nearly absolutist monarchy, for there could be no basis for challenging a power which was shown to be a necessary consequence of the working out of a divine plan. Providential history thus reinforced the political doctrine of obedience. Corroboration for this view comes from the development of historical writing in France. In *The Idea of Perfect History*, George Huppert gives an account of the growth during the sixteenth century of a brilliant French school of historiography, sophisticated in theory and method, secular in manner, objective in attitude, and indifferent to miracles and divine providence; yet, as Huppert points out, with the absolutism that followed the civil wars at the turn of the century providentialism returned to French history.[37] In England, it was the sixteenth century during which political circumstances favored providential history.

Though compatible with the aims and political interests of the monarchy, the providential idea of history embodied in Hall and Holinshed was nevertheless at odds with certain strong currents of thought and feeling in the sixteenth century. The social, religious, and political changes which characterized the age and the stirring events which accompanied them aroused interest in fundamental questions of the nature of government and political power and consequently awareness of the need to provide proper guidance for those who were to manage the affairs of the state. In this respect, strictly providential historians suffered from a serious limitation:

> In their anxiety to detect the general plan of history [writes Collingwood], and their belief that this plan was God's and not man's, they tended to look for the essence of history outside of history itself, by looking away from man's actions in order to detect the plan of God; and consequently the actual detail of human action became for them relatively unimportant.[38]

29

If history's purpose was to trace the workings of providence in the acts and affairs of men, the instruction which history was expected to afford was unlikely to be essentially political. Hall and Holinshed fluctuate between conflicting aims. In contrast is Machiavelli's clear statement of the pleasure and profit to be aimed at in history, as set forth in the opening remarks of his *Florentine History*:

> If anything teaches or pleases in history it is that which is described in detail, and if any reading can be profitable to citizens who may be called upon to govern republics, it is that which reveals the causes of hatreds and dissensions in a state, so that learning wisdom from the perils of others, they may maintain themselves in unity.[39]

The passage defines the spirit of the new history. The new historians are sharp observers, and they are alert to the motives behind intrigues, the machinations of powerful individuals, the dissimulations, the strokes of desperation that animate the political scene. Their attitude is candid, and though they have their heroes, they do not idealize them and are not surprised to find human nature devious and selfish.

A theory of history functioned as a guide to the selection and ordering of the many events of the past, but in addition, if instruction was a primary aim, it also established a scale of probabilities of the possible outcome of certain kinds of actions, and the chances of success or failure. If God's justice and providence are presumed to be everywhere manifest in history, then the consequences of certain acts—a broken oath, a usurpation, the killing of an anointed king, or any other act displeasing to God—may be predicted with some degree of accuracy. Guicciardini, in making the point about the fortunate life of Alexander VI, in effect rejects this idea of creating order out of the past. The new historians concern themselves primarily not with God's ways to man but with second causes, and the past becomes understandable and the future less unpredictable by reference to human nature and the laws of polity and chance. History becomes profitable by looking for causes, as far as possible, in the characters of men, the nature of the state and of political authority, and the mechanism of power. This view of history had gained wide approval. It is how Camden, with an appeal to the example of Polybius, thought that history should be written: "take away from history why, how, and to what end, things have been done, and whether the thing done has succeeded according to reason; and all that remains will rather be an idle Sport and Foolery, than a profitable Instruction: and though the present it may delight, for the future it cannot profit."[40] Thomas More, in *The History of Richard III*, wrote of John Morton, who served during hazardous times and changing dynasties under Henry VI, Edward IV, and Henry VII and became archbishop of Canterbury: "This man . . . by long and often alternate proof, as well of prosperity and adverse fortune, had gotten by great experience, the very mother and mistress of wisdom, a deep insight in politic and worldly drifts."[41] Whatever else a discriminating reader might have sought in his perusal of history, one thing he looked for was precisely a deep insight in politic and worldly drifts.

The kinds of instruction expected of history are illustrated in a popular work of multiple authorship of the late sixteenth century, *A Mirror for Magistrates*, first published in 1559 and republished several times with additions until it received its final form in 1587. It is a collection of verse narratives all taken from the period of English history that is the subject of Hall's work, Daniel's *The Civil Wars*, and Shakespeare's principal history plays. It derives from a medieval literary form exemplified by Boccaccio's *De casibus virorum illustrium* and Lydgate's *Falls of Princes*, and in sentiment some of the verse "tragedies" echo the older celebrations of the capricious rule of fortune and the vanity of human wishes. It is also, however, in a special sense a form of history, and there is some preoccupation with principles of historical writing. The earl of Worcester prefaces his narrative with a plea for truth and for the presentation of causes:

> But seeing causes are the chiefest things
> That should be noted of the story writers,

> That men may learn what ends all causes brings,
> They be unworthy the name of chroniclers,
> That leave them clean out of their registers.[42]

Occasionally a direct providential moral will appear: a note to
the reader following Jack Cade's narrative affirms the doctrine
that no rebellion against a king is justified, but points out that
rebels are always agents of a divine plan: "Although the devil
raise them, yet God always useth them to his glory, as part of his
justice."[43] The dedication of William Baldwin, the original editor and compiler, warns princes that God in his justice punishes
those of his officers who are themselves unjust, with "shameful
death, diseases, or infamy,"[44] and refers the reader to Boccaccio
for older examples. At the same time, he lays the responsibility
for the welfare of the realm on the ruler: "For if the officers be
good, the people cannot be ill. Thus the goodness or badness of
any realm lieth in the goodness or badness of the rulers."[45] The
purpose of the collection is, accordingly, to encourage self-exami-
nation and reform for possibly erring rulers: "For here as in a
looking glass you shall see (if any vice be in you), how the like
hath been punished in other heretofore, whereby admonished,
I trust it will be a good occasion to move you to the sooner
amendment."[46] A Mirror is an earnest but, on the whole, not a
very sophisticated work; but in its very simplicity it shows more
starkly the continued presence of older attitudes along with the
newer enthusiasm for politically directed history and for accounts
of the characters and the destinies of men who found themselves
involved in affairs of state in times of crisis.

There is no simple way of summing up or defining the idea
of history which Shakespeare—or any other dramatist for that
matter—must have derived from the reading of his sources, since
he was subject to a variety of influences and attitudes concerning
the nature and uses of history, sometimes within a single work.
Shakespeare's principal sources underscore heavily the providential implications of their narratives, but there are also to
be found in them shrewd observations about men and politics

and, occasionally, reservations about how far a historian can push dependence on divine intervention and punishment, as in the following comment by Hall on the imprudent marriage of Edward IV to Lady Grey:

> By this marriage the Queen's blood was confounded, and utterly in manner destroyed. So that men did afterward divine, that either God was not contented, nor yet pleased with this matrimony, or else that he punished King Edward in his posterity, for the deep dissimuling and covert cloaking, with his faithful friend the Earl of Warwick. But such conjectures, for the most part, be rather more of men's fantasies than of divine revelation.[47]

If assurance about the minutiae of God's calculus of justice could sometimes be too much for Hall, we may safely conjecture that it was probably too much for Shakespeare. Only by imposing on these plays—with a consistency not followed by Tudor historians themselves—a rigid theory of history as providence and politics as "Tudor myth" is it possible to opine that "the political doctrines of the History Plays fascinate partly because they are remote and queer."[48] It is an observation belied by the impression the plays themselves produce. The variety and diversity of the political situations they depict, the panorama of vividly delineated characters enmeshed in affairs of state, and the astuteness and yet compassion with which these characters are depicted required something more than the view of man in history that Shakespeare found in the most doctrinaire statements of his sources.

III

Ideas of History:
1, 2, and 3 *Henry VI*,
Richard III

Shakespeare is so much a dramatist that he will readily sacrifice historical accuracy in matters of detail to dramatic effectiveness and dramatic logic. He will bring Henry VI's queen, Margaret, back to England during the last years of Edward IV and the reign of Richard III to act as a chorus, an expositor of past events, and an avenging nemesis; he will make Hotspur a young man about the same age as Prince Hal; and he will create a dramatic scene in which Aumerle's mother pleads before Bolingbroke and against her husband for the life of her son, although she had been dead several years at the time of Aumerle's plot. But where large issues are concerned, Shakespeare is certainly not without historical perspective and a strong awareness of historical differences and of the changes wrought by time. The world of his Roman plays is distinctly different from that of his English plays; his Romans are Epicureans and Stoics and conform to models more readily discernible in Plutarch than in Holinshed. Even within the English plays, the sense of changes and of differing times is strongly suggested. There is a strong impression of an older, passing world in *Richard II* which contrasts with that of

Henry V. We accept without resistance the idea of a trial by combat in the former, whereas in the latter it would seem clearly out of place and absurd. To what extent does Shakespeare also imply a philosophy of history in his plays, an idea of the forces which govern the destinies of men in great place and which influence the movement of the action and the form of the play?

Shakespeare would have encountered a philosophy of history in his two principal sources, Hall and Holinshed, and it seems natural to look for it in the first four history plays, especially as *Richard III*, which completes the narrative sequence of this series, contains unmistakable echoes of the providential sentiments found in the two main sources. This interpretative approach has had wide appeal, for the providential idea provides a common theme and a causal scheme which help tie together the many episodes and characters of the three parts of *Henry VI*, give a semblance of unity to their prodigal richness, and bind them all to *Richard III*, which completes the cycle and confirms the theme. However, the intellectual and artistic order thus created among the four parts is achieved with some loss. Is there not something specious about the unity which has been imposed? Does the view of the tetralogy thus achieved do justice to the originality and dramatic power of the early plays? It is necessary only to detach the three parts of *Henry VI* from *Richard III* to appreciate the force of such questions, for once the plays are given an independent identity the compelling influence of the providential idea seems to disappear. The grand organizing theme is lost, but as a result the distinctive character of the trilogy becomes more evident, and the series, loose though it is, reveals a shape of its own.

One character is conspicuously present in all three plays—Henry VI himself. As the embodiment of the sovereign power of the state, the luckless king combines just about every serious disability that can befall a monarch and haunt his nation. He inherited the throne as an infant—a classic piece of bad luck, in the opinion of all political commentators and theorists. He followed one of the glamorous hero kings of England, a handicap

35

which would have made any succeeding king look weak and unattractive by comparison, but particularly serious for Henry VI
since he was by temperament and inclination unfit to be a king.
To make matters worse, he inherited from his father a nagging
unfinished war in France. He also made a politically imprudent
marriage. His title was beclouded because his grandfather was
a usurper, and he was therefore intimidated by those descendants
of Edward III who challenged the legitimacy of the Lancastrian
claim to the throne. Every conceivable political danger and every
conceivable political complication is inherent in this complex of
unfortunate circumstances, and Henry experiences just about
all of them. Considering Shakespeare's youth and inexperience
as a playwright, his dramatization of the numerous possibilities
arising from the central situation is simply brilliant, though
along with the plenitude there is a corresponding lack of neat-
ness of form. Still, too much can be made of the formlessness.
There is a well-defined line of progression discernible through
the trilogy. The first play opens with a political struggle to gain
control over the infant king, and the personal rivalries and ambitions which are aroused at the outset and flourish in so favorable a climate are responsible first for the loss of France, then
for the collapse of political stability at home, and finally for the
outbreak of civil war.

In each play there is a dominant figure who provides a central
focus of interest in the midst of the diversity and even occasional
diffuseness. In Part 1, in which the rivalries and struggles for
power at home result in the loss of France, the most conspicuous
character in the military action is Talbot, who dies in a battle
which was lost because of the mean-spirited and petty rivalry
between York and Somerset. His death provides the final touch
of pathos in the spectacle of a useless sacrifice of the traditional
military virtues of valor, courage, loyalty, and honor, which are
helpless against the fierce personal ambitions, disloyalty, cynicism, and political intrigue which have taken over and will
destroy the nation. Humphrey, duke of Gloucester, representing
the political virtues of loyalty, honesty, and dedicated service

to his king, is to Part 2 what Talbot is to Part 1. We may suppose that this parallel was deliberate, since the Gloucester that Shakespeare found in his sources is quite different from the honorable Protector of *2 Henry VI*. Shakespeare's Gloucester is a dedicated, if at times high-tempered, civil servant, a shrewd and loyal counselor. His reliance on the inviolability of his own truth and honesty makes him a powerless victim of the machinations of the clever and ruthless seekers after power who systematically cut him down, neutralize his influence, and finally have him murdered. With his death there is nothing to stand between them and the inexperience and uncertainty of the king, and the nation moves toward the breakdown of all order. Part 3 presents the grim picture of the horrors of civil war and Henry's total loss of control and power. But, paradoxically, as the king becomes more helpless and indecisive and the conduct of the war is assumed by the queen, the very qualities which make him inept as king now place him in a central position as the only character who retains his humanity, and he comes to occupy the position of the compassionate and pure man through whose eyes we see and pass judgment on the savagery which has taken over. In the last scene but one, Henry is shown face to face with Richard, a character who has been growing in importance and vividness, and this juxtaposition provides a measure of the enormity of the genius whom the savage times have spawned and who is to carry his extraordinary but perverted abilities into the next play in the person of Richard III.

This scheme provides a framework better suited to a political rather than a providential interpretation of events.[1] The solemn scene which opens Part 1—"Hung be the heavens with black"—combines a sense of catastrophic loss in the death of Henry V with a feeling of apprehension for the future, yet among all these gloomy forebodings there is no trace of a suggestion that Henry V, for all his greatness, might nevertheless have carried the taint of his father's sin, and hence no foreshadowing of a doom hanging over Henry VI as the one to whom the curse of Bolingbroke's crime has passed and who will be the victim of God's justice.

What does command attention is the political danger in the new situation and the passions of the leading figures who will try to take advantage of it, for the grave opening speeches lead at once to the envious bickerings which, in the absence of a forceful king, will tear the country apart. The opening scene, moreover, establishes a standard of comparison between the virtues of the previous monarch and his rule and the deficiencies of his heir, a contrast frequently appealed to in the course of the trilogy. What emboldens the Yorkist claimants to the title is not simply the presumed legal taint in Henry's title, and certainly not moral revulsion at what Bolingbroke did to the Lord's anointed, but Henry's ineptness for rule. In pushing his claim in Part 2, York declares himself not only "far better born than is the King," but "More like a king, more kingly in my thoughts" (5.1.28–29). In his first speech of defiance York upbraids Henry for his failings: "King did I call thee? No, thou art not king, / Not fit to govern and rule multitudes" (5.1.93–94), and pronounces himself better in comparison: "Here is a hand to hold a sceptre up" (5.1.102). Edward, the son who takes over York's claim in Part 3, asserts that it was the king's lack of his predecessor's abilities and his impolitic marriage to a proud, ambitious woman that provoked them to push their claim:

> His father revelled in the heart of France,
> And tamed the King, and made the Dauphin stoop;
> And had he matched according to his state,
> He might have kept that glory to this day;
> . . . .
> For what hath broached this tumult but thy pride?
> Hadst thou been meek, our title still had slept;
> And we, in pity of the gentle King,
> Had slipped our claim until another age.
> (2.2.150–53, 159–62)[2]

All parties seem agreed that a Henry V, however tainted his title, would not have had to face such disorderly challenges as have marred his son's rule. Clifford is on Henry's side but, in Part 3, indignant at Henry's plea for patience while York sits in the

king's chair in Parliament, he exclaims, "Patience is for poltroons, such as he: / He durst not sit there had your father lived"
(1.1.62–63). He dies in the king's cause uttering similar sentiments:

> And, Henry, hadst thou swayed as kings should do,
> Or as thy father, and his father did,
> Giving no ground unto the house of York,
> They never then had sprung like summer flies.
>   (2.6.14–17)

Even the king himself, at the moment when, in Part 2, he is
threatened by York on one side and Cade on the other, comments
ruefully: "Come wife, let's in, and learn to govern better; / For
yet may England curse my wretched reign" (4.9.47–48).

Hall has a rebuke for those who attempt to explain Henry
VI's failure in human terms, setting these aside in favor of his
providential theory; Shakespeare, on the contrary, gives the
providential view scant attention, but presents in detail the
human causes for Henry's failure. As the plays move on through
the manifold consequences of inadequate leadership, lust for
power, sedition, revolt, and national disorder, it is the picture of
a nation in the throes of one of the major upheavals and political
crises in its history that stands out, not the fate of a nation under
the curse of God being punished for its past sins. Such random
suggestions of the providential view as do appear are muted and
ambiguous. In Part 1 there are a few hints of a guiding power
behind events. Both sides, French as well as English, attribute
their victories to God (1.6.14; 2.1.26; 3.2.117), but pious affirma-
tions of divine favor amid the chances of war were a commonplace, and both sides are repeating a conventional sentiment of
victorious generals. The sense of a preordained destiny is introduced in a speech by Exeter who, after expounding the natural
consequences of the "late dissensions grown betwixt the peers"
recalls a prophecy common in Henry V's time, "That Henry
born at Monmouth should win all, / And Henry born at Wind-
sor should lose all" (3.1.198–199). Joan declares, "Assigned am

39

I to be the English scourge" (1.2.129), and that is the sole hint that the English reverses are a retribution of which she is but the agent. War was sometimes thought of as an instrument of divine punishment, an idea reflected in Clifford's speech in Part 2 as he stands over the body of his dead father and invokes war as the "son of hell, / Whom angry heavens do make their minister" (5.2.33–34), but this speech has no general applicability, for its chief sentiment is that of personal vengeance on the slayers of Clifford's father. These scattered phrases have a conventional and rhetorical air, and they can hardly be said to add up to the controlling idea of the series of plays or provide evidence for a comprehensive theory about their meaning.

The one consistent spokesman for God's providence and justice is the king. He looks to God for support, and he accepts the trials and calamities which befall him as God's will. When, in Part 2, he dismisses Humphrey, duke of Gloucester, as Protector and assumes power in his own name, he places himself in God's hands:

> Henry will to himself
> Protector be, and God shall be my hope,
> My stay, my guide and lanthorn to my feet.
> (2.3.23–25)

This is more than the habitual sentiment of a pious man. Henry literally accepts everything that happens to him as the will or justice of God. His response later in Part 2 when he hears of the loss of France is, "Cold news, Lord Somerset; but God's will be done!" (3.1.86). At the sight of Cade's head he exclaims, "Great God, how just art Thou!" (5.1.68). His simple faith is the source of his resignation, and in a crisis he becomes infuriating to others, as at the battle of Saint Albans:

> *Queen.* Away, my lord! You are slow; for shame, away!
> *Henry.* Can we outrun the heavens? Good Margaret, stay.
> *Queen.* What are you made of? You'll nor fight nor fly.
> (5.2.72–74)

In Part 3 Henry gives up all pretense of kingly leadership. He awaits the outcome of the battle of Towton alone: "Here on this molehill will I sit me down. / To whom God will, there be the victory!" (2.5.14–15). When he is captured by two gamekeepers who command him in God's name and King Edward's to go with them, he resigns himself:

> In God's name, lead; your king's name be obeyed:
> And what God will, that let your king perform;
> And what he will, I humbly yield unto.
>
> (3.1.98–100)

These invocations to God's providence and justice serve not so much to establish the philosophical thesis of the play or the causal scheme which explains the sequence of events and binds the plays in the series together, but rather to establish Henry's simple, passive submissiveness and his pious acquiescence to the will of God. In the background is the image of Henry V, who bequeathed a throne to his son but not the temperament of a king. The opposing parties talk a good deal in these plays about the legal claims to the throne, but to the politically minded characters who people the trilogy the ability to rule has as much to do with the right to rule as the sanctions of undisputed inheritance and divine ordinance.

What is distinctive about these three plays is their originality and power in presenting in dramatic form the conduct of men in the world of statecraft and politics, struggling selfishly for power and the gratification of their private interests, under circumstances in which the established means of controlling such aberrant forces are feeble and in time break down utterly. The political emphasis of the plays alters the impression of Henry VI from the chronicles as the long-suffering victim of divine judgments for errors of his own (like his imprudent marriage) and for the past wrongs which he did not commit, to that of a king who came to the throne under circumstances which only a political genius could have overcome, and who by his own ineptness and indecision became a cause of the very evils he deplores. Politically the king is a dismal failure, yet Shakespeare manages to arouse a measure of sympathy and even, finally, admiration for this wretched saintly man, not, however, as a victim of the long arm of God's justice, but as the conscience of his ravaged country.

Beyond the three parts of *Henry VI* lay *Richard III*, and in the final play of the trilogy there are clear anticipations of the next play. The character of Richard introduces a fascinating new note in Part 3, and the full outline of the man emerges in his remarkable soliloquy in act 3. There also appear, late in the play, foreshadowings of the events and conclusion of *Richard III* in a manner that suggests the presence of a guiding force beyond the passions, ambitions, and wiles of men. Henry marks a youth in the care of Somerset, and on learning that it is Henry, earl of Richmond, he lays his hand on the youth's head and pronounces him the future king:

> Come hither, England's hope. If secret powers
> Suggest but truth to my divining thoughts,
> This pretty lad will prove our country's bliss.
> His looks are full of peaceful majesty;
> His head by nature framed to wear a crown,
> His hand to wield a sceptre; and himself
> Likely in time to bless a regal throne.
> Make much of him, my lords, for this is he
> Must help you more than you are hurt by me.
> (4.6.68–76)

During Part 3 Henry's piety and humanity set him so completely apart from others that his speech at this point has the effect not of a personal hope but of a prophecy from a specially endowed man for this youth whom he seems not to have seen before. Somerset calls it a "presaging prophecy" (4.6.92). The same quality of prescience, rather than simply shrewd political prognosis, animates his speech to Richard before his death:

> And thus I prophesy: that many a thousand
> Which now mistrust no parcel of my fear,

> And many an old man's sigh, and many a widow's,
> And many an orphan's water-standing eye—
> Men for their sons', wives for their husbands',
> Orphans for their parents' timeless death—
> Shall rue the hour that ever thou wast born.
>
> (5.6.37–43)

Richard interrupts Henry's recital of the prodigies which attended his birth by striking down the king with his dagger: "I'll hear no more. Die, prophet, in thy speech. / For this amongst the rest was I ordained" (5.6.57–58). It is typical of Richard that the last line should carry a fleer at the prophetic pretensions of Henry, yet in context the line becomes a part of Henry's inspired projection of the future and suggests that Henry is indeed the mouthpiece of an ordaining power. These speeches, coming at the end of the series, do not, however, color retrospectively the events of the *Henry VI* plays, but rather they cast their shadow ahead to the next play.

Richard III is more thoroughly permeated by suggestions of a providential order and the operations of divine retributive justice than any of the other history plays. It is as the instrument of God's vengeance and of the fulfillment of his will that Richmond prays before the battle of Bosworth Field:

> O thou whose captain I account myself,
> Look on my forces with a gracious eye!
> Put in their hands thy bruising irons of wrath,
> That they may crush down with a heavy fall
> The usurping helmets of our adversaries!
> Make us thy ministers of chastisement,
> That we may praise thee in the victory!
>
> (5.3.109–15)

The fact that Richmond has played no part so far in the action, that there is no detailed presentation of his claims to the throne (unique in this respect among all the monarchs in the histories), and that he emerges as a victor with little dramatic preparation for this role (compare the build up of Malcolm and Macduff in *Macbeth*) removes this speech from any association with aspects

43

of character or political controversy. Shakespeare follows the virtually universal disposition of his age in regarding the career of Richard and his defeat by the future Henry VII, who brought peace and unity and established the new Tudor dynasty, as an order of events which was not readily explicable by the probabilities that usually govern events in affairs of state, and which could be accounted for only by assuming divine intervention. Throughout the play there are prophecies of dire events that will ensue, laments over the consequences of former crimes, and appeals to God's justice to right old and new wrongs. It has accordingly become a commonplace of recent criticism to view the action of the play as the unfolding of the providential theme; for example:

> In this play Shakespeare dramatizes the fall of the evil prince and the restoration of political order through the marriage of Richmond and Elizabeth. This is, of course, Hall's theme. . . . The historical theme is counterpointed by the theme of expiation. Margaret becomes an Old Testament prophetess, the ghosts become divine agents; and behind the dramatic action we sense the hand of providence.[3]

Such statements are not so much wrong as oversimplified. God's providence and justice are frequently appealed to, but *Richard III* is not a play whose form and meaning result from adherence to the providential thesis as exemplified in Hall and Holinshed. It is more in the nature of a dramatic examination of the concept.

The issue of God's retributive justice enters the play directly in the third and fourth scenes of act 1. The third scene begins with the factious quarrels of the court, and is then dominated by Margaret, Henry VI's widow, and her imprecations and curses on those who have reaped the fruits of her defeat. The fourth scene begins with Clarence's recital of his dream to his keeper, Brakenbury, which is followed by his murder, carried out on his brother Gloucester's orders. What connects the scene of the murder with the preceding scene is the lengthy discussion of

44

crime and punishment, of duty to the king's law and to God's, and of justice and vengeance, which takes place between Clarence and the two murderers. This debate, following closely on the prophecies and curses of Margaret, reflects back on the previous scene as a commentary on the whole question of divine and human justice and revenge raised by Margaret's performance, as well as by Clarence's crimes, and indeed by the entire play.

Clarence construes his dream as the prompting of conscience for wrongs he has committed, for which, he believes, he stands in jeopardy of divine vengeance:

> Ah, keeper, keeper, I have done these things
> That now give evidence against my soul
> For Edward's sake, and see how he requites me!
> O God! if my deep prayers cannot appease thee,
> But thou wilt be avenged on my misdeeds,
> Yet execute thy wrath in me alone.
> O, spare my guiltless wife and my poor children.
>
> (1.4.66–72)

If nothing had intervened between this speech and Clarence's murder, the clear implication would have been that God had indeed avenged himself on Clarence's misdeeds and that the hired assassins and ultimately Gloucester who hired them were the divine instruments. But the murderers do not act simply as killers; they assume the role of subtle disputants, for which purpose they take on a new character. The sudden change in the tone of their speeches, from the comic banter of common men to the solemn accents of their replies to Clarence, endows the debate with great seriousness. They first alter their role from that of hired thugs to instruments of the king's power:

> *Clarence.* Thy voice is thunder, but thy looks are humble.
> *First Murderer.* My voice is now the King's, my looks
>   mine own.
>
> (1.4.166–67)

Yet neither in their minds nor in Clarence's is their act an official execution, and they do not challenge his use of the word "murder" for what they are about to do. Clarence's insistence on his innocence—in spite of his confession to his keeper of a guilty soul—is thus technically correct, because Clarence uses the word "innocent" in the sense of not having been found guilty in accordance with the forms of law:

> Are you drawn forth among a world of men
> To slay the innocent? What is my offense?
> Where is the evidence that doth accuse me?
> What lawful quest have given their verdict up
> Unto the frowning judge? Or who pronounced
> The bitter sentence of poor Clarence's death?
> Before I be convict by course of law,
> To threaten me with death is most unlawful.
>
> (1.4.180–87)

In these circumstances their act will be a crime: "The deed you undertake is damnable" (1.4.191). Their defense is that "he that hath commanded is our king" (1.4.193). To which Clarence replies—in an argument that calls to mind one of the great issues of our own times—that loyalty and duty to a secular power cannot be used as an excuse for violating higher laws of God or conscience or humanity:

> Erroneous vassals! The great king of kings
> Hath in the table of his law commanded
> That thou shalt do no murder. Will you then
> Spurn at his edict and fulfill a man's?
> Take heed; for he holds vengeance in his hand
> To hurl upon their heads that break the law.
>
> (1.4.194–99)

The concluding two lines shift the issue from the execution of human justice to God's own way with those who transgress his law; but the murderers turn the argument against Clarence:

> And the same vengeance doth he hurl on thee
> For false forswearing and for murder too.
> . . . .

How canst thou urge God's dreadful law to us
When thou hast broke it in such dear degree?

(1.4.200–201; 208–9)

They now speak not as obedient instruments of the king's commands but as agents of God's vengeance on Clarence, the vengeance he feared in his speech of remorse to Brakenbury. Clarence rejects their argument: God executes his vengeance not secretly or lawlessly:

If God will be avenged for the deed,
O, know you yet he doth it publicly.
Take not the quarrel from his powerful arm.
He needs no indirect or lawless course
To cut off those that have offended him.

(1.4.214–18)

But the murderers refute Clarence from his own past:

Who made thee then a bloody minister
When gallant-springing brave Plantagenet
That princely novice, was struck down by thee?

(1.4.219–21)

Does this imply that Clarence, having then taken the right to vengeance on himself, cannot now with justice complain when others assume the same right against him? Or does it mean, as the word "minister" suggests, that just as Clarence, while supporting Edward's fight for the crown, became the means by which the Lancastrians were punished for their former crimes, so the murderers, hired by Gloucester in the name of Edward IV, become God's agents to punish Clarence for his crime committed as avenger? When the murderers inform Clarence that Gloucester has betrayed him, and urge him to make his peace with God, Clarence returns to his first argument, that murder is damnable:

Have you that holy feeling in your souls
To counsel me to make my peace with God,

47

And are you yet to your own souls so blind
That you will war with God by murdering me?
(1.4.250–53)

If all murder is against God, then it cannot be God's way of
achieving his own justice. Clarence warns them, too, that even
in worldly terms they will fail, since "they that set you on / To
do this deed will hate you for the deed" (1.4.254–55). At this
point the Second Murderer hesitates: "What shall we do?"
(1.4.256). Now the style changes again; the murderers speak once
more like ordinary men hired to do a dirty job, and the performance of the murder shows it for what it is, a brutal act which
leaves the Second Murderer penitent and unwilling to share
in its rewards:

A bloody deed and desperately dispatched!
How fain, like Pilate, would I wash my hands
Of this most grievous murder!
(1.4.271–73)

Measured against the simple, naïve assurance of Hall and Holinshed, this scene stands out for its subtlety and penetration in
confronting a commonplace of the age. It does not encourage
a dogmatic resolution of the debate that it contains, but for that
very reason it demonstrates that Shakespeare was fully aware of
the difficulties, intellectual and human, inherent in the idea of
God's retributive justice and providence in the affairs of men.[4]
It also provides a gauge with which to measure the self-appointed
proclaimers and interpreters of God's justice who populate
this play.

The counterpoint of curses and prophecies that recall the past
and prognosticate the future enters with dramatic flourish when
Queen Margaret, against all historical authority, walks on the
scene to interrupt the wrangling between Richard and Edward's
queen and her relatives. Though divided among themselves, they
all unite to turn on her, and she appreciates the irony:

> What! were you snarling all before I came,
> Ready to catch each other by the throat,
> And turn you all your hatred now on me?
>
> (1.3.188–90)

It is a fierce scene in which almost nothing is spoken in reason but nearly all in venomous hatred, self-justification, and lust for vengeance. Margaret's first speech—an aside to Elizabeth's plaint, "Small joy have I in being England's queen" (1.3.110)— is a prayer that her successor may be further plagued: "And lessened be that small, God I beseech him! / Thy honor, state, and seat is due to me" (1.3.111–12). She makes her appearance before them to challenge their right to her privileges and to demand an eye-for-an-eye measure of compensation for her wrongs: "A husband and a son thou ow'st to me, / And thou a kingdom; all of you allegiance," (1.3.170–71). But the calculus of blood vengeance is not that simple. Richard reminds her of the curse his father laid on her when she crowned York with the paper crown and offered him a handkerchief steeped in the blood of his son to dry his tears; and now, by the rigid mechanism of the moral world according to the view of it which all seem to share with Margaret, the curse has fallen on her, and Richard is not behind the rest in pointing out this harsh divine logic: "God, not we, hath plagued thy bloody deed" (1.3.181). Elizabeth for the moment joins with her mortal enemy to second this pious judgment: "So just is God to right the innocent" (1.3.182). And all the others express their horror at the recollection of Margaret's bloody deed. But Margaret has her own way of calculating the exchange:

> Did York's dread curse prevail so much with heaven,
> That Henry's death, my lovely Edward's death,
> Their kingdom's loss, my woeful banishment,
> Should all but answer for that peevish brat?
>
> (1.3.191–94)

If York's curse can result in such large dividends, then she shall ask for her share: "Can curses pierce the clouds and enter

49

heaven? / Why then, give way, dull clouds, to my quick curses"
(1.3.195–96). So she proceeds to address her demands to heaven
for the death of Edward IV by surfeit, for the death of Elizabeth's
son Edward for her Edward, for the prolonged suffering and
sorrow of Elizabeth, and for the violent deaths of Rivers, Dorset,
and Hastings because they stood by when her son was killed. The
climax is a long, fierce denunciation of and curse on Richard,
and a final warning to Buckingham. Her hopes for success rest
on her belief that these her prayers will reach God: "I will not
think but they ascend the sky / And there awake God's gentle-
sleeping peace" (1.3.287–88). Because her curses sum up precisely the fate that awaits all the principal characters, she has been
generally regarded as an inspired prophetess brought into the
play against the facts of history to give choral voice to its providential meaning. But can we assume that her lust for retributive
vengeance binds or anticipates or correctly interprets the justice
of God?[5] The debate between Clarence and his murderers in the
scene which immediately follows casts doubt on such simplicities.

There is something perverse and even blasphemous in the way
the characters in the third scene bandy about their rights in the
scheme of God's dispensation of justice. Margaret does not pray
for justice but for revenge with interest. She dismisses the killing
of Rutland as merely getting rid of a "peevish brat," not worth
all that York's curses got in exchange—though if that is the way
the system works, then she is now entitled to more and will ask
for it. She exults when she learns of the death of the child prince—
it has evened up the score: "Plantagenet doth quit Plantagenet, /
Edward for Edward pays a dying debt" (4.4.20–21). And in what
must be one of the ugliest prayers ever uttered, she thanks God
for Richard because he is the agent of this gratifying justice:

> O, upright, just, and true-disposing God,
> How do I thank thee that this carnal cur
> Preys on the issue of his mother's body
> And makes her pewfellow with others' moan!
>
> (4.4.55–58)

The belief of these characters in a divine justice is entirely self-serving, without a serious ethical base. In the moral logic to which they appeal, a broken oath brings about necessary punishment irrespective of the merit or purpose of the oath, and a curse on an enemy for a real or presumed wrong places a judgment on him which must be paid in full. Condemned to death by Richard, Rivers proclaims his guiltlessness, but Grey looks on their doom as the fulfillment of Margaret's curse "When she exclaimed on Hastings, you and I, / For standing by when Richard stabbed her son" (3.3.16–17); and hearing this, Rivers takes comfort that on the same terms his enemies too will die, and he reminds God of this outstanding account before he is led off to execution:

> Then cursed she Richard, then cursed she Buckingham,
> Then cursed she Hastings. O, remember, God,
> To hear her prayer for them, as now for us!
> And for my sister and her princely sons,
> Be satisfied, dear God, with our true blood,
> Which, as thou knowest, unjustly must be spilt.
>   (3.3.18–23)

If he is guiltless, it is remarkable that justice should require his death, and if his fate leads him to hope for a similar fate for his enemies it is also remarkable that he takes the trouble to intercede for Elizabeth and her sons who seem to be caught up in the same mechanism. For these people, living in a frightful and disordered world, belief in the operation of a divine retributive justice provides a sense of moral order, mechanical and perverse but dependable; but it helps keep alive the urge for private vengeance and relieves them of a feeling of responsibility for wrongs suffered by others—"So just is God to right the innocent," says Elizabeth to Margaret.

But in *Richard III* there are no innocent, except the children. Their fate, as measured by the calculus of divine justice employed by these people, seems especially shocking because Shakespeare has taken pains to make the children appealing as well as pitiful. The sons of Edward IV, the famous princes in the Tower, are not simply two characters brought in for the sake of the plot; they are made to appear bright and wholesome, and the older one reveals precocious intelligence, a token of the great promise he holds for the future of the throne. These touches alone would be sufficient by themselves to arouse distress at their fate and revulsion against those who bring it about, but Shakespeare does not neglect opportunities to magnify this effect. Buckingham, who has been Richard's willing ally in his devious way to the throne, draws back from becoming implicated in their death. Tyrrel reports that the murderers "wept like two children in their death's sad story" (4.3.8). Against this dramatic preparation, Margaret's inhuman thanks to "true-disposing" God for the fulfillment of her prayers for their death can only produce dislike for her and all the others who insist on identifying the fulfillment of their ugly wishes with the moral order of the universe. Shakespeare twice introduces a note of pathetic irony in a hidden allusion to the fate of Clarence's children. Lily Campbell calls attention to the effect that Clarence's prayer asking that his wife and children be spared the penalty of his crimes must have had on those of the audience familiar with history: "Clarence is murdered before an Elizabethan audience that knew his last prayer had not been answered, for the destruction of his wife and children by Henry VII and Henry VIII, who feared their possible claims to the throne, was an oft told tale."[6] Shakespeare recalls their fate a second time when he brings two of Clarence's children briefly on to the scene. They have learned of their father's death, and one of them in his simplicity believes that the fault lies with King Edward, and that Richard is their true friend:

> Then you conclude, my grandam, he is dead.
> The King mine uncle is to blame for it.
> God will revenge it, whom I will importune
> With earnest prayers all to that effect.
>
> (2.2.12–15)

Paradoxically, the prayer is answered, since the one guilty of Clarence's death is punished in the end; but the overriding effect of the speech is one of pathos for the innocent boy, so confident of God's justice, who was to die in the interest of cold politics at the command of the man who accounts himself God's captain and who emerges at the end of this play as the agent of God's justice and providence to usher in an age of peace and just rule. Shakespeare heightens every opportunity to gain pathos for the children whose destiny brought them to the center of power and placed them in the path of ruthless men and women in an age of evil and disorder, and he does nothing to mitigate the sense of loss and injustice; on the contrary, in the case of the princes he sets the pity in relief by the shock of Margaret's prayer of thanks to God for having provided Richard to perform this act of "justice" in the Tower. The providential historians pointed to the fate of the children as evidence of God's justice in retribution for the sins of their parents; in *Richard III* their plight speaks out against the inhumanity which surrounds them.

It is possible, of course, to trace the action of the play in entirely naturalistic terms. The emergence of the malevolent Richard is certainly a predictable outgrowth of the years of unrelenting and bitter civil strife and conscienceless politics, and his destruction can be reckoned as the inevitable response of outraged humanity which has finally been pushed to the limit. And it is possible to regard the fulfillment of the curses and prophecies as the inevitable consequence of violent deeds that provoke similar responses, the evenhanded justice which Macbeth understood as the judgment which is rendered here simply because

> we but teach
> Bloody instructions, which, being taught, return
> To plague the inventor.
>
> (1.7.8–10)

In Buckingham's phrase, "wrong hath but wrong, and blame the due of blame" (5.1.29). Such a reading of the play would be in some respects better, and truer, than saying that the main end is "to show the working out of God's will in English history,"[7] or pointing to it as Shakespeare's propagation of the "Tudor myth." But there still remains to be accounted for an impression which survives after Margaret and her fellow profaners of divine justice have been reckoned with, that something other than the wills of individual men affects the outcome of human affairs, and does so in a way that gratifies a feeling for equity. The commonplace and hackneyed trivializing of divine justice is exposed, but the validity of the concepts themselves is not in the process wholly discredited. There is a difference between the dying Edward's remorseful awareness of a moral universe ruled by God and the vengeful quibblings and curses of his court. Edward responds to the news of Clarence's death with contrition and fear of just retribution: "O God, I fear thy justice will take hold / On me and you, and mine and yours for this!" (2.1.131–32). Richard immediately attempts to embarrass the queen and her relatives by hinting that Clarence's death was their doing, and then hypocritically adds, "God will revenge it" (2.1.138). His tactic contrasts the sincerity of Edward's fear with the misuse of the idea of God's justice and Richard's vast cynicism. The dying Edward, anxious to neutralize rivalries and hatreds before he dies, warns those on whom he has urged an oath of amity against any later failure to preserve the concord they have just sworn to keep:

> Take heed you dally not before your king,
> Lest he that is the supreme King of kings
> Confound your hidden falsehood and award
> Either of you to be the other's end.
>
> (2.1.12–15)

An oath falsely taken on this solemn occasion would be a crime against a fragile civil order. Of this cynical oath-taking Buckingham is a principal victim, and he acknowledges the justness of the retribution:

> This is the day which in King Edward's time
> I wished might fall on me when I was found
> False to his children and his wife's allies.
> . . . .

54

> That high All-seer which I dallied with
> Hath turned my feigned prayer on my head
> And given in earnest what I begged in jest.
> (5.1.13–15, 20–22)

Buckingham acknowledges the existence of influences that over-reach the premises of his cynical realism.[8]

Portents and mysteries have a part in *Richard III.* Some instances of presaging signs probably do not carry any deep significance. Hastings not only brushes aside prudent warnings, but he also disregards several omens (3.4.82 ff.). Clarence complains that he is being imprisoned because some wizard told Edward "that by G / His issue disinherited should be" (1.1.56–57), and although he and Richard jest about this superstitious notion, Edward's issue is in fact disinherited by G, the duke of Gloucester. Such riddling omens are a common feature of Shakespeare's dramatic rhetoric in establishing an ominous sense of danger and doom. Of a different order, however, is the reintroduction of the prophecy of Henry VI from *3 Henry VI,* which is recalled by Richard after Tyrrel has left to murder the princes, and which stands out because of Richard's strange restless mood:

> I do remember me, Henry the Sixth
> Did prophesy that Richmond should be king
> When Richmond was a little peevish boy.
> A king! perhaps, perhaps,—
> How chance the prophet could not at that time
> Have told me, I being by, that I should kill him?
> (4.2.94–97, 99–100)

But the cynicism of the concluding lines fails to reassure, and Richard recalls an enigmatic prognostication:

> Richmond! When last I was at Exeter,
> The Mayor in courtesy showed me the castle,
> And called it Rugemont; at which name I started,
> Because a bard of Ireland told me once
> I should not live long after I saw Richmond.
> (4.2.102–6)

We might take this to indicate merely that Richard reveals deeply hidden uncertainties and is losing his nerve; but an equally likely inference is that he too is beginning to sense that there are forces influencing the outcome of events which are well beyond even his control. Among Margaret's curses, her denunciation of Richard has a special quality of its own, and it is indicative of the sometimes baffling art of this play that we sense a sudden exaltation in the style and tone when she leaves the petty creatures upon whom she asks for blood vengeance and turns her attention to Richard, whom she describes, with uncharacteristic breadth of feeling, as "the troubler of the poor world's peace" (1.3.221). And there are the ghosts, not scary ghosts, but ritual messengers of divine vengeance on Richard and of fulfillment of divine promise for Richmond. The providential outcome predicted by these spirits is reinforced by Richmond's prayer before the battle and his final speech, which includes a reference to the union of the rival houses "by God's fair ordinance" (5.5.31).[9]

This, it has often been remarked, is Hall's thesis. It was, in fact, just about everyone's thesis who dealt with the history of this period or commented on Richard and his overthrow. The traditional picture of Richard was that of a man so monstrous that the evil he performed was beyond explaining by reference to the usual motives and energies which prompt men to do wrong, and the removal of this evil by an obscure young man who established a new and successful dynasty was an outcome that lay outside the normal consequences of political calculation and military luck. Shakespeare adopted this view—indeed, it would have been surprising if he had not. He makes Richard a brilliant genius in the art of ruthless politics, but he succeeds also in making his malevolence and lack of scruple seem not only unnatural but awesome and even somewhat mysterious. Richard's birth was prodigious, and he imposes his will on innocent victims like Anne, even as he succeeds in fascinating the reader who knows he must wish his final destruction. The ghosts, though derived from Senecan tradition, bear out the suggestion of a justice which does not lie merely in the hands of men. Even the most advanced historians of Shakespeare's age sometimes resorted to providence in dealing with extraordinary events which seemed to follow a persistent logic that appeared to transcend the usual probabilities on which we depend for understanding the everyday world of human affairs, and this aspect of providential history does enter into the scheme of *Richard III*. Shakespeare is, however, a world away from the simplicities of the "Hall thesis" and the "Tudor myth"; *Richard III* is, in fact, a critical exploration and to a degree a rejection of these commonplaces.

There is, finally, one more perhaps not so minor consideration to reckon with. To the strict providentialist, God's justice is not only beyond human power to comprehend in every instance, but also inexorable. Bolingbroke's crime had to be finally punished no matter how long the punishment was deferred, no matter how much piety or how much innocence had to be disregarded or sacrificed to effect it. It appears likely that Shakespeare refused to accept the total rigor of this view. Richard, attempting to persuade Elizabeth that marriage with her daughter is an absolute necessity in the interest of national concord, excuses his murder of the princes by pleading the necessities of fate: "Lo, at their birth good stars were opposite," to which Elizabeth replies, "No, to their lives ill friends were contrary" (4.4.216–17). It was not willed by the stars that friends who might have acted to save them proved mean, self-seeking, and indifferent. Richard repeats his excuse more forcefully: "All unavoided is the doom of destiny" (4.4.218). Elizabeth's answer raises a possibility nowhere else mentioned in the play:

> True, when avoided grace makes destiny.
> My babes were destined to a fairer death
> If grace had blessed thee with a fairer life.
>   (4.4.219–21)

The verbal wit of these lines lends the speech an air of paradox, of an unexpected possibility that cuts across the commonplaces appealed to by Richard. The phrasing of this unexpected statement does not lend itself readily to precise theological explication, but Elizabeth's sentiments clearly allow some escape from the trap of conventionally construed providential destiny and retributive justice through the exercise of powers available to man to gain freedom from evil through grace. It is one more detail which enlarges and humanizes the idea of God's ways to man. Shakespeare, like all his contemporaries of whatever intellectual bias, approached Richard III through the providential idea of history, but he left the idea more complex, less rigid, more humane than he found it in any of his sources. He was thus liberated of its conventional pieties and mechanistic rigor, and free to place the primary emphasis on the phenomenon of power divorced from all considerations of humanity and to create a protagonist worthy of representing its human embodiment.[10]

IV

Ideas of History:
Richard II, I and 2
Henry IV, Henry V

The plays which follow *Richard III* are in subject matter quite similar to those which precede it. They, too, deal with crises in the struggle for power—with the dethronement and murder of a king, with rebellion, with war. However, in these later plays the events do not overwhelm by the sheer volume of disorder and fearful chaos as in *Henry VI*, and the atmosphere is less deeply charged than in *Richard III* with omens, portents, prophetic warnings, and the mysterious operation of a moral universe. The presentation of the crises and conflicts which develop in these later plays appeals more directly to rational judgment and worldly knowledge; interest is more sharply focused on the nature of the political situation out of which the conflicts grow, and on the characters of the men who are caught up in it and are put to the test as they face the consequences of their failures and respond to the challenges or tribulations of power.

In these plays, moreover, Shakespeare provides explicit indications that he is clearly aware of the rationale of the kind of history which sought the meaning and form of events in second causes and in an analytical approach to political conduct, and that he understands how this conception of history might determine the causal scheme of his plays and guide the sequence of events. The evidence consists of a series of related passages in *Richard II* and the two parts of *Henry IV*. The first of these speeches occurs when Northumberland interrupts the leave-taking of the now broken Richard from his queen and announces that Richard must go not to the Tower but to Pomfret. Richard is the firmest believer among all of Shakespeare's kings in the divine right of kingship, with a faith in the idea so great that he once thought that for every soldier on Bolingbroke's side God for his Richard had a glorious angel who would fight for him. It might therefore be expected that he would call down God's wrath and pronounce the doom of divine justice on those who have deposed the Lord's anointed and now move to end his life. On the contrary, with the analytical assurance of a Guicciardini or a Bacon, he unfolds the necessary consequences of Northumberland's actions:

> Northumberland, thou ladder wherewithal
> The mounting Bolingbroke ascends my throne,
> The time shall not be many hours of age
> More than it is, ere foul sin gathering head
> Shall break into corruption. Thou shalt think,
> Though he divide the realm and give thee half,
> It is too little, helping him to all;
> He shall think that thou which knowest the way
> To plant unrightful kings, wilt know again,
> Being ne'er so little urged, another way
> To pluck him headlong from the usurped throne.
> (5.1.55–65)

This is in miniature the plot of *1 Henry IV*. It also anticipates the kind of thinking on which Worcester in that play justifies the rebellion against Henry:

> And 'tis no little reason bids us speed
> To save our heads by raising of a head;
> For, bear ourselves as even as we can,
> The king will always think him in our debt.

60

> And think we think ourselves unsatisfied,
> Till he hath found a time to pay us home.
>
> (1.3.277–82)

There is a striking and pointed repetition of Richard's prognosis in *2 Henry IV*, with direct reference to the earlier play, at the moment when, ill and dejected, Henry recalls the treachery of his former friends and supporters:

> But which of you was by—
> You, cousin Nevil, as I may remember—
> When Richard, with his eye brimful of tears,
> Then checked and rated by Northumberland,
> Did speak these words, now proved a prophecy?
> "Northumberland, thou ladder by the which
> My cousin Bolingbroke ascends my throne"
> (Though then, God knows, I had no such intent,
> But that necessity so bowed the state
> That I and greatness were compelled to kiss)
> "The time shall come,"—thus did he follow it—
> "The time will come that foul sin, gathering head,
> Shall break into corruption"—so went on,
> Foretelling this same time's condition
> And the division of our amity.
>
> (3.1.65–79)

In his reply Westmoreland does not attribute prophetic insight to the deposed king, nor does he appeal to fortune or God's justice; instead he expands the lesson of the specific case into a general truth—prophecy is the art of projecting our knowledge of the past into a possible future:

> There is a history in all men's lives
> Figuring the nature of the times deceased;
> The which observed, a man may prophesy,
> With a near aim, of the main chance of things
> As yet to come to life, who in their seeds
> And weak beginning lie intreasured.
> Such things become the hatch and brood of time,
> And by the necessary form of this
> King Richard might create a perfect guess

That great Northumberland, then false to him,
Would of that seed grow to a greater falseness,
Which should not find a ground to root upon
Unless on you.

(3.1.80–92)

To this the king submits as to a law of nature: "Are these things then necessities? / Then let us meet them like necessities" (3.1.92–93). Distributed among three plays, these explicit expressions of a naturalistic scheme of causation, based on universal properties of men and the nature of political power, serve, in sequence, first to adumbrate the action of the second and third plays, then to underscore the political realities which motivate the action in the second, and finally to provide in the third a retrospective understanding of the events dramatized and establish a firm line of association among the plays of the series which begins with *Richard II.*

In *Richard II* occurs the dethroning of a legitimate monarch and the break in the line of succession which was to divide England for decades thereafter. It was, according to the providential interpretation of these events, an impious crime which aroused God's displeasure and brought about the long train of national disasters which did not cease until by a series of acts of divine justice the nation was properly punished and purged of the initial sin and its evil consequences, and God could confirm anew his special concern for England. Considering the momentous significance attached to the abdication and murder of Richard II and the usurpation of his throne by Bolingbroke, Shakespeare's dramatic presentation of this episode is singularly lacking in solemn, mysterious prefigurings of disaster and sorrow, and comparison with *Richard III* serves to point up how indifferent Shakespeare seems to have been to these opportunities in *Richard II.* Premonitions of disaster are few and fairly conventional. The queen is troubled with anticipations of nameless woes:

methinks
Some unknown sorrow ripe in Fortune's womb
Is coming towards me, and my inward soul

62

> With nothing trembles; at some thing it grieves,
> More than with parting from my lord the King.
>
> (2.2.9–13)

The Welsh Captain and his men will no longer wait for Richard, persuaded by signs hallowed by local superstition and time-honored regard:

> 'Tis thought the King is dead; we will not stay.
> The bay-trees in our country are all withered,
> And meteors fright the fixed stars of heaven,
> The pale-faced moon looks bloody on the earth,
> And lean-looked prophets whisper fearful change;
> Rich men look sad, and ruffians dance and leap—
> The one in fear to lose what they enjoy,
> The other to enjoy by rage and war.
> These signs forerun the death or fall of kings.
>
> (2.4.7–15)

These are familiar accompaniments of tragedy: Juliet's divining soul sees doom ahead, Hamlet's mind misgives him before the duel, and Calphurnia warns Caesar that "When beggars die there are no comets seen. / The heavens themselves blaze forth the death of princes." Even the idea that heaven will avenge the shattering of the divinely ordained order of the kingdom is given less emphasis than might have been expected. The clearest and most impressive statement of this idea is given by Richard, when, confronted with the insolent Northumberland, he admonishes him to think on God's punishment of such irreverence:

> And though you think that all, as you have done,
> Have torn their souls by turning them from us,
> And we are barren and bereft of friends,
> Yet know, my master, God omnipotent,
> Is mustering in his clouds, on our behalf,
> Armies of pestilence, and they shall strike
> Your children yet unborn and unbegot,
> That lift your vassal hands against my head,
> And threat the glory of my precious crown.
>
> (3.3.82–90)

Singularly prophetic though this is, it has still some of the boastful impotence with which Richard invoked God's angels to come to his aid against the armies of Bolingbroke on his return from Ireland. The lines which conclude the speech are more political in content and more mindful of the practical consequences of Bolingbroke's action than of heaven's ultimate vengeance:

> Tell Bolingbroke, for yon methinks he stands,
> That every stride he makes upon my land
> Is dangerous treason. He is come to open
> The purple testament of bleeding war;
> But ere the crown he looks for live in peace,
> Ten thousand bloody crowns of mothers' sons
> Shall ill become the flower of England's face,
> Change the complexion of her maid-pale peace
> To scarlet indignation, and bedew
> Her pastures' grass with faithful English blood.
> (3.3.91–100)

In the same spirit as these concluding lines is Carlisle's long denunciation of the proceedings at the abdication and his prediction of disaster in consequence. The substance of Carlisle's speech is the impropriety and illegality of a subject's pronouncing judgment on a king, "the figure of God's majesty, / His captain, steward, deputy elect" (4.1.125–26):

> What subject can give sentence on his king?
> And who sits here that is not Richard's subject?
> (4.1.121–22)

The consequence of Bolingbroke's treason will be a divided kingdom and the horrors of civil war:

> My Lord of Hereford here, whom you call king,
> Is a foul traitor to proud Hereford's king;
> And if you crown him, let me prophesy—
> The blood of England shall manure the ground,
> And future ages groan for this foul act,
> . . . .

> O, if you raise this house against this house,
> It will the woefullest division prove
> That ever fell upon this cursed earth!
>
> (4.1.134–38, 145–47)

It is the consequences of destroying the traditional sanctions of kingship and of raising "house against house" that Carlisle inveighs against; and though he does truly prophesy, since what he predicts comes to pass, he does not prophesy in quite the sense that the saintly Henry VI does when he looks at an unknown youth and pronounces him the hope of England, but rather in the sense of predicting from their seeds the "hatch and brood of time." One of the very few direct pronouncements about God's purpose in these events is that of York, in commenting on the humiliating treatment of Richard by the populace:

> had not God for some strong purpose steeled
> The hearts of men, they must perforce have melted,
> And barbarism itself have pitied him.
> But heaven hath a hand in these events.
> To whose high will we bound our calm contents.
> To Bolingbroke are we sworn subjects now,
> Whose state and honor I for aye allow.
>
> (5.2.34–40)

God's purpose, York seems to believe, was to stop up the natural springs of pity in men in order to facilitate a peaceful acceptance of Bolingbroke as king, a view of God's providence well enough suited to York's political aims at the moment but sadly at odds with Richard's convictions about the support which God must provide for his anointed representative. York usually takes a more pragmatic and political view of things. He rebukes Richard (as does Gaunt) for the murder of Woodstock, but he does not predict ruin for him on account of this particular crime. It is the seizure of Bolingbroke's inheritance that finally breaks his patience, because by setting aside the law of primogeniture Richard has undermined the legal foundations of his own title as king—"For how art thou a king / But by fair sequence and

65

succession?" (2.1.198–99). It is significant too that the one scene in the play—that of the gardeners (3.4.29–71)—which, because it is completely isolated from any involvement in the action or with the principal characters, has an emblematic and symbolic force, is a political parable. It contrasts the well-ordered garden and the responsible gardener with the disordered kingdom and the imminent destruction of its irresponsible king. The action of *Richard II* puts to trial Richard's idea of kingship and Richard as a man. This is a dramatic concept which does not lend itself to providential interpretation.

Richard II is a preparation for *1* and *2 Henry IV*, not simply because the sequence of events is continuous, but because the political consequences of *Richard II* are worked out in the two Henry plays. These two plays subject events to the hard light of political analysis more thoroughly and consistently than any of the other plays in the series. The nature of the dramatic conflict calls for such treatment. In both plays the dramatic movement is sustained by a rebellion against the king. Since the king is a usurper, he is not in a very strong position to appeal to the sanctity of his crown; and since the rebels are the ones who put him on the throne, they cannot make their cause a crusade against a usurper who committed the sin of deposing the deputy elected by the Lord, and they are therefore hard put to it to defend either their past action or their present one on high principles. It is a purely political situation, and the adversaries play it out largely on the basis of political maneuvering and military challenge. Significantly, the real leader of the rebellion in Part 1 is Worcester, a totally political man. Hotspur is the figurehead, allowed the role in order to bring honor, glamor, and the tone of moral integrity to the enterprise. Hotspur rants against his father and Worcester for their former support of Henry and lusts for the honor of destroying him, yet, ironically, his generous sentiments and his hatred of "that vile politician Bolingbroke" are being used by a master politician, Worcester, to ensnare him and make him an eager partner in the rebellion. Hotspur himself is innocent of what is happening to him at this point, but even he is not above being used. He is not entirely honest about whether he did or did not categorically refuse to turn his prisoners over to Henry, and why; though, to do him justice, it is clear that he seems unaware that he was put up to this challenge of Henry's right to the prisoners in order to provide an occasion for challenging Henry. Worcester realizes the value to their enterprise of Hotspur's lofty and heroic impulses, but his own motives are coldly realistic. The position of Henry's former supporters has become difficult: the king is too much indebted to them to remain at ease now that they have challenged his power. It is for similar reasons that Worcester refuses to report to Hotspur Henry's offer of pardon and accepts the risk of battle against odds:

> It is not possible, it cannot be,
> The King should keep his word in loving us.
> He will suspect us still and find a time
> To punish this offense in other faults.
>
> (5.2.4–7)

He remains in character to the end. His is not a hero's death in battle, but the resigned, impenitent acceptance of death by a man who failed in a dangerous game:

> What I have done my safety urged me to;
> And I embrace this fortune patiently
> Since not to be avoided it falls on me.
>
> (5.5.11–13)

There is no concession to the notion that God's justice is heavy for the sin of rebellion; there is no denouncing of fickle fortune. Worcester took certain unavoidable calculated risks in a political gamble and he lost. He is a thorough professional.

In Part 2 the figurehead leader is not a warrior hero and worshipper of honor like Hotspur, but an archbishop. The enterprise, however, does not essentially change in character. The remaining leaders of the first rebellion review their position in a thoroughly realistic spirit. Hotspur, Morton reflects, was unfortunately a man whose "forward spirit / Would lift him where most trade of danger ranged" (1.1.173–74). The archbishop puts it in less flattering terms: ". . . with great imagination / Proper to madmen, led his powers to death" (1.3.31–32). Besides, the first effort was sullied in the minds of the soldiers from the outset with the taint of rebellion: "For that same word 'rebellion' did divide / The action of their bodies from their souls" (1.1.194–95). The advantage of the new leadership is that it will color the enterprise with holiness:

> But now the Bishop
> Turns insurrection to religion.
> Supposed sincere and holy in his thoughts,
> He's followed both with body and with mind,
> And doth enlarge his rising with the blood
> Of fair King Richard, scraped from Pomfret stones.
> (1.1.200–205)

No one, however, really believes that this is a war in a holy cause, not even the archbishop, who is not a naïve tool like Hotspur but as aware as the rest of his fellow conspirators of what is being planned. They now realize that it was a mistake to place the whole burden of moral justification on Hotspur—Lady Percy characterizes the battle of Shrewsbury as

> a field
> Where nothing but the sound of Hotspur's name
> Did seem defensible.
> (2.3.36–38)

There will be a better chance to arouse public approval with an archbishop ("supposed sincere and holy in his thoughts") as the leader, and the display of relics in the form of scrapings of Richard's blood. It is as calculating as anything Worcester might have thought up, though not as bright or hard-headed. These men weigh their chances more cautiously, and have neither the chivalric coveting of honor of Hotspur nor the political boldness of Worcester. Circumstances, the archbishop thinks, make their enterprise reasonably safe: "The commonwealth is sick of their own choice; / Their over-greedy love hath surfeited" (1.3.87–88). And he supports this view with pessimistic reflections on the giddiness of the vulgar multitude who applaud Bolingbroke one day and now are become enamored of the grave of Richard whom they formerly rejected for Bolingbroke—"what trust is in these times?" (1.3.85–108). The imagery of disease appears again in the archbishop's reply to Westmoreland, the king's emissary:

> we are all diseased,
> And with our surfeiting and wanton hours
> Have brought ourselves into a burning fever,
> And must bleed for it; of which disease
> Our late king, Richard, being infected, died.
>
> (4.1.54–58)

Their aim is medicinal, to

> show awhile like fearful war
> To diet rank minds sick of happiness,
> And purge th' obstructions which begin to stop
> Our very veins of life. (4.1.63–66)
>
> (4.1.63–66)

These analogies portraying the political disturbances of the times as disease and the rebellions as cures and purges imply a naturalistic view of the nation's woes. Significantly, the archbishop applies the disease image to Richard as well as to the present regime, as though his abdication and death were due to natural causes; considering that he is a churchman, his failure to condemn the present king for having committed the crime of usurpation is conspicuous, and the tone is so conciliatory that one would never guess that Henry IV was thought guilty of regicide. The talk is thoroughly political, and the rebels do not seem to regard themselves, as does Richmond, as the instruments of God's vengeance. The arguments in the confrontations before the battles in both plays sound like the positions of a party line, and the same can be said for Hotspur's justification of their cause to Blunt before Shrewsbury, as though it was a piece which he had been made to study for the occasion. There is, however, more passion and personal involvement in the debates of Part 1, and even the tough Worcester speaks feelingly of breaking his staff of office and deserting Richard for Bolingbroke, in the accents of a bitterly disappointed man. Not much of this depth of feeling remains to animate the cautious political maneuverings of Part 2.

In both plays, war, for the mature leaders of both sides, is an instrument of policy, a final means of gaining or securing power. Battles are not the pitiless, bloody, revengeful affairs they are in *3 Henry VI*, and they are not referred to as instruments of God's punitive justice. In Part 1, there is a coloring of chivalry in the gallantry of Hotspur and Douglas, and of the prince, with his final gesture of placing his "favors" on the dead foe after his fight with Hotspur at Shrewsbury. But these gestures seem special and have an air of anachronism about them. The purely political man does not long for battles, like Hotspur, or waste them. Better to persuade Richard to abdicate, as Bolingbroke does in *Richard II*, than take to the battlefield. Shrewsbury was unavoidable—Worcester was too much a student of *Realpolitik* to accept the king's offer of amnesty. But the conspirators of Part 2 are a tame breed. The archbishop rightly diagnoses the king's mood—"The King is weary / Of dainty and such picking grievances" (4.1.197–98)—but he misjudges the cure. Prince John of Lancaster persuades them to dismiss their troops on his acceptance of their articles and his promise that these will be scrupulously observed—and then arrests them for high treason and sends them off to be executed. He did not, after all, mention amnesty. The purely political forces at work in Part 1 have taken over completely; there is no battle, and instead of the chivalric fight to the death of Hotspur and Hal, we have the cynical brilliance of Prince John's action.[1]

It was one of the troublesome details of Henry's position that, on his return from exile, he had sworn an oath that he had come only to claim the inheritance which Richard had illegally confiscated on Gaunt's death, and that he had no further aim. Hot-

70

spur lists this breach of faith in Part 1 in reciting the justification
of their rebellion to Blunt (4.3.60–65), and Worcester repeats
the same charge in his talk with the king before Shrewsbury
(5.1.41–46, 58). The charge is not pressed, however, and in Part
2, it is not even mentioned among the grievances uttered by
the leaders of the insurrection. With neither side in a clear
position, there cannot be a strong appeal to political idealism
or to high moral imperatives, and there is no appeal to the just
retribution which must come to those who break a vow solemnly
made. In raising the matter of the oath in *1 Henry IV* Shakespeare is faithful to history, and honest about Henry's failings
and disabilities, but he does not play up the issue, nor does he
use it in such a way as to undermine what sympathy he manages
to create for Henry. The king and his cause are made to seem the
more acceptable alternative, because his practice of the art of
politics is aimed at a reasonable goal—whatever the past, to
restore the authority of the sovereign, check the forces that produce disunity, and maintain the equilibrium necessary to preserve the peace. In both plays, both sides, in the last analysis,
justify their position on political grounds (except Hotspur, who
justifies his on honor), but the king has the advantage of appealing to national loyalty, and in Part 2 his concern for the welfare
of his nation becomes a major obsession.

In two plays permeated throughout with political realism,
Henry alone raises the question of divine retribution for the
wrongs he has committed. It is a minor matter, but an interesting
one, and grows out of his worry over the prince. It is the substance
of his opening remark to the prince in their first interview in
Part 1:

> I know not whether God will have it so
> For some displeasing service I have done,
> That, in his secret doom, out of my blood
> He'll breed revengement and a scourge for me;
> But thou dost in thy passages of life
> Make me believe that thou art only marked

> For the hot vengeance and the rod of heaven
> To punish my mistreadings.
>
> (3.2.4–11)

We know from the prince's soliloquy which concludes act 1 scene 2 that he will not be a disappointment to his father, and he demonstrates his intentions at Shrewsbury in Part 1 and again before his father's death in Part 2. Thus, Henry IV's one fear of divine retributive justice ends in irony. He never loses a troubled sense of his grave wrongdoing in the past, and in Part 2 he confides to the prince:

> God knows, my son,
> By what by-paths and indirect crooked ways
> I met this crown. . . .
>
> (4.5.183–85)

Neither play, however, is haunted by an overpowering sense of guilt or the shadow of God's anger. This king's principal worry, especially in Part 2, is the state of his kingdom:

> Then you perceive the body of our kingdom
> How foul it is, what rank diseases grow,
> And with what danger, near the heart of it.
>
> (3.1.38–40)

The metaphor of illness suggests, as does the archbishop's use of similar imagery in the same play, that what troubles the land is within the order of nature. Warwick's reply is like that of a consulting physician who concludes that though the patient is indeed quite sick, it is nothing that proper medication, bed rest, and a healthful regimen will not cure:

> It is but as a body yet distempered,
> Which to his former strength may be restored
> With good advice and little medicine.
>
> (3.1.41–43)[2]

The world of the *Henry IV* plays is almost completely secular. These are men dealing with practical matters in a contingent world, and this impression increases in Part 2. When the conspirators led by the archbishop have reviewed their chances in a second rebellion, Hastings remarks, "We are time's subjects, and time bids begone" (1.3.110). Something in the ever-shifting circumstances beyond any individual's control provides the conditions within which men must act—"the times do brawl" (1.3.70) is Hastings' phrase. The same attitude is reflected in Westmoreland's plea to the leaders of the insurrection:

> O, my good Lord Mowbray,
> Construe the times to their necessities,
> And you shall say indeed it is the time,
> And not the King, that doth you injuries.
> (4.1.103–6)

It is on similar grounds that the archbishop justifies the rebellion:

> The time misordered doth, in common sense,
> Crowd us and crush us to this monstrous form
> To hold our safety up.
> (4.2.33–35)

And though the king expresses regret about the way he gained the crown, he can nevertheless say, "necessity so bowed the state, / That I and greatness were compelled to kiss" (3.1.73–74), as though he did not have much choice in the matter.[3] These people face the world in the spirit of Bacon's aphorism in "Of Innovations," that "time is the greatest innovator, and if time of course alter things to the worse, and wisdom and counsel shall not alter them to the better, what shall be the end?"

In this tough and demanding world the king manages to stay on, acting neither as a man cursed by God nor yet as the providential agent of some great plan, but rather as one who finds himself required to play a principal role in a time of national troubles and uses his gifts and powers as well as he can. He enters upon the battle of Shrewsbury in Part 1 without pondering the meaning of signs and portents. He comments on the ominous bloody sun, and the prince in replying predicts a tempest, but the king ends forthrightly: "Then with the losers let it sympathize, / For nothing can seem foul to those that win" (5.1.7–8). It is the same weather for both sides, and confidence belongs to the potential victor.[4] No one after the decisive battle of Shrewsbury attributes the victory to God. In Part 2, when the king is dying, Gloucester and Clarence talk about unnatural events— "loathly births of nature," "the river hath thrice flowed no ebb between," and the like—but it is the merest conventional decoration and theatrical rhetoric. There is only one authentic touch that carries the events of the play outside the interplay of natural forces: the prophecy that Henry IV would die in Jerusalem, which turns out to be the Jerusalem Chamber at Westminster:

> Laud be to God! Even there my life must end.
> It hath been prophesied to me, many years,
> I should not die but in Jerusalem,
> Which vainly I supposed the Holy Land.
> But bear me to that chamber; there I'll lie;
> In that Jerusalem shall Harry die.
>
> (4.5.235–40)

Historically, this prophecy is not uniquely associated with Henry IV, and has the status of a myth.[5] It is, nevertheless, appropriate in an odd way to Shakespeare's treatment of Henry and his career. At the end of *Richard II*, Henry promises to undertake a journey to the Holy Land as an act of expiation. In *1 Henry IV* this project has taken on a political character, as a means of unifying contentious and restless forces in a common cause—a characteristic move for one who must perforce make political use of everything. The fulfillment of the prophecy comes in the form of a paradox. Because of continuing disturbances at home, Henry is disappointed in his hopes of undertaking a crusade to the Holy Land, but he does nevertheless die in "Jerusalem"—a fulfillment in name only, but for which he thanks God. The detail of the oddly fulfilled prophecy can stand for Henry's career: a kingship inspired by a national aim with hopes for a notable success, both for himself and for the nation, carried out with talent and intelligence, yet ending in apparent failure and disappointment. But in an unexpected sense Henry did succeed politically: he maintained the title and the nation intact to pass it on to a son who was not a scourge for his sins, as he had feared, but the future hero king.

There is a striking difference in tone between *2 Henry IV* and *Henry V*. We move from a world controlled by the natural history of politics and the struggle for power to one in which it is acknowledged that the will and justice of God govern the doings of kings and magistrates and the comings and goings of armies. As much as does Henry VI, Henry V recognizes that the final course of events is controlled by a higher power. After his flashing defiance of the dauphin to the French ambassadors, he adds, "But this lies all within the will of God" (1.2.289). At Agincourt he orders his troops to action with resignation to the divine will: "Now soldiers, march away; / And how thou pleasest, God, dispose the day" (4.3.131–32). He is not as complacent as Richard II, who believed that God would of course come to the rescue of his anointed representative, yet at times he speaks with almost as much assurance of divine support. Montjoy, aware of the desperate plight of the English forces, demands ransom of Henry in arrogant terms, but instead Henry returns defiance in a courageous speech which admits the seemingly disastrous state of affairs but nevertheless concludes:

> Yet, God before, tell him we will come on,
> Though France himself and such another neighbor
> Stand in our way.
>
> (3.6.162–64)

Henry VI's piety and his unfailing submission to events because they are God's will rendered him inept, indecisive, and inactive; Richard II's assumption that God would always be on his side because he was His anointed encouraged him to be indifferent to the nation's welfare, inconsiderate, and politically unprepared and imprudent. Henry V suffers from no such disabilities. Neither his submissive piety nor his reliance on God's favor interferes with his energetic and effective exercise of the responsibilities of his office. In his case the providential view of history

takes on a special—one is tempted to say a pragmatic and utili-
tarian—flavor.

Of Henry's devoutness we are left in no doubt. The very first
mention of his name in *Henry V* is accompanied by references
to his religious temperament:

> *Canterbury.* The King is full of grace and fair regard.
> *Ely.* And a true lover of the holy Church.
>
> (1.1.22–23)

None of Shakespeare's kings appeals so often to God or utters
God's name so frequently, and considering his success, Henry
does not utter it in vain. He is mindful of the retributive justice
of God, and in the dark moments before Agincourt he prays that
God will not exact punishment on him and his nation for his
father's usurpation in this battle:

> O God of battles! steel my soldiers' hearts;
> Possess them not with fear; take from them now
> The sense of reckoning, if the opposed numbers
> Pluck their hearts from them. Not today, O Lord,
> O not today, think not upon the fault
> My father made in compassing the crown!
> I Richard's body have interred new,
> And on it have bestowed more contrite tears
> Than from it issued forced drops of blood.
> Five hundred poor I have in yearly pay,
> Who twice a day their withered hands hold up
> Toward heaven, to pardon blood; and I have built
> Two chantries, where the sad and solemn priests
> Sing still for Richard's soul. More will I do;
> Though all that I can do is nothing worth,
> Since that my penitence comes after all,
> Imploring pardon.
>
> (4.1.295–311)

But Henry is not haunted, as is his son in the first trilogy, by
the blot on his title, and while he prays that God will not possess
his soldiers' hearts with fear, it is evident in all that he does
before and during the battle that his own heart is not possessed

76

with fear, or at least that he is master of it.[6] He acknowledges his father's sin, but he has done as much as a man can do in the way of public and private atonement and he has reason to hope that God will take his earnest efforts into account in this moment of crisis for his army and his country. The outcome confirms his confidence.

The context of some of his expressions of resignation to God's will is significant in this connection. It is true that in his speech to the French ambassadors he acknowledges that all depends on the will of God, but the defiance which precedes is charged with confidence:

> But tell the Dauphin I will keep my state,
> Be like a king and show my sail of greatness
> When I do rouse me in my throne of France:
> For that I have laid by my majesty
> And plodded like a man for working-days,
> But I will rise there with so full a glory
> That I will dazzle all the eyes of France,
> Yea strike the Dauphin blind to look on us.
>
> (1.2.273–80)

After the reiteration of the first person singular pronoun, the resignation to God's will comes rather as a confirmation of support than an acknowledgment of submission. In his second refusal of ransom to Montjoy, Henry speaks feelingly of the wretched state of the English forces and their chances of death, but declares by way of transition to his positive statement, "Let me speak proudly" (4.3.108), and it is a proud speech, praising the appearance of his men as "working day" soldiers bearing the marks of their hard marches and confident in their valor:

> And my poor soldiers tell me, yet ere night
> They'll be in fresher robes, or they will pluck
> The gay new coats o'er the French soldiers' heads
> And turn them out of service. If they do this,
> As, if God please, they shall, my ransom then
> Will soon be levied.
>
> (4.3.116–21)

77

The phrase, "if they do this," does not refer to the "fresh robes" which they would wear in heaven if they died, but to their triumphant plucking of the gay coats of the French, and "if God please," at the end of so eloquent and brave a speech, comes close to implying that indeed he will. There can be no greater support to self-reliance than belief that the will of God is supreme in the affairs of men, coupled with the reasonable certainty that God is on your side.

This inner strength of conviction which provides positive courage to action is something which Henry seems to take for granted, and it contributes greatly to his success. A comparison of the king's speech at Agincourt with its sources effectively illustrates the importance Shakespeare attached to this aspect of Henry's character. The speech begins with a reply to Westmoreland's rueful reflection on their few troops:

> O that we now had here
> But one ten thousand of those men in England
> That do no work today!
>
> (4.3.16–18)

The first half of the king's speech builds on the theme "not one man more":

> What's he that wishes so?
> My cousin Westmoreland? No, my fair cousin;
> If we are marked to die, we are enow
> To do our country loss; and if to live,
> The fewer men, the greater share of honor.
>
> (4.3.18–22)

This idea, which is developed through a little more than twenty lines and which concludes the speech, is derived from a passage in Holinshed (Hall does not have this detail):

> It is said that as he heard one of host [sic] utter to another thus: "I would to God there were with us now so many good soldiers as are at this hour within England!" the king an-

78

swered: "I would not wish a man more here than I have, we are indeed in comparison to the enemy's but a few, but, if God of his clemency do favor us, and our just cause (as I trust he will) we shall speed well enough. But let no man ascribe victory to our own strength and might, but only to God's assistance, to whom I have no doubt we shall worthily have cause to give thanks therefore." [7]

What Shakespeare omits is the conditional statement, "if God of his clemency do favor us," and the command to ascribe the victory only to God (there will be enough of this after the battle). The spirit of confidence (Holinshed's "as I trust he will") animates the speech, but what comes through magnificently as an addition to Holinshed is the instinct for heroic action irrespective of the circumstances: "We would not die in that man's company / That fears his fellowship to die with us" (4.3.38–39). Holinshed reports the oration to the troops in summary form:

> Calling his captains and soldiers about him, he made to them a right grave oration, moving them to play the men, whereby to obtain a glorious victory, as there was hope certain they should, the rather if they would but remember the just cause for which they fought, and whom they should encounter, such fainthearted people as their ancestors had so often overcome. To conclude, many words of courage he uttered, to stir them to do manfully, assuring them that England should never be charged with his ransom, nor any Frenchman triumph over him as a captive; for either by famous death or glorious victory would he (by God's grace) win honour and fame. [8]

None of this is reflected in the Crispin Crispian day portion of the speech—the appeal goes beyond the cliché "play the men," there is no disparagement of the French, there is no talk of famous death or glorious victory, and the decision not to be taken or ransomed appears not in this public utterance but in his conference with the French herald. Hall reports his version of the oration in full:

79

Wellbeloved friends and countrymen, I exhort you heartily think and conceive in yourselves that this day shall be to us all a day of joy, a day of good luck and a day of victory: for truly if you well note and wisely consider all things, almighty God under whose protection we be come hither, hath appointed a place so meet and apt for our purpose as we ourselves could neither have devised nor wished which as it is apt and convenient for our small number and little army so is it unprofitable and unmeet for a great multitude to fight or give battle in: and in especial for such men in whom is neither constant faith nor security of promise, which persons be of God neither favored nor regarded, nor he is not accustomed to aid and succor such people which by force and strength contrary to right and reason detain and keep from other their just patrimony and lawful inheritance, with which blot and spot the French nation is apparently defiled and distained: so that God of his justice will scourge and afflict them for their manifest injuries and open wrongs to us and our realm daily committed and done.[9]

Hall pushes the providential line very hard—God is clearly on their side because he has brought them to a site ideally suited to an outnumbered army, the foe cannot expect God's favor, defiled as they are by having broken the law of inheritance, and God's justice requires that they be punished. Shakespeare disregards this text completely. He has deliberately set aside all the inducements provided by his sources for a demonstration of Henry's piety and his belief in God's providence and God's support of his aims. Shakespeare's Henry appeals to the pride of those who will have fought on this heroic occasion and lived to tell the story—

> He that outlives this day, and comes safe home,
> Will stand a tip-toe when this day is named,
> And rouse him at the name of Crispian.
>
> (4.3.41–43)

—and to the sense of equal fellowship among those who must share the ultimate mortal danger:

> we band of brothers;
> For he today that sheds his blood with me
> Shall be my brother; be he ne'er so vile,
> This day shall gentle his condition.
>
> (4.3.60–63)

In his critical hour Henry is at once most kingly and most independent.

With the victory won, Henry returns to his role as the humble instrument of God's purpose. "Praised be God, and not our strength for it!" (4.7.89), he exclaims when the French herald admits defeat. What follows goes well beyond the common acknowledgment of divine assistance by victorious generals, just as the battle goes well beyond most courageously fought victories. While defeating a much larger army, better nourished and better equipped, the English have lost only four men of rank "and of all other men / But five and twenty" (4.8.107–8). The king exclaims,

> O God, thy arm was here;
> And not to us, but to thy arm alone,
> Ascribe we all! When, without stratagem,
> But in plain shock and even play of battle,
> Was ever known so great and little loss
> On one part and on th' other? Take it, God,
> For it is none but thine!
>
> (4.8.108–14)

It is proclaimed that it will be death "To boast of this or take that praise from God / Which is his only" (4.8.117–18). The casualty figures may be made public, but only "with this acknowledgment, / That God fought for us" (4.8.121–22). The scene ends with orders for appropriate acts of piety, the singing of *Non nobis* and *Te Deum*, and the decent burial of the dead. The chorus to act 5 reports how the king forbade display of his "bruised helmet and his bended sword" (l. 17) as signs of ostentation calling attention to his own valor rather than to the aid of God. Henry's conduct after the battle confirms in detail the first statement about him in the play, and the authority of all the sources, that he was a devout and religious man. ⌉

The battle of Agincourt occupies a special place in sixteenth-century histories of Britain as one of those notable occasions which could not be accounted for as a product of superior military skill (the historians comment favorably on the strategy, which Shakespeare completely disregards), or passed off as a case of fabulous good luck. Like Bosworth Field, what happened seemed beyond cleverness and the power of human will, and was thought therefore to be divinely ordained. Shakespeare adopts this view of Agincourt in *Henry V*, but he manages with great skill to incorporate the miracle of Agincourt into his total conception of the Christian hero king. The impression which Shakespeare's Henry leaves is not that he was a pious and God-fearing man who for that reason was favored of God. Alas, the wretched and luckless Henry VI was far more genuinely pious and God-fearing. ⌈Henry V regularly defers to God's will, but everything he says and does tells us that he is pretty sure that God's will and his own efforts must cooperate toward the same end. He is endowed with the energy, the personal authority and attractiveness, and the political insight which a king needs for success, whether he is devout or not.⌋ In the last act, where he pushes through all the favorable terms for the peace, it is these characteristics which are prominent, and there is no mention of guidance or aid from God. In the moment before Agincourt he stands alone as a man, and asks of his soldiers no more than he can give himself. If God favors him in everything he does, it is because he has earned the favor. Thus, while acknowledging that the affairs of this world are in the hands of a higher power, he can also believe that he is its chosen agent; and so he is not intimidated by the contingent world and does not despair of being able to exercise a measure of control over it. ⌈To become the mirror of all Christian kings it is necessary to be a Christian, but the mirror of all Christian kings must first of all be a king. The providential idea of history and the idea of a great king are brought together in the person of Shakespeare's Henry V. ⌋

V

The Foundations and Limits of Sovereign Power

The dominant form of political organization which emerged out of the turmoil and violence of the fifteenth and sixteenth centuries in Europe was the powerful national monarchy. During the Middle Ages there were two major restraints on any pretensions to absolute kingly power. One was the pope, who as the spiritual head of a presumably united Christendom could exert considerable political pressure through the wealth and widespread institutional influence of the church and through the threat of excommunication. The second was the feudal nobles, who were at times as well off financially and as powerful militarily as the king. Both these checks to sovereign power were eroded and finally rendered politically impotent by the social and economic changes of two centuries, by devastating wars, and by the Reformation. The consolidating power of a strong national monarch came to seem not only the most effective means for reorganizing the human, economic, and military resources of a country, but also the only hope of providing order and putting an end to turbulence, uncertainty, and suffering. By the middle years of the sixteenth century, the sovereign national king appeared less as a threat to liberty than as a welcome savior from chaos.[1]

This development was not as simple and uniform, and certainly not as complete, as it sounds in a brief summary. The city-states of Italy, in spite of their vigor, wealth, and culture, proved unequal to the challenge of centralized national government, and Italy became the unhappy battleground for Spanish and French ambitions, the victim of the new monarchical order which it was itself unable to achieve. Moreover, the Reformation gave a special direction to political thinking; political theory became inextricably bound up with questions of church government and the promotion of true religion. Some of the political organizations which were most closely associated with new religious reforms were highly specialized and radical, for instance, Calvin's Geneva and—what became a proverbial cautionary example—Münster under the Anabaptists. In Germany, no single political figure of national stature emerged out of the upheaval produced by the Reformation, but the princes of the chief principalities achieved the power of heads of minor kingdoms. By the middle years of the sixteenth century, however, three major monarchies had established themselves—England, France, and Spain—which had achieved, or were rapidly achieving a strong national administration in which the king claimed, or conducted himself as though he claimed, absolute or near absolute power. In the course of these extraordinary changes, fundamental questions were raised and debated about the source and sanction of sovereignty, the nature of the state, and the forms of good government. In the end, however, the principal problem of political theory was that of coming to terms with the absolutist pretensions of the king in the new national state.[2]

In England, the change to the new monarchical order was brought about by two men, Henry VII and Henry VIII. Henry VII, by defeating Richard III at Bosworth Field and then by marrying the princess Elizabeth, daughter of Edward IV, put an end to the Wars of the Roses and resolved the fierce quarrels over the succession. Henry VIII destroyed the last vestiges of papal and church power by the Act of Supremacy, which made him head of the church in England as well as head of the state and thus gave him more authority than any previous English monarch. Between them, they produced a revolution, without being by temperament or even intention revolutionaries. They managed to gain a wide measure of support, but they also found it prudent to provide justification for their political actions. Henry VII claimed the throne through a tenuous and distant connection with John of Gaunt, and he acquired the crown only after a military invasion with French aid and a battle in which the already crowned king, Richard III, was killed. He gained respect by governing with skill and concern for the needs of the nation, but he also took pains to prove that the authority he exercised was truly his. Because of his Welsh ancestry he sought to establish an ancient lineage through descent from King Arthur, and he named his first son Arthur to capitalize on this claim. Henry VII's reputed interest in history may have been largely a reflection of his desire to advance the new learning in England, but he could not have been unaware of its possible usefulness when he appointed Polydore Vergil to write a history of England. Vergil's work, which was not published until 1534, was a disappointment in one respect; it attacked the historicity of Arthur and thus invalidated the claim of the Tudors to ancient royal British descent, for which Vergil was much condemned by English historians and antiquarians of the sixteenth century even while they made extensive use of his materials.[3] He did, however, provide support for Henry VII's legitimacy from another direction, by making him the providential agent for ending national discord: after reviewing Henry's prudent acts immediately after becoming king, Vergil adds: "He then took in marriage Elizabeth, daughter of Edward, a woman indeed intelligent above all others, and equally beautiful. It is legitimate to attribute this to divine intervention, for plainly by it all things which nourished the two most ruinous factions were utterly removed."[4] Henry VIII did not need to concern himself seriously about his title. The great questions of his rule resulted

from the Act of Supremacy, the most important political consequence of the divorce from his first wife. To his virtually absolute secular power as head of state was now added, as head of the
church, power over the administration of the national church
and even over matters of faith. Royal authority could extend no
further. Henry VIII was a great patron of letters, and thus he
had available well-educated, talented men to establish the legal
grounds and supply the moral and political justification for his
actions, and the relatively new technology of printing was used
to that end through the royal press with the skill of certain modern political figures in taking advantage of radio and television.[5]
But the new monarchy raised problems that went beyond the
immediate political involvements of the two Henrys to become
the center of philosophical analysis and vigorous partisan debate
throughout the sixteenth century and well into the seventeenth.
What was the ultimate sanction of such sovereign power? From
what source was it derived? Could any limits be imposed on it?

Since early Christian times the king was regarded as God's
deputy on earth. The distinctive meaning which this common
assumption had acquired for the fifteenth and sixteenth centuries was a consequence of the long controversy during the
Middle Ages between the pope and the emperor over the question of who had the ultimate power and the right to pronounce
final judgment. If the pope could claim primacy because he was
the divine vicar and head of the Christian church, the defenders
of the emperor's right could also claim, on the basis of historic
and biblical precedent, that the secular ruler was the true representative of God's power on earth. When in the course of time
the flimsiness of the emperor's pretensions to being the sovereign
head of Christian nations became evident, the challenge to the
pope's claim to supremacy over the secular power was taken over
by the individual national monarchs who were becoming the
true centers of power. Henry VIII's resolution of the conflict
had the advantage of combining the claims of the pope and the
emperor in his own person, but at the same time it sharpened
the issue of the nature and the management of absolute power.

86

Sovereign power, except when it is simply and candidly claimed on the basis of military might and political callousness, can be effectively exercised only when the ruler does not owe its possession and legitimacy to some human agency to which he must therefore be somehow beholden. The idea that the king was God's representative on earth, exercising divine authority, and must for that reason he obeyed was widely accepted because it gave sanction to a degree of central power which appeared to be politically necessary.[6] "There is no power," wrote Tyndale, closely paraphrasing Romans 13:1–2, "but of God (by power understand the authority of kings and princes). The powers that be are ordained of God." And he adds, with a glance at Henry VIII and the Act of Supremacy, "Whosoever therefore resisteth power resisteth God: yea though he be Pope, Bishop, monk, or frere."[7] Tyndale has much to say by way of admonition about the king's obligations and responsibilities, but in a frequently cited passage, he affirms in simple straightforward language the absolute nature of a king's powers: "The king is in this world without law and may at his lust do right or wrong and shall give accounts but to God only."[8] The general acceptance of such views is evidenced by that popular source of historical narrative and political theory, *A Mirror for Magistrates*. The note to the reader that follows Jack Cade's narrative states:

> For indeed officers be God's deputies, and it is God's office which they bear, and it is he which ordaineth thereto such as himself listeth, good when he favoreth the people, and evil when he will punish them. And therefore whosoever rebelleth against any ruler either good or bad, rebelleth against GOD, and shall be sure of a wretched end: for God can not but maintain his deputy.[9]

The same idea is stated with more felicity in a work of far greater literary merit than the *Mirror*, *The Faerie Queene*:

> He [God] maketh kings to sit in sovereignty;
> He maketh subjects to their power obey.[10]

And Spenser's image of the queen is an embodiment of this idea:

> Dread Sovereign Goddess, that doth highest sit
> In seat of judgment in th' Almighty's stead,
> And with magnific might and wondrous wit
> Dost to thy people righteous doom aread
> That furthest nations fills with awful dread.[11]

It was an accumulation of impressions like these which was conveyed by the phrase "the Lord's anointed," which in popular usage was not accompanied by a sense of the legalistic tangles and subtleties with which it was becoming encrusted; it conveyed the complex notion of the divine origin and sanction of kingly power and the biblical aura associated with the story of the anointing of Saul and of David.

This notion of kingship was strengthened by the principle of strict hereditary succession based on primogeniture. Indeed, legitimacy through hereditary succession became essential to secure possession of the throne. It insured that the king was not selected by men but designated by the mysterious process of being conceived and born as the oldest child of the established king, and hence in the strictest sense was "the deputy elected by the Lord." As one of the speakers puts it in the discussion following the narrative of the Blacksmith in *A Mirror*, "in my judgment, there is no mean so good . . . as the natural order of inheritance by lineal descent: for so it is left in God's hands, to create in the womb what prince he thinketh meetest for his purpose."[12] A king with an undisputed hereditary title was in a position to wield the enormous powers of the English monarchy without feeling the need to justify his exercise of them to others who might have a taste for power, for he owed his authority to no man but to nature and to God.

This view was vigorously supported by Hooker, who, writing late in Elizabeth's reign, condemned as "strange, untrue, and unnatural" the notion that succession might be determined by the will of the people and the merits of a particular claimant,

88

a view which he believed to be the work of rebellious minds, and maintained that "unless we will openly proclaim defiance unto all law, equity, and reason, we must (there is no remedy) acknowledge that in a kingdom hereditary birth giveth right unto sovereign dominion."[13] The statement implies awareness of challenges to this position. Starkey, writing during the reign of Henry VIII, rejected the theory that succession by inheritance was demanded by nature and right reason, and viewed it rather as a system imposed by "tyrants and barbarous princes," yet he approved of the practice as an expedient way of avoiding "discord, debate, and confusion."[14] Starkey may have been reacting to the practice of rulers, especially Henry VIII, of multiplying and intensifying statutes against treason to protect themselves against rebellion and assure the succession. The extreme position resulted usually from religious pressures in politics, as in the case of the notorious Catholic Robert Parsons (Doleman) who, in *A Conference about the Next Succession to the Crowne of Ingland* (1594), contended that hereditary succession was a matter of law and could therefore be altered, and that under certain circumstances kings could be deposed.[15] However, the strength of the principle that the best claim to the title was by lineal descent is demonstrated by the tenacity with which it was appealed to by every claimant. No king was ever simply "deposed," and even those who secured the throne by force or fraud or assassination took pains to establish a proper lineal right to the sovereign power they had assumed. The preoccupation with royal genealogies, the tragic fate of some who gambled on the wrong side when the case for a particular succession seemed ambiguous, the great issue of Elizabeth's successor—all indicate how important hereditary right had become as a principal means of endowing royal power with legitimacy and freedom from restricting political obligations.[16]

The sixteenth-century idea of kingship implied as a necessary corollary that the king may not be resisted. It is, in fact, almost impossible to find a statement which defines the king as the vicegerent of God without the accompanying statement that the king must be obeyed. The prevailing opinion on the Continent as well as in England was that resistance to the prince was not only dangerous to the realm and eventually self-defeating but, because it was aimed at God's representative on earth, it was indeed a sin. On this point there is no difference between Luther and Calvin and between them and Tyndale and Hooker. The doctrine of obedience received its official statement in England in two homilies which appeared in a collection of sermons required to be read at prescribed occasions in all churches. The first of these appeared in the collection, *Certayne Sermons, or Homelies*, in 1547, and was entitled "An Exhortation concerning Good Order and Obedience to Rulers and Magistrates." It describes the disorder and chaos which would accompany the taking away of kings, magistrates, "and such estates of God's order," and urges nonresistance as a divine command: "Whereby Christ taught us plainly, that even the wicked rulers have their power and authority from God, and therefore it is not lawful for their subjects to withstand them, although they abuse their power." It ends with a simple admonition: "Therefore let us all fear the most detestable vice of rebellion, ever knowing, and remembering that he that resisteth or withstandeth common authority, resisteth or withstandeth God and his Ordinance." Evil commands of wicked kings should not be obeyed, but he who follows his conscience must accept the consequences to himself after the example of the apostles and the early Christians:

> We may not obey Kings, Magistrates, or any other (though they be our own Father) if they would command us to do anything contrary to God's commandments. In such a case we ought to say with the Apostle, We must rather obey God than Man. But nevertheless in that case we may not in any wise withstand violently, or rebel against Rulers, or make any insurrection, Sedition, or Tumults, either by force of Arms (or otherwise) against the anointed of the Lord, or any of his officers. But we must in such case patiently suffer all wrongs and injuries, referring the judgment of our cause only to God.

The "Homilie against Disobedience," which was added to the collection in 1571, contributes nothing essential to the "Exhortation." The main arguments are expanded, new illustrations introduced and earlier ones amplified—for instance, the allusion to David's refusal to slay Saul becomes a narration of the episode in some detail. The purpose of the new homily was to confirm the doctrine following the excommunication of Elizabeth in 1570, which released her Catholic subjects from obedience to her, and the Northern Rebellion (the sermon concludes with a prayer of thanksgiving "for the suppression of the last Rebellion"). The doctrine, however, remains unchanged. "An Exhortation" supports its principal line of argument with an appeal to the idea of universal order and degree:

> Almighty God hath created and appointed all things in Heaven, Earth, and Waters in a most excellent and perfect order. In Heaven he hath appointed distinct and several orders and states of Archangels and Angels. In Earth he hath assigned and appointed Kings, Princes, with other governors under them, in all good and necessary order. The water above is kept, and raineth down in due time and season. The Sun, Moon, Stars, Rainbow, Thunder, Lightning, Clouds, and all Birds of the Air, do keep their order. The Earth, Trees, Seeds, Plants, Herbs, Corn, Grass, and all manner of beasts, keep themselves in order. All the parts of the whole year, as Winter, Summer, Months, Nights, and Days, continue in their order. All kinds of Fishes in the Sea, Rivers, and Waters, with all Fountains, Springs, yea, the Seas themselves keep their comely course and order. And Man himself also hath his parts both within and without, as soul, heart, mind, memory, understanding, reason, speech, with all and singular corporal members of his body in a profitable, necessary, and pleasant order.

The order of nature is the design of God. When Alexander Pope, in his later and more systematic presentation of the idea of the great chain of being in *An Essay on Man*, exclaimed,

> All this dread ORDER break—for whom? for thee?
> Vile worm!

he expressed something of the feeling which was implied some two centuries earlier in the more luxuriant phrasing of "An Exhortation," except that the homily is addressed less abstractly to Man, as in Pope, and more politically to restless mobs, unruly nobles, fomenters of plots, and religious militants.

This complex of ideas had the appearance of a set of self-evident propositions, but in fact it was not free of uncertainties and was vulnerable to challenges arising out of shifting political circumstances. In its pure form it was too simple for the realities of the times. It allowed no avenue for redress of grievances by politically authorized means, and so when there were irreconcilable conflicts of conscience there were always those who did not yield to the demands for submissive obedience and raised questions about the doctrine itself. Reginald Pole, for example, could not accept Henry VIII's Act of Supremacy, and accordingly advocated the right of the people to depose a king when they were severely oppressed. Mary Tudor came to the throne determined to do God's will in her own way, which proved to be diametrically opposed to that of her father, and many who could not obey a Catholic queen died at the stake, martyrs not only to their faith but to the doctrine of nonresistance. But some who fled and had the opportunity to think matters out in the atmosphere of Continental Protestant debate came to the conclusion that the doctrine was incorrect. John Ponet maintained that it is lawful to remove kings who act contrary to the law of nature.[17] In Scotland, John Knox, faced with what seemed to him the intolerable position of having to obey Mary Stuart, a woman and a Catholic, finally abandoned Calvin's consistent stand on nonresistance. It was part of the idea of nonresistance that evil kings were assigned by God to punish nations. The prospect of Mary Stuart was enough to convince Knox that this view was infamous:

> For now the common song of all men is, We must obey our Kings, be they good or be they bad; for God hath so commanded. But horrible shall the vengeance be, that shall be poured forth upon such blasphemers of God his holy

name and ordinance. For it is no less blasphemy to say that God hath commanded Kings to be obeyed when they shall command impiety than to say that God by his precept is author and maintainer of all iniquity.[18]

Both Ponet and Knox, faced with an extreme test of their belief in the standard doctrine, felt unable at that point to follow it. Thomas Starkey, writing under Henry VIII and as one of his servants, also denied that tyranny comes from God:

> For to say, as many men do, that the providence of God ordaineth tyrants for the punishment of the people, this agreeth nothing with philosophy nor reason; nor yet to the doctrine of Christ and good religion. . . . Therefore never attribute tyranny (of all ill the greatest) to the providence of God, except you will, consequently, attribute all ill to the Fountain of goodness.[19]

These views are unusual; the common opinion, as these statements acknowledge, did attribute evil rulers to the providence of God. What such minority opinions call attention to is that the idea of tyranny introduced a nagging contradiction into the conventional attitude toward the doctrine of obedience, a contradiction that was never fully resolved during the century.

To some English writers on politics the issue of tyranny would have seemed unimportant because they believed that there already existed certain limits to the absolute power of an English king. To begin with, no English writer maintained that only monarchy was ordained by God or that it was necessarily the ideal form. Hooker wrote: "The case of man's nature standing therefore as it doth, some kind of regiment the Law of Nature doth require; the kinds thereof being many, Nature tieth not to any one, but leaveth the choice as a thing arbitrary."[20] Thomas Smith regarded the English monarchy as a product of history: "By old and ancient histories that I have read, I do not understand that our nation hath used any other general authority in this realm, neither Aristocratical, nor Democratical, but only the royal and kingly majesty. . . ."[21]

Monarchy was, simply, the best form for England: "it doth appear that the mutations and changes of fashions of government in commonwealths be natural, and do not always come of ambition or malice: And that according to the nature of the people the commonwealth is to it fit and proper."[22] The extreme English position would be to consider monarchy the best generally among the three possible forms described by Aristotle, which is the position of Thomas Elyot.[23]

A more important consideration is that for most English writers the monarchy of England was circumscribed by Parliament and by law. Of the two, the presumed limitation placed on the king by Parliament was the more real check on absolutism. Henry VIII himself contributed to the power of Parliament by the very steps he took to enlarge his own, for the Reformation Parliament of 1526–36 was the means through which the required changes were made to bring about the revolution which made the king the head of the church. There was, moreover, the traditional function of Parliament of providing special appropriations in times of national emergency and great need, such as war, which made the king occasionally dependent on Parliament of necessity. Among English writers Thomas Smith is the most outspoken on the importance of Parliament. Writing less as a theorist than as a delineator of the merits of the British system, he does acknowledge the considerable actual power of the crown:

> The prince is the life, the head, and the authority of all things to be done in the realm of England. And to no prince is done more honor and reverence than to the King and Queen of England, no man speaketh to the prince nor serveth at the table but in adoration and kneeling, all persons of the realm be bareheaded before him; inasmuch that in the chamber of presence where the cloth of estate is set, no man dare walk, yea though the prince be not there, no man dare tarry there but bareheaded.[24]

Only a very awesome power can command such ceremonies of submission. Yet, according to Smith, there was one power greater than that of such a prince: "The most high and absolute power of the realm of England," he wrote, "consisteth in the Parliament." He describes Parliament as an organization made up of members of the three highest estates deliberating and determining "what is good and necessary for the commonwealth," which "the Prince himself in presence of both parties doth consent unto and alloweth." "That is," concludes Smith, "the Prince's and the whole realm's deed: whereupon justly no man can complain, but must accommodate himself to find it good and obey it."[25] Aside from the forthright declaration of the supremacy of Parliament, the statement is also somewhat unusual in that it derives obedience not from divine injunction but from implied consent in an action involving both the king and representative national participation—"the whole realm's deed." What is not unusual is the notion that the powers of the king, while very considerable, acquire their absolute force by the presence of the king in Parliament.[26]

It was also a commonly held opinion that the king should regard himself as subject to the law. This followed from his position as God's representative. Tyndale cautioned kings to "remember that they are in God's stead and ordained of God not for themselves but for the wealth of their subjects. . . . The king is in the room of God, and his law is God's law and nothing but the law of nature and natural equity which God graved in the hearts of men."[27] If the law of nature be of God, then the king is not above the law. According to Sir John Fortescue, the most distinguished political writer of the late Middle Ages, the king was bound to rule by the laws to which his people assented, and morally obligated to obey the highest law himself: "Wherefore as oft as such a king doth anything against the law of God, or against the law of Nature, he doth wrong notwithstanding the said law declared by the prophet."[28] The notion of the law of nature and the king's subordination to it persists throughout the sixteenth century. The reference to nature as a fundamental norm occupies a central place in the thought of Hooker, and one of its implications is that the king is bound by the law:

I cannot but choose to commend highly their wisdom, by whom the foundations of this commonwealth have been laid; wherein, though no manner person or cause be unsubject to the king's power, yet so is the power of the king over all and in all limited, that unto all his proceedings the law itself is a rule. The axioms of our royal government are these: "lex facit regem;" the king's grant of any favour made contrary to the law is void; "rex nihil potest nisi quod jure potest." [29]

This idea placed a profound philosophical limitation on aspirations to absolutism, but it was impotent by itself to check it. Political writers could urge the king to consider his duty to his people and his obligation to obey the law, but the idea could not compel—it could act only as moral suasion.[30] Parliament, on the other hand, was an established political institution and hence potentially a real restraint, for although it was subject to the king's pleasure and invoked only when he found it useful, nevertheless it could exert political force.

These restraints on total power were recognized by most English political writers. The great Tudor monarchs were successful in achieving near absolute rule by working hard at the business of being sixteenth-century national sovereigns—by gaining public admiration and approval, by not defying Parliament, and by avoiding overt conflict between the practical exercise of power and the idea of ruling lawfully. But the sensitive issue of obedience and nonresistance was never quiescent, and sharp confrontations arose for groups of people and for individuals between the doctrine of divine authority and nonresistance, and between religious conscience and political conviction. Not all who faced dilemmas of conscience were willing to agree that political repression or individual martyrdom was the sole answer, and some of them challenged the doctrine itself. Even when no crisis of faith was involved, an individual could be placed in a difficult situation if he was commanded to commit a deed he knew to be wrong. It was not easy to deny a king, or convenient to remember that although it might be deemed a sin to disobey a king, it was also a sin to obey a command that violated the laws of nature or the laws of God. *A Mirror for Magistrates* presents such a case in the unfortunate plight of John Tiptoft, earl of Worcester, who was charged with the crime of killing the earl of Desmond's sons at the behest of Edward IV. His narrating ghost asks sympathy for his cruel dilemma:

> either I must procure to see them dead,
> Or for contempt as a traitor lose my head.

> What would mine enemies do in such a case,
> Obey the king, or proper death procure?
> They may well say their fancy for a face,
> But life is sweet, and love hard to recure,
> They would have done as I did I am sure.

His final word of advice is:

> Let none such office take
> Save he that can for right his prince forsake.[31]

A discouraging conclusion, for how many courageously virtuous men would be left to undertake the king's business? Men with profound convictions know how to be martyrs, but they are not fair models for those who are servants in the daily work of running the state. How do such men challenge the wisdom of that fearsome power?

In 1598 a celebrated dramatic incident took place in which a subject had the opportunity to ponder this question. During a heated debate with his queen on the question of peace with Spain and the choice of someone to send to Ireland, Essex so far forgot himself as to earn a box on the ear from his sovereign, upon which he intemperately laid his hand on his sword. The Lord Keeper, in what Camden describes as "a grave and sober letter," advised him to humbly ask the queen's mercy: "If he had justly offended his Prince, he could not make her satisfaction; if she had offended him, prudence, duty, yea religion itself did require that he should submit himself to the Queen, to whom he was so much engaged, forasmuch as there is no equality between a prince and a subject." Essex replied "stomachfully and passionately," in a letter which expresses the feelings of a proud subject who thinks himself wronged by a ruler who is beyond a subject's criticism:

> What I owe as a subject I know, and what as an Earl and Marshall of England I know: but how to serve as a drudge and a slave I know not. If I should acknowledge myself guilty, I should do wrong to the truth, and to God the author of truth. My whole body is wounded by that one blow. Having received this indignity, it were impiety in me to serve longer.

And he then asked with equal passion those improper questions: "Cannot princes err? Can they not wrong their subjects? Is any earthly power infinite? . . . They which get advantage by princes' errors and misdoings, let them take injuries at princes' hands. They who believe not the infinite omnipotency of Almighty God may acknowledge an infinite power in royal majesty."[32] Essex was an unruly spirit, quite capable himself of being "violent and outrageous," but to how many other men, less temperamental and ambitious, did similar thoughts occur, in spite of their familiarity with the *Homilies?*

The point has been made in connection with the political views and attitudes of Elizabethan dramatists that they would have been unavoidably influenced by the doctrine of the official sermons on obedience, and that we may be sure that Shakespeare must have listened to them and absorbed their teachings. It does not necessarily follow, however, that Shakespeare, or any other Elizabethan dramatist for that matter, was by that process brainwashed. We cannot properly see them as men of their time by belying the complexity of their world. If Shakespeare could not fail to attend to the annual readings of the homilies, neither could he escape an awareness of the great events and the diversity of opinion of the extraordinary times in which he lived, and in consequence he must have been conscious of the theoretical difficulties involved in the doctrine, the challenges which the times repeatedly threw up against it, and the dilemmas of great as well as ordinary men whom the realities of power and the inflexibility of the official doctrine tempted to entertain rebellious thoughts.

It is true that for the most part the English plays that deal with the theme of civil rebellion in the 1580s and the 1590s are conservative in outlook and unprovocative in their approach to the redress of wrongs.[33] This is not surprising in view of the nature of the patronage of dramatic companies, the licensing of plays before production, and the fact that the only serious bias in the censorship of plays was political. There are sufficient reasons, however, why we should not adopt these premises as a guide to the history plays of Shakespeare. A political philosopher or propagandist will devote his rhetoric to making one view prevail, but a dramatist is by the nature of his art directed to present a diversity of men working with or contending against each other and representing a variety of individual attitudes. The more impressive and original the talents of a dramatist, the more flexible will be his use of the conventions of the theatre and the more wide-ranging his capacity to enter into the action of his characters. Beyond all other dramatists of his age, Shakespeare approached the involvements of his characters with a degree of understanding which comprehends a measure of sympathy for them. Their enmities, their mortal conflicts, their expedient alliances and oppositions arise out of their whole being, and that involves their political attitudes and prejudices. These cannot be dissociated from the passions that move them and the choices which they make, and in consequence political beliefs acquire a vitality and human attachment which makes them something more than topics and commonplaces in a formal argument. What emerges from the plays is not a doctrine, but understanding. One is persuaded from a reading of these plays that their author had certain convictions and attitudes of his own, though trying to formulate them precisely seems always to end in disappointing results. But whatever we may finally determine to be Shakespeare's individual political attitudes, we can be reasonably certain that if we read the history plays with official pronouncements on disobedience as the primary gloss and chief touchstone we will miss out very badly. And we will miss out in more than one way. We will fail to perceive the intricate way in which the political ideas enter into the design of the plays, and we will also be in a less advantageous position to go beyond these to an appreciation of the plays as a remarkable representation of political man in action and of the ways of power.

VI

Legitimacy and Sovereign Power:
1, 2, and 3 Henry VI

"Why is it that the poor are crushed beneath wrongs and out-
rages, made lean with exactions, despoiled by manifold and
often repeated rapine, why are the peoples bidden to clash together in arms and shake the world, to no end but that princes
may be succeeded by their natural heirs?"[1] This was written by
John of Salisbury in the late twelfth century, but the question
he asked troubled England throughout the long period of dispute, uncertainty, and warfare which followed the abdication
of Richard II, and it had not yet been fully answered in the
reign of the Tudors.

For nearly two centuries the succession to the throne of England had been a troublesome and often bloody business. Edward II was deposed and then cruelly murdered some seventy
years before Richard II had to endure the same experience. Between Richard II and Henry VIII only two kings of England,
Henry V and Henry VI, inherited the throne as acknowledged
heirs on the death by natural causes of the previous monarch.
Two—Richard II and Henry VI—were forced to abdicate. One—
Edward V — was never crowned and was deposed by Parliament

and later murdered in the Tower. The rest—Henry IV, Edward IV, Richard III—made their way to the throne by unconventional and illegal means. Henry IV returned to England from exile with the support of many of his peers and backed by troops, and he willed the murder of the king whom he forced to abdicate. Edward IV became king only after a bloody civil war. On the path to the throne he had supported his father in breaking an oath that Henry VI would be permitted to live out his rule in exchange for allowing the succession to pass to the house of York on his death, an action which renewed the civil war; he had been implicated in the death of Edward, son and heir of Henry VI; and he seems to have acquiesced in the death of Henry VI, presumably murdered by Edward's brother Richard in the Tower. Whatever may be the historical truth about Richard III, at least one thing is clear: that neither of Edward's male heirs was crowned. Richard himself was killed in a battle contesting his right to the throne; and though his successor was generally accepted, in part by virtue of a prudent marriage resolving the claims of the Yorkist line, his own claims were tenuous, and he was challenged twice by impostors who found support. Henry VIII succeeded by direct inheritance, but the irregularities of his marital life and his frustrations in producing a male heir vastly complicated the problem for the future. Henry's heirs succeeded not in natural order but in that prescribed in his will; moreover, the legitimacy of Mary or Elizabeth could be questioned and hence their right to the crown. Before Mary was officially crowned, Lady Jane Grey lost her life in consequence of a scheme to promote her claims to the throne, and the ramifications of Henry's divorce kept alive the claim of Mary Stuart until she was finally beheaded. As for Elizabeth's successor, it remained a problem during her entire reign and was a touchy issue with the queen.

Political considerations, even force, entered into many of these successions to the throne, and in every instance Parliament intervened to consent to the abdication or approve the lineal claim, and thus became an important instrument in determining succession. Moreover, each case left its mark on the constitutional issue. Legitimacy was an essential condition for the confident exercise of power, but what determined a clear and unquestionable succession was not fixed by a single law or even a firm and unbroken tradition.

The issue of legitimacy and power is at the center of the *Henry VI* trilogy. It divides loyalties, arouses passions, and becomes a touchstone that exposes character and temperament, and it unfolds in the course of these plays with a complexity that would have delighted Jarndyce and Jarndyce and kept them in fees for years. But in *Henry VI* its involvements produce a more than Dickensian plot and lead to all the evils that can beset a commonwealth. Each play of the trilogy has its own particular center of conflict, but the principal one which is introduced in Part 1 and grows in importance until it takes over completely arises from the claims of the Plantagenets to the throne. Who has the right to be king of England—the duke of York and his heirs, or Henry VI and his?

As the play opens, the raising of such a question would have appeared shocking, if not treasonable. A great king has just died. Men who later reveal themselves to be bitter enemies join in common praise of the heroic Henry V whose like had never been seen before and is unlikely to appear again. His father may have technically been a usurper, but no one raises this objection; in the atmosphere of the opening speeches an allusion to a defect in the title of the dead hero would have been near blasphemy. There is no hint of a weak title or of divine disfavor. There is only a chorus of praise mixed with lament:

> *Bedford.* Henry the Fifth, too famous to live long!
> England ne'er lost a king of so much worth.
> *Gloucester.* England ne'er had a king until this time.
> (1.1.6–8)
>
> *Winchester.* He was a king blessed of the King of kings.
> (1.28)

Though these same men break out into quarreling almost before the laments die on their lips, they unite again in taking steps to crown the infant heir of Henry V as the new king—casually, as though there could be no other step to take, no other succession thinkable. The quarrels which begin the play and grow in intensity and scope have nothing to do with the rightness of the succession. They are centered rather in a struggle for power behind the throne of the infant king, initially between the Protector, Humphrey duke of Gloucester, and the bishop of Winchester, but eventually involving others who take selfish advantage of the confusion produced by the political disputes at home and the unfinished war abroad. Late in Part 1, Exeter, who several times during these plays exercises a choric function, sums up the dangerous situation:

> no simple man that sees
> This jarring discord of nobility,
> This shouldering of each other in the Court,
> This factious bandying of their favorites,
> But sees it doth presage some ill event.
> 'Tis much when scepters are in children's hands;
> But more when envy breeds unkind division:
> There comes the ruin, there begins confusion.
> (4.1.187–94)

These quarrels invite unrest and create the environment which the Yorkists take advantage of. The first indication of the great division which will end in civil war is the unhistorical episode in the Temple Garden (2.4) in which the disputants pluck white and red roses from the garden as a sign of their partisanship. The "jarring discord" which Exeter refers to in the speech just quoted is a quarrel between Basset and Vernon, an outgrowth of the Temple Garden episode, "about a certain question in the law" (4.1.95). It is never revealed just what the legal question was which had been argued so loudly in the Temple itself that the disputants saw fit to remove to the garden, but it could not have been York's claim to the throne since at this point such a question would have been treasonous, and the debate in the garden would have taken a different form. The argument is ominous nevertheless because it creates a cleavage that is bitter and irreparable, and the quarrel produces an insult which leads Plantagenet to inquire into his rights and arouses the sense of injustice that eventually prompts him to challenge the king's title. The scene has another interest as well, because as the disputants explain their position on the question at issue, they reveal attitudes which anticipate those that will become decisive when the important dispute over the title to the throne is finally made explicit.

Plantagenet opens the scene: "Great lords and gentlemen, what means this silence? / Dare no man answer in a case of truth?" (2.4.1–2). Suffolk's reply expresses an indifference to "truth" and law:

> Faith, I have been a truant in the law
> And never yet could frame my will to it,
> And therefore frame the law unto my will.
>
> (2.4.7–9)

Legalities and claims of truth, that is, are trivial and unimportant; what counts is to bend the law to one's will. Warwick also refuses to become mired in legalities; the future kingmaker's attitude is pragmatic:

> Between two hawks, which flies the higher pitch;
> Between two dogs, which hath the deeper mouth;
> Between two blades, which bears the better temper;
> Between two horses, which doth bear him best;
> Between two girls, which hath the merriest eye—
> I have perhaps some shallow spirit of judgment;
> But in these nice sharp quillets of the law,
> Good faith, I am no wiser than a daw.
>
> (2.4.11–18)

Somerset, no less than Plantagenet, claims the truth for his side, but the feelings become so intense as the two sides divide with the plucking of the roses that when Plantagenet demands of Somerset, "where is your argument?" (2.4.59) the latter replies,

"Here in my scabbard, meditating that / Shall dye your white rose in a bloody red" (2.4.60–61). The scene is prophetic. In the very sanctuary of the common law, a dispute over an undesignated legal question has generated such fierce controversy that the disputants have had to leave the Temple hall and carry their argument in the garden, and the legal issue ultimately gets lost among differences which are neither legal nor intellectual. What hope, then, that later a legal claim involving the succession and steeped in so much history could get settled on its legal merits alone?

What fixes the direction of this quarrel is a calculated insult by Somerset—"We grace the yeoman by conversing with him" (2.4.81). This is a reference to the loss of the family title and lands through the execution of Plantagenet's father, the earl of Cambridge, for treason against Henry V; it provides the incentive to start the fiery Plantagenet on the road that brings his son to the throne. He begins by visiting his dying uncle, Mortimer, in prison to learn the truth about his father's attainder and execution. Mortimer expounds the anti-Lancastrian version of the title of Henry VI—the deposition of Richard II, the "usurpation" of his throne by Henry IV, and the unjust exclusion of Mortimer's and Plantagenet's rights as descendants of Lionel, the third son of Edward III. To these circumstances he ties Plantagenet's loss of inherited title and lands: Plantagenet's father lost his life because he had levied arms in support of Mortimer's claim against that of Henry V. With his dying voice Mortimer hints darkly at future possibilities: "Thou art my heir, the rest I wish thee gather; / But yet be wary in thy studious care" (2.5.96–97). To Plantagenet the execution of his father by the hero king, whose death is universally lamented at the opening of the play, "was nothing less than bloody tyranny," but Mortimer advises caution:

> With silence, nephew, be thou politic:
> Strong-fixed is the house of Lancaster,
> And like a mountain, not to be removed.
>
> (2.5.101–3)

Whatever the legal rights, Henry IV and Henry V have turned a usurper's slippery footing into a strong foundation. With Warwick's assistance, the blot on the family is removed and Plantagenet is "restored to his blood" as duke of York by the king (3.1.149 ff.); but now York has a greater goal to aspire to. Yet in the atmosphere of admiration for Henry V which characterizes the opening scene, the complex legal claims of the Plantagenets would have been neither self-evident nor compelling enough in themselves to force their consideration; it is the occasion which in time gives life and reality to the legal question. And when it does, the decisive arguments are found not in law but, as Somerset says in the Temple Garden scene, in a scabbard.

The matter of legal right is not, of course, without persuasive power. In Part 2 the legality of the Yorkist claim is the argument by means of which York persuades Warwick and Salisbury to support his claims. He reviews for them the complicated lines of inheritance and intermarriage on which his claim rests, and his friends are persuaded.

> What plain proceeding is more plain than this?
> Henry doth claim the crown from John of Gaunt,
> The fourth son; York claims it from the third.
> Till Lionel's issue fails, his should not reign:
> It fails not yet, but flourishes in thee,
> And in thy sons, fair slips of such a stock.
> (2.2.52–57)

Warwick and Salisbury kneel and acknowledge York their true king. Without the support of the principle of nearest in blood and indefeasible right, they would be nothing but traitors; as it is, they can regard themselves as supporters of law and justice. Nevertheless, what fires York's ambition is not so much his complicated legal rights as his contempt for the gentle Henry in comparison with his own spirit and abilities. This is the theme of his long soliloquy which concludes the first scene of Part 2. York deplores the loss of "his" lands in France, while Henry, "the silly owner of the goods,"

> Weeps over them, and wrings his hapless hands,
> And shakes his head, and trembling stands aloof,
> While all is shared and all is borne away,
> Ready to starve, and dare not touch his own.
>
> (1.1.227–30)

Henry is the usurper who holds "the scepter in his childish fist" (246), whose "church-like humor fits not for a crown" (248), and whom York is determined to replace: "And force perforce I'll make him yield the crown, / Whose bookish rule hath pulled fair England down" (1.1.259–60). In the course of the play this conviction becomes a passion. He returns from Ireland with his troops, determined to demand his right:

> From Ireland thus comes York to claim his right,
> And pluck the crown from feeble Henry's head.
> Ring bells, aloud; burn bonfires, clear and bright,
> To entertain great England's lawful king.
> Ah, sancta majestas, Who would not buy thee dear?
> Let them obey that know not how to rule;
> This hand was made to handle nought but gold.
>
> (5.1.1–7)

The angry discontent of Part 1 has been transformed into a fierce aspiration echoing Tamburlaine; right is won not by birth only but by virtue: "I am far better born than is the King, / More like a king, more kingly in my thoughts" (5.1.28–29). This is spoken in an aside when Buckingham demands to know why he comes to England armed at a time of peace, and for the moment York temporizes, claiming that he came only to remove Somerset's influence over the king; but when Somerset, who is supposed to have been imprisoned, suddenly appears, he speaks his mind in open defiance in the royal presence:

> King did I call thee? No, thou art not King,
> Not fit to govern and rule multitudes,
> Which dar'st not, no, nor canst not rule a traitor.
> That head of thine doth not become a crown;
> Thy hand is made to grasp a palmer's staff,
> And not to grace an awful princely scepter.

> That gold must round engirt these brows of mine,
> Whose smile and frown, like to Achilles' spear,
> Is able with the change to kill and cure.
> Here is a hand to hold a scepter up,
> And with the same to act controlling laws.
> Give place: by heaven, thou shalt rule no more
> O'er him whom heaven created for thy ruler.
>   (5.1.93–105)

The contrast which York insists on between himself and the
king is supported by Henry's conduct and the opinion of others,
including his queen. She compares him unfavorably to Suffolk:

> I thought King Henry had resembled thee
> In courage, courtship, and proportion:
> But all his mind is bent to holiness,
> To number Ave-Maries on his beads;
> His champions are the prophets and apostles.
> His weapons holy saws of sacred writ,
> His study is his tilt-yard, and his loves
> Are brazen images of canonized saints.
> I would the College of the Cardinals
> Would choose him Pope and carry him to Rome,
> And set the triple crown upon his head:
> That were a state fit for his Holiness.
>   (1.3.53–64)

Unkind and unwifely this may be, but the queen perceives correctly that in consequence of the king's character they have to
endure not only "the haughty Protector," but the dangerous
exercise of power by Beaufort, "the imperious churchman," as
well as Somerset, Buckingham, and "grumbling York" (1.3.68–
70). In the important matter of whether Somerset or York shall
be regent of France, Henry is indifferent—"all's one to me"
(1.3.102), and the queen has to remind the wrangling nobles
where the power lies: "Because the King, forsooth, will have it
so" (1.3.115). Even during a hunting party the insolent rivalries for power trouble the occasion and Henry, tormented by
the undercurrent of quarreling, has to admonish his attendant
nobles and the queen:

> I prithee peace,
> Good Queen, and whet not on these furious peers,
> For blessed are the peacemakers on earth.
> (2.1.32–34)

They are blessed, but not, as Henry uses his powers, kingly, for it is precisely the decency and pacific gentleness of Henry that nourishes the quarrels in his court which finally undo him.

The inability of Henry to make his sovereignty felt and thus insure justice and harmony for his kingdom finds its most poignant dramatic expression in the indictment and murder of Gloucester. This is a critical episode in Part 2. Gloucester is the only important character in this play whose conduct is not guided by selfish personal interest, and his defeat removes from the scene the only honest and strong person close to the king. In contrast to York, he never dreams of taking advantage of the times to push his own lineal descent from Edward III, and recoils when his wife, foreshadowing Lady Macbeth, urges him to seize the throne: "Put forth thy hand, reach at the glorious gold. / What, is't too short? I'll lengthen it with mine" (1.2.11–12). The queen, however, does not scruple to hint at such possibilities as a way of poisoning Henry's mind against Gloucester:

> Small curs are not regarded when they grin,
> But great men tremble when the lion roars;
> And Humphrey is no little man in England.
> First note that he is near you in descent,
> And should you fall, he is the next will mount.
> (3.1.18–22)

York takes no part in the undermining of Gloucester. His strategy is to allow the contending ambitions of Suffolk, Beaufort, Somerset, Buckingham, "and all the crew of them" to destroy Gloucester, and when the wolves have "snared the shepherd of the flock" to move against the king (2.2.69–75). The king's inability to protect Gloucester is therefore more than a humiliating failure to secure justice; it makes him vulnerable to York's plans. And the humanity which distinguishes him from the rest serves only to deepen his suffering at the injustice which is being done, for he is fully persuaded of Gloucester's innocence:

> but, shall I speak my conscience,
> Our kinsman Gloucester is as innocent
> From meaning treason to our royal person
> As is the sucking lamb or harmless dove.
>
> (3.1.68–71)

All he can offer Gloucester after hearing the formal charges is reassurance:

> My lord of Gloucester, 'tis my special hope
> That you will clear yourself from all suspense.
> My conscience tells me you are innocent.
>
> (3.1.139–41)

Neither the despairing speech of Gloucester nor the evidence of implacable malice on the part of those, including the queen, who bring the charges is enough to compel the king's prudent attention to his responsibilities, for when Gloucester is led out, Henry rises to leave also, assigning the exercise of his office to those he mistrusts: "My lords, what to your wisdoms seemeth best, / Do, or undo, as if ourself were here," (3.1.195–96). Even the queen is astonished: "What, will your Highness leave the Parliament?" (197). In reply he reaffirms his belief in Gloucester's integrity and innocence, but all he can do is to pour out his grief and bewail

> good Gloucester's case
> With sad unhelpful tears and with dimmed eyes
> Look after him and cannot do him good,
> So mighty are his vowed enemies.
>
> (3.1.217–20)

"So mighty"—mightier than the king, the heir of Henry V? The queen's comment to the nobles is contemptuous: "Henry my lord is cold in great affairs, / Too full of foolish pity," (3.1.224–25). Out of their contempt they plot the murder of Gloucester, for they realize that in any lawful trial they have "but trivial argument" (3.1.231–43). Thus, when Henry opens the trial with a show of regal firmness it is an act of futility:

> Proceed no straiter 'gainst our uncle Gloucester
> Than from true evidence of good esteem
> He be approved in practice culpable.
>
> (3.2.19–21)

The only purpose of the meeting for the others is to receive the news of Gloucester's death; yet Henry cannot act on the conviction that the death was not natural:

> O thou that judgest all things, stay my thoughts,
> My thoughts that labor to persuade my soul
> Some violent hands were laid on Humphrey's life.
> If my suspect be false, forgive me, God,
> For judgment only doth belong to Thee.
>
> (3.2.135–39)

But here, on earth, judgment also belong to God's magistrate, and shortly, but too late and only after the commons rise up in revolt at the news of Gloucester's death to demand the death of Suffolk, Henry does act, without recourse to law, on his own prerogative to protect his crown and the country. He exiles Suffolk. Ironically, in this entire episode, Henry has unwittingly been playing a role in York's scenario. Gloucester is dead, Suffolk exiled, the plotters for the moment discomfited, and the rabble-rouser Cade, a product of York's intrigues, is creating a dangerous diversion. It is the moment that York has been planning for.

In the confrontation between the king and York after the latter's return from Ireland, York proclaims himself the rightful king, and the question of his legal claim comes up briefly. Salisbury affirms that his conscience tells him York is "the rightful heir to England's royal seat" (5.1.178). But the complicated claims and counterclaims now have a faintly academic air. There is an amusing scene (4.2.125 ff.) in which Cade justifies his rebellion by a fanciful line of descent beginning with Adam who was a gardener, proceeding through Mortimer's marriage to the duke of Clarence's daughter, by whom he had twins, and thence to the theft of one of these by a beggar woman who brought him up to be a bricklayer—a ludicrous parody of genealogical claims to the throne based on a circuitous pedigree which intervening events have rendered tenuous if not irrelevant. The real issue in this play is the capability of the ruler to maintain whatever claims he does have by the forceful exercise of the powers and responsibilities which belong to the office. It is significant that when Buckingham and Clifford face Cade and his mob they ask for allegiance to the king in the name of "Henry the Fifth, that made all France to quake," and when the mob cries, "We'll follow Cade," it is checked with, "Is Cade the son of Henry the Fifth?" (4.8.17, 33–34). Cade observes ruefully that "the name of Henry the Fifth hales them to an hundred mischiefs and makes them leave me desolate (4.7.56–58).[2] The rival legal claims have become meaningless in the face of the steady erosion of the powers of kingship through Henry's failure to exercise them and the disruption of all order which this failure has produced. Nothing can now avert civil war, the first battle of which concludes the second part. Even here Henry proves a frustrating monarch. As his forces flee from the defeat in the first battle of Saint Albans and the queen urges haste, Henry replies, "Can we outrun the heavens? Good Margaret, stay." Margaret is not an appealing character, but sympathy at this moment surely goes to her: "What are you made of? You'll nor fight nor fly" (5.2.73–74).

The primary impression of Part 3 is the dehumanizing effects of the civil war, and against this background the arguments over legitimacy continue, manifesting at once their obstinate futility and their tragic power. The play opens on this theme. York and his sons enter the Parliament House mixing boasts of their exploits at Saint Albans with scoffing references to the "fearful king," the "bashful Henry," "whose cowardice / Hath made us by-words to our enemies" (1.1.25, 41–42). York has already seated himself on the throne before Henry enters, and Henry proves the justice of their epithets by urging patience on his followers. Clifford breaks out in exasperation: "Patience is for poltroons, such as he. / He durst not sit there had your father lived" (1.1.62–63). Once more the point is made in the name of Henry V that kingly bearing and conduct are proof against challenges to royal power. Nevertheless, it is the presumption of legal right that nourished York's aspirations and gave his allies moral courage and justification for armed rebellion. "Will you we show our title to the crown?" asks York. "If not, our swords shall plead it in the field" (1.1.102–3). Henry takes up the challenge:

> What title hast thou, traitor, to the crown?
> Thy father was, as thou art, Duke of York;
> Thy grandsire, Roger Mortimer, Earl of March.
> (1.1.104–6)

Henry conveniently leaves out the question of Lionel's precedence, and supports his title by appealing to his descent from the hero king:

> I am the son of Henry the Fifth,
> Who made the Dauphin and the French to stoop
> And seized upon their towns and provinces.
> (1.1.107–9)

It is an unfortunate reference, for it merely enables Warwick to make the obvious comparison: "Talk not of France, sith thou hast lost it all" (1.1.110). It is futile for Henry to plead, "when I was crowned I was but nine months old"; he only opens himself to an insult from Richard: "You are old enough now, and yet methinks you lose" (1.1.112–13). The dispute brings Henry to one of his few resolute moments:

> Thinkst thou that I will leave my kingly throne,
> Wherein my grandsire and my father sat?
> No: first shall war unpeople this my realm,

114

Ay, and their colors, often borne in France,
And now in England to our heart's great sorrow,
Shall be my winding sheet. Why faint you, lords?
My title's good, and better far than his.
                                    (1.1.128–34)

The mood does not last. Warwick challenges him—"Prove it
Henry, and thou shalt be King" (1.1.135)—and Henry is soon
baffled. He begins bravely enough, going back to the beginning—"Henry the Fourth by conquest got the crown"—but this
introduces the ancient question of Bolingbroke's moral wrong:
" 'Twas by rebellion against his king," and Henry confesses to
himself, "I know not what to say; my title's weak" (1.1.136–38).
But he perseveres: if a king may adopt his heir, as Richard did
Bolingbroke, then he is heir by right of descent from Henry IV.
But York objects that the resignation was "perforce" and Warwick raises the question whether, even if the resignation were
unconstrained, " 'twere prejudicial to the crown" (1.1.146–48).
The answer comes from Exeter: "No; for he could not so resign
his crown / But that the next heir should succeed and reign"
(1.1.149–50). This argument rests on the principle of indefeasible right—that neither the continued occupancy of the throne
by Henry IV and his heirs nor the great success of Henry V had
wiped out the rights of the descendants of Lionel. On these
grounds Exeter takes his stand for York: "My conscience tells
me he is lawful king" (1.1.154). But Clifford, with the memory
of his slain father on his mind, sweeps away all such abstruse
technicalities: "King Henry, be thy title right or wrong / Lord
Clifford vows to fight in thy defence" (1.1.163–64).

The immediate conclusion of this perplexed, finespun argument evades all its serious implication, irrespective of which side
one takes. It is a political deal. The king asks for and is granted
the right to reign during his lifetime on condition that he disinherit his son "unnaturally" and confirm the succession to York
and his heirs, provided that York take an oath to end the civil
war. It is an impossible settlement. The prince protests, "Father,
you cannot disinherit me: / If you be King, why should not I

succeed?" (1.1.233–34). When Henry explains that he was forced, Margaret exclaims, "Enforced thee! Art thou King, and wilt be forced?" (1.1.237). What, indeed, does it mean to be a king if the title is dubious and cannot therefore be passed on by the laws which govern inheritance? And what does it mean to be king when one is intimidated and commanded by the most aggressive of one's subjects? The agreement is equally inconsistent and ineffectual on the other side. If York believes his title to be superior, he cannot in justice agree to defer the taking of it. As his son Richard points out, "Your right depends not on his [Henry's] life or death" (1.2.11). As for the oath York swore to preserve this odd arrangement, his young son knows that such outmoded technicalities can be argued away by sophistries, and that his father will yield to a direct appeal to his fierce aspiration (1.2.28–32). The civil war breaks out anew.

The rival claims are disputed for the last time before King Lewis of France. Margaret has come to plead for aid, and Warwick to propose marriage for the new king, Edward IV, with Lady Bona, Lewis' sister. Margaret argues that Edward is a usurper, since he has seized the throne of a legally crowned king, and therefore a tyrant; but Warwick maintains that Henry is the original usurper (3.3.65–80). Oxford reviews the hereditary basis for Henry's legitimacy:

> Then Warwick disannuls great John of Gaunt,
> Which did subdue the greatest part of Spain;
> And after John of Gaunt, Henry the Fourth,
> Whose wisdom was a mirror to the wisest;
> And, after that wise prince, Henry the Fifth,
> Who by his prowess conquered all France:
> From these our Henry lineally descends.
>
> (3.3.81–87)

Oxford does trace an unbroken succession, but the emphasis is rather on the wisdom and prowess of the line from John of Gaunt, and nothing is said of the crucial matter of the deposition of Richard II. Significantly, Warwick's rebuttal begins with a reference to the failings of Henry VI in comparison with his forebears:

> Oxford, how haps it, in this smooth discourse
> You told us not how Henry the Sixth hath lost
> All that which Henry the Fifth had gotten.
>
> (3.3.88–90)

When he does refer to the question of inheritance, it is not to raise the legal issue of indefeasible right of York and his heirs but the weakness of a dynastic claim based on a brief period of tenure:

> But for the rest: you tell a pedigree
> Of threescore and two years—a silly time
> To make prescription for a kingdom's worth.
>
> (3.3.92–94)

Lewis cuts through most of the legalities of the situation. "Is Edward your true king?" he asks Warwick, "is he gracious in the people's eye?" (3.3.114, 117), and he rejects Margaret's plea for assistance chiefly on the basis that Edward's title seems the stronger since he is successful:

> But if your title to the crown be weak,
> As may appear by Edward's good success,
> Then 'tis but reason that I be released
> From giving aid which late I promised.
>
> (3.3.145–48)

Yet all this is reversed in a moment when news comes that Edward has married Lady Grey and broken off the negotiations for Lady Bona. Warwick, dishonored, asks, "Did I put Henry from his native right? / And am I guerdoned at the last with shame?" (3.3.190–91). Once more political and personal considerations become decisive.

Repeatedly, the question of Henry's right to rule turns on the question of whether he can rule. Edward, in fact, admits that had it not been for Henry's lack of those kingly qualities his father had, his imprudent marriage, and Queen Margaret's aggressive tactics, his family would not have pushed their claim (2.2.150–62). Clifford is a supporter of Henry, and Edward an ambitious enemy, but both agree in their estimate of him. Dying, Clifford judges the man he has supported with his life:

> And, Henry, hadst thou swayed as kings should do,
> Or as thy father, and his father did,
> Giving no ground unto the house of York,
> They never then had sprung like summer flies;
> I and ten thousand in this luckless realm
> Had left no mourning widows for our death;
> And thou this day hadst kept thy chair in peace.
>   (2.6.14–20)

The three parts of *Henry VI* present a comprehensive view in debate and in action of the legal and political aspects of the problem of legitimacy and power. Neither the triumph of Edward nor the death of Henry can be thought of as resolving conclusively the issues around which the long contest has raged. However, one strong inference seems to emerge, that although an undisputed legal succession provides the strongest moral support for the exercise of sovereign power, the right to govern cannot be separated from the ability to govern—from the capacity and talent for the exercise of power in the person of the man who occupies the sovereign office. The name of Henry V runs through all three plays as a universally recognized symbol of kingly greatness. Henry V's father was a usurper with the blood of Richard II on his conscience, yet Henry V had made his authority legitimate and respected because he had exercised power with talent and public approval. In comparison with his father, Henry VI is shown to lack the ability to wield power in such a way as to command authority and inspire confidence and awe. In comparison with York, he is shown to be insecure and to have no taste for the power and glory of his office. Lacking these kingly qualities he is unable to control the disruptive actions of the ambitious men who surround him—in fact, his ineffectuality as a king breeds these ambitions and invites the contempt which inflames the aspirations and the petty greeds that tear his kingdom apart.

Henry is not a despicable figure, however, and in time he comes to arouse sympathy. The first two plays of the trilogy contain characters who stand out for their integrity and honorableness in the midst of the predators who take advantage first of Henry's infancy and then of his weakness. Talbot holds this position in Part 1, and Gloucester in Part 2. In Part 3 only Henry stands out in the midst of the slaughter and outrage as a decent and sympathetic character. In his piety, his distaste for conflict and his hopes for peace, in his longing for a life of simple content, and in his horror at the spectacle of the woes, fierce passions, and cruelty of the civil war, he remains the only one who redeems humanity. Yet he cannot redeem his kingdom. Henry is admittedly an extreme case among all the monarchs represented in the histories, but for that very reason he sets in the sharpest relief the terrible dilemma of power.

VII

Tyranny and Resistance:
Richard III

Just before the battle of Bosworth Field, Richard restores his courage by reaffirming his principles:

> Let not our babbling dreams affright our souls;
> Conscience is but a word that cowards use,
> Devised at first to keep the strong in awe;
> Our strong arms be our conscience, swords our law!
>
> (5.3.309–12)

Richard's lack of conscience stands him in good stead, but it is not swords that cut his path to the throne, it is not might that establishes his right. He gains the crown through becoming the legal heir by right of hereditary succession and the securing of public approval. Though he makes a mockery of the solemn traditions and legal sanctions of legitimacy, he does not challenge them; he makes them his ladder to the throne.

Richard's opening soliloquy gives the impression of a time shortly after the death of Henry VI and the possession, at last, of the throne by Edward IV of the Yorkist line, and this impression is confirmed by the appearance of Anne with the body of Henry VI being carried to burial. Yet we hear almost immediately of the illness of Edward which shortly proves fatal, although some twelve years separated these two events in history (Henry VI was killed in 1471 and Edward died in 1483). The restless spirit which animates the opening soliloquy could hardly have been content to wait so long, and Shakespeare radically contracts historical time so that the question of Richard's action during the interval does not arise. There is no indication that he ever contemplated shortening Edward's reign as a step in his progress to royal power. His scheme is to eliminate the principal heirs so that on Edward's death he will remain the sole survivor among Edward's kin whose claim to the throne could be considered.

The first victim is Clarence, who is murdered before Edward dies to eliminate him as a possible contender. Richard marries Anne "for a secret close intent" (1.1.158), never explained; presumably Richard sees some advantages in her former connections as daughter of the late earl of Warwick and as wife (really betrothed) to Prince Edward, son and heir of Henry VI. On the death of Edward IV, Richard breaks the power of the queen and her family by arresting Rivers and Grey as they are accompanying the two princes to London for the coronation of Edward V. The princes are placed in the Tower for "safekeeping," and Richard has Rivers and Grey executed. Hastings loses his life for declaring his loyalty to the princes as heirs of the former king. Next the princes are declared illegitimate. Then, with the help of Buckingham who acts as Richard's public-relations man, an image of Richard is created as a pious Christian prince who will only reluctantly take on the cares of state because the public demand that he do so is overwhelming. He thus becomes king with a legal title by hereditary succession, official solicitation, and public acclaim, though the title is obtained by fraud, the official approval nothing more than a timorous request by a bamboozled Lord Mayor without parliamentary action, and the public acclaim a contrived piece of stage business. It remains to make the crown secure. The princes are murdered in the

Tower; Anne, no longer useful, is done away with, and Richard goes to Edward's queen to arrange for a politically advantageous marriage with her daughter. But this last move fails. Elizabeth will promise her daughter to Richmond, and the whole extraordinary tour de force of intrigue and murder ends on the field of battle at Bosworth. Richard emerges from Shakespeare's presentation of his progress to the throne as the classic image of the tyrant; he is tyrannical because of the means by which he achieves the throne and tyrannical because he uses power selfishly and not for the welfare of the commonwealth—a "tyrant both in title and regiment," as Bacon succinctly puts it in the opening sentence of his life of Henry VII. Richmond, who replaces him, is accordingly cast in the role not of a usurper but of a national savior, in the tradition of heroes who rid their country of a tyrant.

Tyranny has never proved an easy concept to deal with, because where constitutional provisions for the removal of an inept or evil ruler do not exist, the alternative means can only be forceful and violent, producing disruption and even threatening the idea of legitimacy as a source of power. Political writers since antiquity have recognized tyranny as a political phenomenon and described its nature, but whereas all agree in deploring its evils and warning of its dangers, there is disagreement on how it should be dealt with and especially on the necessity of removing the tyrant at all costs. Aristotle's definition of tyranny as debased monarchy is frequently cited, but Aristotle does not provide authority for the means by which tyrants should be removed. Cicero approved of tyrannicide in extreme cases, and Seneca portrayed tyrants in several of his plays in a way that gave a sympathetic picture of their opponents. The Old Testament provided examples of the killing of tyrants, but the New Testament could be cited to prove that Paul and even Christ forbade resistance to the emperor, and the example of the Christian martyrs confirmed the idea of passive nonresistance in the face of tyranny. All these classical and biblical precedents became sources for the discussion of tyranny and tyrannicide in the Middle Ages and the Renaissance.[1] The earliest medieval work on tyranny, the *Policraticus* of John of Salisbury, was written near the end of the twelfth century. It describes a tyrant as one who "oppresses the people by rulership based upon force, and regards nothing accomplished under laws unless laws are brought to nought and the people reduced to slavery."[2] In contrast, the good prince rules by law. Since all power is of God, tyrants also are of God, sent because of men's sins, and hence to be endured. God will judge and punish tyrants. At the same time, John also argues, God can employ a human hand to remove a tyrant if he wishes, as the examples of the Old Testament show, and therefore tyrannicide is justified. One should not undertake to kill a tyrant if bound to him by oath or fealty, but for another, "it is as lawful to kill a tyrant as to kill a condemned enemy." Nevertheless, John counsels prayer and dependence on God, instancing David who spared Saul. The two parts of the argument are never reconciled: the *Policraticus* could be cited as a recommendation of passive submission to tyranny providentially ordained, or as a defense of tyrannicide by individuals.

Aquinas attempts to resolve this difficulty and to correct the danger of anarchy inherent in any forthright defense of tyrannicide by individuals. Aquinas' views became generally known through a compilation under the title *De regimini principium*.[3] He defines tyranny in terms of the manner of rule: "If an unjust government is carried on by one man alone, who seeks his own benefit from his rule and not the good of the multitude subject to him, such a ruler is called a *tyrant*—a word derived from *strength*—because he oppresses by might instead of ruling by justice."[4] If the tyranny is but mild it should be tolerated, because sedition is a mortal sin, but Aquinas recognizes that tyranny can become intolerable, in which case the tyrant may be removed, but only by lawful means. What is lawful depends on the source of the king's power. If the king owes his throne to election, "it is not unjust that the king be deposed or have the power restricted by that same multitude if, becoming a tyrant, he abuses the royal power." If he owes his throne to "a higher power," then "a remedy against the wickedness of a tyrant is to be looked for from him." But tyrannicide by an unauthorized individual is unlawful. It may seem to some "a virtue for strong men to slay the tyrant and to expose themselves to the danger of death in order to get the multitude free," but though this means may seem to be supported by biblical precedents, it is not supported by apostolic teaching. Where no help is forthcoming, "recourse must be had to God, the king of all, who is a helper in due time in tribulation." [5] When this was written, feudal barons and great ecclesiastics, in particular the pope, were powerful enough to threaten and even depose a wicked monarch through presumably lawful means, but Aquinas is nevertheless reserved and ambiguous about just how a tyrant is to be removed.

Writing at the very beginning of the fifteenth century, Coluccio Salutati in *De tyranno* summed up the medieval view, though at the same time his work reflects a changing political climate in its almost completely secular treatment of the issue. He distinguishes two types of tyranny; "a tyrant is either one who usurps a government, having no legal title for his rule, or one who governs *superbe* [with rigor and violence] or rules unjustly or does not observe law or equity." [6] Both types of tyrant may be "lawfully resisted, not merely by a party of the people, but by an individual, and . . . such a monster may be put down by force even to the point of murder." [7] Salutati insists on the lawfulness. He recognizes that "a successful and fortunate crime passes for a virtuous deed"—the successful tyrannicide occupies a curious place among the heroes of history—but he condemns such actions as tyrannical themselves if not done by authority of an overlord or by a decree of the people or with their consent, express or implied.[8] He grants, moreover, that a usurper may eventually become acceptable; one who is a tyrant by virtue of violently and illegally seizing power may in time, through decent rule, acquire tacit consent, and "may come to have the semblance of a lawful ruler." [9] Precisely what lawful procedures may be used to remove a tyrant remains vague and troublesome, and Salutati demonstrates once more how difficult it is to agree on who is a bona fide tyrant. The liveliest portion of his treatise is his attack on Cicero for not denouncing the assassins of Caesar—a man of humane spirit who was "raised to power constitutionally and through his own merits," who ruled sensibly, and who saved a deteriorating state. The reason for Salutati's approval of Caesar is to be found in his political preferences influenced no doubt by growing disturbances in his native Florence: "There is no greater liberty than obedience to the just commands of a virtuous prince. As there is no better or more divine rule than that of the universe under one God, so human sovereignty is the higher the more nearly it approaches that idea." [10]

In 1407 there occurred an event that brought to a focus the whole traditional argument about tyranny. John (the Fearless), duke of Burgundy caused to be murdered Louis, brother of Charles VI of France, on the street in front of the queen's residence. He acknowledged the act, but justified it as a worthy deed, the killing of a hateful tyrant, and his defense before his peers was successfully presented by his attorney, Jean Petit. The case was brought up again, however, before the Council of Constance (1414–18) in an effort to have a judgment brought against Jean Petit and the favorable action of the Paris tribunal. The argument against Petit was presented by Jean Gerson, and the debate was accompanied by intrigues and pressures by the partisans of both sides. The council of learned churchmen did not formally condemn Jean Petit, though it did express general disapproval of tyrannicide. The episode provided the occasion for a learned review of the arguments for and against tyrannicide, and it left the issue ambiguous against a background of political expediency.[11]

For the emerging absolutist monarchies of the sixteenth century much of this debate must have had an academic air. Increasingly the emphasis fell on the arguments supporting obedience. The charge of tyranny came usually from militants and disaffected persons. To the Marian exiles, Mary Tudor was a tyrant; to John Knox it was Mary of Scotland; to dedicated Catholics it was Elizabeth. Yet even conservative English political theorists acknowledged the special case of tyranny and were aware of the traditional arguments relating to its removal, though uncertain and even timid about the means for correcting the evil. For example, Thomas Smith observes that a question may arise under an unjust and repressive ruler "whether the obedience be just, and the disobedience be wrong," and he takes note of the good and upright men of "great and haughty courages" who have struck down tyrants. But at the tight spot he slips out and gives no encouragement for removing a tyrant by whatever means: "Certain it is that it is always a doubtful and hazardous matter to meddle with the changing of the laws and government or to disobey the rule or government which a man doth find already established." [12] In fact, such arguments as those of Aquinas and Salutati no longer quite applied. Since an absolute national monarch recognized no "higher power" or "overlord" who might lawfully command the removal of a bad king, and since monarchy was not by election and any demand from the people was viewed as the ultimate danger to civil order, there could be no lawful way of removing a tyrant. Nevertheless, the idea of the tyrant and condemnation of the wrongs of tyranny persisted well into the sixteenth century, and this persistence is itself of some significance.[13] It had the effect of acknowledging by implication the grave dangers inherent in granting total power to any man, while at the same time acceding to the practical political necessity of doing so. "What is more repugnant to nature," writes Starkey, "than a whole nation to be governed by the will of a prince?" For Starkey, unlimited power "is the open gate to all tyranny." [14] Starkey wrote these lines while remaining a faithful servant of Henry VIII. The age-old idea of a tyrant remained a warning against the inflexibility of the idea of obedience to God's representative in its pure form, and may perhaps have served as a deep but unacknowledged moral reservation about orthodox absolutist dogma. It also left an avenue open for explaining away a difficult case like that of Richard III.

The image of the tyrant received important support and a special heightened coloring from the plays of Seneca, the principal model for the classical idiom in tragedy during the sixteenth century. Seneca's fullest delineation of tyrannical power is that of Atreus in *Thyestes*, but also exemplifying the type are Lycus in *Hercules furens*, and Nero in *Octavia* (probably not by Seneca but often attributed to him). Seneca's tyrants, like most of his major protagonists, are victims of violent compulsions. It has properly been said of them that Seneca "presents them not as statesmen or leaders of nations, but as embodiments of a mastering passion, who are victims of spiteful gods or are doomed by the taint of an hereditary sin." It is less accurate, however, to assert that "Seneca's wicked kings are not tyrants in any broad political sense."[15] The political aspect is certainly not lacking. There are extended discussions about the use of kingly power; for example, the debate in act 2 of *Thyestes* between Atreus and an attendant on the advantages of the ruthless exercise of royal power versus virtuous and just rule, or a similar debate in *Octavia* between Seneca and Nero, or the remarks of Lycus in *Hercules furens* about the superiority of a ruler who gains his throne by force rather than inheritance. To the Elizabethans especially, with their taste for sententiousness, the plays would appear full of political wisdom. Some of the aphorisms have a distinctly "Machiavellian" flavor: for instance, such remarks as that of Nero that a caesar should be feared, of Lycus that a ruler must have the capacity to experience hatred without being moved, of Eteocles in the fragment *Phoenissae* that one who would reign must not fear to be hated and that any price is worth paying for a kingdom, or of Atreus during the long debate with the attendant that a king's will is the law and that his are not the virtues of a private man. To their fierce and unnatural passions Seneca's tyrants added a lust for power supported by a political philosophy that exalted fear over love, power over legitimacy, and the will over law. In these respects Shakespeare's Richard III is a distant blood relative of Seneca's tyrants, and the association is implied by the fact that *Richard III* has more Senecan characteristics than any of the other history plays.[16]

The idea of the tyrant entered English drama during the 1560s and 1570s in a series of plays of mixed character, some clearly marked by Senecan influence, and all in varying degrees employing morality play devices.[17] Their choice of historically remote and legendary stories—for instance, *Cambises, Jocasta*—avoided direct application to recent events, and the occasional use of morality devices renders the question of how men must meet unjust rule by a tyrant somewhat abstract (Justice and Reward rescue Virginia in *Apius and Virginia*). The solutions are either conventional or unreal. In this respect the appearance of the figure of Richard III in English drama represented something strikingly different. Richard was a historical figure whose violent removal through death in battle was a matter of historical record generally regarded with approval. It was less easy to disguise the political implications of this episode. The earliest play on the subject in England was the Latin *Richardus tertius* of Thomas Legge, performed at Cambridge in 1580. The treatment is unmistakably, even studiously, Senecan, and Richard is represented as a tyrannical monster.[18]

It is unlikely that Shakespeare knew Legge's play. It is more likely that he was acquainted with the anonymous *True Tragedy of Richard III*, though the relation of this play to that of Shakespeare is full of uncertainties. Stylistically it is not particularly Senecan, and often it is colloquial even in the speeches of Richard, but in one respect it follows the image portrayed in the Latin play; Richard emerges as a tyrant and is labeled as such. The idea of the tyrant which dominates the presentation of Richard is also embodied in a nondramatic work which Shakespeare must have known, the narrative of Richard's ghost in *A Mirror for Magistrates*. Richard describes himself as one

Who entered by rigor, but right did not regard,
By tyranny proceeding in killing king Edward
Fifth of that name.[19]

A tyrant was expected to die an awful death, and the *Mirror* gives Richard his just due:

My body it was harried and tugged like a Dog,
On horseback all naked and bare as I was born.
My head, hands, and feet, down hanging like a hog
With dirt and blood besprent, my corpse all to torn.[20]

There is also the expected moral:

Lo here you may behold the due and just reward
Of tyranny and treason which God doth most detest.[21]

The standard version of Richard's political career is summed up in the headnote to the narratives: "How Richard Plantagenet, Duke of Gloucester, murdered his brother's children usurping the crown, and in the third year of his reign was most worthily deprived of his life and kingdom in Bosworth plain by Henry Earl of Richmond after called King Henry the Seventh." [22] A regicide, a child-murderer, and a usurper, therefore a tyrant and hence "worthily" defeated in battle, slain, and replaced.

How did Richard III come to occupy this bad eminence? Henry IV and Edward IV were duly judged in the pages of history for their sins in compassing the crown, yet neither was branded a tyrant. Henry IV was regarded a usurper who suffered for his crime, harrassed by rebellions and disappointed in his son; but he was nevertheless reconciled to his son before his death and it is nowhere suggested that justice or the nation would have been better served if the rebellions had been successful. Moralizing historians could surmise that Henry's crime was finally punished in the miserable reign and death of his grandson. Edward comes off lightly, considering that he joined his father in breaking the oath to Henry VI, broke his own oath made before York, was implicated in the death of Henry VI's son and heir, and probably also acquiesced in the murder of Henry VI, presumably by Edward's brother Richard. Thomas More speaks well of his reign, and other historians strain to detect the operation of divine justice in the fact that he died of "surfeit"—a conventional piece of piety that Richard III in Shakespeare's play unctuously takes up as part of his strategy of casting slurs at Edward and his family (1.1.139–40). The full punishment for Edward's sins was posthumous, in the death of his sons at the hands of Richard.[23] The providentialists managed to discover in the past workings of divine justice a useful political meaning for the times in which they wrote. They were somewhat sparing of erring monarchs like Henry IV and Edward IV, even if this required that innocent victims like Henry VI and the princes in the Tower had to be used to balance the scales of divine justice; but for reasons of state the sins of Richard III had to be made black and without redemption. "There could not be," writes Hall, "a more crueller tyrant appointed to achieve a more abominable enterprise."[24] His violent overthrow by the first of the Tudors could thus appear as an act of salvation and not just another in the long series of depositions of God's representatives. Holinshed sums up this view of history and of Richard: "And now to conclude with this cruel tyrant king Richard, we may consider in what sort the ambitious desire to govern in the house of York, was punished by God's just providence."[25] By the time Shakespeare took up the subject, Richard III was as unmistakably branded a tyrant as Cain was a murderer.

Shakespeare shows a preoccupation with the idea of tyranny in the *Henry VI* plays, though the interest is largely incidental and the concept loosely applied. Even the gallant soldier Talbot is accused of tyranny by the French countess (*1 Henry VI*: 2.3.39–41). Gloucester, more appropriately, denounces the united efforts of his enemies to destroy him as tyranny (*2 Henry VI*: 3.1.149), and Henry VI uses the word to describe Suffolk's fierce ambition: "Upon thy eyeballs murderous Tyranny / Sits in grim majesty to fright the world" (*2 Henry VI*: 3.2.48–49). To Queen Elizabeth, Warwick, having changed sides and captured Edward, has become a tyrant (*3 Henry VI*: 4.4.26–32). Tyranny stands for ruthless exercise of and inconsiderate lust for power. In a more technical sense, it expresses the partisan feelings of the contenders for the throne against their enemies. For York, the execution of his father by Henry V "was nothing less than bloody tyranny" (*1 Henry VI*: 2.5.99–100). Henry VI himself is referred to by the Yorkists as a usurper and never as a tyrant, but the Lancastrian dynasty is charged with tyranny by the lieutenant who executes Suffolk because the family of York was

> thrust from the crown
> By shameful murder of a guiltless king [Richard II]
> And lofty proud encroaching tyranny.
> (*2 Henry VI*: 4.1.93–95)

On the other hand, for Queen Margaret pleading her case before King Lewis of France, Edward IV is a tyrant, and the proof lies in the fact that the former king, Henry VI, still lives. What and who is a tyrant? Who is to decide? What are the tolerable limits beyond which tyranny must be resisted? The *Henry VI* plays present a situation within which tyranny cannot be accurately identified. In the fiercely competitive world of ambitions, complicated claims, frustrated expectations, fierce hatreds, and savage wars, any precise political meaning is lost in the partisan exchange of epithets.

No such ambiguity exists in *Richard III*. Shakespeare fixes the title "tyrant" unmistakably on Richard. Except for Buckingham's reference to Edward's "tyranny for trifles" (3.7.9) in his efforts to undermine the reputation of the former king, the term is applied to no one else except Richard and the accusation comes from all sides. Only in *Macbeth* do the words "tyrant" and "tyranny" appear more frequently. With the news of the arrest of Rivers and Grey by Richard, Queen Elizabeth, seeing the ruin of her house, exclaims, "Insulting tyranny begins to jet / Upon the innocent and aweless throne" (2.4.51–52). Tyrrel, repenting of his crime, bemoans the "tyrannous and bloody act" (4.3.1) of the murder of the princes. Queen Margaret names Richard "that excellent grand tyrant of the earth" (4.4.52). His one-time right-hand man, Buckingham, joins the ghosts before the battle to proclaim himself both an abbetor and victim of tyranny: "The first was I that helped thee to the crown; / The last was I that felt thy tyranny" (5.3.168–69). The charge of tyranny comes from all, irrespective of their former loyalties, so that when toward the end Richmond repeatedly proclaims Richard a tyrant, he does so not as a man using damaging epithets against his enemy to justify his challenge of established authority, but as one who represents a universal consensus. Richard is "the wretched, bloody, and usurping boar" (5.2.7) and the nation "bruised underneath the yoke of tyranny" (5.2.2). In the address to his troops Richmond characterizes his adversary as "a bloody tyrant and a homicide" (5.3.247), and promises peaceful rule free of a tyrant's oppression: "If you do sweat to put a tyrant down, / You sleep in peace, the tyrant being slain" (5.3.256–57). The dramatic strategy focuses the idea of tyranny to make it appear that the accusation of Richard does not arise from partisan zeal but is a verdict of all men.

Setting aside for the moment the vivid qualities which Shakespeare has breathed into the character of Richard and considering only the moral and political significance of what he says and does, the portrait of Richard is without any saving merits. He is deformed in mind and body, he is totally lacking in human scruples, and he offends not only those who stand to lose by his success but also men like Hastings, who will support him but not to the extent of being disloyal to Edward's sons, and Buckingham, who is his willing agent but short of killing the princes, and he is the despair of his mother. We know that he is a tyrant, by title, not merely from the evidence of his actions and the testimony of others, but by his own admission that his claim to the throne is unfounded and that he secures it with falsehood and murder. That he is also a tyrant by regiment both his actions and his gloating over them confirm.

132

In the murder of the princes his acts of tyranny reach a climax. The murder of Clarence is a crime for which Edward himself bears some share; the execution without trial of Hastings has many parallels in the annals of ambitious men on the road to power, and Hasting's glee over the beheading of his enemies gives his own fate a touch of poetic justice. The murder of the princes, however, is made to appear as though without parallel and beyond forgiveness. Early in the play the separation of the two boys from their mother and friends is ominous in its dramatic juxtaposition of the innocent princes and the master of calculating malevolence. The princes are made appealing—they are helpless in the hands of the unfeeling politician, but they are also bright, perceptive, and mature for their years—and thus the effect of their death is as though England's hope had been snuffed out. The sense of an awful moment being reached is created by the reactions of others. Hastings, tested out by Catesby, unhesitatingly rebels at the mere suggestion that the sons of Edward might not succeed their father. And there is that remarkable scene in which Buckingham, the willing agent of Richard on his fraudulent path to the throne, recoils and hesitates at the indirect hints and finally the outright demand that the princes must die, and Richard perceives that his most dependable confidant and tool has proven himself untrustworthy and must be cast off. At this moment Richard's isolation from ordinary human association seems complete. The sense of horror is worked over in detail following the murder. Tyrrel is given a scene of remorse over his involvement in the deed—

> The tyrannous and bloody act is done,
> The most arch deed of piteous massacre
> That ever yet this land was guilty of.
>
> (4.3.1–3)

And his description of the penitent murderers, who "wept like two children in their death's sad story" (4.3.8), and their account of the childrens' death is heavily embellished with pathetic touches:

"O, thus," quoth Dighton, "lay the gentle babes."
"Thus, thus," quoth Forrest, "girdling one another
Within their alabaster innocent arms.
Their lips were four red roses on a stalk
And in their summer beauty kissed each other.
A book of prayers on their pillow lay. . . ."

(4.3.9–14)

It is almost too much. There follows, finally, the scene of lamentation of Queen Margaret, Queen Elizabeth, and the duchess of York—the duchess sitting down on "England's lawful earth, / Unlawfully made drunk with innocent blood" (4.4.29–30), while the old Queen Margaret, almost surfeited with the killings she has hoped for, prays for one more, that of Richard, that she "may live to say, 'The dog is dead' " (4.4.78). Nothing is omitted to stamp this act as unique in the annals of British kings.[26] In other respects, Shakespeare avoids any mitigating details offered him by the historians. More indicates the existence of some doubt regarding Richard's responsibility for the death of the princes, but there is no hint of such doubts in the play. Richard's title was approved by Parliament, but in place of any formal approval Shakespeare provides the episode of the befuddled and compliant Lord Mayor and the odds and ends of rabble that are persuaded to cheer for Richard, a patched-up substitute for official and popular approval.

To the difficult question of who is to determine whether a ruler is a tyrant, Shakespeare provides a dramatically convincing, if legally and politically evasive, answer: in Richard III everyone proclaims Richard a tyrant. There is no official source of indictment; it is a national consensus expressed in the suffering and pathos or the repentance of his victims and in the wailing of the survivors. And how is the tyrant to be removed? Shakespeare's answer is again dramatically effective, but reflects the evasiveness not only of many writers on tyranny but specifically of the historians who recorded Richard's infamous doings. For the great national monarchies of the sixteenth century, there was simply no legal or constitutional way of indicting and removing an unjust and cruel king. The removal of a tyrant had to be by violent means, yet his successor had somehow to be spared the guilt of achieving the throne through violence. It was only by applying the providential theory to the rebellion against Richard III that the historians could designate Henry VII as unquestionably the deputy elected by the Lord, and this in spite of awkward questions which remained. Even after the death of the princes, there survived Edward IV's daughter, Elizabeth, who could properly have inherited the throne; the arrangement that Richmond was to marry Elizabeth and thus unite the rival claims represented a tacit acknowledgment of her rights. There were, moreover, the children of George, duke of Clarence, Edward's brother. Their possible claims to the throne were just troublesome enough to bring about their elimination, along with that of their mother, by Henry VII and Henry VIII; one of Henry VII's first acts was to imprison Clarence's oldest son.

The crowning of Henry VII was, in fact, a pragmatic solution to the question of succession, and judged against the uncertainty and warfare brought on by a more fastidious concern for legitimacy based on strict inheritance, it was to be preferred to the Wars of the Roses. Nevertheless, seen against the minute examination of genealogies and the legalistic claims in the three parts of *Henry VI*, the absence of any statement about the claims of Richmond to the throne in *Richard III*, or in the *Henry VI* plays for that matter, is striking. There is one allusion to his Lancastrian origins in the speech of Clarence's ghost: "Thou offspring of the house of Lancaster, / The wronged heirs of York do pray for thee" (5.3.137–38). The more important line is the second: the issue of title is subordinate to the need for a savior, and in this respect the prayer of Clarence's ghost is like the prayers of the rest. It has often been noticed that Richmond plays no role in this play until the end. Whether one decides that this was a result of dramatic immaturity or of artistic skill is immaterial at this point. The effect of this strategy is to introduce Richmond as one chosen to answer the call of outraged humanity. The slight characterization adds to this impression;

we do not understand his triumph as a consequence of any qualities of mind or character. In *3 Henry VI* Henry has prophetically blessed a youth whom he points to as England's hope, and the ghost of Henry recalls this in *Richard III*:

> Virtuous and holy, be thou conqueror!
> Harry, that prophesied thou should'st be king,
> Doth comfort thee in thy sleep. Live and flourish!
> (5.3.129–31)

Virtuous and holy: everything contributes to the impression that what Richmond does he does as an agent of God.[27] It is thus that Richmond understands his mission in invading England: "O thou whose captain I account myself, / Look on my forces with a gracious eye" (5.3.109–10). References to God are also sprinkled throughout his oration to his troops—they fight God's enemy, God will reward them, they fight in the name of God, and the battle cry is "God and Saint George! Richmond and victory!" (5.3.237–71). In representing the one "legitimate" rebellion in his series of eight plays, Shakespeare followed the accepted view, and in consequence the providential determination of events is more conspicuously and continuously suggested in *Richard III* than in any of the others.

In some respects, however, Shakespeare does not adhere to all the details of the stereotype. It was conventional to insist that tyrants did not enjoy power very long, that they suffered from a bad conscience, and that they died terrible or humiliating deaths. History took care of the first of these criteria of tyranny: Richard's reign lasted three years. His troubles of spirit are touched on—Shakespeare shows him losing his self-possession as events turn against him: he orders Catesby to go to the duke of Norfolk and then forgets to tell him why, he commands Ratcliffe to go to Salisbury and then changes his mind, and he strikes a messenger before he learns his news, which turns out to be favorable. He also has bad dreams, induced by the ghosts, on the night before the battle, and for the first time expresses a sense of fear. But these are momentary lapses, and he takes on

the enemy courageously and dies a soldier's death. It is significant that Shakespeare does not follow the cliché about the tyrant's death, as does, for example, *A Mirror for Magistrates* and
also the anonymous *True Tragedy of Richard III*:

> *Richmond.* I will it be proclaimed presently, that
>   traitorous Richard
> By our command, drawn through the streets of Lester,
> Stark naked on a collier's horse let him be laid,
> For as of others' pains he had no regard,
> So let him have a traitor's due reward.

Shakespeare spares his Richard this ignominy. Our last view of
him is in combat with Richmond, by whom he is slain. The
numerous satanic images associated with him (e.g., "foul devil,"
"the son of hell," "thou'st made this happy earth thy hell") convey the idea of total evil, but they also reinforce a sense of
satanic power, of the fascination of a Lucifer who can say, "Evil
be thou my good."

The solution to the problem of the tyranny of Richard in
Richard III through the agency of Richmond is not political.
A final end to the long fight over the succession, a brilliant solution to the rivalry for the crown which had torn and divided
the nation, and the successful establishment of a strong national
monarchy and a new dynasty—all these achievements were perforce subordinated to a public myth about this succession. Acceptance of this myth almost of necessity required that the
emphasis should be placed not on the brilliant political schemes
of Richmond but on the evil of Richard. (There seems to have
been no play written on the life and acts of Henry VII.) And
since he was forcibly resisted and removed, the situation required that he be branded a tyrant and that his removal be
depicted as an act of divine providence and justice. Accepting
the established pattern, however, Shakespeare carried the political meaning of these events well beyond the providentialism
of his historical sources and the didacticism of the *Mirror*. It is,
in fact, from its political features that the play derives its bril-

liance and originality. Shakespeare's Richard represents the ultimate limits of political action unscrupulously and inhumanly employed, an embodiment of the exercise of power as a science divorced from considerations of morality and just rule. In Richard, Shakespeare gave to the idea of tyranny a new image and a new meaning.[28]

VIII

Divine Right and the Politics of Legitimacy: *Richard II*

In the strictest technical sense, the phrase "divine right of kings" cannot be accurately applied to English political theory before the seventeenth century.[1] In a loose, pragmatic sense, however, it summarizes a complex of ideas characteristic of political thinking under the Tudors. The widely held belief that resistance to a king is a sin rests on the assumption that the source of a king's power is divine: "There is no power but of God," wrote Tyndale in *The Obedience of a Christian Man*; ". . . The powers that be are ordained of God."[2] Such deceptively simple phrases as "the Lord's anointed" or "anointed king" were, for precise theorists, fraught with legal problems arising from the historic issue over the powers of the pope or any other churchman in designating or confirming a nation's ruler, an issue which Cranmer was careful to make clear on the occasion of the coronation of Edward VI:

> [Kings] be God's anointed not in respect of the oil which the bishop useth, but in consideration of their power which is ordained . . . and of their persons which are elected of

God and indued with the gifts of his Spirit for the better
ruling and guiding of this people. The oil, if added, is but
ceremony: if it be wanting that king is yet a perfect monarch
notwithstanding, and God's anointed as well as if he were
inoiled.[3]

In common usage these phrases stood for the idea of the divine
sanction of a king's authority and the corollaries which followed from it. This complex of ideas and sentiments, useful in
supporting and enhancing a king's power, could also be invoked
to suggest the gravity of the king's responsibilities. To refer to
kings as gods, as Baldwin does in his dedication to *A Mirror for
Magistrates*, is to call attention to the exalted nature of a king's
calling and to the great evil of the misuse of power:

> For as justice is the chief virtue, so is the ministration
> thereof the chiefest office: and therefore God established it
> with the chiefest name, honoring and calling kings, and all
> officers under them, by his own name, Gods. Ye be all Gods,
> as many as have in your charge any ministration of justice.
> What a foul shame were it for any now to take upon them
> the name and office of God, and in their doings show them-
> selves devils.[4]

It is possible, accordingly, to apply loosely the concept of the
divine right of kings to certain widespread tenets of sixteenth-
century English political thought—that the king is God's representative on earth, that the designation of kings is of God and
not of men, that obedience to kings is the obligation of all subjects, and that the judgment of a king's conduct in office rests
with God. To refer to Tyndale again:

> God hath made the king in every realm judge over all, and
> over him is there no judge. He that judgeth the king judgeth
> God, and he that layeth hands on the king layeth hands on
> God, and he that resisteth the king resisteth God and
> damneth God's law and ordinance. If the subjects sin they
> must be brought to the king's judgment. If the king sin he
> must be reserved unto the judgment, wrath, and vengeance
> of God.[5]

Such considerations have a bearing on discussions of *Richard II*, for the divine origin and sanction of the king's power is at the center of the conflicts in the play. Does *Richard II* provide a basis for determining Shakespeare's own attitude toward kingship? For some critics it does, and not unexpectedly there is a variety of opinions, from those who regard the play as a reflection of the most conservative opinion on the sinfulness of rebellion to those who read it as encouragement for the removal of an ineffective or unjust king.[6] Alfred Hart, who inclines with reservations to the view of Shakespeare as a believer in divine right theory, writes: "Shakespeare outdoes every important dramatist of his time in the number and variety of the allusions made to the divine right of the reigning monarch, the duty of passive obedience, enjoined on subjects by God, and the misery and chaos resulting from civil war and rebellion," and he adds, "*Richard II* is the main Shakespearean storehouse of passages relating to divine right."[7] It is indeed the case that Richard's eloquent expressions of the divine sanction of his power, Gaunt's submission of the king's wrongdoings to God, and Carlisle's rebuke to the council which gives official approval to the abdication all add up to an impressive presentation of the royalist position. These statements, however, arise out of the dramatic circumstances, and if the play is a storehouse of passages relating to divine right it need not follow that their cumulative force necessarily produces a favorable response to the idea. Richard II is the only one of the kings dealt with in Shakespeare's histories who is a king by virtue of natural inheritance in a line established by a long uninterrupted tradition of rule by lineal descent, and whose legitimacy is acknowledged by everyone; he is also neither statesmanlike nor much interested in the serious problems of rule, and he uses power self-indulgently. He is therefore the ideal protagonist in an action which represents the Lord's anointed as unworthy of this awesome title. In making Richard an advocate of divine right, and to a degree not stressed by his sources, Shakespeare sets the conflicts and dilemmas of the play in their most acute form. What can loyal, honorable, and mighty subjects do when the power of the state is vested unquestionably, and sacramentally, in one who seems irresponsible and unjust in its exercise? Every important character in *Richard II* has occasion to ponder this question.

As the only one among the gallery of Shakespeare's monarchs who could wear the crown completely secure in the knowledge that it was his, Richard is the only true believer in the divine origin of the kingly office. His statements of the idea of divine election are memorable. When he learns of Bolingbroke's invasion he proclaims confidently:

> Not all the water in the rough rude sea
> Can wash the balm off from an anointed king
> The breath of worldly men cannot depose
> The deputy elected by the Lord.
>
> (3.2.54–57)

Even when threatened, he manages before the insolent Northumberland to recover his magisterial tone:

> Show us the hand of God
> That hath dismissed us from our stewardship,
> For well we know no hand of blood and bone
> Can gripe the sacred handle of our sceptre
> Unless he do profane, steal, or usurp.
>
> (3.3.77–81)

Richard's conviction that the powers and privileges which kingship carries are beyond question his to use is a source of his weakness. The possession of royalty so long taken for granted as an inherited authority has dulled the king's sense of the personal qualifications and the political demands of the office, and nothing remains except an appreciation of the traditional forms and ceremonies which mark its public exercise and the sense of personal power which is the most conspicuous prerogative of kingship. Inheriting the glory and power of the office without any serious pressure on him to make prudent use of the instruments of royal power—councils, courts of law, responsible delegation

142

of authority, military support—Richard has come to rely chiefly on the idea of the king as divinely ordained and supported. Aumerle and Carlisle sense this fatal weakness in the king upon his return from Ireland as they try to urge practical steps on him to meet the threat of Bolingbroke's invasion:

> Fear not my lord. That power that made you king
> Hath power to keep you king in spite of all.
> The means that heavens yield must be embraced
> And not neglected; else, if heaven would,
> And we will not, heaven's offer we refuse,
> The proferred means of succor and redress.
>
> $(3.2.27-32)$[8]

But Richard extravagantly places his reliance on the divine support of his legitimacy:

> For every man that Bolingbroke hath pressed
> To lift shrewd steel against our golden crown,
> God for his Richard hath in heavenly pay
> A glorious angel.
>
> $(3.2.58-61)$

This indifference to the practical instruments of power is not, however, a sign of reluctance to play fully the role of king as Richard understands it, and to enjoy the part. He appreciates the opportunity for ceremonial which the office requires of him, and as the most sensitive of Shakespeare's monarchs, he takes delight in the indulgences which being a king allows. He also appreciates the vast personal power which accompanies the office, and he does not hesitate to use it when he can. If the circumstances under which he became a king and his own temperament combined to encourage a disregard of the political skill, moral strength, and sound judgment which kingship at its best demands, they did not induce a lack of interest in being king or in making full personal use of its opportunities.

A good deal of what we learn about Richard during the course of the play is there below the surface in the first scene. It is one of those opening scenes (another is in *Hamlet*) which is at first almost misleading and whose full significance becomes clear only later. On the surface the scene may be viewed as a virtuoso performance by Richard in the ritual of his office, the exercise of a "stereotyped social institution," in the discharge of which Richard comes off "creditably enough."[9] Richard's performance reveals considerably more than this, however. Below the surface there is great tension, and the king just barely saves the situation. Bolingbroke's challenge to Mowbray is in effect an oblique way of attacking the king. The various charges against Mowbray are part of the strategy of bringing out into the open the murder of Thomas of Woodstock, duke of Gloucester, seventh son of Edward III and one of Richard's uncles, and it is significant that Mowbray answers all the other charges directly, but answers the important one ambiguously. Richard does indeed act his part well. There is wit and shrewdness in his reply to the fulsome assertions of loyalty by the two appellants: "We thank you both, yet one but flatters us" (1.1.25). He expresses his impartiality, and he pleads with the two men for a peaceful settlement. Yet given the situation—known to him and to the assembled nobles but not yet explained to the audience—he must feel threatened, and there is a trace of this in his assertion of impartiality to Mowbray:

> Mowbray, impartial are our eyes and ears.
> Were he my brother, nay, my kingdom's heir,
> As he is but my father's brother's son,
> Now by my sceptre's awe I make a vow,
> Such neighbor nearness to our sacred blood
> Should nothing privilege him, nor partialize
> The unstooping firmness of my upright soul.
> He is our subject, Mowbray; so art thou:
> Free speech and fearless I to thee allow.
>
> (1.1.115–23)

This is impressive, but the reference to Bolingbroke's remoteness from the throne is unnecessarily pointed in this context, and the real thrust of the speech is not so much to reassure Mowbray as to put Bolingbroke on notice. It is surely to Richard's advantage to have this crisis passed over without being forced to its final issue, and his strategy throughout is to act as peacemaker, as a judicious sovereign, and as a king who can command if need be as a final resort; but he fails not only to persuade the appellants to make peace, but also to make them obey his command to return the gages they have picked up. Bolingbroke refuses to heed his father's plea that he accede to the king's wishes, and Mowbray will not obey when the king demands, "Norfolk, throw down; we bid—there is no boot" (1.1.164). Richard finds it necessary to reassert his power: "Rage must be withstood. / Give me his gage; lions make leopards tame," (1.1.173–74). It is to no avail. The lion fails, yet he can pretend to have succeeded by the command which ends the scene:

> We were not born to sue, but to command;
> Which since we cannot do to make you friends,
> Be ready, as your lives shall answer it.
> At Coventry upon Saint Lambert's day.
>   (1.1.196–99)

Ironically, then, the king ends up by commanding the appellants to do what they have insisted on doing at the risk of disobeying the king's command that they disengage themselves. The scene of the lists (1.3), where he permits the two to proceed up to the moment of the charge and then forbids the combat, has produced considerable puzzlement. Nevertheless, Richard's behavior here is not inconsistent with his difficulties in the first scene where he felt threatened, for he will now demonstrate safely what a king's will can mean. He assembles his council to advise on the issue, but since this is the only time he confers with this body it is a case of making use of an available form to his own advantage. The two men are exiled—Mowbray for life, a judgment that shocks the loyal subject who had served Richard: "A dearer merit . . . / Have I deserved at your Highness' hands!" (1.3.156, 158). The one man in whom is locked the secret of the murder of Gloucester is never to be in a position to worry the king again. These two scenes are a brilliant display of Richard's "monarchizing"—Richard's own word in a later mood of despair—but they epitomize the uneasy unstable equilibrium which sustains the impressive façade of Richard's style of rule.

Bolingbroke's challenge is his response to the question of what a subject can do who must live under injustices committed by a king. He does not accuse Richard directly but indirectly through the king's presumed instrument, Mowbray. In 2 *Henry IV* (4.1.131–33) Westmoreland dismisses the complaint of Mowbray's son that his father was prevented from securing justice at the lists by pointing out that it was just as likely that Bolingbroke might have won; trial by combat is subject to fortune and has nothing to do with justice. In the more hardheaded and politically sophisticated world of the *Henry IV* plays Westmoreland's argument is unanswerable, but in the more ceremonial world of Richard II it was the one avenue open to Bolingbroke short of rebellion. His attempt fails, for in the matter of ceremonial forms the king is preeminent, and he dismisses the proceedings with the simple gesture of throwing down his warder. What is more important, the king's responsibility is hidden behind the charges leveled at Mowbray, and this circumstance produces Mowbray's evasiveness in answering Bolingbroke's most serious charge and Richard's brilliant but puzzling conduct in the first scene. It is the second scene which introduces the information that places the king's behavior in a new light, and also prepares for a better understanding of the next scene, the lists. In a dialogue between Gaunt and the duchess of Gloucester we learn that Richard was responsible for Gloucester's death. The king's guilt for this murder is confirmed later in the play (2.1.124–31, 165), when both Gaunt and York accuse Richard directly and he fails to contradict them. Gaunt's response to the king's misconduct is different from that of his son. To the duchess' plea that he seek justice against the murderer of her husband, his brother, Gaunt gives the conventional answer required by all those sixteenth-century political writers who urged obedience to the king, the vicegerent of God on earth: the king is guilty of the murder, but a subject cannot judge a king, who can be judged and punished only by God:

> But since correction lieth in those hands
> Which made the fault that we cannot correct,
> Put we the quarrel to the will of heaven
>
> God's is the quarrel; for God's substitute,
> His deputy anointed in His sight,
> Hath caused his death, the which if wrongfully,
> Let heaven revenge, for I may never lift
> An angry arm against His minister.
>
> (1.2.4–6, 37–41)

Gaunt urges patience, the virtue invoked by all those for whom loyal obedience was an inescapable corollary of the king's position as God's substitute on earth, but the duchess rejects the advice: "Call it not patience Gaunt, it is despair" (1.2.29). The pathos of the duchess' concluding speech which ends the scene casts a shadow over the counsel of Gaunt. Hers are the embittered outpourings of a victim of royal injustice who cannot be reconciled to the conventional answer, because it does end in despair: "Desolate, desolate will I hence and die; / The last leave of thee takes my weeping eye" (1.2.74–75).

The murder of Gloucester was an old crime for which, given the circumstances, Gaunt may have provided the only prudent answer. However, the king precipitates a new situation by seizing Gaunt's estate on the latter's death, thus disinheriting Bolingbroke, who is in exile. Faced with this outrage there are subjects who will refuse to resolve this new dilemma in Gaunt's way, and among them are some of the most powerful nobles of the realm, including, finally, Gaunt's brother, the duke of York.[10]

The arbitrariness, and even insolence, of Richard's act is placed in relief by the setting of the episode. Dying, Gaunt calls Richard in a last effort to hold up his failings to him and urge his reform. York, seeing the indifference of the young king even after the death of Gaunt, also tries to influence him by describing Richard's father, Edward, the Black Prince, as the image of a good king whom Richard resembles so far only in appearance. The failure of a king to hearken to good counsel is a commonplace of manuals on kingship as a sign of a bad ruler, but the primary emphasis in this scene falls not on this but on the politically important constitutional issue which is raised by the seizure of Gaunt's estate. It is York who makes the point, a man as loyal and in most respects as conventional as Gaunt, but in whom conventional loyalties, and patience, are running out: "How long shall I be patient? Ah, how long / Shall tender duty make me suffer wrong?" (2.1.163–64). What York tries to point out to Richard is that his seizure of Bolingbroke's inheritance is wrong, not simply because a just king should respect his own laws, but because in breaking this particular law Richard threatens the very foundations of his legitimacy:

> Take Hereford's rights away, and take from time
> His charters and his customary rights.
> Let not tomorrow then ensue today;
> Be not thyself. For how art thou a king
> But by fair sequence and succession?
>
> (2.1.195–99)

Richard is king by hereditary succession—it is by this means that he is identified as the deputy elected by the Lord, and lineal succession is therefore the source of his legitimacy. Can he break the law of inheritance in the case of Bolingbroke without undermining the foundations of his own sovereignty?[11] The breaking of order was usually thought of in terms of rebellion by subjects against the authority of the king. What York implies is that since the basis of order is law, of which the king is the custodian, the king also can disrupt order by violating the law and thus inviting chaos: "Let not tomorrow then ensue today; / Be not thyself." The king possesses the power to disregard the law if he wishes, but if he does so he risks disaster:

> You pluck a thousand dangers on your head,
> You lose a thousand well-disposed hearts,

148

> And prick my tender patience to those thoughts
> Which honor and allegiance cannot think.
>
> (2.1.205–8)

York finds himself in a trying dilemma when Bolingbroke appears to claim his inheritance, for York is the king's appointed deputy during the king's absence in Ireland, and Bolingbroke's return from exile is an act of treason. Bolingbroke's position is, to be sure, intolerable:

> What would you have me do? I am a subject
> And I challenge law; attorneys are denied me,
> And therefore personally I lay my claim
> To my inheritance of free descent.
>
> (2.3.132–35)

York confesses a "feeling of my cousin's wrongs," yet he is "loath to break our country's laws"; and unable to resolve this dilemma he declares himself a neuter (2.3.140, 168, 158). There are situations when to proclaim neutrality is in effect to take sides. By offering Bolingbroke the hospitality of the castle, York has already decided that between the king's breaking of the law in this instance, and Bolingbroke's, a choice can be made. It is not surprising to find York later taking an active part in the arrangements for the abdication. It is he who conveys to the assembled lords Richard's alleged willingness to resign, who escorts the king to them, and who then kindly but firmly instructs Richard

> To do that office of thine own good will
> Which tired majesty did make thee offer:
> The resignation of thy state and crown
> To Henry Bolingbroke.
>
> (4.1.177–80) [12]

What now is Bolingbroke's position? The scene in which Gaunt dies presents a serious case against Richard. In addition to the rebukes of Gaunt and York, there is the long list of charges made against Richard by the nobles who speak their minds after

149

the seizure of Gaunt's lands. They cite the king's submission to parasitic flatterers, his plundering the commons, exacting money by unscrupulous means from the nobility, farming out the crown lands, and now the illegal confiscation of Bolingbroke's inheritance (2.1.225 ff.). This list of grievances amounts in effect to a charge of tyranny by regiment sufficient to justify involving themselves in the scheme revealed by Northumberland to join an eminent group of nobles led by Bolingbroke, who are already making for England with aid from the duke of Brittany. Though there is a metaphorical vagueness in Northumberland's exhortation to his fellow nobles to join him, there is no mistaking his purpose:

> If then we shall shake off our slavish yoke,
> Imp out our drooping country's broken wing,
> Redeem from broking pawn the blemished crown,
> Wipe off the dust that hides our sceptre's gilt,
> And make high majesty look like itself,
> Away with me in post to Ravenspurgh.
>
> (2.1.291–96)

Northumberland can mean only one thing by "shake off our slavish yoke." In view of the arguments about Bolingbroke's oath and the charge made later in the *Henry IV* plays by the Percys that Bolingbroke had deceived them about the purpose of his return, it is important to notice that from the beginning Northumberland and his fellow nobles joined Bolingbroke at Ravenspurgh with every intention of dethroning Richard and making Bolingbroke king. On his part, however, Bolingbroke nowhere directly depicts his role as that of a Richmond coming to save his country from a tyrant. He vows that he has come only to claim his inheritance, and he is careful always to make the proper ceremonial gestures and to refer to Richard as his king; and though he comes supported by an army, he does not challenge the king in battle.

This propriety of conduct is part of a legalistic and highly sophisticated plan to secure the throne without damaging the

mystique of divinely ordained sovereignty and the authority
which comes with legitimately acquired power. In other ways,
however, Bolingbroke's ultimate aim becomes apparent. When
he arrives in England the ceremonial tone of the speeches of his
adherents is more fitting for address to a sovereign than to an
equal whose rights are to be restored (2.3.1 ff.). He commands
the execution, without trial, of Bushy and Green on the charge
of their having misled a prince, an action questionable and arbitrary even in a crowned king. In his personal relations to Richard, he is conspicuously correct and respectful; in his actions,
he not only threatens Richard but anticipates the actual taking
over of power. But Bolingbroke is not interested merely in seizing power, which he is in a position to do at any time after Richard's return from Ireland, and with public approval and the
support of the nobility. The power he already has, but he is too
astute a politician not to realize that power and authority are not
the same thing. Authority is in part a consequence of what the
possessor of sovereign power can bring to the office in the way of
personal attractiveness, or genius for leadership, or infectious
ideals, or a combination of these; but there is the authority which
comes simply from unimpeachable legitimacy, the authority
which inheres in the office itself by virtue of legality based on tradition and common consent. It is this which Bolingbroke seems
bent on preserving for himself. He takes steps to become a king
without force, without circumventing law and tradition, and thus
without shattering the mystique of divine election and inheritance. Richard is to abdicate the throne and adopt him as heir.
The king is to be persuaded to play the role of "tired majesty"
resigning with his own good will the "state and crown to Henry
Bolingbroke." With the throne empty and the succession established, Parliament will approve these arrangements and Bolingbroke will be crowned Henry the fourth of that name. It is significant that when Northumberland tries to bully the tearful Richard into reading a list of the accusations against him so that "the
souls of men / May deem that you are worthily deposed"
(4.1.226–27), Bolingbroke stops him—"Urge it no more, my Lord

Northumberland" (4.1.271)—a detail which goes counter to the source where Richard does read the charges against him. It is an act of kindness on Bolingbroke's part, but Bolingbroke can afford the gesture because he realizes that the public reading of his sins by Richard is not necessary. The idea of Richard as a tyrannical king who must be deposed may have been necessary to inspire the nobles to flock to Bolingbroke and bring him back from exile, but it is no longer essential if there is to be a succession based on abdication by "tired majesty" in favor of an heir he has publicly adopted.

It is Richard who perceives the fatal error in this plan. If the legitimacy of kingship derives its power from divine election through inheritance, no one presumably can remove a king but God. If he is indeed the deputy elected by the Lord then not even Richard can wash the balm off with his tears or for any reason abdicate the throne which succession by lineal inheritance has designated to him. He realizes that to divest himself of the title is as much an act of treason as is Bolingbroke's forcibly placing him in this extremity:

> Nay, if I turn mine eyes upon myself,
> I find myself a traitor with the rest;
> For I have given here my soul's consent
> T'undeck the pompous body of a king;
> Made glory base, and sovereignty a slave,
> Proud majesty a subject, state a peasant
>
> (4.1.247–52)

By his act he has tarnished the idea of his legitimacy as much as has Bolingbroke; he has made glory base and sovereignty a slave, and the title could not descend now to anyone with the same authority.[13]

As a justification of the possession and exercise of sovereign power by one man, the idea of the divine right of kings has proved itself to be a very durable political idea. It was invoked in classical antiquity and during the Byzantine Empire, and it was a concept which, in varying degrees of preciseness, served the political needs of the sixteenth century. *Richard II* is one of

Shakespeare's most moving plays, and Richard's tenacious dedication to divine right is at the center of a dramatic conflict so engrossing as to arouse even today a sympathetic appreciation of the potency of this outmoded concept for those who believed in it or dared to challenge its power. But in the most general sense, the fate of Richard reveals how fragile are those vital assumptions on which rests the authority of the sovereign power of a great state. Irrespective of the form a particular state may take, philosophical justification of its sovereignty on grounds other than those of practical effectiveness or accommodation to past and present circumstances leads finally to some sort of myth or fiction. Thomas Jefferson, setting forth principles of a new state in the new world, declared, "We hold these truths to be self-evident; that all men are created equal; that they are endowed by their Creator with certain unalienable rights; that among these are life, liberty, and the pursuit of happiness." The sentence breathes out the air of the Enlightenment, yet it comes very close to proclaiming the divine right of citizens. Such conceptions are most powerful when they remain unquestioned. To undermine a myth of sovereignty seriously is to threaten the political institutions and arrangements which it has fostered; conversely, to attack the political arrangements is to damage the myth. The words which Shakespeare gives to Richard when he realizes what he has done—made glory base and sovereignty a slave—describe the damage done to the idea of sovereign power when the intangible basis on which its authority has been thought to rest is shattered. By their actions, Richard and Bolingbroke have shown the myth of divine right to be vulnerable, and Bolingbroke, for all his fastidious efforts to preserve it, cannot depend on it to provide him with the same unquestioned authority and respect, and therefore the same degree of power, which it carried before.[14]

The source of Bolingbroke's authority is now pragmatic. When York announces that Richard "with willing soul / Adopts thee heir" (4.1.108–9), the bishop of Carlisle challenges this proceeding on the basis of the established doctrine that the king is by definition beyond the judgment of his subjects:

What subject can give sentence on his king?
And who sits here that is not Richard's subject?
Thieves are not judged but they are by to hear,
Although apparent guilt be seen in them;
And shall the figure of God's majesty,
His captain, steward, deputy elect,
Anointed, crowned, planted many years,
Be judged by subject and inferior breath,
And he himself not present?

(4.1.121–29) [15]

The only effective answer to this argument is Carlisle's arrest for capital treason, after which Bolingbroke commands that Richard be brought in so that "in common view / He may surrender; so we shall proceed / Without suspicion" (4.1.155–57). It is York who by his words and conduct defines and establishes the conditions for the survival of the new regime. When he has finished his account to his duchess of the triumphant public progress of Bolingbroke and the appalling degradations heaped by the populace on the dethroned Richard—a spectacle he can explain only as inspired by Heaven for some inscrutable divine purpose—he concludes: "To Bolingbroke are we sworn subjects now, / Whose state and honor I for aye allow" (5.2.39–40). The alternative to Bolingbroke now is political chaos. York has an immediate opportunity to put his new political loyalties to the test. When he discovers that his son Aumerle is implicated in a plot to kill the new monarch, without hesitation, he hastens to inform Bolingbroke and accuse his son of treason. The king must be supported at all costs in the expectation that by his superior abilities and statesmanship he will make himself accepted and thus validate the fiction of his divine election by adoption.

Bolingbroke demonstrates that this is precisely the policy he intends to follow. Even before the abdication he launches an investigation into Gloucester's death (4.1), and the obvious contrast between his performance and that of Richard in the first scene is clearly to his advantage. He also displays magnanimity and statesmanship in forgiving Aumerle and sparing Carlisle's life. On the other hand when he believes the situation calls for

154

the utmost rigor, he does not hesitate to act, as in the instance of sending Bushy and Green to execution. The severest test of his political realism is in disposing of Richard, for he knows, as Aumerle's conspiracy demonstrates, that neither he nor his new regime is safe as long as Richard is alive. Richard could not be tried and publicly executed; he could not be allowed to live.[16] The death of Richard was to haunt Henry IV in many ways, but ironically in the end the real impediment to success was, as Richard himself discerned when adversity had brought him a measure of political wisdom, that those who aided Bolingbroke in forcing the abdication and gaining the throne would expect more than gratitude, and the act of unseating a rightful king would only show how it could be done again (5.1.55–68). The play ends with news of rebellions in the land, and with Bolingbroke's remorse over the dead Richard. These are to be the principal themes of his reign.[17]

IX

Richard II
and the Idea of Tragedy

The anatomizing of power in the form of a contest for kingship is what establishes *Richard II* as a political play; what makes it a tragedy is the way Richard responds to his fall as the victim of the struggle for power. In treating the fall of an English king as a tragedy, Shakespeare was taking advantage of the opportunity which the history play afforded for innovation and originality. The history play—for all practical purposes an English invention of the sixteenth century—was not bound by established dramatic conventions and traditional modes. In dramatizing the events of English history from the abdication of Richard II to the death of Richard III Shakespeare created a variety of dramatic forms, inventing where necessary and adapting whatever was available in the drama of the past and of his own day to the requirements of the material he had selected for a given play.[1] The recognized dramatic model for tragedy in the sixteenth century was Seneca, and Shakespeare found some features of the model useful in *Richard III* in the dramatization of the fall of a tyrannical king,[2] but the story of Richard II did not lend itself to the Senecan idiom. Marlowe's *Edward II* suggested an appropriate structural pattern, but, although Shakespeare's indebtedness to Marlowe was considerable, the similarities between the two plays do not go very deep. In investing the fall of Richard with tragic significance, Shakespeare was exploring new territory.

One literary tradition with which *Richard II* has been frequently associated is that of the narrative tragedies of the Middle Ages, characteristically a collection of stories recounting a fall from high place and felicity and celebrating the pervasive power of fortune in human life. The classic form was given to this genre by Boccaccio's *De casibus virorum illustrium*, a collection of narratives in Latin which begins with Adam and Eve and continues with selected examples from world history, concluding with the plaint against fortune of King John of France captured by Prince Edward of England. This work was translated into English by John Lydgate, with additions and interpolations, and it was the model for Chaucer's "The Monk's Tale," which acknowledges Boccaccio in the subtitle, "Heere begynneth the Monkes Tale *De casibus virorum illustrium*." It is easy to oversimplify Boccaccio's dominant theme. Fortune is ubiquitous in the stories, but Boccaccio also affirms (for example, the opening of book 3) that men bring about their bad fortune through their own excess of ambition, covetousness, or other wickedness, that men are rewarded for their merits as they are punished for their vices, and that princes should cultivate prudence. In the case of Nero the specific political moral is that tyrants end in misfortune. To the extent, however, that an idea of tragedy illuminates the collection, fortune is the key. In a long disputation between Fortune and Poverty which opens book 3, Poverty wins because she holds Fortune in subjection; the virtue in adversity is patience. Where a specific prudential moral is not stressed, the emotional effect of the fall is in the spectacle of the loss of worldly happiness and glory. The pervasive impression of mutability is emphasized in Lydgate's translation by the addition of a chapter on fortune, the burden of which is that men are most subject to the whim of fortune when they are at the top, and that fortune spares no man, whether virtuous or evil, thrifty or idle. The refrain is,

> Unto Fortune this mateer doth applie:
> She maketh oon rise, another to dissende.

What gave substance to the primary role of fortune in medieval tragedy was an underlying attitude toward man and his earthly destiny. Medieval tragedy is permeated with the notion of the fickle inconstancy of worldly affairs. Chaucer begins the fourth book of his "litel tragedy," *Troilus and Criseyde*, with an invocation to fortune:

> But all to litel, welaway the whyle,
> Lasteth swich joie, ythonked be Fortune,
> That semeth trewest when she wol bygyle.
> And kan to fooles so hire sone entune,
> That she hem hent and blent, traitour commune!
> And whan a wight is from hire whiel ythrowe,
> Than laugheth she, and maketh hym the mouwe.

The medieval Christian preoccupation with fortune fostered contempt for the world: since men are subject to the capricious whims of fortune, success and mastery in the affairs of the world is no triumph and losing worldly felicity no disgrace, for this world is but a proving ground for the next, and to place hope for happiness in worldly success and pleasure is to ask for sorrow. Chaucer's Troilus is granted a glimpse of the final truth when, after he dies, he sees from the height of the eighth sphere,

> This litel spot of erthe, that with the se
> Embraced is, and fully gan despise
> This wretched world, and held all vanite
> To respect of the pleyn felicite
> That is in hevene above.

In medieval narratives of the fall from high fortune, individual qualities of character are not very significant as determinant factors in the outcome. Aristotle is careful to prescribe the kind of character required of a good tragedy, but the point about the inconstancy of fortune can be made with any type of character—good or bad, active or passive. The effectiveness of Boccaccio's collection of stories depended not so much on a gallery of striking individual portraits as on a series of variations on the theme of fortune, demonstrating by its very repetitiveness the truth of the leading idea and sustaining interest by showing the many ways in which chance can interfere with the lives of eminent and notorious persons. Individual stories in such collections may call for different emotional responses. In "The Monk's Tale" Chaucer expresses gratification for the doom which befell the wicked Holofernes, but for the "worthy Petro, glorie of Spayne," he reflects, "Wel oghten men thy pitous deeth complayne." The main theme, however, arises above these differences in emotional appeal: "Lat no man truste on Blynd Prosperitee; / By war of thise ensamples trewe and olde." The tragic idea is inherent in the mere possession of happiness or prosperity.

During the sixteenth century the ideas underlying the form and sentiments of medieval tragedy underwent certain important modifications. Among these was an enhanced view of man's capacities and their proper use, effectively illustrated, with an explicit contrast to the otherworldly view, in the following:

> We may not only have regard of the life to come, but also of this here present, procuring evermore such things as pertain to the maintenance thereof, with all good civility, to the intent that we here, well using this worldly prosperity, may, at the last attain to such end and perfection as by the providence of God, is ordeyned to the excellent nature and dignity of man.[3]

The primary emphasis here falls not on fortune, the vanity of human wishes, and contempt of the world, but on respect for the powers and gifts with which God has endowed man and regard for their proper use. This emphasis is a major theme of the humanists of the sixteenth century. The well using of worldly prosperity and of the gifts of fortune and nature is, moreover, the chief aim of the treatises devoted to the education of princes and courtiers, the elite who must assume the responsibility of governing society and setting an example of human excellence.

Thomas Elyot, for example, in the opening sentence of the chapter in *The Governour* entitled, "The education or form of bringing up of the child of a gentleman, which is to have authority in a public weal," wrote:

> For as much as all noble authors do conclude, and also common experience proveth, that where the governors of realms and cities be founden adorned with virtues, and do employ their study and mind to the public weal, as well to the augmentation thereof as to the establishing and long continuance of the same: there a public weal must needs be both honorable and wealthy.[4]

The conduct of princes and courtiers was understandably a matter of serious concern to an age which was emerging out of great political, religious, and social upheavals and witnessing the creation of a new nobility and strong centralized monarchies. The welfare of the nation called, moreover, for an understanding of the means by which the affairs of state could be controlled, and was, in consequence, somewhat at odds with the notion that fortune ruled and that contempt of worldly power was the highest wisdom. In the twenty-fifth chapter of *The Prince*, "The Power of Fortune in Human Affairs, and to What Extent She Should Be Relied on," Machiavelli acknowledges the old and still widespread belief "that the affairs of this world are so under the direction of Fortune and of God that man's prudence cannot control them," and he grants that events of the recent past might encourage one to accept this belief and "let Chance control." But Machiavelli could not have submitted to this view and written *The Prince*. He concludes that "because the freedom of the will should not be wholly annulled, I think it may be true that Fortune is arbiter of half our actions, that she still leaves us the control of the other half."[5] Fortune is still fortune, but there is a considerable margin of influence and control left for a knowledgeable and talented ruler.

It is considerations of this nature which help to account for the new emphasis in the last of the important English collections on the *De casibus* plan, *A Mirror for Magistrates*. The change is apparent not only in the title but in the statement of the original compiler and editor, William Baldwin:

> The goodness or badness of any realm lieth in the goodness or badness of the rulers. . . . For here as in a looking glass you shall see (if any vice be in you) how the like hath been punished in other heretofore, whereby admonished, I trust it will be a good occasion to move you to the sooner amendment.[6]

Like Boccaccio's collection, *A Mirror* is not rigidly consistent in maintaining the primary theme. The mood and sentiments of the older narrative tragedy break through. Thomas, earl of Montague, killed by a cannon shot after many victories, reflects simply on "the uncertainty of Glory," and warns princes "The happiest Fortune chiefly to mistrust." The old conventional imagery appears too. Mortimer announces himself as "Among the riders of the rolling wheel / That lost their holds," and Salisbury observes that "this Goddess guideth all the game." The editor strains to find a moral on the death of Edward IV ("How king Edward through his surfeiting and untemperate life sodainly died in the midst of prosperity"), but the poem that follows is simply a plaint against mutability and the inevitability of death. And finally, in the most admired single item, Sackville's Induction, fortune is celebrated as a goddess sent by providence "To wail and rue this world's uncertainty," and the personified figure of Sorrow shows us the vanity of this world's pomp and happiness. Such traditional sentiments call attention to what is permanently and universally appealing in the medieval tragic attitude; they are natural accompaniments of the doom of men who struggled for power and fame in the affairs of the world and found sorrow and catastrophe. In the context of the whole collection they are minor notes which place in relief the dominant themes and ideas which distinguish *A Mirror* from the earlier compilations in the *De casibus* tradition. It is Baldwin's statement that strikes the keynote. The difference is reflected in the choice of materials. The selection of stories is not random and universal: the examples are chosen from that period of turbulence and change in English history which fascinated the Elizabethans and which also provided the subject matter for Hall's *The Union of the Two Noble and Illustrate Fameles of Lancastre and Yorke,* Daniel's incomplete poem, *The Civil Wars,* and Shakespeare's historical cycle. The bias in many accounts in *A Mirror* is political. The interest in the compilation is sustained not by the variety of ways in which the men who tell their stories met ill fortune, but why they fell. John, earl of Worcester, criticizes historians who fail to inquire into specific causes,

> seeing causes are the chiefest things
> That should be noted of the story writers
> That men may learn what ends all causes brings.[7]

In such a scheme fortune must be relegated to a secondary role. Cade asks, "Shall I call it Fortune or my froward folly?" but the question is clearly rhetorical. Mowbray asserts, "I blame not Fortune though she did her part." Sometimes the story points to a bit of practical political wisdom: Henry, duke of Buckingham, who, as the chief agent of Richard III's machinations, might have ended on a pious moral, attributes his fall not to fortune, or the fates, or Jove, but simply to the fickle commons, and his advice is "O, let no prince put trust in commonty." In a comment to the reader following the narrative of the poet Collingbourne who had the misfortune to write an epigram that displeased Richard III, there is the shrewd observation that Richard should have winked at such scribblers because they reflect public opinion, "and so might have found mean either by amendment (which is best) or by some other policy to have stayed the people's grudge, the forerunner of Rulers' destruction." The narrators sometimes raise difficult questions. John earl of Worcester, had to choose between obeying the orders of an unjust king and losing his life. Thomas, earl of Salisbury, asks why his father should die defamed because he plotted to restore Richard II to his throne: "What cause can be more worthy for a knight, / Than save his king and help true heirs to right?" Such disturbing questions do not remain long unresolved. The world of *A Mirror*, like that of Hall and Holinshed, is governed by divine retributive justice. The earl of Salisbury comes through with the conventional moral: "God hateth rigor though it further right," and "To every vice due guerdon doth belong." And the editorial comment following Cade's narrative could have come out of the "Homilie against Disobedience": "and therefore whosoever rebelleth against any ruler either good or bad, rebelleth against GOD."

By imitating the scheme which gave medieval tragedy its most characteristic expression, *A Mirror* continued the association of the falls of eminent men with the old idea of tragedy, but the basic vision was a different one. The disasters recounted in *A Mirror* are those of men who failed in a politically active world largely through error or evil intent, and the moral of the tales is generally prudential in conformity with the expressed aim of the compilers. *A Mirror* implies a view of man and his world in which there is merit in achieving mastery over one's human powers and using one's talents and position to exert a beneficent influence over events, especially by those whose failure could bring distress to those who depend on them as superiors and rulers. By selecting episodes from a fairly recent struggle for sovereignty in English history, *A Mirror* associated the fall from great place with the problems which confront men at the center of political power: the *mise en scène* of tragedy becomes the political arena. The reputation of *A Mirror* is now one of poetic dreariness, but it was very popular in its day, as witness the numerous editions and enlargements. The question of its influence on the dramatists may be left undecided.[8] Its existence and popularity make clear that by the middle years of the sixteenth century the fall from greatness and happiness had acquired a significance which went beyond the thoughts and sentiments long associated with it—the capricious turn of fortune's wheel as the cause, and contempt for the world as its primary lesson.

Richard II has very strong associations with the *De casibus* tradition. The story could serve as an ideal model for the type, and the precipitous fall of Richard from the high point of royal splendor and authority of the first scene, accompanied by the spectacular rise of Bolingbroke from banished man to king, had unavoidable associations with a long tradition of iconography and literature. Shakespeare nowhere refers to the conventional and ubiquitous image of fortune's wheel, but critics find it implied in the structural pattern of the play. "His grief," writes Pater of Richard, "becomes nothing less than a central expression of all that in the revolutions of Fortune's wheel goes *down* in the world." [9] Shakespeare's avoidance of the image, Wilson believes, "is part of his subtlety. For the wheel is constantly in his mind throughout the play. Indeed, it determines the play's shape and structure, which gives us a complete inversion." [10] Shakespeare's choice for expressing vividly the fall from greatness is not the wheel but the shooting star:

> Ah Richard! with the eyes of heavy mind
> I see thy glory like a shooting star
> Fall to the base earth from the firmament.
> Thy sun sets weeping in the lowly West,
> Witnessing storms to come, woe and unrest.
> Thy friends are fled to wait upon thy foes,
> And crossly to thy good all fortune goes.
>
> (2.4.18–24)

This appears at the end of the brief scene in which Salisbury reports the departure of the Welsh troops and foresees the inevitable disaster. Much is to happen between Richard's return from Ireland and his abdication and, finally, his death, but Richard does not experience a step-by-step decline to ruin. He is broken in one scene. Shakespeare achieves the effect of a sudden plunge from high station and felicity by Richard's response to the return of Bolingbroke. The ill news imparted in a series of messages casts him into a despair that precipitates his eloquent outpouring of feeling at the loss of all worldly happiness, and with the speech,

"For God's sake let us sit down upon the ground / And tell sad stories of the death of kings" (3.2.155–77), the association with the *De casibus* collection of stories recounting the fall of princes becomes unmistakable. However, the identification of Richard's fall with the design of medieval tragedy is only tentative. Though it is possible to make too much of Shakespeare's omission of the wheel of fortune which some critics have insisted on supplying for him, its evidently calculated absence suggests that he was trying to avoid a reductive cliché.[11] Where the sensibilities appealed to by tragedy in the *De casibus* vein represented a universal response to the spectacle of a sudden fall from greatness, Shakespeare retained them and gave them a fresh richness. But the vivid evocation of the form and mood of medieval tragedy was not an end in itself but rather a means of defining the fall from greatness in new terms.

In contrast to the *De casibus* narratives, and in this respect bearing more resemblance to *A Mirror for Magistrates*, the political interest is strongly underscored in *Richard II*. The play concerns the dethronement of a king who relies for his power on his unquestionable legal right supported by a long tradition of unbroken succession. All the other principal characters are viewed in relation to the idea of kingship and Richard's conduct as king. The various responses to Richard's rule and the idea of sovereignty and legitimacy on which it is based represent differing attitudes toward state power, and the particular attitude which each individual adopts becomes a test of his convictions and the touchstone of his character. Richard's trial begins when he awakens from the illusion of security in his God-given authority to find himself threatened by naked political power operating in the name of justice and the public good.

The initial effect of power is to deprive its victim of the customary forms and objects which help him to express his identity and establish his status among his fellows. Mowbray terms his exile to foreign lands a "speechless death" (1.3.172). "Such is the breath of kings," remarks Bolingbroke (1.3.215); and to his father's consolations he replies:

Nay, rather every tedious stride I make
Will but remember me what a deal of world
I wander from the jewels that I love.
Must I not serve a long apprenticehood
To foreign passages, and in the end,
Having my freedom, boast of nothing else
But that I was a journeyman to grief?

(1.3.268–74)

It is Lear's vague sense that Goneril intends to deprive him of all that gave him a place in the world and strip him of the familiar objects of his self-esteem that makes him desperate at the thought of losing his hundred knights. Ultimately, the victim of power becomes a helpless, manipulable object, and finally a mere thing, a corpse. Richard makes this grim progress—from king to man, from man to a political pawn, thence to a despised and castoff object, and finally to a lifeless body.

None of Shakespeare's tragic characters comes more ill prepared to such an ordeal. He is a king and knows no other way of being himself. He can put on an impressive, if misleading, public spectacle as a judicious and fair ruler (the opening scene), he has a flair for the ceremonials of his office (the lists), and he knows how to use its opportunities for pleasant indulgence (the scene with his favorites). But he also reveals a relish for the power which it gives him (the exiling of Mowbray and Bolingbroke) and for the arbitrary exercise of his office (the confiscation of Gaunt's estate). His nobles complain of oppression and seek to replace him (they list their grievances after Gaunt's death). He shows a scant regard for the limits which law places on authority (York's rebuke after the confiscation of Gaunt's estate), and he is careless about maintaining the instruments which protect and assure the survival of his legal authority—capable officers, wise advisers, and adequate military protection. He thus has at his command neither the practical instruments of royalty nor the resources of character with which to meet a threat to his kingly state. For these he substitutes a deeply felt belief in the mystique of his office and in the public awe inspired by its divine ordinance. It is this belief which initially sustains him when he returns from Ireland and learns of the rebellion. When his companions suggest tactfully that "the means that heaven yields must be imbraced / And not neglected" (3.2.29–30), he replies with assurance that the crown rests on an unshakable authority:

> Not all the water in the rough rude sea
> Can wash the balm off from an anointed king;
> The breath of worldly men cannot depose
> The deputy elected by the Lord.
>
> (3.2.54–57)

But God does not provide for his Richard a glorious angel for every soldier in Bolingbroke's pay, and the Welsh soldiers have dispersed. Though Richard recovers for a moment—"Am I not king?" (3.2.83)—the bad news mounts and the truth has to be faced. He lacks soldiers, his favorites have been executed, and his officers have fled to Bolingbroke.

Out of his collapse and despair he finds a bitter answer to his question, Am I not king? To be a king is to be the hero in a tragic cycle so universal that it has become a standard literary form. Story after story has celebrated the fall of kings, for the tragic pattern is inherent in their very greatness. To this he now appeals (3.2.155–56), and seeing the pomp and power of a monarch under the aspect of ever-present death he can appreciate the irony of its pretensions:

> within the hollow crown
> That rounds the mortal temples of a king
> Keeps death his court, and there the antic sits,
> Scoffing his state and grinning at his pomp
> Allowing him a breath, a little scene,
> To monarchize, be feared, and kill with looks;
> Infusing him with self and vain conceit
> As if this flesh which walls about our life
> Were brass impregnable; and humoured thus,
> Comes at the last, and with a little pin
> Bores through his castle wall, and farewell king!
>
> (3.2.160–70)

These sentiments reminiscent of medieval tragedy and the dance
of death do not lead to the expected conclusion, contempt of the
world, but move without transition to a new thought. It is as
though the phrase "farewell king" not only expresses the ironic
doom of a king's death but alludes at the same time to the literal
truth of his present position, that having been deprived of all the
accouterments of his power which Bolingbroke now has in abun-
dance, he is no longer a king but a man:

> Cover your heads, and mock not flesh and blood
> With solemn reverence; throw away respect,
> Tradition, form, and ceremonious duty;
> For you have but mistook me all this while.
> I live with bread like you, feel want,
> Taste grief, need friends—subjected thus,
> How can you say to me, I am a king?
>
> (3.2.171–77)

There is left him only his despair—"What comfort have we
now?" (3.2.206)—and all that remains of his royalty will be the
majesty of his sorrow; his grief will be kingly: "Go to Flint Castle,
there I'll pine away— / A king, woe's slave, shall kingly woe
obey" (3.2.209–10).[12]

As the scene opens at Flint Castle, Richard has momentarily
recovered his kingly bearing, and if it is only to be a final performance of regality it is nonetheless impressive—"Yet looks he
like a king," says York (3.3.68). He revives his conviction that
he is king by divine election, and the thought is sufficient to
enable him to defy the arrogant Northumberland:

> We are amazed, and thus long have we stood
> To watch the fearful bending of thy knee,
> Because we thought ourself thy lawful king;
> And if we be, how dare thy joints forget
> To pay their awful duty to our presence?
> If we be not, show us the hand of God
> That hath dismissed us from our stewardship.
>
> (3.3.72–78)

Richard is at his best when he expresses belief in the divine origin of his power. Only then does any serious sense of royal dignity and sincere conviction shine through. It is when he realizes that he cannot sustain this belief in the face of the facts and that he is powerless against the practical threats to his office that he turns to helpless despair and seeks consolation in fictions. He has scarcely uttered the splendid affirmation of the divine source of his power in defiance of Northumberland when the realities once again cast him down, and he now despairs even of being equal to kingly woe: "O that I were as great / As is my grief, or lesser than my name" (3.3.136–37). He submits, when Northumberland returns, as a deposed king even before he learns what demands will be made on him:

> What must the king do now? Must he submit?
> The king shall do it. Must he be deposed?
> The king shall be contented. Must he lose
> The name of king? a God's name let it go.
>
> (3.3.143–46)

And upon this act of submission his mind turns once again to sentiments associated with medieval tragedy, the rejection of worldly pomp and escape into the retirement of the holy life, or obscure death:

> I'll give my jewels for a set of beads;
> My gorgeous palace for a hermitage;
> My gay apparel for an almsman's gown;
> My figured goblets for a dish of wood;
> My sceptre for a palmer's walking staff;
> My subjects for a pair of carved saints,
> And my large kingdom for a little grave,
> A little, little grave, an obscure grave,
> Or I'll be buried in the king's highway,
> Some way of common trade, where subjects' feet
> May hourly trample on their sovereign's head;
> For on my heart they tread now whilst I live:
> And buried once, why not upon my head?
>
> (3.3.147–59)

The sincerity of Henry VI pining for a similar escape from his royalty can be accepted—we know him to be pious and we do not see him luxuriating in his role as monarch. But the same thoughts in Richard here convey no conviction. More convincing is the injured sense of rejection—his subjects trampling on his buried head; and frustration and despair drive his thoughts to such extravagance that he realizes their impotence: "Well, well, I see / I talk but idly, and you laugh at me" (3.3.170–71). Neither the form nor the accompanying sentiments of medieval tragedy offer any serious grounds for consolation or any appropriate imaginative projection of himself in his new role as fallen king, and so they fail him as a design for acting out his tragedy.

To reject the false consolations of these fictions requires that he become aware of his own betrayal of his deepest convictions about his divine ordinance, that he acknowledge his failure as king. The path to such awareness, however, is not direct. In a manner similar to Lear's reluctant glances at the wrong he did Cordelia, Richard's moments of self-knowledge come without premeditation, arising suddenly out of self-pity or grief, amid the fluctuations of feeling that mark his efforts to understand and cope with the utter collapse of everything that gave form and meaning to his life. The earliest of these flashes of insight occurs when at the command of Northumberland he descends to the "base court": "Down, down I come, like glist'ring Phaeton / Wanting the manage of unruly jades" (3.3.178–79). These lines are sometimes cited to show the similarity between *Richard II* and *De casibus* tragedy, and Phaeton does indeed provide a notable image of a spectacular fall from a glorious height; but Richard is employing the image of the glittering descent not to identify himself as a victim of fortune, but rather as an emblem of his own incapacity. The sun is Richard's symbol. He describes his return from Ireland as the rising of the sun whose light will dispel the dangers of the night (3.2.36–53), and this symbol is revived on Richard's entrance in the next scene by Bolingbroke, who refers to him as the "discontented sun" when morning clouds threaten to dim his glory (3.3.62–67). But in this speech Richard does not represent himself as the true sun god: he is the over-weening Phaeton, an upstart who could not manage the horses of the chariot of the sun. Expressed indirectly through the myth, this is Richard's first suggestion of an acknowledgment that the fault lies within himself.[13] His descent to the court, he knows, disgraces everything which gave honor to his kingship—"Base court, where kings grow base" (3.3.180)—and the thought drives him to a frenzy of grief that "makes him speak fondly like a frantic man" (3.3.185). He has now become a pawn in Boling-broke's politics of power: "Set on to London, cousin, is it so? . . . Then I must not say no" (3.3.208, 209). Nevertheless, his ac-knowledgment of failure is a turning point. Before the scene ends, he shows calm and resignation in his comfort of York: "Uncle, give me your hands; nay, dry your eyes— / Tears show their love, but want their remedies" (3.3.202–3). And he addresses Bolingbroke not with frenzied grief or self-pity but with ironic wit and paradox, a touch of the antic disposition by means of which clever minds exercise control over their feelings and em-barrass their oppressors: "Cousin, I am too young to be your father / Though you are old enough to be my heir" (3.3.204–5).

Before Richard enters upon his next scene a new and momen-tous circumstance has been introduced. He has already agreed to abdicate, and he can therefore no longer challenge his oppres-sors or support his self-esteem by appealing to the divine sanc-tions of his royalty. His consent to accept the role of "tired maj-esty" willingly resigning the crown, far from resolving his inner conflicts, has added a new complexity to them. Renouncing his throne has not prepared him to be a subject:

> Alack, why am I sent for to a king
> Before I have shook off the regal thoughts
> Wherewith I reigned?
>
> (4.1.162–64)

His sorrow therefore remains, and it becomes, though with a difference, a major theme of the scene. He can now think of it as something of a discipline: "Give sorrow leave awhile to tutor me / To this submission" (4.1.166–67). Everything becomes a vehicle for it. The figure of two buckets and a well with which he describes his decline and Bolingbroke's rise appears occasionally in medieval depictions of the reversals of fortune,[14] but it becomes for Richard primarily an image of his sorrow: "That bucket down and full of tears am I, / Drinking my griefs, whilst you mount up on high" (4.1.188–89). To Bolingbroke's, "I though you had been willing to resign" (4.1.190), Richard replies:

> My crown I am, but still my griefs are mine.
> You may my glories and my state depose,
> But not my griefs; still am I king of those.
>
> (4.1.191–93)

This is not the same as his saying, as in an earlier speech, that being a king his woe will be kingly; what this says is that his sorrow is the only kingdom he now possesses.

Having agreed to give up his crown, he relieves his frustrations by denouncing those who once stood in awe of him as the Judases who betrayed him and the Pilates who delivered him to his sour cross (4.1.170–71). This speech has inspired efforts to interpret Richard as a Christ figure, but this symbolic identification is far-fetched. Is this not one more attempt, given his extravagant feelings in this scene, to find a consoling fiction in which he can play a role that justifies and ennobles his failure? He does not, however, persist in it, for these denunciations conceal an element of self-deceit. Richard cannot now rightly depict himself, as in an earlier circumstance he might, as a pawn of fortune or, in this instance, a helpless victim of a great betrayal. In consenting to the abdication he has become an accessory to his own ruin. Yet it is out of these very denunciations that an important truth comes to him, for the word "traitor" strikes a chord within himself:

> Mine eyes are full of tears, I cannot see.
> And yet salt water blinds them not so much
> But they can see a sort of traitors here.

> Nay, if I turn mine eyes upon myself,
> I find myself a traitor with the rest;
> For I have given here my soul's consent
> T'undeck the pompous body of a king;
> Made glory base, and sovereignty a slave,
> Proud majesty a subject, state a peasant.
>
> (4.1.244–52)

The one thing that has dignified Richard's possession of the crown is his profound belief that his authority comes from God. His expressions of this conviction have an eloquence combined with exactness that makes them memorable among statements of the divine right of kings. Even at his first appearance in this scene he hints that abdication may not release him from his divine ordinance: "God save the king! although I be not he; / And yet amen, if heaven do think him me" (4.1.174–75). If not all the water in the rough rude sea can wash the balm off from an anointed king, then not even his own tears can do so (4.1.207). Richard's predicament now is that of a man who lacks the will and courage, under pressure from superior power and political shrewdness, to abide by his most passionately held belief, and who comes to know what he has done.[15] This confession of weakness, however, implies an unexpected source of strength. He has been brought to this scene to be finally stripped of everything—"I have no title; / No, not that name was given me at the font" (4.1.255–56)—to be made a pawn of power, and to be humiliated by being forced to read publicly a prepared list of his sins. But to acknowledge his own failure of integrity and moral strength in agreeing to unking himself, and to express his own knowledge of wrongdoing, is in an important sense to demonstrate a moral courage that undermines the effort to degrade him utterly and to destroy him not only as a king but as a man.

The scene of the abdication, in spite of its outbursts of passion and its moments of self-pity, thus becomes something other than the total humiliation which Northumberland tries to make it. Richard takes the lead, and before he is finished with this extraordinary episode, he has passed through another stage on the way to knowing himself. He asks for a mirror, "That it may show me what a face I have / Since it is bankrupt of his majesty" (4.1.266–67). The mirror carries complex iconographic and literary echoes.[16] It was used as a symbol of vanity and pride, and at the same time as an image of truth, and in the latter aspect it was associated with the cautionary tale in which the reader could find instruction by contemplating the image of folly, or evil, or imprudence. That latter sense was conveyed in the title *A Mirror for Magistrates,* and whether this particular literary association was intended or not, the general idea was inescapable: a monarch whose story is a perfect *exemplum* of the fall from greatness calls for a mirror at a low point in his fall, just after he has acknowledged his share of responsibility for his overthrow. Richard himself calls attention to this association. While he is waiting for the mirror, Northumberland continues his bullying insistence that Richard publicly read a list of his crimes that the commons may be satisfied. Richard replies:

> They shall be satisfied. I'll read enough
> When I do see the very book indeed
> Where all my sins are writ, and that's myself.
>
> (4.1.273–75)

At this point, as the mirror is brought to Richard, he concludes: "Give me that glass, and therein I will read" (4.1.276). The mirror thus reinforces Richard's discovery of his own failure and guilt: but the effect of Richard's tragedy is not that of the story of the fall with a moral attached to it, as in the narratives of the ghosts in *A Mirror.* The mirror becomes an emblem of Richard's search for truth and understanding about himself, a variation of the self-examining sorrow which runs through the scene.

> No deeper wrinkles yet? hath sorrow struck
> So many blows upon this face of mine
> And made no deeper wounds?
>
> (4.1.277–79)

It is a "flattering glass," for what it shows is the face which once dazzled a kingdom, and not the reality of the moment. When he asks, "Is this the face which faced so many follies, / That was at last outfaced by Bolingbroke?" (4.1.285–86), it is to balance the truth which he has been discovering about his follies against the image in the glass where this truth is not yet reflected. The glory which the face in the mirror still reflects is a brittle glory, brittle like the image of the face itself which Richard shatters into fragments. The moral of the sport, as he tells the "silent king," is, "How soon my sorrow hath destroyed my face" (4.1.291). Sorrow has shattered the illusions of the past, and brought a measure of self-knowledge. Just as the evocation of the fall of princes becomes the prelude to a departure, ultimately, from the sentiments of *De casibus* tragedy, so the scene with the mirror recalls, and then departs from, the associations of the simple cautionary tale. He ends his exchange with Bolingbroke, Hamlet-like, contrasting the "external manners of lament," the "shadows," with the "unseen grief / That swells with silence in the tortured soul" (4.1.296–98). His final remark to Bolingbroke after this exchange on shadow and substance, is, as in an earlier scene, a witty speech condensing poignant feeling into paradox:

> Fair cousin! I am greater than a king;
> For when I was a king, my flatterers
> Were then but subjects; being now a subject,
> I have a king here to my flatterer.
>
> (4.1.305–8)

The scene with the queen is largely given over to expressions of sorrow, but there is a suggestion of passion spent or under restraint. In Richard's opening speech the sorrow is tempered with resignation:

> Join not with grief, fair woman, do not so,
> To make my end too sudden. Learn, good soul,
> To think our former state a happy dream;
> From which awaked, the truth of what we are

175

> Shows us but this. I am sworn brother, sweet,
> To grim Necessity, and he and I
> Will keep a league till death. Hie thee to France
> And cloister thee in some religious house.
> Our holy lives must win a new world's crown.
> Which our profane hours here have thrown down.
>
> (5.1.16–25)

The words "truth" and "necessity" strike a note in contrast to the make-believe by which he had earlier sought to mask the truth. The contrite closing lines suggest an admission of irresponsibility in the "profane hours," and this time the reference to cloisters and holy lives is not an empty gesture of escape to a conventional symbol of retreat. The queen's astonishment that he shows none of the rage of the wounded lion, the king of beasts, serves to point out how far he has come from trying to prove his kingliness by making his woe kingly. Instead, he tells her to think of him as dead, a subject for a sad tale:

> In winter's tedious night sit by the fire
> With good old folks, and let them tell thee tales
> Of woeful ages long ago betid;
> And ere thou bid goodnight, to quit their griefs
> Tell thou the lamentable tale of me,
> And send the hearers weeping to their beds;
> For why, the senseless brands will sympathize
> The heavy accent of thy moving tongue,
> And in compassion weep the fire out,
> And some will mourn in ashes, some coal-black,
> For the deposing of a rightful king.
>
> (5.1.40–50)

This is not quite the same as the "sad stories of the death of kings" which it recalls. His story is not the typical plunge from greatness of the medieval collections; it is the story of the crime of the deposing of a rightful king. And the emotional suggestions are also different: this is not the vanity of human wishes nor a moral for magistrates. The "tales of woeful ages long ago betid" conveys rather the more general mood of the long annals of human tragedy and sorrow.

His final scene Richard must play alone, bereft of everything and having no expectation but death. He who had the kingdom for his stage must now, in a final soliloquy, people the world of his prison with his thoughts, and since they are "in humours like the people of this world," "no thought is contented" (5.5.10, 11). Thoughts of divinity end in contradiction, and thoughts of ambition end in frustration and "die in their own pride" (5.5.22).

> Thoughts tending to content flatter themselves
> That they are not the first of fortune's slaves,
> Nor shall not be the last—like silly beggars
> Who, sitting in the stocks, refuge their shame,
> That many have and others must sit there;
> And in this thought they find a kind of ease,
> Bearing their own misfortunes on the back
> Of such as have before indured the like.
>
> (5.5.23–30)

There is a hearkening back here to the form and themes of medieval tragedy, but the comparison of fortune's slaves seeking consolation in the calamities of others with beggars in the stocks degrades both the lesson and the consolation. Richard does not proceed from this rejection to the self-awareness of the abdication scene or the resignation of the scene with the queen. Instead, he recalls that he is a rightful king who was unkinged by Bolingbroke and now is nothing, and the finality of that word leads him to the conclusion that peace from discontent comes only in the final nothingness of death.

> But whate'er I be,
> Nor I, nor any man that but man is,
> With nothing shall be pleased, till he be eased
> With being nothing.
>
> (5.5.38–41)

It is as though his isolation has brought him philosophically to a state of total spiritual nakedness and bankruptcy. This state of mind is jarred by the unexpected intrusion of music, a reminder not of the power and glory of his former life but of its amenities and its refinements of sensibility. An imperfection in the music prompts him to associate this lack of concord with the disharmony of his own life, and moves him to a final admission of his own former failings:

> Music do I hear?
> Ha, ha! keep time—how sour sweet music is
> When time is broke and no proportion kept!
> So is it in the music of men's lives.
> And here have I the daintiness of ear
> To check time broke in a disordered string;
> But for the concord of my state and time
> Had not an ear to hear my true time broke:
> I wasted time and now doth time waste me.
>
> (5.5.41–49)

No calm resolution comes to him, however, with this confession. The idea of being wasted by time brings him back to a realization of the harshness of his present condition, and in a complex figure of time and the clock he expresses his tedium, his grief, and his frustrating humiliation, concluding with the image of himself, the king, reduced to Bolingbroke's jack of the clock, a mechanical mannikin striking his hours. What concludes the soliloquy, however, is as remarkable as it is unexpected:

> This music mads me. Let it sound no more;
> For though it have holp mad men to their wits,
> In me it seems it will make wise men mad.
> Yet blessing on his heart that gives it me,
> For 'tis a sign of love; and love to Richard
> Is a strange brooch in this all-hating world.
>
> (5.5.61–66)

As a reminder of his old life and his present woe, the music becomes a fiendish torment, but with a suddenness that often marks Richard's grasp of a new perception he sees the music not as it affects him, but from the point of view of the musician as an offering of love.[17] The sudden, unexpected appearance of the thought at the end of the soliloquy produces the effect of a discovery. As if to confirm it, the lowly groom enters the dungeon at the risk of his life to see his old master. Shakespeare does not allow us to linger over this sentiment. The groom tells the story of Richard's roan Barbary carrying Bolingbroke to the coronation, and the irony of this plunges Richard into ill thoughts again. Only a faint echo in Richard's touching concern for the safety of the groom restores the humanity of feeling on which the soliloquy had ended: "If thou love me, 'tis time thou wert away" (5.5.96).[18]

The concluding episode of the scene shows Richard turning angrily on the keeper and meeting his murderers not passively but with fierce courage, dispatching two of them before Exton can give him his death blow. It is possible to object to this scene as introducing a heroic quality which does not appear in the character before and which presents him as something other than the vacillating, inept king who submitted even before he was asked and who up to this point has displayed a gift for language but not for courageous personal action. There is, however, an unpredictable quality in Richard. His moments of discovery come in flashes, brought into being by some unexpected association which produces its consequences without the intervening steps, like some metaphor or enthymeme. It could be argued that Richard's fluctuations between self-justification and self-pity on the one hand and self-knowledge on the other have led to this moment, and that with the Pomfret soliloquy the poetry of passion and self-examining sorrow has accomplished its purpose and there is no more left for speech to do. To grant Richard this act of resolution reaffirms in the language of the theatre the impression of Richard's refusal to be utterly broken. The instrument of power reaches into the isolation of his loathsome dungeon prison to perform the last step of turning him into a convenient corpse, and it finds him still a man.

It does not follow that with his final gesture of defiance Richard proves himself to be a tragic hero of impressive proportions.

But perhaps the point has already been more than sufficiently made in criticism that he is not an admirable figure and that he fails to measure up to such titans among Shakespeare's protagonists as Hamlet and Lear. That is a truth, however, from which it is difficult to proceed to a sympathetic understanding of what *Richard II* is about on its own terms, or to an appreciation of how extraordinary an accomplishment it was for Shakespeare at this stage in the growth of his art.

Richard and Bolingbroke are seen in relation to their political ambitions and skills, their response to the legalities of sovereignty, and their capacity to manage the realities of power. Here Richard is found wanting. It was, however, precisely the political nature of *Richard II* which gave Shakespeare the opportunity to explore new avenues for tragedy and to enlarge its possibilities. The lines of Richard's story rendered the admired conventions of Senecan tragedy inappropriate, but they had the classic contours of the medieval tragedy of fortune, the sentiments of which still had great appeal during the sixteenth century and which Shakespeare strongly suggests in the early portions of the play. However, viewing the conflict between Richard and Bolingbroke in the pitiless light of the natural history of politics, Shakespeare left far behind the causal scheme and the conventional pieties of the *De casibus* tradition. For one thing, the failure and fall of a king meant for the politically minded sixteenth century the ruin of the embodiment of the power and order of the state, and of the sacerdotal figure who held the state together. All the characters, with the possible exception of Northumberland, sense the importance of what is happening, that in dethroning Richard they are not simply removing a bad ruler for a capable one but touching the awesome mystery of sovereign power. For all his personal limitations and errors as a ruler, Richard manages to convey this aspect of royalty. The political nature of the play had also the more important effect of placing greater importance on character than was required by the design of *De casibus* tragedy. The king bore a responsibility for the catastrophe he brought on his nation through his failures. He could ill afford the luxury of contempt for the world, and pity for him as a victim was not enough.

In these respects *Richard II* shows superficial similarities with the design of *A Mirror for Magistrates*. In Shakespearean tragedy fortune is not the sole or principal cause of the catastrophe but the contingency which the protagonist must meet and against which he is tested, and this is so in *Richard II* as it is in many stories in *A Mirror*. But *A Mirror* was unsuitable as a model for the tragedy of a fallen king as Shakespeare depicts it in *Richard II*. It was didactic in aim, and its lessons were simplified and conventional. A tragedy framed on such a model would go beyond the *De casibus* pattern but not beyond *Gorboduc*. Richard's limitations of character and statesmanship produce the circumstances which lead to his fall and make him a ready victim of superior power and political skill. That he suffers in consequence of his failings makes him an object of pity. But Shakespeare also endows him with imagination and sensibility and thus renders him capable not only of feeling keenly and expressing his sorrow with eloquence, but also of searching within himself for the meaning of his sorrow. He thus carries the play beyond the prudential didacticism of such works as *A Mirror* and *Gorboduc*; he endows the theme of fallen greatness with new significance and anticipates the later tragedies in which the action leads the protagonist to self-knowledge and to the kind of anagnorisis in which he experiences an understanding of his own tragedy.[19]

What, finally, is striking about the play is that the movement of the action toward its conclusion seems at the same time to convey a sense of movement toward a new idea of tragedy. The traditional form and sensibilities of stories of fallen greatness are alluded to and even exploited, and then either reshaped or replaced to suit the quite different needs of the play. And the principal instrument of this progress is Richard himself. From the moment Richard apprehends the extent of his ruin on his return from Ireland, his response ceases to be one of meeting

181

the rebellion by the practical means of statecraft and war, and becomes instead a search for consolation and identity as he grasps and relinquishes various ways of acting out his true tragedy. The movement of the protagonist toward awareness and understanding and the emergence in the play of a new idea of tragedy are substantially one and the same.

X

The Politics of
a Conscientious Usurper:
I and *2 Henry IV*

In comparison with *1* and *2 Henry IV*, *Richard II*, the previous play, seems a closed, hothouse environment of kings, nobles, and retainers. In the two *Henry IV* plays, the canvas broadens to include all England. The vignettes of life in the inns, on the roads, the rural shires, and the London taverns create a vivid impression of a national setting, a lively and diversified world within which the political action appears as something more than the private affair of kings and nobles, and indeed sometimes seems in danger of becoming lost amid the fascinating variety of persons and incidents which crowd these plays. It is the political action, however, which holds all these diverse elements together. Henry IV is not the central figure in the way that Richard III and Henry V are central characters in the plays which bear their names, but all the events of the two plays find their meaning in relation to him and his main concerns and activities.

At the center of the plays is Henry's effort to establish himself firmly on the throne he had seized from Richard II, to legitimize the succession, and to pass it on to his heir. It is a measure of his political talents that no one has a shrewder perception of the situation he faces than Henry himself, or is more candid in passing judgment in retrospect on what he has been able to accomplish. Near the end of the second play, in his final talk with his son, who will shortly be king, Henry IV explains why his own reign had been a failure: his title had been "snatched with boisterous hand," he was beholden to others who later resented his power, and accordingly he had to fight to retain his throne (4.5.190–98). All this, Richard II had foreseen and predicted in a speech to Northumberland, "the ladder wherewithal / The mounting Bolingbroke ascends my throne" (*Richard II*: 5.1.55–56). The one serious flaw in a brilliantly arranged usurpation was Henry's dependence on powerful men for the support necessary to take the crown from Richard, while at the same time seeking to maintain the independence and inherent power of the office. The "willing" abdication, the public adoption by the resigning king as his heir, the formal approval by Parliament, and the enthusiastic popular support were not sufficient to provide the total legitimacy which endows the sovereign with an authority beyond that which derives from the power available to the office. Bolingbroke could not have obtained Richard's resignation without the military support provided in part by his fellow nobles. Though the troops themselves were never actually used, the threat behind them was made explicit in the message Bolingbroke sent to Richard, who had taken refuge in Flint Castle on his return from Ireland:

> Henry Bolingbroke
> On both his knees doth kiss King Richard's hand,
> And sends allegiance and true faith of heart
> To his most royal person; hither come
> Even at his feet to lay my arms and power,
> Provided that my banishment repealed
> And lands restored again be freely granted;
> If not, I'll use the advantage of my power
> And lay the summer's dust with showers of blood
> Rained from the wounds of slaughtered Englishmen.
> (*Richard II*: 3.3.35–44)

The forces which supported Bolingbroke's claim to his lands and title remained to provide the motive for Richard's abdication, and not surprisingly Henry's crown came to seem "an honor snatched with boisterous hand." The boisterousness might in good time have been forgotten, and even the murder of Richard—the ultimate moral price Henry paid for his throne as it was the ultimate political necessity for its protection—might have been forgiven. There have been monarchs who managed to overcome handicaps as great as these. Far more damaging politically was the debt of obligations which the personal and military aid from his fellow nobles had placed on Bolingbroke. Angered by Richard's misrule and outraged by his seizure of Bolingbroke's estate, they rushed with enthusiasm to Ravenspurgh to greet the exile as a savior, but they came, in time, to resent the fact that the man who was made king by their connivance and support seemed determined to be a king in fact as well as in name. Hotspur calls the king "this vile politician Bolingbroke." The new king was a full-time politician of necessity, playing the role of a man who owes his office to others who have no intention of forgetting what the incumbent owes them.

All these considerations are there below the troubled surface in the first scene in *1 Henry IV*, and they break through in the third scene to separate Henry and his former friends and allies. The king's opening speech expresses a hope for peace, but the dominant impression is that of violence and war, and any suggestions of respite and calm are overwhelmed by their opposites: peace is "frighted" and "panting," and the "flourets" are "bruised" with the "armed hoofs of hostile paces" (1.1.2, 8–9). Henry's broad policy during the course of the play will be to unify his kingdom and insure peace, and his immediate goal is to prevail on the forces which fought each other in civil butchery to "March all one way, and be no more opposed / Against acquaintance, kindred, and allies" (1.1.15–16). To this end Henry revives the idea, announced at the end of *Richard II* as an act of penance, of leading a crusade to the Holy Land as a means of bringing together in a national and religious cause the unruly forces which now seem bent on turning on one another. It is a plan which has earned Henry the contempt of many critics; but Henry's position now is such that he cannot afford to neglect the political value of any action or gesture. If a noble impulse can yield political dividends, so much the better; if it interferes with politically necessary actions, it must give way. Unfortunately, border enemies, taking advantage of the unsettled state of affairs within the kingdom, have been attacking, and success in one quarter is balanced by failure in another. That paragon of honor, Hotspur, has won a victory over the Scots, but the "noble Mortimer" has been captured in Wales by Glendower. And there are some unpleasant overtones from the victory in Scotland over a small matter of the king's share of the prisoners, for fortune will never give to this king with both hands. The expedition to the Holy Land must be postponed.

The meaning of these reverberations becomes clear in the third scene. The king's opening lines plunge precipitously into the central political problem:

> My blood hath been too cold and temperate,
> Unapt to stir at these indignities,
> And you have found me, for accordingly
> You tread upon my patience.
>
> (1.3.1–4)

Henry has tried to placate his powerful supporters and be attentive to their sensibilities, but the result has been not increased friendliness but the undermining of his regal status. Henry has decided that he cannot continue to behave as though he were still a mere equal, now greatly beholden to his former allies, without undermining the authority of his office. No king (or any other head of state for that matter) can be placed in the position of being simply a man indebted to others as powerful as himself, without becoming a mere political tool and figurehead. Henry decides that the moment has come to make this point:

> I will from henceforth rather be myself,
> Mighty and to be feared, than my condition,

Which hath been smooth as oil, soft as young down,
And therefore lost that title of respect
Which the proud soul ne'er pays but to the proud.
                                    (1.3.5–9)

Worcester's reply is a direct challenge of the king's intent:

Our house, my sovereign liege, little deserves
The scourge of greatness to be used on it,
And that same greatness too which our own hands
Have holp to make so portly.
                                    (1.3.10–13)

The respectful phrase, "sovereign liege," is contradicted by the words that follow. The one thing Henry cannot permit and still remain a king in fact is the expressed conviction that his power is a gift from powerful men whose wishes can determine what he shall do and how long he can stay in office. He dismisses Worcester unceremoniously:

Worcester, get thee gone, for I do see
Danger and disobedience in thine eye.
O, sir, your presence is too bold and peremptory,
And majesty might never yet endure
The moody frontier of a servant brow.
                                    (1.3.14–18)[1]

The withholding of the prisoners is a less overt attack on Henry, but it represents a slight that is equally menacing. It is generally agreed that by the laws of combat the king was entitled to the earl of Fife but not to the rest of Hotspur's prisoners, but Shakespeare does not represent the Percys as making an issue of this point, and indeed they are defensive. Northumberland explains that the prisoners were "not with such strength denied / As is delivered to your Majesty" (1.3.24–25). Hotspur insists, "I did deny no prisoners" (1.3.28), and explains that he took offense at the manner of the popinjay courtier who questioned him about the prisoners after the battle, when, tired and wounded, he answered impatiently he knew not what. This speech has been much admired,[2] but Henry sees through the evasion of Northumberland's "not with such strength denied," and is therefore not as moved as is Blunt by Hotspur's defense. The point which nettles Henry, and which Westmoreland suspects is Worcester's doing (1.1.95–98), is that the prisoners are being used as a bargaining point, a tactic of which Henry rightly suspects the motive. In typical fashion he goes directly to the essential issues: "Why, yet he doth deny his prisoners / But with proviso and exception" (1.3.76–77). The proviso is that Henry should ransom Mortimer, earl of March, the "noble Mortimer" of the first scene but now for Henry "the foolish Mortimer," who had not done well in the expedition against Wales and had married Glendower's daughter—a treasonable act under the circumstances. Henry knows that this demand is not an innocent desire of the Percys to secure the freedom of a relative of Hotspur's by marriage, for Mortimer, as a descendant through the female line from Lionel, the third son of Edward III and, according to the Percys, the person designated by Richard II as the next in line, could well claim the throne. Hotspur, it turns out, is innocent of these complications and motives, though Northumberland and Worcester certainly are not (1.3.139–57), and it is unlikely that so astute a man as Henry would not see through Hotspur's attractive performance to its source in the defiance and plottings of Worcester and Northumberland. If in this instance Henry is lacking in the kind of magnanimity that he could show to Mowbray, Aumerle, and Carlisle in *Richard II*, it is not because he has suddenly become a stickler over a technicality about prisoners of war, but because of the proviso which Hotspur has been schooled to introduce. Like Worcester's statement about what Henry owes to them, the proviso represents a disregard amounting to contempt for the dignity and authority of his kingship, without which Henry knows his office is empty and cannot be effectively used to do his country good. It is, in fact, a very menacing tactic, since it implies that the Percys will now use Mortimer's claim as a threat against Henry.

Thus far the preparation of the political groundwork of the play has been precise and brilliant, but the oppositions are not merely those of abstract principles and political choices but of people who establish various claims on our sympathies. So far we have been seeing the situation from the viewpoint of the king. We see the next episode largely through the eyes of the chivalrous and attractive Hotspur. Worcester and Northumberland explain to him the reason for Henry's anger about the prisoners. They report that Richard proclaimed Mortimer "the next of blood" before going to Ireland, and that they had witnessed the proclamation. This information immediately places in a questionable light their own support of Bolingbroke, and might well justify Henry's reaction to their present machinations. Hotspur rebukes them, in fact, for having "set the crown / Upon the head of this forgetful man" (1.3.158–59), but for the moment the impression of Henry's understandable anger is diminished in the presence of the more engaging anger of Hotspur, for whom Henry is an infamous and ungrateful politician. As the scene develops, however, it becomes clear that "politician" might better be applied to Worcester, though Hotspur is hardly the one to perceive either this or the fact that he is being manipulated to serve the ends of his kinsmen. Worcester provides throughout an interesting comparison with Henry. Both are astute men with strongly developed political instincts, and Worcester is, like Henry, a political realist. His analysis of their position and his justification for plotting a rebellion are an explicit statement of what Henry fears:

> For, bear ourselves as even we can,
> The King will always think him in our debt,
> And think we think ourselves unsatisfied,
> Till he hath found a time to pay us home.
> (1.3.279–82)

This is shrewd and calculating, but does it do full justice to Henry? Worcester usually judges on narrower grounds and on the basis of more personal ends than the king. We have the opportunity to compare the conspirators with Henry when they gather to coordinate their plans (3.1.). Dramatically it is one of the finest scenes in the play, and it includes a splendid characteristic performance by Hotspur, but what emerges is that these men are ready to carve up the kingdom and so are motivated by a feudal-minded policy quite the opposite of Henry's "march all one way."

We have a final opportunity to compare the two parties in the scenes of confrontation before the battle of Shrewsbury. In the first of these Blunt, as spokesman for the king's party, talks with Hotspur in the rebel camp. To Hotspur's flattering wish that Blunt did not stand against them as an enemy, Blunt replies that he cannot do otherwise "So long as out of limit and true rule / You stand against anointed majesty" (4.3.39–40). Nowhere does Henry claim that he is king by divine right. "Anointed majesty" refers to the public ceremony of coronation, by virtue of which he regards himself as lawful king and entitled therefore to the respect which the office requires. Hence those who oppose him by force are outside the law and therefore rebels. But Blunt also brings concessions, which reflect the king's awareness of the limitations which his illegitimate path to royal power has imposed upon him in spite of the technical and practical rightness of his position—the king has not forgotten the "good deserts" of his onetime allies, and promises to redress any grievances:

> You shall have your desires with interest,
> And pardon absolute for yourself and these
> Herein misled by your suggestion.
>
> (4.3.49–51)

In reply Hotspur recounts the events leading to Henry's coronation. It is not exactly an inaccurate account—the facts are there—but it is necessary only to recall *Richard II* to realize how twisted the events have become in retrospect. Northumberland and Worcester "did give him that same royalty he wears"; Henry was then but "a poor unminded outlaw sneaking home";

Northumberland, "in kind heart and pity moved," swore to assist him; the king forgot the vow he made to Northumberland (did not Northumberland also forget it?); and the king but seemed "to weep / Over his Country's wrongs," in order to take advantage of the need for reform to further his private interests (4.3.52–88). Most disingenuous is the reason alleged for the rebellion: Henry's harsh treatment of his former friends, which drove them to look after their own safety, also prompted them

> to pry
> Into his title, the which we find
> Too indirect for long continuance.
>
> (4.3.103–5)

By their own admission, Worcester and Northumberland knew exactly where the title stood when they aided Bolingbroke and presented Richard with a bill of his crimes in order to justify their support of the new king. Blunt quite rightly dismisses all this elaborate rationalizing. The real question now is whether the rebels will accept Henry's offer of "grace and love"; and surprisingly—until we reflect on his generous and impulsive nature—Hotspur replies, "And maybe so we shall" (4.3.113).

The next confrontation is between the king and Worcester, and the tone of this interview is quite different. Here are two men of similar political temperament, and both know that events have placed them in equivocal positions. Worcester's account of the past and of the circumstances which brought them to challenge the king is, of course, partisan and intended to be damaging to the king, but it is more honest and fair than Hotspur's. His statement of what happened after Henry broke his oath— that he had come only to claim his own—goes far to picture Henry's accession not as an act of calculated villainy and political cynicism, but largely as a consequence of circumstances which converged to create an almost irresistible opportunity. In view of what critics have written about Henry's sinful path to the throne, the passage is worth considering in detail:

> You swore to us,
> And you did swear that oath at Doncaster,
> That you did nothing purpose 'gainst the state,
> Nor claim no further than your new-fall'n right,
> The seat of Gaunt, dukedom of Lancaster.
> To this we swore our aid: but in short space
> It rained down fortune showering on your head,
> And such a flood of greatness fell on you,
> What with our help, what with the absent King,
> What with the injuries of a wanton time,
> The seeming sufferances that you had borne,
> And the contrarious winds that held the King
> So long in his unlucky Irish wars
> That all in England did repute him dead:
> And from this swarm of fair advantages
> You took occasion to be quickly wooed
> To gripe the general sway into your hand;
> Forgot your oath to us at Doncaster,
> And being fed by us, you used us so
> As that ungentle gull the cuckoo's bird
> Useth the sparrow.
>
> (5.1.41–61)

Grudgingly, Worcester acknowledges their complicity and also the compulsion in these circumstances. The real grievance, the only expressed justification for the rebellion, is the alleged loss of the king's favor, and their consequent fear for their own safety, for which Worcester blames the king:

> Whereby we stand opposed by such means
> As you yourself have forged against yourself
> By unkind usage, dangerous countenance,
> And violation of all faith and troth
> Sworn to us in your younger enterprise.
>
> (5.1.67–71)

The king, like Blunt, dismisses all this as rationalization for rebellion, and with better chance of being understood than had Blunt in the case of Hotspur. It is pointless, both men must know, to rake up the past, since both were parties to his elevation to kingship. If Henry does not have clean hands, neither do they, and he can reproach them for their present revolt as an act of disloyalty—"You have deceived our trust" (5.1.11). He can also maintain with good reason that if his rights as king are not respected, and are challenged by rebellion, the nation cannot escape a time of "pellmell havoc and confusion" (5.1.82). The only practical issue is whether they will accept pardon and abandon the rebellion:

> No, good Worcester, no.
> We love our people well, even those we love
> That are misled upon your cousin's part;
> And, will they take the offer of our grace,
> Both he, and they, and you, yea, every man
> Shall be my friend again, and I'll be his.
> So tell your cousin, and bring me word
> What he will do. But if he will not yield,
> Rebuke and dread correction wait on us
> And they shall do their office.
>
> (5.1.103–12)

There are those who will read a mean motive in every utterance of this capable if not very appealing usurper, but taking his measure only as a political man we can grant that the offer was made in good faith, because the alternatives Henry offers to the rebels are the only ones available now, and to survive he must, if his offer of pardon is accepted, try to make his promise work. In its context within this one play and having no reference to what happens in Part 2, the offer must be accepted as genuine, with some hope on the king's part that its acceptance by the rebels might resolve the immediate problems that confront the realm. We have an explicit verification of this view in Worcester's decision not to report Henry's terms to Hotspur: "O no, my nephew must not know, Sir Richard, / The liberal and kind offer of the King" (5.2.1–2). Shakespeare did not place such words as "liberal and kind" in the mouth of this hard-bitten politician with a design of irony.[3] But Worcester remains consistent. The reasons he gives to justify deceiving Hotspur arise from the same premises that led to the rebellion: Henry must now remain suspicious of them, and so "It is not possible, it cannot be, / The King should keep his word in loving us" (5.2.4–5). Hotspur may be spared because, as Worcester candidly admits, "We did train him on" (5.2.21), but he cannot believe the others would be left in peace. These are shrewd reasons, but they come from a narrower and less imaginative politician than Henry. And so the battle will have to be fought.

Looking back over the political action of the play from this point it appears remarkable how dramatically effective and at the same time how sharp has been Shakespeare's definition of the political situation, in spite of his sympathetic approach to the characters in both camps. And one mark of his success is that though critics have judged the king in many ways and often with a savage lack of sympathy, no one has ever suggested that the play leaves us with the impression that the country would have been better off if Hotspur and his fellow rebels had won the day at Shrewsbury.

The defeat of the rebels at Shrewsbury successfully checked the most serious threat to Henry's power and to his policy of uniting the kingdom, but Part 1 does not end on a note of finality. In his last speech, the king is giving orders for further military action—he and the prince will go to Wales to continue the fight against Glendower, while Prince John and Westmoreland will take troops north to fight Northumberland and Scroop. It is with the latter action that Part 2 begins. It has been often noted that Part 1 is characterized by a spirit of energy and youthful buoyancy in contrast to Part 2, in which the king seems old and ailing and images of disease appear throughout. The changes in tone affect all the principals. As far as the king is concerned, they reflect the failure of a bold and confident plan, which he began as Bolingbroke in *Richard II*, to reform the conduct of the kingly office, to sweep aside a decaying order, and to introduce a fresh new energy in guiding the affairs of the nation. The rebellion of Part 2 is also a less spirited enterprise than that of Part 1. It is cautiously planned as a holy war in the name of Richard II and led by an archbishop, and no one involved

in it is as tough politically as Worcester or as glamorous in
arms as Hotspur. The animus against Henry is less fierce, and
when the time comes for the rebels to present their case, while
the armies wait for battle at Gaultree Forest, their arguments
sound tired, they complain chiefly of neglect and of the harsh
necessities of the sick times, and they end up asking for a
review and redress of grievances. The climax of this part of the
action has no resemblance to that of Part 1, a combat between
two youthful representatives of military valor, the one "the
theme of honor's tongue" and the other a onetime truant to
chivalry who will recover his lost honor in this victory. Instead,
the cautious and reflective archbishop accepts the offer made in
the name of the king by Prince John that their grievances will
be met, only to have John arrest them for high treason and
send them off to execution on the technicality that he promised
to redress their grievances but said nothing about pardon. It is
a morally offensive act which can be justified, if at all, solely on
the grounds of the most desperate political necessity.

It is, however, a mistake to use this episode retrospectively to
impugn the motives of the king in Part 1 when he offers redress
of grievances and amnesty to Worcester. For one thing the
terms are not quite the same. Westmoreland promises in Part 1
not only redress "with interest" but also "pardon absolute"
(4.3.49–50), and the king offers his grace and promises friendship. But these are secondary considerations. The whole spirit
of Part 1 is different, as is the general situation. No one expresses Henry's plight in Part 2 better than the archbishop before the fateful interview with Prince John:

> Full well he knows
> He cannot so precisely weed this land
> As his misdoubts present occasion.
> His foes are so enrooted with his friends
> That, plucking to unfix an enemy,
> He doth unfasten so and shake a friend.
> So that this land, like an offensive wife
> That hath enraged him on to offer strokes,

As he is striking, holds his infant up
And hangs resolved correction in the arm
That was upreared to execution.

(4.1.204–14)

Each such episode hurts the king as much as it does his foes. John performs a ruthless piece of radical political surgery, sparing the lives of his troops and breaking the source of further rebellion, but this is not the kind of victory which casts fame on the victor or inspires love in his people. In Part 2 the king does not enter on the scene until the beginning of act 3, and what we see is an unhappy man, worried over matters of state, reflecting on how he was deceived in his trust in his former friends, brooding over the disappointments of the past, and hoping once more to undertake a crusade to the Holy Land: "And were these inward wars once out of hand, / We would, dear lords, unto the Holy Land" (3.1.107–8). This thought still troubles him in a later episode as he waits for news from Westmoreland and John:

Now, lords, if God doth give successful end
To this debate that bleedeth at our doors,
We will our youth lead on to higher fields
And draw no swords but what are sanctified.

(4.4.1–4)

The never-to-be-taken crusade becomes a sign of his failure to achieve national unity. The king in Part 2 knows that his initial hopes will not be fulfilled, and that the nation will never "march all one way" under his leadership.

Henry is not, however, ultimately defeated either as a man or as a foresighted politician, and the play ends with greater finality and with a greater sense of something important achieved than does Part 1. Having failed in his first goal, he is now motivated by a new aim. He will preserve the title at all costs— even if it means Gaultree Forest—and pass it on to his son, for an uncontested succession seems now the only hope for bringing unity and internal peace where his questionable title could not.

196

Henry's continued worry over his son's waywardness goes far deeper than the disappointment of a father over a son from whom he had expected a great deal. What merit would there be in fighting and conniving to provide for an uncontested succession if the heir will not be worthy of the office? In a despairing mood he exclaims to his son:

> O my poor kingdom, sick with civil blows!
> When that my care could not withhold thy riots,
> What wilt thou do when riot is thy care?
> O, thou wilt be a wilderness again,
> Peopled with wolves, thy old inhabitants.
>
> (4.5.133–37)

It is no achievement to save the country from the chaos of rebellion only to secure for it the chaos of misrule. What relieves the prevailing impression of illness and death in the latter portions of the play is the emergence of the prince as a fitting heir with political sagacity the equal of his father's. Shortly before the interview which produces the cry of despair quoted above, the prince reveals a clear understanding of the importance of an uncontested succession and an appreciation of Henry's efforts to establish it. The action which brings on Henry's most bitter sorrow over his disappointment in the prince, the prince's removal of the crown from the pillow of the dying king and placing it on his own head, is, ironically, the occasion for the soliloquy which reveals the prince's awareness of the meaning of his political inheritance:

> My due from thee is this imperial crown,
> Which, as immediate from thy place and blood,
> Derives itself to me. Lo where it sits,
> Which God shall guard; and put the world's whole strength
> Into one giant arm, it shall not force
> This lineal honor from me. This from thee
> Will I to mine leave, as 'tis left to me.
>
> (4.5.40–46)

As soon as the king is relieved of his anxiety about the prince, he feels once more secure in his grasp of the political situation.

His own crooked, boisterous, and almost inadvertent path to the throne is now a thing of the past, and in his mind the troubles it brought him need not be those of his heir:

> And now my death
> Changes the mood, for what in me was purchased
> Falls upon thee in a more fairer sort.
>
> (4.5.198–200)

The dynasty, to be sure, is still not an ancient one: "Yet though thou stand'st more sure than I could do, / Thou art not firm enough, since griefs are green" (4.5.202–3). And so, if there is not to be a crusade, the general policy of using some similar stratagem to achieve a united nation still holds good: "Be it thy course to busy giddy minds / With foreign quarrels" (5.4.213–14). Henry is persuaded that his death purges the title of its taint, and that his sin need not be visited on the sons even to the third and fourth generation:

> To thee it shall descend with better quiet,
> Better opinion, better confirmation,
> For all the soil of the achievement goes
> With me into the earth.
>
> (4.5.187–90)

The crime is between Henry and God, and his son may hope to wear the crown in peace: "How I came by the crown, O God forgive, / And grant it may with thee in true peace live!" (4.5.218–19). For the prince, this hard-won succession assures him of a legal crown:

> My gracious liege,
> You won it, wore it, kept it, gave it me.
> Then plain and right must my possession be,
> Which I with more than with a common pain
> 'Gainst all the world will rightfully maintain.
>
> (4.5.220–24)

With this great business finished Henry's work is over, and he can retire to Jerusalem Chamber to die.[4]

XI

The Honor of Princes, Warriors, and Thieves: *1* and *2 Henry IV*

One consequence of the variety and breadth of scale of *1 Henry IV* is that the play provides numerous points of reference against which we can measure the principal characters. As we move from court to tavern, from robbery on the road to the field of battle, we become aware of a number of different challenges to the values of the king and the prince. Prominent in this scheme of direct and implied comparisons are Falstaff and Hotspur, two brilliantly conceived and attractive characters who draw on our sympathies and in consequence puzzle and tease our judgment. They are key figures in the development of a major preoccupation of the persons in the play, the idea of honor. Hotspur and the prince are compared as young men whose birth and social obligations demand their services in arms and therefore their dedication to the ideals of chivalry. Falstaff, a renegade from the cultivated world of the court and its preoccupations, is the foil to Hal, a truant from the life of princely responsibilities. And on the issue of honor, Hotspur and Falstaff are also contrasted, though this comparison reflects as well on the values and choices of the prince.

The word "honor" occurs frequently in Part 1, and its presence has raised some troublesome questions. What place can honor have in a world in which subjects rebel against a usurper whom they placed in office, the prince plays at robbery with a dissolute knight, and the contending parties in government seem guided by "policy" rather than principle? Superficially, the answer appears to be that honor has little to do with the conduct of most of the characters, and where it is invoked the concept often seems narrow. At first glance honor seems to mean no more than a reputation for prowess and skill in arms gained in battle by noblemen and knights. That is the implication when the word first appears in the opening scene, in which the king contrasts the victorious Hotspur, "the theme of honor's tongue," with his son, who was not at the battle and whose brow is stained with "riot and dishonor" (1.1.80, 84), and also when, later in the play, the king upbraids the prince, comparing his son's dissoluteness and negligence with the boldness of young Hotspur leading his rebellious followers "to bloody battles and to bruising arms" and to the "never-dying honor" which he gained against Douglas (3.2.105–6). It is also the prince's meaning when he promises to redeem his bad reputation against the "child of honor and renown" and exchange his own shames "for every honor sitting on his helm" (3.2.139, 142). Hotspur glorifies the honor to be gained in battle against worthy foes, and the more hazardous the enterprise the greater the chance of gaining honor. The extravagance of his speech about plucking "bright honor from the pale-faced moon" and "drowned honor by the locks" (1.3.199 ff.) is inspired by Worcester's warning that the matter he is about to reveal is "deep and dangerous" (1.3.188).[1]

Even in this narrow military context, however, honor demands from these warriors something more than bravery and success in battle. This is a society in which the nobility constitutes an elite expected to bear arms, and honor stands for the special virtues which distinguish this class in the exercise of its vocation—gallantry in combat with a worthy foe, adherence to the accepted code of arms, and individual loyalty to friends, family, and comrades in arms. These qualities are taken seriously and have currency in *1 Henry IV*, even though men accuse each other of breaking their solemn word, rebellions are plotted, and warriors fight for something less than the highest moral principles and national glory. It says something for the world of *1 Henry IV* that such distinctions can be made. In *Troilus and Cressida*, Hector can fight for the honor of his family and the city of Troy in a war which he believes to be wrong because he is faithful to the highest standards of the code of arms, and he is accordingly admired on both sides for his exemplary conduct; but Troilus upbraids him for being so fastidious in an ugly, war-tired world, and the great Achilles takes advantage of a Hector so foolish as to fight fair. The battle of Shrewsbury is a deadly serious affair, yet the prince can call Hotspur "a valiant rebel of that name" before engaging him in fair fight to the death.

There are further shades of meaning which extend the idea of honor in *1 Henry IV* beyond the demands of chivalry and war. Even for Hotspur honor can mean something more than meeting dangers and triumphing over great warriors in battle. His first use of the word is, in fact, not in connection with warfare at all. He upbraids his father and uncle for having dishonored themselves by putting down Richard, setting the crown on Bolingbroke, and having to endure the humiliation of being discarded by him now that he is Henry IV. From these shames, he urges,

> time serves wherein you may redeem
> Your banished honors and restore yourselves
> Into the good thoughts of the world again.
> (1.3.178–80)

The dishonor that the king attributes to his son is not simply that he failed to distinguish himself in battle, but that by indulging in riot and bad company at a time when the king's interest was in danger he failed in a principal obligation of a prince. The king rejoices when his son joins him, not only because Hal has promised to use Hotspur's glory to redeem his own, but because he has returned to his proper princely role. "A hundred thousand rebels die in this," Henry exclaims (3.2.160). Honor, then, goes beyond chivalry and military fame.[2]

Nevertheless, at its broadest it is a concept with serious limitations. Henry's perjury is a case in point. It is charged against him by his former supporters that in taking the crown from Richard II he had broken an oath which he made to them on returning from exile, that he had come only to claim his inheritance; but, in spite of the gravity of this charge, little enough is made of it, because the oath was taken for expedient reasons and broken with the connivance of his then allies, now his enemies. And yet for most of the characters, including the king, honor is a serious matter. Judgment of conduct is referred to it, and it is invoked to bind men to a cause and to inspire the exercise of such private virtues as are demanded by one's public obligations. Its prominence is thus a mark of the secular atmosphere of *1 Henry IV*, in which the characters do not normally look beyond the immediate present to a cosmic scheme of justice or expect the wrath of God for neglecting a solemn obligation. In a world of politics and civil war it functions as a substitute for moral principle. It is not a static or a univocal concept, however; in the changing patterns of the play its merits are revealed, its limitations exposed, and in due course even the reality of honor is questioned.

The most direct, and indeed the only, denial of the reality of honor comes from Falstaff. His soliloquy on honor is a virtuoso performance of clever negation. It comes just after the king has ended his interview with the rebel leaders and the royal party awaits the almost certain sign for battle. Falstaff, the realist, says apprehensively, "I would 'twere bedtime, Hal, and all well." The prince's casual reply, "Why, thou owest God a death," provides the cue to the opening line of Falstaff's reflections, " 'Tis not due yet, I would be loath to pay him before his day"

(5.1.125–28). Restricting honor to its limited sense of the intangible rewards for valor in battle, Falstaff rejects it as empty and valueless, incapable of repairing wounds or surviving detraction after death. The sight of Sir Walter Blunt dead on the field of battle confirms him in his views—"There's honor for you" (5.3.32–33)—and it leads him to his final word on the subject: "I like not such grinning honor as Sir Walter hath. Give me life, which if I can save, so; if not, honor comes unlooked for, and there's an end" (5.3.58–61). " 'Tis not due yet," "Give me life"—these phrases sum up Falstaff's determination to hold on to life as the final good, even if it is only a precarious hold defiantly maintained against the decay of youth and the coming of age, the loss of moral virtue and of the world's esteem. The direct opposite of this is summed up in Hotspur's remarks shortly before the battle. A messenger comes with letters and Hotspur dismisses them—"I cannot read them now"; and as though this incident has suddenly brought home to him the realization that nothing matters now until the dangerous business is over, he continues,

> O gentlemen, the time of life is short!
> To spend that shortness basely were too long
> If life did ride upon a dial's point,
> Still ending at the arrival of an hour.
>
> (5.2.81–84)

There are things which are more important to Hotspur than life. Though addressing his men, Hotspur seems in these lines almost to be speaking to himself, surprised by the circumstances into a moment of self-revelation which suggests something of the depth of feeling that underlies his earlier extravagant sentiments about honor or the apparent flippancy of his comment when he learns of the big odds against them in the battle, "Doomsday is near; die all, die merrily" (4.1.134).

Shakespeare has made both of these spokesmen for opposing attitudes attractive, each in his own extraordinary way. They have, moreover, some basic traits in common. Both conduct their lives and make their choices in accordance with a settled principle. Both have a distaste for the reserve and calculation of official public life. Their loyalties are narrow. Falstaff's loyalty is to himself and his cronies when they are useful, and Hotspur's is personal and clannish. Both reveal a lively extravagance at times when they feel challenged or aroused, and both display a trace of desperation in seeking to extract the full measure of gratification out of life. Both men have a zest for life, though Falstaff's inclinations carry him to dissoluteness and even degeneracy, and Hotspur's valor and sense of personal integrity sometimes express themselves in discourtesy, eccentricity, and foolhardiness. It is in the aberration of qualities which can enhance life that the danger lies in these two men. Hotspur's sense of honor which makes him despise Henry as a "vile politician" and a "king of smiles" also makes him the victim of politicians who need his virtues to glamorize a rebellion, and his wholly personal coveting of honor "without corrival" inspires him to seek out occasions to exercise his youth and virtues in the destructive enterprise of war. Falstaff's ridicule of honor is a corollary of his guiding principle, "give me life," as he understands it; honor at Shrewsbury involves the danger of self-sacrifice, and so he will not seek it. If we see his position as a reply to the extravagances of Hotspur, we may be inclined to agree with him that honor is an empty illusion—Falstaff would not have ordered the charge of the Light Brigade. But by strictly limiting the scope of the term, Falstaff excludes its usefulness in defining a secular idea of loyalty and of dedication to the best demands of a serious calling, and thus as a means of maintaining one's self-esteem. Oddly enough, Falstaff has not completely lost the need for some modicum of that last quality. When they decide to do a play extempore and the prince proposes, "the argument shall be thy running away," Falstaff replies, "Ah, no more of that, Hal, and thou lovest me" (2.4.277–78). But Falstaff's chief use for the respectable world is to exploit it for his own purposes. He welcomes the rebellion as an opportunity to replenish his purse: "Well, God be thanked for these rebels, they

offend none but the virtuous; I laud them, I praise them"
(3.3.189–91). Lacking a sense of honor, he is capable of leading
his wretched recruits to the thick of the battle where most of
them will be killed so that he can keep their pay for himself.

It takes some reluctant second thoughts to arrive at the conclusion that Hotspur and Falstaff are both dangerous to the
well-being of a normal society. Given free rein to their inclinations, Hotspur is a source of division, turbulence, and war, and
Falstaff of degeneracy and anarchy. Yet we are sympathetic to
both because they are undeniably interesting and attractive in
a human way. Any talented young actor would rather play Hotspur than the prince, and what mature actor offered the part of
Falstaff would ask to play the king? For the first time in Shakespeare's histories, agents of disorder are made to appear in a
sympathetic, life-enhancing guise. The dangers to the order of
the state in the other plays arise for the most part from obviously
menacing and unattractive sources. Hotspur does not lead a
rebellion out of the fierce ambitions, petty selfish animosities,
and blood revenges which are responsible for so much of the
turmoil in the *Henry VI* trilogy, and there is no trace in him of
the pathological lust for power of Richard III. Thus we sense
something false in the prince's epitaph over his dead rival, "Ill-
weaved ambition, how much art thou shrunk" (5.4.87). Falstaff
is not an immediate threat to the state, but he brings a spirit of
scoffing, irresponsible selfishness to any serious enterprise of
which he is a part and he represents the kind of crookedness
which disgraces and inevitably corrupts any army. Their danger
lies in their attractiveness, because the form which their likeable
qualities takes is not suitable for emulation.

The prince, early in the play, shows a distaste for the questing
after military victory that is the bad side of Hotspur's love of
honor:

> I am not yet of Percy's mind, the Hotspur of the North, he
> that kills me some six or seven dozen of Scots at a breakfast,
> washes his hands, and says to his wife, "Fie upon this quiet
> life, I want work." "O my sweet Harry," says she, "how

many hast thou killed today?" "Give my roan horse a
drench," says he, and answers, "Some fourteen," an hour
after, "a trifle, a trifle."

(2.4.99–106)

Just before this he had described a drinking bout with a group
of tapsters at the inn, and tells Poins, "I tell thee, Ned, thou
hast lost much honor that thou wert not with me in this action"
(2.4.19–21). This fleering use of "honor" may represent an indirect attempt to justify his present truancy, but the use of the
military term "this action" to describe the heavy drinking and
the "honor" gained by staying with it may also express some
impatience with the cant of the warrior class. In comparison
with Hotspur, Hal's attitude toward honor may be likened to
Starbuck's attitude toward courage in *Moby Dick*—"one of the
great staple outfits of the ship in their hazardous work of whal-
ing, thought Starbuck, and, like her beer and bread, not to be
wasted." The prince accepts the idea of honor as a mark of the
warrior when he promises to exchange his shames for Hotspur's
honors, but it is not an exact exchange. There are certain features of Hotspur's code which Hal does not take on. He does not
have an excessive craving for military exploits or gloat publicly
over his success—he is willing, for the sake of a joke, to allow
Falstaff to claim credit for killing Hotspur; and his sense of
loyalty is not as clannish as Hotspur's nor as provincial ("this
Northern youth" [3.2.145], he calls him)—it is to his father as
king and therefore to the nation. It is an idea of honor more
befitting a London courtier than a northern earl, and more useful to a national king than to a feudal lord. Hal appreciates
Hotspur's gallantry—he honors the dead Hotspur by placing his
"favors" on the body of his adversary; and in this connection
Falstaff shows up to disadvantage, for we see him dishonoring
Hotspur's corpse with a coarse comic bravado that is as unpleasant as it is funny.

This view of the significance of the scheme of multiple comparisons is in keeping with the way the conflicts are resolved at
the end. The victory of the king's party seems the only acceptable

206

conclusion—not merely the one imposed by history—and even the most unsympathetic critics do not express offense at the defeat of the rebels at Shrewsbury as they do, for instance, at the sophistry of Prince John at Gaultree or the rejection of Falstaff in Part 2. Nevertheless, it is questionable whether Shakespeare ever fully redresses the balance in favor of Henry and his son in *1 Henry IV*, for the rebels are not pictured in a wholly reprehensible light. Once the rebellion gets under way, Hotspur's leadership lends it an air of gallantry and glamor. Aside from Worcester, who seems incapable of controlling the enterprise of which he was the political engineer, the others all have an almost amateurish quality which contributes to their undoing. This comes out in the one scene in which they all assemble to map out their strategy (3.1); they quarrel and show themselves more eager to divide the spoils of a hoped-for victory than to resolve the divisions within the kingdom, and hence appear as a worse choice politically than the king. Nevertheless, the conclusion which Shakespeare contrives for this episode comes as a surprising close to a scene of rebellious plotting. Glendower ushers in their wives, and there follows an engaging exchange of sentiments between Mortimer and his Welsh wife, with Glendower acting as interpreter, the contrasting affectionate sparring of Hotspur and his Kate, and finally the ethereal music invoked by Glendower which accompanies the Welsh song sung by Mortimer's wife. And these are the men who are threatening the center of order in the kingdom! There is nothing in the whole play that associates the king or the prince with as much charm and genial humanity.

It is, however, primarily the scenes involving Falstaff that play on the sympathies in a way which tips the balance in his favor in the dialectic on honor and encourages conclusions at odds with the common-sense line of political development in *1 Henry IV*, including the actions which lead to the success of the king's party and the prince's triumph over Hotspur. Criticism in our century, which has shown great interest in discovering and relating the parallelisms and analogies suggested by

Falstaff and his companions, has also made the most damaging use of these to render the king and his enterprise shabby and evil. The method is now so well established that it is necessary only to call attention to a parallelism in order to be sure that a damaging inference will be made. It is reasonable to assume, for instance, that the effect of following the first scene of act 1 with one involving Falstaff and the prince is more than comic relief to contrast with a serious political episode; "both express disorder and a prince's misconduct; in both a campaign is prepared—defiance to the Percies, robbery at Gad's Hill; and Hal's soliloquy at the end of I.ii knots both together."[3] What inferences are to be drawn from such a parallelism if no distinction is made between the kinds of disorder and misconduct alluded to—between, for example, the defiance to the Percys, which is a response to a serious threat to a fragile political order which the Percys themselves helped to create, and the robbery at Gad's Hill? Is the "prince's misconduct" identical in the two cases, and does it involve the same degree of reprehensibility or necessity? Not to raise such questions is to imply that there is no difference between the two—a conclusion which, if stated, would at least warn the reader where he is being led. "That Gad's Hill robbery," writes A. P. Rossiter, "is not mere farce. If we 'realize' it in an Usurper's state where Henry's right is might, might only—then what are the Percies and Bolingbroke's but Gadshills, Bardolphs, Petos in Bigger Business?" The starting point for this conclusion is the observation that the *Henry IV* plays make use of "a constant shifting of appearances, like the changing lights of an opal, so that every event, every person, becomes equivocal—as Falstaff made honor."[4] It is possible, however, to accept this observation about the nature of the play and not necessarily every conclusion derived from it. Initially, at least, Henry's right was not based on "might only," though he had the backing of might to bring it about. Henry's might would not have come into existence if the nobles who flocked to him at Ravenspurgh had not been fed up with what they believed to be the capricious and tyrannical rule of Richard II, if

Bolingbroke had not aroused great public enthusiasm, and if Parliament had not approved the abdication and succession. Henry IV became, nonetheless, a usurper, and suffered the disabilities which that unenviable state brought on him in part, at least, because his might is scarcely equal to the might of those who helped him to the throne and now wish to unseat him. If we allow the parallelisms to become reductive, it becomes impossible to distinguish between Richard III and Henry IV, or for that matter between Richmond and Bolingbroke, and Shakespeare's fascinating political discriminations are flattened out.

Since the scheme of comparisons and analogies does indeed have the effect of placing the king and the prince at times in an ambiguous light, it is understandable that critics who are not sympathetic with them will extract whatever they can from the parallelism to support their distaste, but it is a method that can lead to some unexpected interpretations. It can, for example, result in a reading of *1 Henry IV* as satire.

> The account of the proposed crusade is satiric. . . . The satire is general, directed against statecraft and warfare. Hotspur is the chief representative of chivalry, and we have only to read his speeches to understand Shakespeare's attitude towards "honour"; there is no need to turn to Falstaff's famous soliloquy.[5]

Falstaff is the key figure in establishing this satiric measure: "The Falstaff attitude is . . . in solution as it were throughout the play even when he is not on the stage," and since to all ideas of war, blood, and the like, "Falstaff, as a walking symbol, is of course opposed," the general conclusion is clear—"once the play is read as a whole the satire on war and policy is apparent."[6] This is like making Touchstone Shakespeare's walking symbol and *As You Like It* a satire on love and courtship in youth: what after all, are Rosalind and Orlando but Audrey and William in fancy clothes and with court manners? Comparison with the comedies is not out of place. Written at the same time as the histories, they employ parallelisms and analogies extensively:

Proteus is opposed to Valentine, Petruchio and Katherine are set off against Lucentio and Bianca, and Benedick and Beatrice against Claudio and Hero. In *As You Like It* the myth of pastoralism is taken apart and critically viewed from several angles, and is further used to provide a whole series of comparisons and analogies bearing on love and courtship. Commentators tend to refine on the distinctions suggested by these comparisons rather than to make them reductive. But then the comedies do not involve us in politics.[7]

Shakespeare's hold on our admiration and affection is so great that we are reluctant to concede that he can ever disappoint us by not being entirely on our side. If his art or taste in some particular offends us, we can put the blame on his audience.[8] And if he appears to espouse or even allow a sympathetic view of ideas which would arouse our opposition and indignation if we found them expressed in an editorial, we hasten to make the necessary critical adjustments required to make him our ally. One form of critical overcompensation tends to produce an equal reaction on the other side. J. Dover Wilson's learned and detailed effort to repair the damage caused by the politically unsympathetic critics of the prince results in a picture of Hal as the beau ideal of Renaissance princes, and in its own way overlooks important distinctions in the process. One turns almost in relief to Empson's insistence on ambiguity, only then to feel uncomfortable about a *Henry IV* which has become all things to all men.[9]

What tends to happen to criticisms which begin in impatience with the calculation and human detachment of professional politicians is that the dramatic comparisons of *1 Henry IV* are read in only one direction. In fact, they cut both ways. "The Prince and Falstaff," as Traversi points out, "imply by their very existence a criticism of the other."[10] Hotspur's honor, which involves not only a lust for military glory but a dislike of politicians, is measured against Falstaff's, which involves a cynical view of warriors as well as of politicians. And each is being looked over appraisingly by the prince. If we think of Hotspur and Falstaff as participants not simply in *Henry IV* but in the great human comedy, we are likely to feel that a world in which they exist is more interesting and engaging than one from which they are excluded, and we can indulge in such feelings because they have been given moments of great appeal in the play. But then we are brought back sharply to their role in the more restricted context of the political world in which Henry IV is fighting to preserve national unity and to pass an undisputed title to his son, who in turn is measuring himself for the kingly role he is destined to play. From that practical if specialized bias it does not seem good that Hotspur should be in a position of political leadership and power, or that Falstaff should have a continuing influence on the prince, or that his values should become the vogue among those who are by circumstance charged with preserving order and civility in the realm. Something of this must surely come through in any experience with *1 Henry IV*; otherwise the success at Shrewsbury would be felt to be a disaster, like the victory over Cordelia in *King Lear*. Shrewsbury is, however, a triumph with mixed feelings. It is impossible not to respond with a sense of pity and loss when Hotspur is killed (Shakespeare revives this sense in Part 2 in the touching tribute of Hotspur's wife), and the impressions of Falstaff in Part 1 are so strong that they extend into Part 2 and cast their shadow over his rejection. It is not necessary to renounce the appeal of these characters in order to be aware of a critical approach to their values and the use they put them to; by the same token, Shakespeare does not require us to love Henry IV or to admire his son without reservation in order to understand that their political role goes beyond ambition and includes a sense of honor that neither Hotspur nor Falstaff could understand.

The word "honor" is ubiquitous in the history plays, but it is only in *1 Henry IV* that the dramatic scheme is directly used to probe the possible meanings underlying the term. Some issues, however, which appear to be settled dramatically in Part 1 are continued in Part 2, and honor is one of these. On only a few occasions in the second part does the idea of honor acquire significance, but in these it adds to our understanding of the play and suggests comparisons with the more systematic treatment of the idea in Part 1.

The opening scenes of Part 2 are practically continuous with the earlier play. *2 Henry IV* opens with an Induction personifying the rumors following the battle of Shrewsbury, and the first scene shows Northumberland, who failed to appear at the battle, receiving the shifting and contradictory news of the engagement in his castle and learning finally of the military disaster and the death of Hotspur. When we next see Northumberland, he is trying to persuade his wife and daughter-in-law that he must join forces with the new conspiracy against Henry, and that his going is a matter of honor: "Alas, sweet wife, my honor is at pawn / And, but my going, nothing can redeem it" (2.3.7–8). Honor is not here a matter of valor and success in the impending battle, but simple loyalty to his peers with whom he was joined in an enterprise of danger. He had failed them once and thus pawned his honor; he can restore his right to it by not failing them again. The comparison suggested at this point with Hotspur and the battle which Northumberland failed to join is reinforced by the splendid eulogy to Hotspur which forms a part of Lady Percy's reply; the failure to his son, she argues, cannot be redeemed by keeping his word to his new allies:

> There were two honors lost, yours and your son's.
> For yours, the God of heaven brighten it!
> For his, it stuck upon him as the sun
> In the gray vault of heaven, and by his light
> Did all the chivalry of England move
> To do brave acts.
>
> (2.3.16–21)

The idea of chivalry, like a twilight glow from the previous play, adds a quality of romantic splendor to the honor of Hotspur which was lost by his death, and it is difficult to resist the inference that what it stood for was lost for good. The honor Northumberland appeals to is less comprehensive and heroic, and in his case less compelling, and Lady Percy can measure its limits:

> Never, O never, do his ghost the wrong
> To hold your honor more precise and nice
> With others than with him. Let them alone.
> (2.3.39–41)

Northumberland falls back on prudence:

> But I must go and meet with danger there,
> Or it will seek me in another place,
> And find me worse provided.
> (2.3.48–50)

Hotspur would have sought danger for no better reason than that it was there. For Northumberland, the demands of his honor do not outweigh the advantages of prudence, and he finally decides for Scotland and safety.

The other conspirators prove also to be prudent men. Mowbray alone seems determined to see the issue settled by arms, impelled by the thought of the "unequal hand / Upon our honors" laid by the king, and the recollection of the honor of his father which in Richard's day was not permitted to redeem itself against Bolingbroke (4.1.99–104, 113–29). The others are willing to listen to Westmoreland's assurances that their griefs will be heard and that

> wherein
> It shall appear that your demands are just,
> You shall enjoy them, everything set off
> That might so much as think you enemies.
> (4.1.143–46)

In view of what happens, the word "enjoy" conceals a cruel deceit. Prince John reads their demands and expresses his approval of them in cordial terms:

> I like them all, and do allow them well,
> And swear here, by the honor of my blood,
> My father's purposes have been mistook.
>
> (4.2.54–56)

He seals "our restored love and amity" with a drink and an embrace (4.2.65), And then comes the betrayal. To the archbishop's incredulous question, "will you break your faith?" (4.2.112), Prince John replies,

> I pawned thee none.
> I promised you redress of these same greivances
> Whereof you did complain, which, by mine honor,
> I will perform with a most Christian care.
> But, for you rebels, look to taste the due
> Meet for rebellion and such acts as yours.
>
> (4.3.112–17)

Technically quite unexceptionable, no doubt, but what kind of honor is Prince John offering as a guarantee that the terms of the agreement will be observed?

The kind of honor which is so important a preoccupation in Part 1 is noble and serious, but it has shallow roots, which do not always go down deep enough to be nourished by moral principles. It is almost invariably limited to serving as a code for a special group, whose members acknowledge it and thus bind themselves to high standards of conduct; but anyone who observes the code in the expectation that others within the group will also do so is helpless against one who decides arbitrarily not to conform—this was Hector's case against Achilles. Moreover, the idea of honor can become separated from the ethical principles which give it serious meaning and degenerate into little more than a guide to etiquette for a particular class. When Hamlet asks Laertes' pardon before the fencing match, Laertes says, "I am satisfied in nature," but this does not end the matter, because satisfaction "in nature" is less important to him than that demanded by the code:

But in my terms of honor
I stand aloof, and will no reconcilement
Till by some elder masters of known honor
I have a voice and precedent of peace
To keep my name ungored.
(*Hamlet*: 5.2.258–62)

One so punctilious about honor can nevertheless agree to use a poisoned foil in a sporting engagement governed by well-understood rules which certainly exclude unbaited and poisoned weapons, and he expects to get away with it only because Hamlet, as Claudius observes, being "Most generous and free of all contriving, / Will not peruse the foils" (4.7.136–37). As long, however, as the terms of honor are respected, even though restricted in scope or in sense, the possibility for approved conduct exists, and deceit such as that practiced by Achilles or Laertes is immoral not simply because deceit itself is so, but because it undermines the conditions for any sort of social honesty. The defect in the kind of honor talked about by Hotspur, or Hal, or Hector is that it is not proof against desperation, cynicism, or the needs of political expediency.

It is the last that explains the betrayal by Westmoreland and Prince John, though it does not acquit them of the ugliness of their deed. Both had deliberately implied in their dealings with the rebels that their negotiations were being conducted within certain tacitly understood rules—that they were, in short, behaving as "honorable" men. Westmoreland assures the rebel leaders that if they will submit to peaceful negotiations they will "enjoy" the benefits of whatever terms they agree to. John swears by the honor of his blood that his father the king had been misunderstood, and he confirms his promise in the immemorial ritual of a drink and an embrace by which men have sealed a bargain arrived at in good faith. And then he restricts the meaning of honor to exclude everything implied in his words and actions, leaving nothing but a legal obligation to follow the terms of the peace, an obligation which depends on no more than his now badly damaged notion of honor. Nothing better confirms the deterioration which has taken place between Part 1 and Part 2 than the fading out of the gallantry and the sense of obligation which honor meant to Hotspur and which it no longer means to his father, and—especially—the sophistry by which Prince John can claim to abide by honor while deceiving his opponents as to the meaning he attached to the concept, and thus lulling them into a trap that leads to their execution. In *1 Henry IV* honor is still a serious idea to reckon with, and men believe that their dedication to honor will be respected by others, and so they seriously consider what honor demands of them. It is left for the political expediency of Worcester to deceive Hotspur, and for the mocking genius of Falstaff to deny the idea of honor and, by his own comic disregard and even burlesque of it, expose the fragile foundations on which it rests. These two anticipate the debasement of the idea in the world of Part 2, a world in which political disorder and frustration and civil war have lasted too long for honor.

A change takes place in *2 Henry IV* following the death of the king, and a new spirit seems to animate the closing portions of the play. A youthful king takes on his responsibilities in a manner that signalizes a break with his frivolous past, and the play seems to turn to the future and away from the failures and desperate stratagems of Henry IV, whose illness and worry colored the political scenes of the earlier portions of the play. The degradation of the idea of honor by Prince John belongs to the earlier half. The one significant use of honor in the closing portion appears in a wholly new context and introduces a whole new range of possible meanings. The Chief Justice, apprehensively awaiting the appearance of the new king, explains to the king's equally apprehensive brothers why he had once sent Prince Hal to prison:

> Sweet Princes, what I did, I did in honor,
> Let by the impartial conduct of my soul;
> And never shall you see that I will beg
> A ragged and forestalled remission.

If truth and upright innocency fail me,
I'll to the king my master that is dead,
And tell him who hath sent me after him.

(5.2.35–41)

For the Chief Justice, too, there are things that matter more
than life, but they have nothing whatever to do with chivalry.
He was moved by no quest for personal glory, but "by the impartial conduct of my soul," and he was not merely following
the code of a class or profession but safeguarding the integrity
and dignity of the law, which, as he explains later to the young
king, is the authority of the king himself and the source of political and social order. The roots of this kind of honor take their
nourishment from ideas of private morality and public justice.
The reconciliation of the young king with the Chief Justice is
more than restoration of a proper formal relationship:

There is my hand.
You shall be as a father to my youth.
My voice shall sound as you do prompt mine ear,
And I will stoop and humble my intents
To your well-practiced wise directions.

(5.2.117–21)

The reconciliation at the end of Part 2 suggests a parallel with
the recapture of lost honor at the end of Part 1 through the
defeat of Hotspur, and the honor which is embraced by this later
recovery from princely misconduct goes well beyond the narrower idea of it in the earlier play. Significantly, the speech in
which the new king adopts the Chief Justice as a second father
is the one in which he proclaims his idea of the proper exercise
of kingly power:

Now call we our high court of parliament,
And let us choose such limbs of noble counsel
That the great body of our state may go
In equal rank with the best-governed nation;

That war, or peace, or both at once, may be
As things acquainted and familiar to us,
In which you, father, shall have foremost hand.

(5.2.134–40)

The enlargement of the idea of honor through the Chief Justice becomes a part of the making of a king. The honor which the Chief Justice sought to preserve is the kind which kings must be able to command whose ambition it is to rule over "the best-governed nation."[11]

XII

The Morality of Power:
The Case of
Bolingbroke / Henry IV

> But many a king on a first-class throne
> If he wants to call his throne his own,
> Must manage somehow to get through
> More dirty work than ever I do,
>   Though I am a Pirate King.
>   —*The Pirates of Penzance*

The Pirate King rests his apologia on what he assumes to be a
universal sentiment about heads of state. A century and a half before him, in the opening aria of *The Beggar's Opera*, Peachum,
the receiver of stolen goods, appeals to the same popular convictions to support his claim to respectability:

> The priest calls the lawyer a cheat
>   The lawyer be-knaves the divine,
> And the statesman, because he's so great,
>   Thinks his trade as honest as mine.

Hotspur's attitude toward politicians has much in common with
the bias in these satirical verses. When he tells Henry IV that
his kinsman Mortimer was never guilty of "base and rotten

policy," he is not distinguishing one form of "policy" from another, but characterizing policy in general, just as when he cries out against "this vile politician, Bolingbroke," he is simply saying that any politician is vile, Bolingbroke being one of the vilest. Hotspur has found a sympathetic response among Shakespearean critics; it is in the same spirit that Henry IV has often been judged by them.

On a serious philosophical level the acknowledgment of the impurity of political action is summed up in the concept of *raison d'état*, or, to use the phrase of the man generally recognized to have been the first modern writer to expound the concept in clear and uncompromising terms, *ragione di stato*.[1] Machiavelli himself believed that he was propounding something quite new, and says as much in chapter 15 of *The Prince*:

> It now remains to see what should be the methods and conduct of a prince in dealing with his subjects and friends. And because I know that many have written on this topic, I fear that when I too write I shall be thought presumptuous, because, in discussing it, I break away completely from the principles laid down by my predecessors. But since it is my purpose to write something useful to an attentive reader, I think it more effective to go back to the practical truth of the subject than to depend on my fancies about it. And many have imagined republics and principalities that never have been seen or known to exist in reality. For there is such a difference between the way men live and the way they ought to live, that anybody who abandons what is for what ought to be will learn something that will ruin him rather than preserve him, because anyone who determines to act in all circumstances the part of a good man must come to ruin among so many who are not good. Hence, if a prince wishes to maintain himself, he must learn how to be not good, and to use that ability or not as is required.[2]

The concept as well as Machiavelli's association with it must have been commonplace by the end of the sixteenth century. In *Volpone*, the egregious Sir Politic Would-be, who urges new-

comers to Venice to read "Nic. Machiavel and Monsieur Bo-
dine," records among the items of one day in his diary,

> I went and bought two toothpicks, whereof one
> I burst immediately, in a discourse
> With a Dutch merchant, 'bout *ragion' del stato.*

The idea of *raison d'état* and the phenomenon it deals with
did not, certainly, originate in the Renaissance. The distinction
between private and state morality which is at the center of the
idea is as old as the state. Since antiquity, it has been recognized
that the state must use power to protect and advance its interests, that in the exercise of this power it can use whatever means
seem to be required by the circumstances, and that in consequence a distinction has to be made between the moral judgments passed on private individuals and those on states and men
who act as servants of states. A continual tension, therefore, has
always existed in political theory between the philosophical
search for the good state and the good governor, and the concept of *raison d'état*, which assumes that the actual state cannot
at all times conform to the demands of the ideal state, or the
good governor to those of the good man, without being destroyed. The debate in Plato's *Gorgias* is centered on this issue,
and Plato adds to the seriousness of the argument by allowing
Callicles to present a persuasive defense of the power state and
of the ruthless amoralist statesman. Aristotle describes the
methods of such a statesman in book 5 of the *Politics*, which
deals with the rule of the tyrant. There are numerous other
treatments of this theme in antiquity, including the plays of
Seneca, whose tyrants deliver themselves of maxims which exalt
the uses and privileges of power. Machiavelli is known to have
drawn from Aristotle, Livy, and Xenophon; he could have used
many others.

It was the intervening years that provided the background
for Machiavelli's distinctive position in the history of political
ideas. Early Christian writers thought of the state as evil. Later

writers, Aquinas and Dante, for example, modified this view because they conceived of the state and ruler as subject to the laws of nature and the divine will. As Cassirer has stated, "The earthly city and the city of God are no longer opposite poles; they are related to each other and complement each other."[3] Machiavelli's accomplishment was that against this background he faced what he believed to be an evasion of historic and political truth, and analyzed the science of power and the art of its administration without confusing the issue by the introduction of moral and theological considerations. He did for political science what Bacon was to do for natural science in urging that natural knowledge be kept clear of religion and that men "do not unwisely mingle or confound these learnings together."[4] His approach was the outcome of a long firsthand involvement in a political world which every day gave evidence that what ought to be was helpless against the fierce pressures of what politically was and must be. The sixteenth-century state with its inevitable power politics is often contrasted, to its disadvantage, with the medieval conception of the state as an organization dedicated to peace and justice and the welfare of man's soul, bound to other Christian states under a universal church which could function at need as a second imperium to exercise control over individual rulers. That such a conception existed is true, but that it represented normal political reality will not stand up against a history of the papacy, or of Byzantium, or of the Crusades. That the new doctrine of political amorality found its classic statement first in Italy was the result of a set of largely accidental circumstances, in consequence of which the city-states developed as independent temporal powers and became involved in intense political interaction with one another, with the papacy, and finally with the great emerging national sovereignties of Europe.[5] The increasingly powerful national monarchies were of course not far behind. If Machiavelli succeeded in becoming notorious overnight, it was because he exposed a sensitive nerve.

It is not necessary to rehearse the intrigues, treasons, assassinations, and broken oaths and treaties that characterized the internal and international politics of Europe during these years; but one familiar instance may be briefly recalled to illustrate the demands and the tone of political life in the sixteenth century—the celebrated political drama involving Elizabeth and Mary Stuart which ended with the triumph of state necessity over mercy, kinship, the touchy issue of divine right, and personal feeling. The intrigues which resulted in the flight of Mary, queen of Scotland, from her throne and those which finally ended in her trial and death were international in scope, involving the kings of France and Spain as well as the pope. When Mary took refuge in England, great pressure was put on Elizabeth from her council, Parliament, and popular sentiment to end the anomalous situation by getting rid of the cause. A striking instance of national feeling on this issue was the Bond of Association, which pledged its numerous signatories to prevent, if necessary by assassination, the succession of anyone who plotted against the life of Elizabeth. For a variety of reasons, Elizabeth resisted these pressures; she hesitated on political grounds to execute an anointed queen, she was reluctant to agree to the death of a kinswoman, and she was not bloody-minded like her father. After Mary was tried and condemned, Elizabeth, while hesitating to sign the warrant, was persuaded to evade the issue of executing a duly crowned queen by having Mary assassinated, and instructed Walsingham to communicate this wish to Mary's keeper, Sir Amias Paulet. Paulet's reply assured him his place in history:

> I am so unhappy to have lived to see this unhappy day in which I am required by direction from my most gracious sovereign to do an act which God and the law forbiddeth. . . . God forbid that I should make so foul a shipwreck of my conscience, or leave so great a blot on my poor posterity, to shed blood without law or warrant.[6]

Paulet this conformed to the model of what a subject was supposed to do when commanded by his sovereign to commit an act against the laws of God: he followed his conscience and took the consequences. The consequences in his case, since the sovereign was Elizabeth, were not serious; he was, in fact, subsequently made Chancellor of the Order of the Garter and appointed a commissioner to the Low Countries. But Elizabeth could not resist a cynical comment about "the niceness of those precise fellows," Paulet as well as others, who had signed the Bond of Association but preferred to have Elizabeth assume under pressure the ultimate public responsibility for an unpleasant act of state which she disliked for reasons both political and personal. It is indicative of the political sensibilities of the age that there were representatives of foreign governments who thought Elizabeth would have been better advised to have arranged matters so that Mary would have somehow died in bed. Yet this episode, if only because it was so open and dramatic, was played out with more honor than many of the sordid and violent acts committed in the name of *raison d'état* during the same period.[7]

One thing this episode brings out is the highly exposed position of the sixteenth-century monarch. In the modern vast, bureaucratic corporate state, actions taken for reasons of state often have the effect of impersonal events performed by anonymous instruments remote from the center of authority. The sixteenth-century monarch could not envelop himself in any such corporate cloak of invisibility and anonymity. The power of the state was completely embodied in him; his involvement in morally ambiguous decisions was unavoidably personal and, in the comparatively small and intimate arena of national and international politics, it was also conspicuous. The politics of the sixteenth-century monarchical system thus lent itself admirably to dramatic treatment, and Shakespeare took full advantage of its possibilities. His monarchs are presented as men at the same time that they represent in themselves the authority, power, and responsibility of the state. Questions of state are inseparable from personal questions, and the universal problem of the stress between the morality of *raison d'état* and private morality becomes the immediate personal dilemma of men who find themselves principals in struggles for power during times of great change and crisis.[8]

One situation in particular raised the dilemma of private versus political morality in acute form. The institution of hereditary monarchy in which the king was God's anointed representative on earth made no provision for the removal of an ineffectual or bad king. Rebellion and usurpation were not merely treason, but grave sins against God's deputy. It become inevitable that any change of rule—except that occasioned by the death by natural causes of the reigning monarch—by the very nature of the initial political crime of usurpation, called for the further crime of regicide. The case is put with epigrammatic clarity by Bolingbroke, in John Hayward's account, in his reply to those who urge him to return from exile and replace Richard: "He that aimeth at a kingdom, hath no middle course between the life of a prince, and the death of a traitor."[9] The simultaneous existence of two anointed kings was an anomaly which could not be long sustained; indeed, all possible heirs of the deposed ruler who might conceivably establish a closer hereditary claim to the throne than the new incumbent had perforce to be eliminated. A deposed king was of necessity marked for death, and so were his immediate heirs. This situation is repeated several times in the history plays—Henry VI, his son Edward, the duke of Clarence, the sons of Edward IV, Richard II, and Richard III all die that the one who takes the throne may be secure in his title. In modern democratic states, in which the idea of rebellion has been institutionalized by means of the ballot, a political leader who rises to power by destroying the political career of a rival contender would today be admired as a brilliant politician for precisely the qualities despised in Henry IV, who is compelled to manifest his political genius under the most distressing circumstances and to take ultimate measures to secure his power. In the circumstances of an illegal and forced succession, political morality found its most dramatic and poignant testing ground.

The issue of private and political morality runs throughout

the first trilogy by virtue of the saintly, unworldly character of the king, Henry VI. Henry is not a political man, and he tries to conduct himself throughout as a pious and Christian human being. He does not recognize a standard of conduct for political morality different from that for private morality, and he values personal virtue and peace of mind over success in problems of state achieved by the firm exercise of royal power. The opposition of these values is represented therefore in extreme terms, as illustrated in a sharp clash during an episode shortly before the battle of Towton in Part 3. Henry sees the head of the executed duke of York on the towers of the city of York, and he reacts with horror and remorse: "Withhold revenge, dear God! 'tis not my fault, / Nor wittingly have I infringed my vow" (2.2.7–8). It was York, however, who had, wittingly, broken his oath that he would permit Henry to remain king in exchange for Henry's disinheriting his son in favor of York; and having lost the battle which followed the resumption of the civil war, he was beheaded for treason. Clifford uses the occasion to lecture Henry on the need for a king to be kingly, and reproaches him for having disinherited his own son, but Henry is unmoved, and in his reply virtually renounces the inheritance he received from his father, Henry V, the one monarch admired by everyone throughout the play as the embodiment of all the kingly virtues:

> Full well hath Clifford played the orator,
> Inferring arguments of mighty force,
> But, Clifford, tell me, didst thou never hear
> That things evil got had ever bad success?
> And happy always was it for that son
> Whose father for his hoarding went to hell?
> I'll leave my son my virtuous deeds behind;
> And would my father had left me no more!
>
> (2.2.43–50)

His advice to his son as he knights him is, "And learn this lesson: Draw thy sword in right" (2.2.62). The son's answer—anticipating Hal's assurance to his dying father—comes close to being a rebuke:

> My gracious father, by your kingly leave,
> I'll draw it as apparent to the crown,
> And in that quarrel use it to the death.
>
> (2.2.63–65)

Henry's reign is a disaster, in which those who do attempt to exercise their state functions with honesty and honor—Talbot and Gloucester—are destroyed by selfishly ambitious men whose insubordinate quarrels Henry cannot control. The next play, *Richard III*, presents the very opposite situation, in equally extreme terms. Richard is the complete embodiment of *Realpolitik* without the usual justification of acting in the national interest. He seizes and uses power for purely selfish ends; the philosophic appeal to *raison d'état* cannot be raised to defend his rejection of legality and legitimacy or the claims of pity and justice. Here there is no question: Richard is a moral monster and his philosophy is self-defeating. It is with Bolingbroke-Henry IV that Shakespeare presents at length the career of a man who has political instincts and talents, who recognizes an obligation to the welfare of his country, and who finds himself in a position where he must reconcile with his conscience as best he can the demands made on him for what he believes to be convincing reasons of state. It is a career in which Shakespeare apparently took considerable interest, for he follows it through three plays with the kind of persistent care that calls for something more by way of response than political invective and attempts at ironic wit.[10]

The moral judgment of the sixteenth-century historians is heavy on Henry IV. He bears the infamy of having usurped the throne, willed the murder of the king he had deposed, and thus having begun the long era of troubles which ended only when God was satisfied that these sins had been fully atoned for and England could be restored to peaceful rule under the Tudors. Hall's history is shaped around this theme, and Holinshed supports a similar thesis in his scattered providential comments. And yet, oddly enough, Henry emerges from the pages of these two major sources of Shakespeare as neither an unscrupulous, crafty politician nor a man whose overweening political ambitions drive him to crime.

In their account of the events which led to Bolingbroke's challenge of Mowbray, they leave the impression that he acted from unselfish motives. Hall reports that Hereford initially went to Mowbray as one close to the king to inform him of complaints against Richard, "more for dolour and lamentation, than for malice or displeasure," so that Mowbray might "advise the king to turn the leaf and to take a bitter lesson." [11] The challenge of Mowbray by Bolingbroke takes place in consequence of Mowbray's misrepresentation of this interview to the king. Holinshed's account, which Shakespeare follows at this point, is somewhat different, but it too does not attribute Bolingbroke's challenge to malice or ambition. [12] Both historians, moreover, place the responsibility for Bolingbroke's return from exile upon certain troubled and honorable men of the realm who turned to him in despair at the terrible misrule of Richard:

> While king Richard was in Ireland, the grave persons of the nobility, the sage prelates of the clergy, the sad magistrates and rulers of the cities, towns, and commonalty perceiving daily more and more the realm to fall into ruin and desolation (in manner irrecuperable as long as king Richard either lived or reigned) after long deliberation, wrote into France to Duke Henry . . . soliciting and requiring him with all diligent celerity to convey himself into England, promising him all their aid, power and assistance, if he expelling king Richard as a man not meet nor convenient for so princely an office and degree would take upon him the sceptre rule and diadem of his native country and first nutritive soil. [13]

Not to have received their representatives graciously, Hall suggests, would have been less than natural:

> When he saw the Archbishop his especial friend and
> looked on other his fautors and lovers, if he thanked God
> no man ought to marvel, if he welcomed these ambassadors
> no creature can wonder: but if he rejoiced and applauded
> not at their access and coming, wise men may think folly
> and fools may laugh him to scorn.[14]

In his account of this episode Hall presents at length the eloquent plea which the archbishop delivers to the duke, recounting the wrongs the nation suffers under Richard, and urging the
duke to come to the rescue of his country. Since a widespread
impression prevails that Shakespeare inherited from the historians an idea of Henry as the cunning ambitious usurper who
brought the curse of God on his land, Hall's version of the per-
suasiveness of the appeal to Bolingbroke should be seen in detail. Here is what the archbishop says:

> When your loving and natural kinsmen and countrymen,
> most noble and mighty prince, had much and long time
> considered and debated with themselves of their affairs and
> business in this tempestuous world and season (in the
> which no man of our nation is sure of his life, nor enjoyeth
> his lands and seignories without dread nor possedeth his
> moveables without terror or fear, which outrageous doings
> many years occupied have brought the public wealth of
> our abundant country almost to wreck and utter extermi-
> nation) their last anchorhold refuge and comfort was to
> study and devise how to have a governor or ruler which
> should excell and flourish in wisdom, policy and justice
> above all other. By which reason a great number of the
> nobility and in manner all the commonalty, being led and
> persuaded (when they had well cast their eyes and marked
> all the peers and nobles of the realm of England) they
> could find no duke, nor marques, no earl nor other poten-
> tate within all the realm, to whose empire and authority
> they would be subject and vassals so gladly as to yours. For
> this I assure you (and you know it as well as I) that we
> miserable subjects have so long borne the yoke of wanton
> unwitty king Richard and have patiently tolerate the per-
> nicious persecution of his greedy and avaricious counsel-
> lors, and have winked at the polling and extortion of his

unmeasureable officers, that our backs be so galled that we can no more suffer, and our shin bones so weak that we can no longer carry. And therefore necessity and not will, reason and not affection, constancy and not levity enforceth us to lament and desire your aid and comfort, to whom we be sent by the most part of the nobility and also of the most part of the universal commonalty, to desire and require you to take upon you the high power, governance and sceptre of your native country and right inheritance, and the same to govern, rule and defend according to your approved wisdom and long experimented policy, whom we have ever known to be of that justice, of that prudence and of that integrity that you will not command, admonish or attempt any thing which shall not be just, honest and laudable. Which request if you well consider and diligently ponder privily with yourself, you shall easily perceive that nothing more profitable, more honest or more glorious can by any ways happen or chance to you than to accept and conform yourself to the same. For what can you more expect and wish, than to command and do all things according to right, reason and honesty. We offer not to you gold, silver, pearl, or precious stone, but our country, our bodies, goods and us all to use as yours and not as ours, desiring you to give to us in recompense, indifferency quietness and peace, and to restore to her seat and throne again, the lady justice, which hath so long been banished out of our nation, to thentent that wise, sage and good persons (whose desire and appetite is ever to live well) may honor, love and embrace you as a governor and king sent from God, and that malicious and obstinate persons (whose conscience is grudged with daily offences, and whom the fear of justice and punishment doth continually vere and trouble) fearing you as the scourge and plague of their naughty doings and mischievous acts, may either soon amend, or shortly avoid your country and region. Now occasion is offered, refuse it not, by the which your wisdom, policy, and valiantness shall appear to the universal world, by the which you shall not only bring us into an unity and monacorde but also repress all sedition and cankered dissimulation: then the noble men shall triumph, the rich men shall live without fear, the poor and needy persons shall not be oppressed nor

confounded, and you for your so doing, shall obtain thanks
of your creator, love of your people, favor of your neigh-
bors, fame and honor forever.[15]

Hall makes this plea sound virtually irresistible, and it should
be noted that the archbishop uses the phrases "a governor and
king sent from God" and "obtain thanks of your creator," as
though Henry will be playing a role like that assigned by the
historians to Richmond in removing the tyrant Richard III.
Holinshed does not retain the archbishop's long plea in what
he takes over from Hall, but he leaves no doubt that Henry
was called to assume the throne and had not himself contemplated seeking it:

> This surely is a very notable example, and not unworthy of
> all princes to be well weighed and diligently marked, that
> this Henry of Lancaster should thus be called to the king-
> dom, and have the help and assistance (almost) of the
> whole realm, which perchance never thereof thought or yet
> dreamed; and that king Richard should thus be left deso-
> late, void, and in despair of all hope and comfort.[16]

Shakespeare's principal sources do not support the notion, common among students of the histories, that "the chronicles make
clear the drift of events by which Bolingbroke, having returned
merely to remedy the withholding of his rights, is swept into
usurpation."[17] Both Hall and Holinshed emphasize the pressures which were put on Bolingbroke to return to England for
the express purpose of replacing Richard as king. The same
historians attribute York's inability to mount an adequate defense for the king against Bolingbroke not to any failure to
muster adequate forces but to a general refusal of these forces
to fight against the duke, "whom they knew to be evil dealt
with": "[York] assembled a puissant power of men and arms
and archers . . . but all was in vain, for there was not a man
that willingly would thrust out one arrow against the Duke of
Lancaster, or his partakers, or in any wise offend him or his
friends."[18] According to Holinshed, Henry did not resolve on

the death of Richard until after the Oxford conspiracy, which planned to assassinate Henry and made use of a monk to impersonate Richard:

> And immediately after, king Henry, to rid himself of any such like danger to be attempted against him thereafter, caused king Richard to die of a violent death, that no man should afterward fain himself to represent his person, though some have said, he was not privy to that wicked offense.[19]

Considering the role which Henry IV had been assigned as the initiator of England's great troubles, it is remarkable how considerate the historians are of him and how careful to avoid placing more opprobrium on him than necessary. In reporting how Henry died while completing preparations for a crusade, both Hall and Holinshed—Hall with considerable indignation—reject the notion that Henry was struck down with a loathsome disease by the hand of God: "he was eftsoons taken with a sore sickness, which was not a leprosy, stricken by the hand of God (saith master Hall), as foolish friars imagined; but a very apoplexy, of the which he languished till his appointed hour, and had none other grief nor malady."[20] An ugly death was a conventional mark of the passing of a sinful monarch—even for Edward IV there are references to dying of a surfeit, and dark hints of possible poisoning; but Henry is pointedly spared such ignominy. Finally, there is Hall's summing up of the man, complimentary and respectful:

> The king was of a mean stature well proportioned, and formally compact, quick and deliver and of a stout courage. After that he had appeased all civil dissensions he showed himself so gently to all men that he got him more love of the nobles in the latter days than he had malice and ill will of them in the beginning.[21]

Hall ends his account of Henry IV at this point, but Holinshed, after having reproduced this passage from Hall almost verbatim, surprisingly continues immediately with a contradiction of the favorable final note:

> But yet to speak a truth, by his proceedings, after he had attained to the crown, what with such taxes, tallages, subsidies, and exactions as he was constrained to charge the people with, and what by punishing such as moved with disdain to see him usurp the crown (contrary to the oath taken at his entering into this land, upon his return from exile) did at sundry times rebel against him, he won himself more hatred, than in all his life time (if it had been longer by many years than it was) had been possible for him to have weeded out and removed.[22]

The explanation of this reversal probably lies in the almost compulsive moralizing tendencies of the 1587 Holinshed. The statement with which Hall concluded his characterization of Henry does not point out the ways of divine justice, and allows Henry to depart from history without the unfavorable judgment appropriate to usurpers and regicides. Holinshed corrects this oversight, though in defiance of logic and rhetoric he also retains Hall's favorable judgment, while at the same time calling attention to the less amiable aspects of Henry's reign and the more attractive ones of Richard's. He thus prepares the way for the moral:

> And yet doubtless, worthy were his subjects to taste of that bitter cup, sithens they were so ready to join and clap hands with him, for the deposing of their rightful and natural prince king Richard, whose chief fault rested only in that, that he was too bountiful to his friends, and too merciful to his foes, specially if he had not been drawn by others, to seek revenge of those that abused his good and courteous nature.[23]

The effect of Holinshed's odd conclusion is to reinforce the ambiguity which creeps into almost all accounts of Henry. Nevertheless, as the preceding quotations demonstrate, neither of the two principal accounts which Shakespeare used provides the material out of which an unsavory political villain can be constructed, and though there are differences in treatment, Shakespeare does not seriously modify the broad outlines provided by his sources in the accounts of Henry's seizure of the throne and his reign.[24]

The groundwork for the character of Henry IV and of his lifelong dilemma is laid in *Richard II*. In the opening scene of that play the motives of none of the characters are completely clear, but there is no indication of disloyalty in Bolingbroke's accusation of Mowbray, though he is indirectly aiming at Richard in the matter of the murder of Gloucester, which fact does not escape Richard. Bolingbroke appears to have the advantage in this encounter, for in replying to him on this charge Mowbray seems on the defensive. Nevertheless, Bolingbroke accepts the king's pronouncement of exile as final—"Your will be done" (1.3.144). Bolingbroke's departure, as described by the king, was something of a popular triumph, and Richard comments wryly on Bolingbroke's courteous acknowledgment of the crowd's adulation, but the introduction of this information serves the purpose of anticipating the general acceptance of Bolingbroke on his return, rather than of implying deliberate building up of public support on Bolingbroke's part for the purpose of later challenging Richard. There is no sign that Bolingbroke's intentions were anything except those of an obedient subject, until after Richard makes the terrible mistake of seizing his inheritance. There is nothing in the play comparable to the scene described by Hall in detail and by Holinshed in brief of the delegation that waited on the duke to urge his return, and so the play does not establish as vividly as do the histories the impression of great compulsion placed on Bolingbroke; instead there is a scene showing the sullen discontent of the nobles after the seizure of Bolingbroke's lands and titles and their recital of the misdemeanors and unstatesmanlike conduct of Richard which make him in their opinion a near tyrant (2.1.224–69). Northumberland then reveals that preparations have already been made by important nobles and prelates to bring Bolingbroke back, and thus the play makes it clear as do the histories that the aim of those who urged Bolingbroke to return from exile was, in Northumberland's phrase, to "shake off our slavish yoke" and make Bolingbroke king (2.1.291). Important as this point is, it is one which critics are often careless about. It is misleading, for example, to say of Henry in *2 Henry IV*, "the King, like his unsponsored reign, has lasted too long."[25] In its very casualness, the phrase "unsponsored reign" reflects a common forgetfulness of Shakespeare's carefully worked out distinctions by those bent on explaining Henry away as a despicable, cold usurper, not unlike Richard III except that the latter is a more amiable rogue. Shakespeare and his sources present a different view of the situation. The archbishop in Hall's account even suggests that Bolingbroke would return as "governor and king sent from God," and in *Richard II*, in what may be an echo of this idea, Bolingbroke hints in his inscrutable way that he may be an instrument of God in replacing Richard: when York warns him "the heavens are o'er our heads," Bolingbroke replies, "I know it, uncle; and oppose not myself / Against their will" (3.3.18–19). It is not a matter of being "fair" to Henry, but of apprehending the complexity of Shakespeare's dramatic design. A proper appreciation of Henry's frustrated career depends on understanding that Henry and his supporters both knew what they were doing and believed they were driven to it by circumstances and inspired by honorable motives.

Henry's problems begin the moment he has to confront the practical consequences of accepting the anomalous role of a reform candidate for the kingship, for no matter how meritorious the purpose entertained by those who urged Bolingbroke's return and supported him, the very act of returning and the aim itself required actions expedient and necessary but illegal and morally questionable. There is the matter of the oath which Henry had taken in the presence of his supporters that he was returning only to claim his inheritance. (They upbraid him in *1 Henry IV* for having broken this oath.) Northumberland alludes to this oath when he protests to Richard at Flint Castle that Bolingbroke has returned only "for his lineal royalties" (3.3.113), but, in view of Northumberland's role after the death of Gaunt, he must be aware that what he is saying is untrue. The oath served as a plausible excuse for Bolingbroke's return from exile without permission and with show of force, not very different in intent from the oath Edward takes in *2 Henry VI* at the gates of York in order to gain permission to enter a sympathetic refuge while preparing for his next assault on the title. Bolingbroke's oath was made to be violated or at best evaded, and so the taking of it as a temporary political expedient contradicted the solemn moral obligation which the oath implied. A necessary expedient perhaps, but Bolingbroke in adopting it breaks with his past and abandons the morally unambiguous position of his initial role as unsullied public challenger of wrongs and misdemeanors in high places, which had earned him the right to be called on by his peers to restore good rule. More serious is the execution of Bushy and Green. It breaks the inner circle of Richard's favorites, but Bolingbroke is not king and has no legal right to pass judgment on them, and his recital of their misdemeanors in order "to wash your blood / From off my hands, here in the view of men" (3.1.5–6) is a specious bid for moral approval.

This is Bolingbroke's most drastic act on the way to the throne. For the most part he acts with ambiguity: his main strategy is to remain uncommunicative about his main purpose and maneuver the situation in his own favor, and his reserve becomes so pronounced that Richard cries out in the abdication scene against the "silent king." Bolingbroke is not always silent—he was not, for instance, in the opening scene, nor in his defense of his return to the duke of York. In contrast to the strategy of the Yorkists who seize the throne by military force, he allows Richard—who sees how it must all end and deposes himself in his own mind before he is asked—to make the proper moves, like a reluctant actor who must play out the role assigned to him. Bolingbroke's strategy is to see that Richard continues to act out his part: "I thought you had been willing to resign," he remarks, breaking his silence in the abdication scene (4.1.190).[26] The scenario is played out, and in submitting to its terms Richard renders the question of Bolingbroke's guilt ambiguous: technically no oath was broken and a usurpation did not take place, only a legal and publicly sanctioned succession.

The success of this plan, however, does not avoid a final necessity, which even this brilliant scheme cannot eschew: Richard must die. Holinshed connects the death of Richard with the Oxford conspiracy. In *Richard II* the connection is only implied in the fact that immediately after the scene with York, his wife, and Aumerle in which the conspiracy is revealed to Bolingbroke, there follows the brief scene in which Exton, alone, reports having heard the new king say, "Have I no friend will rid me of this living fear?" and decides to be that friend (5.4.2.). The removal of Richard has nothing in common with the savage vendetta slayings of the *Henry VI* plays, and none of the zest with which Richard III goes about removing impediments. It is a characteristic maneuver for Henry. He drops a hint which he knows will be heeded, and an act necessary to the safety of his title will be performed, but he also understands well enough the moral implications of this act of state to experience regret—"They love not poison that do poison need" (5.6.38). And in time he will learn that it is an act which he cannot expiate and which will haunt him until his death.

His general policy, however, is not to rule by terror. He gives every evidence that he intends to deport himself as far as possible as the legitimate ruler which the abdication presumably made him, and hence to act temperately and with mercy as well as justice. The evidence for this is his handling of York's revelation of the conspiracy. It is a complete misunderstanding of this episode to say of it that York "is ready to sacrifice his own blood for a usurper who has only used him as an instrument and who will from now on distrust him as a possible rival. Fear is the mainspring of his action as it is a sign of the new order."[27]

Henry everywhere treats York with respect, and there is no likelihood that York can ever be a rival. He has already declared where he stands in a private talk with his wife, just before he makes the surprising discovery that his son is involved in a plot against Henry's life: "To Bolingbroke are we sworn subjects now, / Whose state and honor I for aye allow" (5.2.39–40). He informs on his son not out of fear of the new king but out of a more rational fear of further disruption at this point of a fragile political order, and Henry on his part tries to show that his will not be a regime of fear if he can help it. He pardons Aumerle, against York's advice, and he also pardons Carlisle, who was a member of the conspiracy, with these words: "For though mine enemy thou hast ever been, / High sparks of honor in thee have I seen" (5.6.28–29). The only spark of honor displayed by Carlisle in the course of the play is his denunciation of the abdication as illegal and dangerous in the presence of Bolingbroke and his supporters (4.1.115–49). Pardoning such a man is not the act of a king who intends to rule by fear.

As *1 Henry IV* opens, however, Henry has to concede that his policy has been a failure, not so much because of the threats from his foes but because his former allies, now disgruntled, have taken advantage of it: they have no fear of his power and hence no respect for his authority. He admits the fact, and announces to them that he will now show more firmness:

> My blood hath been too cold and temperate,
> Unapt to stir at these indignities,
> And you have found me, for accordingly
> You tread upon my patience; but be sure
> I will from henceforth rather be myself,
> Mighty, and to be feared, than my condition
> Which hath been smooth as oil, soft as young down,
> And therefore lost that title of respect
> Which the proud soul ne'er pays but to the proud.
>
> (1.3.1–9)

At first glance Henry's reaction might seem a little excessive for the circumstances. What these men have asked of the king is something which a monarch completely sure of his legitimacy might well grant—the ransom of a relative made prisoner while in the service of the king. In a normal situation, however, these men would not have dared to bargain the prisoners they have taken in battle against the return of their relative, and the king in this instance rightly suspects their motives and will not accede to their request, knowing that the prisoner, Mortimer, is believed to have a nearer claim to the throne than his own. Henry can pardon Carlisle, but Mortimer is another matter; Henry cannot, either in his own or the public interest, place this threat in the hands of the men who were once principal instigators in elevating him to the throne. Above all, he cannot act as though his throne is a gift at their hands without undermining the monarchical idea, and he must therefore dismiss Worcester when the latter refers to the greatness "which our own hands / Have holp to make so portly" (1.3.12–13). It is to miss totally the political meaning of this scene to say of him at this point, "he winces at a hint of his past by others, as when, in his hasty interruption of Northumberland he covers his pain [at the memory of the past] by an outburst of temper."[28] Henry is not a man to wince at a reminder that those who now behave with insolence toward his office were the ones who begged him to assume it. His anger is as much a politic show of regal authority as it is a show of temper. He has seen through the charade about the prisoners and guessed its intent. Later in the scene when Worcester, sensing that the irate Hotspur can be depended on for their purposes, begins, "And now I will unclasp a secret book" (1.3.186), it becomes clear that rebellion was on their minds all along. Yet, before the issue is finally decided by force, Henry is willing to take the risk that they might accept his offer of grace and friendship and thus avoid civil war (5.1.106 ff.). But Worcester is not Henry; the offer is never reported to Hotspur, and the battle of Shrewsbury has to be fought.

The battle of Shrewsbury with its clear triumph over the rebels and its mixture of chivalric bravado and comic verve ends Part 1 in a buoyant spirit that casts the glow of success over

Henry's enterprise. Had the series ended here, the criticism of Henry would have been quite different. It is in Part 2 that the issue of state morality is presented with uncompromising candor, and the most severe judgments on Henry find their justification in this play. It contains, for one thing, the treachery of Prince John at Gaultree Forest. Shakespeare is unsparing in his depiction of this episode. Not only does Prince John arrest the rebels and have them executed after they dismiss their troops on the promise that he will redress all their grievances, but—a detail that seems to have escaped those who would make the most of this episode to denounce Henry and his family as unscrupulous politicians—he fails to keep his part of the agreement to disband the armies, and after the arrest of the leaders he sends his own intact forces in pursuit of the now leaderless and disbanded rebel troops as though they were a defeated army in rout fleeing a battle (4.3)—which is how Falstaff gets to receive Colevile as a prisoner. There is a final chilling detail in Prince John's insulting comments to his victims:

> Most shallowly did you these arms commence,
> Fondly brought here and foolishly sent hence.
> Strike up our drums, pursue the scattered stray.
> God, and not we, hath safely fought today.
> (4.2.118–21)

It was common for victorious generals to thank God for being on their side, but it seems blasphemous to sneer at the men being led to execution for being naïve politically and then thank God for a victory won not on the chancy and dangerous field of arms but in a cold and calculating political battle of wits. In the historical accounts it is Westmoreland who arranges this piece of official treachery, but Shakespeare gives Prince John the role so that this unpleasant piece of political cleverness will remain in the royal family. It is possible to say things in defense of this action—the rebellion has been broken and the lives of many soldiers have been saved—but it is not possible to make it less distasteful.[29] It is to the *Henry IV* plays what the murder of

Richard is to *Richard II*; both actions can be understood and justified as necessary to gain reasonable political ends, yet both deeply offend private morality. Even Johnson was moved to comment: "It cannot but raise some indignation to find this horrible violation of faith passed over thus slightly by the poet, without any note of censure or detestation."[30] Prince John's treacherous defeat of the rebellion is set into the play like one of those nasty jobs which are discharged by subordinate and confidential agents and which high-minded generals and heads of state are grateful for but remain silent about. The effect on our view of Henry is analogous to that produced by Hal's rejection of Falstaff—something which reason might try to persuade us is not without justification, but which nevertheless throws a glaring light on the price which must sometimes be paid in the exercise of great power. Significantly, Shakespeare presents both episodes without minimizing the shock, and without comment. Critics often display greater revulsion of feeling over this episode than over the murder of Richard II. Henry's moral priorities are different: he accepts the news from Gaultree with relief and gratitude (4.4.91–93), but his regret over the need to kill Richard he carries to the end.

Henry himself is not unaware of the cost of the demands made on him in the name of *raison d'état*. "God knows, my son," he tells Hal, "By what by-paths and indirect crooked ways / I met this crown" (4.5.183–85). As a political man, however, he is reconciled to paying the cost if some reasonable benefits for the state can be purchased at the price. Critics sometimes write about Henry as though his moral awareness makes him the more despicable; but the concept of *raison d'état* is, in fact, meaningless unless the possibility of moral conduct is acknowledged and the gravity of its violation weighed against the possible good which is to be achieved in the name of political necessity. The Bolingbroke who challenged the misrule of Richard II has not been completely lost in the king. He is now older and defeated in his hopes, but if he is sleepless it is not out of fear, like Richard III, or because of guilty nightmares like Macbeth, but from worry

over his country and the cares of his office (3.1.4 ff.). His sorrow
at the state of his kingdom is made to appear genuine:

> Then you perceive the body of our kingdom
> How foul it is, what rank diseases grow,
> And with what danger, near the heart of it.
> (3.1.38–40)

Tyrants do not talk this way. Mingled with his sorrow for the
state of his country there is a sense of personal disappointment
over the failure of his own ambitions, but a seriously political
man can scarcely distinguish between the two. To use power
effectively he must also want it. Critics have pointed out that
the woes Henry deplores are of his own causing, and he himself
never disclaims his share of responsibility for the consequences
of usurping the throne:

> It seemed in me
> But as an honor snatched with boisterous hand,
> And I had many living to upbraid
> My gain of it by their assistances,
> Which daily grew to quarrel and to bloodshed,
> Wounding supposed peace. All these bold fears
> Thou seest with peril I have answered;
> For all my reign hath been but as a scene
> Acting that argument.
> (4.5.190–98)

In the words "scene," "acting," and "argument," however, there
is a suggestion that he found himself cast in a role which, once
assumed, could not be easily resigned but had to be played out.
That he had assumed it at all he attributes to the obligations
placed on him by unusual circumstances, rather than to personal
ambition:

> Though then, God knows, I had no such intent,
> But that necessity so bowed the state
> That I and greatness were compelled to kiss.
> (3.1.72–74)

"Necessity" is a direct appeal to the concept of *raison d'état*, and the political man, Henry discovers, cannot escape its pressures and dilemmas or its sometimes grave and unpleasant consequences. He expresses to Warwick his deep disappointment at the fickleness of ambitious men and his betrayal at the hands of those who "like a brother toiled in my affairs" (3.1.62), but he bows to the inevitable when Warwick explains that the conduct of his one-time allies was predictable, as Richard had foreseen: "Are these things then necessities? / Then let us meet them like necessities" (3.1.92–93). This resolution brings him back to reality—"that same word [necessity] even now cries out on us" (3.1.94)—and he turns with renewed concern to the archbishop's rebellion.

Those who read these plays primarily as moral allegories see this episode in a different light. Referring to the lines about necessity, Matthews writes: "Henry tries to protect himself by a kind of fatalism. . . . In this despair repentance becomes impossible. Richard and Macbeth do not even attempt it, but Henry does, and the most illuminating comparison in his case therefore is one with Claudius."[31] The speech is neither about fatalism nor repentance. "Necessity" is a reference to the demands of political life, and Henry's momentary despair arises not from thoughts of repentance but from his failure to restore health to his kingdom. In this context the not uncommon comparisons with Claudius are misleading: "Henry IV, not yet clear-headed enough to ask with Claudius, 'May one be pardoned and retain the offence?' obviously hopes to 'shove by justice', and dies, as it were, in doubtful repentance."[32] The two cases are not comparable: the differences are fundamental. Henry IV's actions are purely political in motivation and execution; the crimes of Claudius are entirely personal and not political, though they have political consequences. There was no national crisis to which Claudius felt called on to respond, there was no demand placed on him by his countrymen to assume the kingship, and he does not enjoy popular support. And there was also Gertrude, so that he could satisfy his lust and ambition at once by personally murdering his brother and conniving to exclude a perfectly eligible and popular direct male heir to the title. There was no political justification for any of these acts, and his attempts to make a public case for marrying Gertrude and beating Hamlet out of the election as a response to a national crisis are specious.

Henry never forgets that he was guilty of a crime for which he stands in need of expiation and forgiveness, but he sees his political responsibilities as a separate matter. He must "retain the offence" because the only hope he sees for political stability and freedom from internal discord is direct succession on his death to his oldest son. If he were to resign the crown to purge himself of sin, to whom should he resign it?—to Mortimer, married to Glendower's daughter, and a convenient pawn of the Percys? He puts his hopes on the succession, and to this end gives his son political advice whenever he can. In Part 1 he tells him how a prince should behave to gain the respect and admiration of his subjects, comparing Richard's failure in this matter with his own success (3.2.29–89). In Part 2 he warns him not to be too secure about his title, and advises him "to busy giddy minds / With foreign quarrels" (4.5.202–15). Both speeches deal with matters of political prudence and expediency, and they have in consequence been condemned, with some justice, as coldly calculated, in particular the second which has acquired some notoriety in criticism. The idea of a foreign war as a way of removing the threat of civil war was fairly common during the fifteenth and sixteenth centuries, and in that age not very shocking. As Mattingly explains:

> It was a means of avoiding internal dissension, usually the nearest and sometimes actually the cheapest means. Outside Italy, all Europe was saddled with a class in possession of most of the landed wealth, most of the local political power, and most of the permanent high offices of state, who had no business except war and few peacetime diversions as attractive as conspiracy. Before it attained its zenith, the territo-

rial state had no way of ensuring the allegiance of this
class so effective as giving them some foreign enemy to
fight. Leading the nobility and gentry to foreign conquests
eased domestic pressure. Inevitably, writers compared the
expedient to blood letting which reduced excessive humours in the body politic.[33]

What sullies a fairly conventional piece of advice in Henry's case
is that he has hooked this expedient onto the idea of a crusade
which he had originally thought of as an act of expiation. A
morally fastidious man could not have thought of this combination between *raison d'état* and penance before God, but a political genius would see no flaw in it. Just as Henry can separate
his political responsibilities from his personal moral condition,
so he can combine the two if the need is great enough to justify
it. Throughout his entire career he experiences the conflict between the moral man with good aims and the politician who
must use evil means. The equivocal status of the crusade exemplifies his entrapment in this dilemma, but it does not represent
any confusion on his part concerning the separate and distinct
demands of his political and moral self. The necessities which
his role imposes on him he will face as necessities; the sins he
has committed for reasons of state are a matter between him
and God: "How I came by the crown, O God forgive" (4.5.218).
    At the end of *Richard II*, Bolingbroke says over the dead body
of Richard: "Lords, I protest my soul is full of woe / That blood
should sprinkle me to make me grow" (5.6.45–46). The theatrical tableau itself—the new king in state and the dead king at his
feet—is an image of the irreconcilable disharmony between the
harsh act of political necessity and its human and moral consequences; and the speech expresses the new king's awareness of
the evils that accompany greatness.[34] It is the same man in *2
Henry IV*, now older, saddened by experience, and facing death.
In the melancholy mood which follows his soliloquy on the
cares of office, Henry reflects to Warwick that if one might read
the book of fate,

> The happiest youth, viewing his progress through
> What perils past, what crosses to ensue,
> Would shut the book, and sit him down and die.
>   (3.1.54–56)

He expresses this as a general observation about the condition of mankind, but in context these lines sum up a feeling of disenchantment, a recognition that however good the intentions of one who aspires to great place, the glory that accompanies power leaves a taste of dust and ashes.

"In place," wrote Bacon in his essay "Of Great Place,"

> there is license to do good and evil, whereof the latter is a curse. . . . But the power to do good is the true and lawful end of aspiring. For good thoughts (though God accept them) yet towards men, are little better than good dreams, except they be put into act, and that cannot be without power, and place, as the vantage and commanding ground.

That is one aspect of the phenomenon of great place, that pious wishes without the enabling power to make them actual are a sign of inward virtue only, without social consequences. Bacon understood the other side of the phenomenon as well: "The rising unto place is laborious, and by pains come men to greater pains, and it is sometimes base and by indignities men come to dignities."[35] Only a man with a special kind of temperament can accept the daily necessity of living with this dilemma, and he discovers moreover that the condition of exercising state power exerts a reciprocal shaping influence on his character. Reflecting on this phenomenon in a philosophic spirit, with no specific instances in mind, Meinecke writes:

> For *raison d'état* demands first and foremost a high degree of rationality and expediency in political conduct. It demands of the statesman that he should educate and form himself culturally for it, that he should rule himself strictly, that he should suppress his emotions and his personal inclinations and aversions, and completely lose himself in the practical task of securing the common good. He should

also seek, quite coolly and rationally, to ascertain the practical interests of the State and to separate these from any
emotional overtones. . . . But the elimination of emotional motives can never be completely successful for the
very reason that . . . an elemental power-impulse must
already be present in the statesman himself, because without it he could not do his job properly.[36]

He might have been writing about Henry IV. Henry is not a
likeable or attractive character, and one of the several uncertainties about him is that we cannot be sure whether it is the
demands of the role in which he finds himself that compel him
to subdue whatever capacity he has for warmth, impulsiveness,
or compassion, or whether he is suited to the role because he
lacks such qualities. Henry is not devoid of feelings. His indignation at corruption in the state comes out in his challenge of
Mowbray in *Richard II*; his distress at the woes of his country
is deeply personal; and at times he lets his affection for his son
break through his disappointments and his worry about the
political future, as in his interview with Hal in *1 Henry IV*:

> Not an eye
> But is aweary of thy common sight.
> Save mine, which hath desired to see thee more.
> (3.2.87–89)

But indulgence in such feelings is a luxury he can ill afford. It
is sometimes complained of Henry and his son that the one
criterion they apply to themselves is success; but as political men
this has to be their principal concern, for in men who exercise
great power failure is a social evil which can mean disaster and
misfortune to others. Nevertheless, political success, even in its
largest and noblest sense, may confound personal ambition with
public spirit, and may call for the exercise of qualities that are
not laudable while entailing the sacrifice of private virtue and
private happiness. It is one of Machiavelli's serious limitations—though it may also be a source of his epigrammatic brilliance—that he writes as though this aspect of the problem did

not even exist; and it may be that Shakespeare's original contribution to our understanding of political power is the insight he
provides into how men respond to the moral conflicts inherent
in the exercise of power. In support of this view is Meinecke's
opinion: "The ability to think [of *raison d'état*] in terms of inner conflicts, violations and tragic problems, presupposes a more
modern and sophisticated mentality which perhaps only began
in Shakespeare."[37]

The two parts of *Henry IV* fail to resolve the conflict that is
represented in Henry's career, for the probable reason that it is
one which has defied a satisfactory solution for centuries. Henry
IV believes he is acting for the public good, but he cannot fully
separate this aim from his private ambitions and from the harsh
acts of power he feels called on to perform, and in consequence
his political actions are tarnished with deviousness and moral
guilt, and his successes are uncertain and ambiguous. All of
Shakespeare's kings, with the exception of Richard III, at some
time or other lament the cares and vexations of kingship, but
from none of them but Henry IV could the phrase "uneasy lies
the head that wears a crown" (2 *Henry IV*: 3.1.31) come out of
such fullness of experience and such depth of feeling. He represents in extreme form the conflict inherent in the nature of
statecraft, and the difficulty, perhaps the impossibility of recon-
ciling the demands of great place with unsullied private virtue
and happiness. It is a candid and unvarnished presentation, yet
it is not an unsympathetic one; and it adds a sombre quality to
Shakespeare's portrayal of this difficult and aloof man that he
himself is most fully aware of his dilemma and gives the most
forthright expression to the burden of its consequences. It is a
characterization with tragic overtones.[38]

XIII

The Making of a King:
I and *2 Henry IV*

To overcome the disabilities and dangers of a flawed title, the heir of Henry IV had to bring more than ordinary qualifications to the office. As an astute politician, Henry IV understands that very different demands are made on a king who inherits a throne in quiet times from a long established succession, and on one who comes to a newly established title in a period of turmoil. The latter can succeed only by exerting himself to excel in the art of kingship, and must validate a still uncertain, even if legal, succession by conspicuously good rule.[1] Behind Henry's long worry over the waywardness of his son lies this political consideration. For Henry, the indefeasible right of his successor by direct lineal descent—the issue which provokes the bitter struggles in the *Henry VI* plays—is secondary to the qualifications of the monarch, which if excellent and well used will compensate for any technical flaws in the title. If the prince is fit only for riot and vanity, then the kingdom, "sick with civil blows," will be "a wilderness again" (4.5.133–37), and the king's grief "stretches itself beyond the hour of death" (4.4.57). But if the prince can be made to see his responsibilities in a serious light, then the but recently established and *de facto* title might almost become something of an advantage. Because of his own questionable title, Henry IV had to squander all his political talents and resort to the shrewd and desperate stratagems of the realistic politician simply to hold on to his own and pass it on to his son. The situation of the prince is more favorable; nevertheless, it is not to be taken for granted. To establish his throne firmly, the prince must prove himself beyond doubt to be a worthy and wholly admirable king. To this extent, the flawed title is an advantage, because the newly crowned Henry V understands, as Richard II did not, that the power which comes to him is not a personal gift from God to be enjoyed as a private indulgence. Like the concept of the "fortunate fall," the tarnished title is both a challenge and an opportunity. This is the idea behind one of the major developments in the two parts of *Henry IV*. The tarnished reputation of the prince and his father's deep and continuous concern over his unfitness to inherit the crown in unquiet times become the dramatic vehicle which allows us to observe over two plays the education of a future king.

In introducing this theme into his comprehensive overview of the political world, Shakespeare was reflecting one of the great concerns of his day. The large number of works on the subject of educating a king and the numerous references to classical writings which deal with the qualifications of a good ruler are indicative of the importance of this subject in an age when monarchs were acquiring virtually absolute power.[2] The popularity of some of these writings, in view of the highly specialized and limited audience to which they were ostensibly addressed, is also evidence of how important politically was the idea of a good king and how he was to be made. To take one example, Erasmus' *Institutio principis christiani*, addressed to Prince Charles (the future Charles V), was printed three times in 1516, the date of its first publication, and eighteen complete editions were published within two decades of its appearance. There is a sameness about these mirror-for-princes writing, pagan and Christian. If the common elements from all of them are put together, a reasonably representative composite view can be derived of the ideal model which the training of a prince should aim to produce. Such a composite has been provided by Lester Born in his introduction to Erasmus' *Institutio*:

> In summary we can say that the perfect prince of these ten centuries must be wise, self-restrained, just; devoted to the welfare of his people; a pattern in virtues for his subjects; immune from flattery; interested in economic developments, an educational program, and the true religion of God; surrounded by efficient ministers and able advisers, opposed to aggressive warfare; and, in the realization that even he is subject to law and that the need of the prince, and his subjects is mutual, zealous for the attainment of peace and unity.[3]

Such a summary has the effect of exaggerating the conventional and almost academic flavor of many of these writings, but in fact the concerns of sixteenth-century writers on education and its bearing on the conduct of princes and courtiers were not wholly divorced from reality. The ideal they aim at is summed up by Hall in Edward IV's dying admonitions to his court for the proper training of his young sons:

> I have heard clerks say, although I am unlettered, that fortunate is that realm, where philosophers reign, or where kings be philosophers, and lovers of wisdom. In this tender age, you may writhe and turn them, into every form and fashion: if you bring them up in virtue, you shall have virtuous princes: if you set them to learning, your governors shall be men of knowledge, if you teach them activity, you shall have valiant captains, if they practice policy, you shall have both politique, and prudent rulers. On the other side, if by your negligence, they fall to vice (as youth is to all evil, prone and ready) not only their honor, but also your honesty, shall be spotted and appalled.[4]

The program of study recommended was broadly humanistic, and in most instances also included appropriate nonintellectual accomplishments like music, dancing, horsemanship, and the

251

like. Elyot's *The Governour* illustrates this combination of sound learning and courtly attainments, along with the cultivation of qualities of character such as sapience, patience, moderation, and the like. And when we examine the education actually provided for some of the leading princes of the time, we cannot dismiss these writings as simply pious literary efforts. "There is no choice," writes Erasmus, ". . . in the case of hereditary succession of princes. . . . Under that condition, the chief hope for a good prince is from his education, which should be especially looked to." And he adds, "When there is no opportunity to choose a prince, care should be exercised . . . in choosing the tutor of the future prince."[5] On this score the Tudors come out very well. Henry VIII's tutor, John Skelton, might well seem a singular choice to supervise the education of a future king, but Henry became a well-educated man for his day. There can be no question, however, about the care which Henry himself exercised in selecting tutors for his children, especially Edward and Elizabeth. All were men who exemplified the best learning of their day. Sir John Cheke supervised the education of Edward, and acted as a friend and adviser until the young king's early death. Elizabeth had the advantage of instruction by Cheke also, and in addition Grindal and Roger Ascham. What these tutors achieved with their royal pupils can only arouse respect. Elizabeth's accomplishments are well known; they were considerable even though her program of study was not as thorough as that of her brother who was expected to succeed to the throne. Edward's achievements were quite extraordinary, not only in languages and letters, but in the science of his day, in theology, in history, statecraft, and the arts of a courtier. His early death must have been a blow to those who saw in him an exemplary product of the education deemed proper for a prince who was destined to become king of a great nation.[6] For a brief period a coherent and impressive educational program was applied to willing and able princes to the end that potential rulers would be prepared to use their great power in the interest of the welfare of their people.

Shakespeare's reflection of these concerns is, in one respect, fairly conventional. The king who emerges in *Henry V* as the end product of Prince Hal's progress to the throne possesses many of the properties of the model aimed at in the works on the courtier, or governor, or Christian prince.[7] What is distinctly not conventional is the path which Shakespeare's prince follows before becoming the mirror of all Christian kings. From what we observe of the prince in the *Henry IV* plays, we may take it for granted that he had undergone the kind of princely study thought proper under the Tudors. We may suppose that the young man who left the tavern and his boon companions to amaze the flower of his father's army and defeat Hotspur must have had training in arms and chivalry. The youth who can bandy witticisms, improvise plays, and trade biblical and classical allusions with Falstaff must be presumed to have done some reading, and since he is compared directly and by implication with Hotspur we might infer that he did not, like his rival in honor, despise poetry and prefer a kitten crying mew to metre ballad-mongers. Shakespeare does not deny his prince and later king the arts and attributes associated in his day with the well-rounded courtier, and we may therefore suppose that he respected them. His silence in *Henry IV* about how these were acquired would seem to imply that they should be taken for granted in a prince, but do not of themselves necessarily make a king. The real education of the future Henry V as Shakespeare depicts it follows a quite unconventional course.

The progress of the prince in the two *Henry IV* plays is a highly original and extended development of the legend of the wild prince, which was mentioned in every account of Henry which Shakespeare might have looked at. Our first view of the prince is in company with Poins and Falstaff in a scene of merriment that leads to the robbery at Gad's Hill, and it is with such companions that we associate him during most of *1 Henry IV*. This is not the kind of environment which Erasmus would have approved of: "The Prince," he wrote, "should be removed as far as possible from the low concerns of common people and their sordid desires."[8] In Falstaff, Shakespeare provided the explanation of why this prince could give himself to unprincely company and yet return in due time undamaged to his responsibilities. A man who could seduce theatregoers from the start and for centuries afterwards might understandably attract a lively but not fundamentally corrupt, or corruptible, young man. It was a strategy that in some ways succeeded all too well. The prince is witty, but never quite so witty as Falstaff, and he has a taste for practical jokes—the joke at the expense of Francis is really contemptible. In comparison with the fascinating richness of Falstaff's character and the resourcefulness of his lively mind, the prince seems more limited, less engaging, even less humane. This is an impression that is reinforced by the soliloquy which follows the first scene with Falstaff in *1 Henry IV*, in which it is difficult not to discern a trace of calculation, for the prince not only tells us that he knows his companions for what they are, and that he will emerge from this holiday unharmed to assume a responsibility he never sought and "pay the debt I never promised," but that his reformation when it does occur will "show more goodly and attract more eyes" against the baseness of his past (1.2.204, 209).[9] It is a little disappointing to see the prince contriving to make the delights of youth subservient to a future political purpose, but it is possible that too much has been made of this. A future king with no talent for calculation is not fully equipped for his office, and if the prince did not have the capacity which Shakespeare reveals through the soliloquy to see beyond the present moment of enjoyment with his unusual companions he might very well not have had the resources ever to rise above them. The difficulty is that the soliloquy puts one on the alert for any further evidence of unattractive shrewdness. The soliloquy is also significant for what it does not say: the prince does not reveal that he is indulging in his present experiences because they will be a source of useful knowledge for the future. Late in Part 2, Westmoreland, to reassure the ailing king that the prince's continued association with Falstaff is not dangerous, explains:

> The Prince but studies his companions
> Like a strange tongue, wherein, to gain the language,
> 'Tis needful that the most immodest word
> Be looked upon and learned, which once attained,
> Your Highness knows, comes to no further use
> But to be known and hated. So, like gross terms,
> The Prince will in the perfectness of time
> Cast off his followers, and their memory
> Shall as a pattern or a measure live,
> By which his Grace must mete the lives of others,
> Turning past evils to advantages.
>
> (4.4.68–78)

Critics generally agree with Westmoreland that the prince "accepted ['vile company'] as a means to his political education." [10] The prince's declared calculation does not go quite that far. His own explanation of why he seeks the company of Falstaff and his cronies is a simple one; he wants, he tells us in the soliloquy, to snatch while he can some of the delights of youth before necessity puts an end to them:

> If all the year were playing holidays,
> To sport would be as tedious as to work;
> But when they seldom come, they wished for come,
> And nothing pleaseth but rare accidents.
>
> (1.2.199–202)

The wisdom and knowledge which the prince acquires from his experiences are by-products of circumstances which he sought or came by for quite other reasons, though the capacity to transform these experiences for future use must lie within the prince. The traits which make him behave in ways unconventional and risky in a prince might also betoken originality and great curiosity, qualities which could, with luck, enable him to turn to advantage the experiences which he sought in his youth without realizing the value he would later find in them. In this way, the "wildness" of the prince which Shakespeare inherited from the chronicles becomes in *1* and *2 Henry IV* Hal's opportunity to cultivate certain essential qualities of kingship not by academic study and attention to historical example, relied upon in the usual educational program for a prince, but indirectly through experiences which produce knowledge at some cost and risk.

The kingly qualities which Hal must prove he possesses or acquires are few in number, but they are represented as fundamental. Part 1 has to do with military prowess and chivalry. These are not qualities he acquires in the course of the play; he has, as he admits, been a truant to chivalry, but he easily proves to others at Shrewsbury that he possesses the skill in arms and courage required of him in his service to the king, as well as the chivalrous attitudes which make him respect a foe like Douglas and place his favors on the gallant, headstrong Hotspur he has killed—like airmen in the early days of the First World War returning to the scene of a successful dog fight to drop a wreath on the shattered and charred remains of the plane and aviator they had shot down. The world has now been brought to realize that Hal's low associations have not corrupted him, and that in the exercise of those virtues essential to a prince in times of war he can be depended upon. For a gifted and spirited youth it is a gratifying but not an extraordinary achievement. It is, too, a flashy performance, not unlike the star player on the team who has disappointed his coach by staying away from practice and breaking training by roistering in the town, but who appears unexpectedly for the big game and easily makes the winning score. Vernon's description of him to Hotspur enhances the impression of theatrical youthful exuberance. In fact, the description of Hal's comrades in arms, "all plumed like estridges," "glittering in golden coats like images," and of young Harry rising from the ground "like winged Mercury," vaulting all armed into the saddle "As if an angel dropped down from the clouds / To turn and wind a fiery Pegasus" (4.1.97–109) seems excessive, and quite out of key in a play as down-to-earth and politically tough as this one. Hal's proposal to his father that to save lives he be permitted to decide this issue by single combat with Hotspur also has an air of adolescent bravado, quite out of place in a cause in which the real leaders are Henry IV and

Worcester. The prince contributes much of the buoyant and youthful spirit which gives an optimistic tone to the play, and his conduct foreshadows the king who will grow up to lead his troops to victory at Agincourt; but he is still a long way from being the man who will take over a questionable title and a troubled country with confidence and hope.

The serious education of the prince for kingship takes place in the second part.[11] Shrewsbury has not completely won him away from "vanity," and the king's worry in Part 1 is trivial in comparison with his grief over the waywardness of his son in Part 2; for gratifying as the performance at Shrewsbury was, it did not prove that Hal understands what it means to be a king. It is the king's illness that brings the prince to his first moment of mature perception, the discovery that his youthful dissipations have isolated him and diminished him as a serious and thinking man. To what friends can he show his grief that his father, whose patience he has tried for so long, is near death? Poins remarks candidly that if the prince were to weep, "I would think thee a most princely hypocrite," and the prince realizes that "It would be every man's thought" (2.2.51–52). It is the first indication of awareness on Hal's part that his continued cultivation of his unprincely companions has damaged something more than his reputation, that it has deprived him of the opportunity to be himself when the event is not one of frivolity and youthful spirits. This brief episode marks a transition from the old Hal to the man who will inherit the throne, and it is therefore essential dramatic preparation for the episode which not only reconciles him to his father but brings him to an understanding of the grave responsibilities of being a king.

The king's first speech in Part 2 is the long soliloquy that opens act 3, the apostrophe to sleep which ends, "uneasy lies the head that wears a crown" (3.1.4–31). Warwick enters, and the king talks to him about the ills that beset his kingdom and the destruction of his hopes. Later, just before the final reconciliation, the prince finds his father asleep with the crown on his pillow, and his soliloquy on this occasion repeats the sentiments of his father: the crown is a

> polished perturbation! Golden care!
> That keep'st the ports of slumber open wide
> To many a watchful night!
>
> (4.5.22–24)

The sleep of a king is never so "deeply sweet" as that enjoyed by any of his subjects. It is as though the juxtaposition of the dying king and his crown has aroused a sympathetic understanding in the prince of what his father has endured, and the identity of sentiments in the two soliloquies implies a comprehension of the responsibilities of kingship which his father learned at the cost of years of struggle which have hastened his death. And in taking up the crown without fear or regret, the prince duplicates the king's more laconic acceptance of necessity:

> My due from thee is this imperial crown,
> Which, as immediate from thy place and blood,
> Derives itself to me. Lo where it sits,
> Which God shall guard; and put the world's whole strength
> Into one giant arm, it shall not force
> This lineal honor from me. This from thee
> Will I to mine leave, as 'tis left to me.
>
> (4.5.40–46)

In this speech Hal signalizes his real and final rejection of "vanity." The misunderstanding about the crown brings to a dramatic climax the long history of the king's distress over his son, and so the final reconciliation when it comes generates a greater sense of relief and resolution than the parallel scene in Part 1, since the king knows now that the prince is indeed his political heir. The whole episode creates the impression that, in addition to the crown, the prince will inherit his father's political talents, but without the circumstances that thwarted him, or his ever-present sense of guilt, or his personal limitations.[12]

With this understanding of the seriousness of his destiny, the prince is prepared for the next step, the acknowledgment that the responsible exercise of power presupposes law and justice, which is dramatized in the reconciliation with the Chief Justice. Shakespeare reserves for this late moment in the two plays his only reference to the episode in which the prince once struck the Chief Justice in court and was sent to prison for it. To have dramatized this incident as part of the picture of Hal's wild youth, or even to have had it talked about, would have introduced an unnecessary and serious handicap to be overcome in making acceptable the prince's reformation. At this stage in Part 2, this youthful episode can be introduced without damaging the image of the new king. Indeed, it enhances it; it is the young new king himself who brings it up, pretending to rebuke the Chief Justice for his former temerity, and so provides an occasion for the Justice to expound the nature of the law. The Chief Justice explains that he is not simply a man dispensing laws, but that in his place, when the prince struck him, he was "The majesty and power of law and justice, / The image of the King whom I presented" (5.2.78–79). In punishing the king's son, "I then did use the person of your father; / The image of his power lay then in me" (5.2.73–74). The king and the law are one, and the magistrate in office is in effect the king. The young king agrees: "You are right, Justice, and you weigh this well" (5.2.102). And he quotes his father's approval of the action of the Justice at the time the incident took place:

> "Happy am I, that have a man so bold
> That dares do justice on my proper son;
> And not less happy, having such a son
> That would deliver up his greatness so
> Into the hands of justice."
>
> (5.2.108–12)

Usurper though he was, Henry is shown to have understood the nature of law in relation to the king's power, and once again Shakespeare shows through a parallel between a sentiment attributed to the father and one expressed by his son an identity between them in political understanding. The relation of law to sovereign power is an important consideration with Shakespeare, and it is significant that wherever the issue is raised in the history plays the emphasis is not on the law as an instrument to punish the erring subject and to secure order but on the law as a safeguard against the king's arbitrary exercise of his authority. In *Richard II* York warns Richard that the law which he ignores in disinheriting Bolingbroke is precisely the law that insures his own throne, and that for a king to violate the law is to invite chaos. In *Henry V*, the king's insistence on determining whether he has a right to the title in France for which he is prepared to fight may appear today like an expedient legalism rather than a passion for justice, but it is a further indication that for Shakespeare the king in the exercise of his vast power, cannot disregard the restraints of law and justice.

On the way to becoming the complete king, Henry must perform one more act, an act which may be damaging to his reputation for genial attractiveness but which will signalize the taking on of the aspect of the public man by the onetime wayward prince. Shakespeare's staging of this episode is unsparing and pitiless, providing the maximum clash between the new king's sovereign presence and his irresponsible past. Falstaff, impetuous and unthinking to the point of rudeness, places himself in the king's path during the solemn procession following the coronation, and the king's unrelenting public rebuke more than matches Falstaff's thoughtless effrontery. The king banishes Falstaff and publicly renounces his former life:

> For God doth know, so shall the world perceive,
> That I have turned away my former self;
> So will I those that kept me company.
>
> (5.5.57–59)

There is more to this than the fact that the king is a reformed character and will henceforth choose his companions more circumspectly. In rejecting Falstaff and all the merriment, informality, and unconventional—even unlawful—sport which are associated with him, he rejects not only a questionable past but also all the privileges and delights of a private man, and accepts the constricting conditions imposed on a man in whom the public life of the nation is personified. Such a renunciation was, as Erasmus had observed, a necessary consequence of assuming a king's responsibilities:

> In the case of private individuals, some concession is granted to youth and to old age: the former may make a mistake now and then; the latter is allowed leisure and a cessation of toils. But the man who undertakes the duties of a prince, while managing the affairs of everyone, is not free to be either a young man or an old one; he cannot make a mistake without a great loss to many people; he cannot slacken in his duties without the gravest disasters ensuing.[13]

We might imagine the young Henry V remarking on this with appropriate gravity in the words he used to his Chief Justice: "You are right, and you weigh this well." However, unlike the other steps in Hal's progress which redound to his credit, the rejection of Falstaff has produced a considerable reaction against him, and understandably, for there is indeed something appalling about that dreadful line, "I know thee not, old man. Fall to thy prayers" (5.5.47). In spite of the numerous defenses of Hal's conduct in this scene, the rejection of Falstaff is unpleasant, and, I believe, it was meant to be so. It seems entirely likely, considering the skillful dramatic intensification of the possibilities of this episode, that Shakespeare deliberately produced a difficult moment, an intentional shock to genial sensibility, in order to mark the putting on of the public man as the king's renunciation of much that makes a man amiable and easy of access. Shakespeare may have miscalculated its full effect, but there is no mistaking its relation to the whole design.[14] Every important step which the prince takes in his progress to kingship is marked by a situation which places him in an unprincely and sometimes embarrassing position, and the resolution of each such episode marks his acceptance of an important condition of his greatness. His indulgence in vanity was not so much a deliberately chosen, if unusual, course of training for his office as it was a sign of his initial reluctance to assume that office and at the same time a measure of his progress toward it. His riotous youth was a handicap on the human side, just as the flawed title was on the political. He must overcompensate for both—he must prove his right to be a king a fortiori. To the extent that Hal's original indulgence was gay, uninhibited, and irresponsible, the public break with it becomes disturbing and notorious. To become a king in the full sense he must banish the natural, private man and the "offending Adam"—renounce youth, easy companionship, intimate friendships, and become a public, dedicated, and isolated man. We follow the prince in his unconventional progress to the throne up to the final step, when he accepts the formality, the distance, and the chill fearsomeness of his high office.

XIV

Of Diplomacy, War, and Peace:
Henry V

Henry V is constructed on bold, simple lines. It is dominated
by the figure of the warrior king, and it moves in a sequence of
well-defined acts without the complex interrelations of an intrigue plot and subplots, and with strongly contrasting scenes.
There are, however, several clearly established links between
Henry V and the preceding plays. The prince's youthful wildness and later reformation, so large a feature of *1* and *2 Henry
IV*, is the topic of conversation between the two bishops in the
opening scene. In *2 Henry IV* Henry warns his son that his title,
though got by direct succession, is but newly won, and advises
him to busy giddy minds in foreign wars in order to unify his
country; and the last speech of that play, spoken by Prince John,
predicts the easing of civil tensions by means of a war with
France:

> I will lay odds that, ere this year expire,
> We bear our civil swords and native fire
> As far as France. I heard a bird so sing,
> Whose music, to my thinking, pleased the king.
>
> (5.5.105–8)

War with France is the main issue in the first act of *Henry V*. Henry IV confesses to his son in *2 Henry IV* that his own title was dubiously got, and in his prayer before Agincourt Henry V alludes to his father's guilt in compassing the crown. All of Hal's tavern companions are back except Falstaff. The connections are numerous and provocative and it is natural to suppose that, as in the case of the interrelationships among the other plays in the series, the links indicate significant lines of development which may be followed through with some consistency in any serious study of *Henry V*. One consequence of approaching *Henry V* in this way is that the directness and straightforward simplicity of *Henry V* begin to disappear in complexities, and it becomes necessary to ask how far the method can really be applied in this case. The epilogue to *2 Henry IV* promises more of Falstaff, but Falstaff does not appear again; thus anyone unfamiliar with that remarkable figure from the two previous plays would not know what to make of the talk of his death in the early scenes of *Henry V*, and might be puzzled by Fluellen's praise of the king for casting him off. An individual play that is destined for performance must, simply as a condition of its intelligibility in the theatre, be able to stand pretty much alone. To the extent that this consideration determines the primary impression which the play can make, it must be respected in criticism.[1] As a preliminary step, then, it will be useful to consider the principal links between *Henry V* and the two parts of *Henry IV*, in order to determine to what extent they can be regarded as essential to the play considered as an independent performable work.

If *Henry V* were a consistent working out of major prefigurings in the previous plays—to the degree, for example, that *1 Henry IV* is—we would expect to find as a principal feature of *Henry V* a following up of Henry IV's warning about the insecurity of the succession and the consequent need for Hal to gain acceptance of his rule and thus validate his weak title by convincing the nation of his superior merits as a king. However, Henry's flawed title is not the major issue in *Henry V*. On the contrary, the impression is firmly made from the outset that Henry is fully established as the rightful king with the approval and admiration of his people, and no one ever calls him a usurper, not even the French. The diplomatic insult sent by the dauphin contains no slur on his flawed and sin-laden title, but is inspired solely by his reputation for unprincely conduct. Henry alone alludes to the crime which sullied his father's title, in the prayer before Agincourt:

> Not today, O Lord,
> O, not today, think not upon the fault
> My father made in compassing the crown!
> (4.1.298–300)

But there is no indication that he utters this prayer in guilty fear about his own right, but rather out of pious concern for God's justice (he is relentlessly pious), pity for his men who face terrible odds, and care for the honor of his country. It could be argued that the prayer actually reflects a degree of self-assurance, for confession of his father's wrong does not seem to shake his unquestioning conviction that he is the acknowledged and sole lawful leader in this moment of peril. What follows the prayer, we should bear in mind, is the Crispin Crispian speech before the battle, which is spoken in confidence and a sense of brotherhood with his officers and men.

Shakespeare had an opportunity to call attention to the weakness of Henry's title, but he failed to make use of it in this way. Three traitors are discovered just before Henry sails for France—even during the reign of this paragon treason can occur. One of these, the earl of Cambridge, admits his treason as do the others, but disclaims French gold as his real motive:

> For me, the gold of France did not seduce,
> Although I did admit it as a motive
> The sooner to effect what I intended.
> (2.2.155–57)

The significance of these vague hints is to be found in Holinshed, who explains that according to some accounts Cambridge's real aim was to place the earl of March on the throne, or push his own claims, and that he admitted to accepting money from the French king in order to conceal his true purpose and protect his own descendants in the Yorkist line from reprisal.[2] Shakespeare does not provide these details, so that what stands out is not the threat of these claims but Cambridge's repentant renunciation of an unworthy act of betrayal:

> But God be thanked for prevention,
> Which I in sufferance heartily will rejoice,
> Beseeching God and you to pardon me.
>
> (2.2.158–60)

Alone among all of Shakespeare's English kings (Henry VIII excepted), Henry V enjoys, from the start and throughout, general acceptance of his title and universal approval of his right to exercise the power invested in him by its possession. He never has to come to the defense of his title or demonstrate his right to it, a right which seems to be there from the beginning. Indeed, it is only on this assumption that he makes a diplomatic issue of his hereditary claims in France.

Similarly, the idea of a foreign war as a means of diverting civil broils to a national purpose seems to have been left behind and does not enter into any of the serious dramatic features of *Henry V*. Anyone seeing a performance of *Henry V* for the first time without having read or seen *1* and *2 Henry IV* would be able to make good sense out of most of it, barring some puzzlement about the first appearance of the comics in act 2 and the talk about the prince putting bad humors on the knight. He would never gather that the war was being fought for the politically expedient purpose of channeling unruly spirits into a semblance of unity. The image impressed on us from the beginning of *Henry V* is that England is a unified country under a great king. The two bishops who open the play launch into encomia about their extraordinary monarch, and nowhere does the appearance of Henry produce indications of overt unrest or of disaffection below the surface. Even the one discordant note, the discovery of the conspiracy in act 2, serves in a way to confirm this happy condition. It is a close, secret plot of a few venal men, and the conspirators, when discovered, display remorse and an eagerness to embrace the death which they admit they richly deserve. They demonstrate that evil can exist even under the best of kings—just as later we discover that riffraff follows even the most heroic of armies—and if we do recall *Henry IV* at this point, the conspirators will seem but as the last cloud of an expiring storm which has now blown away. Only one possible source of trouble is discussed in the event a foreign expedition is to be undertaken, and that is Scotland, a historic source of danger which, it is pointed out, even Edward III and the Black Prince had to contend with. More troops are left behind than go with the king, but they are insurance against the Scots, not against danger of subversion and civil war. The long discourses on order and degree emerge out of this discussion, and in the context the thought that

> So may a thousand actions, once afoot,
> End in one purpose, and be all well borne
> Without defeat
>
> (1.2.211–13)

seems to refer not to an ideal state but to the state of affairs at home. The surprising thing about *Henry V* when viewed in the light of its anticipations in *2 Henry IV* is that the national unity which a foreign war was to achieve seems already to exist well before the enterprise is undertaken that was, in Henry IV's opinion, necessary to accomplish it. It is an already unified nation that Henry V is to lead to France. In proposing to fight France, Henry can appeal to historic rights of inheritance, to previous military confirmations of these legal rights, to the practical advantages of title to French lands, and to considerations of national honor. In short, he is about to fight France for fairly customary reasons of state and the national interest.[3]

In only one respect does Shakespeare deliberately and conspicuously carry over into the main action an important feature
of *1* and *2 Henry IV*: that is, the youthful wildness of the prince
and his reformation. This is introduced in the opening dialogue
between the two bishops (1.1.24 ff.) and reappears in the next
scene with the French ambassadors (1.2.266 ff.); it is recalled
through the scenes which bring in the king's onetime tavern
associates (2.1. and 2.3); it is talked about in the French court
(2.4.26 ff., 130 ff.), and alluded to in Fluellen's admiring reference
to the dismissal of Falstaff (4.7.48 ff.). Curiously enough, the
effect of this reiteration is not to tie this play closer to the two
previous ones, but to separate it. The admiring speeches of the
archbishop are preparation for the first appearance of the mirror
of all Christian kings as a paragon who for all practical present
purposes had no past. The dauphin's serious miscalculation on
this matter produces the insult which helps precipitate hostilities and it leads him to underestimate the valor and loyalty of
the English. The prominent persistence of this one theme from
the two *Henry IV* plays is in contrast to the effective insulation
of *Henry V* from the other principal associations with the prince
in the earlier plays. There are certain of these allusions to Falstaff in the king's past which do color the total impression the
play makes and must eventually be fully dealt with, but taking
the full measure of their significance is not a precondition of
determining the play's basic structure and essential character.
The hypothetical first viewer of this play, innocent of its predecessors, would learn that this much admired king had spent a
riotous youth but was now a very different man, and that igno-
rance of this change misled the French. He would not learn that
the war was fought for the reasons proposed by Henry IV, nor
that the king had an insecure title which he had to vindicate.
When reference is made in the king's prayer to the fault his
father made in compassing the crown, it would reinforce the
notion of the king's piety but would not at that late point in the
play create an issue of Henry V's title, since it has not been
an issue for anyone anywhere in the play. It would be nice to

discover what such an ingenuous viewer or reader thought of the play, but in the absence of his untutored judgment the alternative is to put aside deliberately our favorite presumptions about the play and ask what kind of a work it turns out to be when it is considered independently as a dramatic whole, complete in itself.

Politically and geographically, *Henry V* represents a distinct change from the previous plays. The scene enlarges to include the Continent, and most of the action takes place across the sea in France. The kinds of political issues which are at the center of the other plays—the struggles for power, the legal questions of legitimacy, the relations of power to sovereign authority, the evils of civil strife, and the crises of ambition and conscience which trouble a nation and distress or destroy its leaders—these cause no major concern here. The internal politics at the outset has to do with the interplay of special interests which influence the decision to go to war, with the internal dangers that must be met, and with the weeding out of a few traitors. These all, however, are ultimately related to the negotiations between the rival nations. The politics of *Henry V* is, in the broadest sense, international politics, or, more specifically, war politics, for the entire play is about war. To this central emphasis the construction is a clue. The effect of the play is not that of a tightly knit series of events, but of a sequence of five large episodes, almost pageantlike in quality, separated by the choruses into the five acts designated by modern editions, each dealing with one stage in the course of events that unfolds when two great nations become involved in war.[4]

The first act is the prelude to war—the debate which justifies the going to war and establishes its aims, and the formal diplomatic confrontation the failure of which leads to hostilities. It is puzzling that Shakespeare introduced *Henry V* with the two bishops worrying over a proposed bill to expropriate temporal lands willed to the church. This topic does lead directly to the laudatory descriptions, amounting to near reverence, of the reformed king, who will shortly appear on the scene, but the connection has its purpose: the bishops see in this "true lover of the holy Church" a possible ally, and their offer of great sums in support of a possible campaign against France is calculated to influence the king in their favor. This heroic play thus opens in an atmosphere of devious politics in undisguised form, and it does not improve our impression of the archbishop when we learn that the church wealth which Parliament proposes to confiscate would be used to

> maintain, to the King's honor,
> Full fifteen earls and fifteen hundred knights.
> Six thousand and two hundred good esquires,
> And to relief of lazars, and weak age,
> Of indigent faint souls past corporal toil,
> A hundred almshouses right well supplied;
> And to the coffers of the King beside,
> A thousand pounds by the year.
>
> (1.1.12–19)

A modest and apparently laudable social revolution. What is further disturbing is that the man to whom the king appeals to expound whether he can "with right and conscience make this claim" (1.2.96) to the French lands is none other than "my gracious Lord of Canterbury," "my dear and faithful lord" (1.2.1, 13), who had made the offer of church funds to support a possible war with France. Thus, before the play is scarcely under way, we find ourselves among people who seem to have been brought up on *The Prince* and Bacon's "Of Negotiating," and it is not surprising that many critics find this conniving distasteful and so turn against Henry. As one of his modern biographers puts it, "If Shakespeare is to be believed, the renewal of what we now call 'The Hundred Years War' was entirely due to the cynical advice of English Churchmen."[5] Shakespeare, it is true, gives a more favorable picture of the churchmen and their efforts to influence the king than do his sources, but even in his modified form the calculated, conniving conduct of the churchmen serves well enough. Aided by recollections of "that vile politician Bolingbroke," the business at Gaultree Forest, and

Henry IV's dying advice, our impulse at the outset is to involve the king in this sad business and mark him down for a sharp and conniving operator.[6]

This is probably a mistake, and subsequent developments might make one think so. Shakespeare does not spare the churchmen, but it is they who are busy being politicians, and not Henry. The odd thing about *Henry V* is that as we look at the king's conduct at home and abroad, he turns out in all his dealings to be the most straightforward, candid political man of the whole lot. Even when he is courting Kate with tedious gallantry, he is blunt about his purpose: "No, it is not possible you should love the enemy of France, Kate; but in loving me you should love the friend of France, for I love France so well that I will not part with a village of it; I will have it all mine" (5.2.176–80). It should be noted, moreover, that negotiations between the countries had been in progress before the offer of the bishops. As the play opens, the French envoys are waiting to present their reply to an embassy sent by the king, before the play begins, to state his claims to France. As Shakespeare arranges the order of events, the offer of money is not the primary incentive to undertaking the war, and so in solemnly warning Canterbury to state the case of his French claims honestly and without sophistry Henry need not be pretending piety or indulging in irony.[7] On the score of learning and logic—too much for us as audience—Canterbury's speech shows that Henry has asked the right man. Today the long harangue on the Salic law is a bore, and whether, as has been alleged, it was more interesting to an age that had to listen to long sermons can be no more than a hopeful guess. But Shakespeare introduces it as though he wished it to be taken as reasonable, and it is doubtful that he put it in for laughs—which is the only way Olivier saw of getting by with it in the film version of the play. By itself the play does not readily support the charge that Henry trumped up an unjust war—a charge, incidentally, which, as the Arden editor points out, would not have been supported by the eminent sixteenth-century jurist, Gentili.[8]

Shakespeare's dramatic strategy has induced numerous unfavorable responses, but it can be accounted for. Henry is presented as a model king, but he rules over an ordinarily imperfect nation—it is one way of bringing a sense of reality into the affairs of this near-perfect epic hero. The play moves on to high moments of patriotism and heroism, but in the course of events there are unsentimental glances now and then at the realities which accompany such great actions of state. The canny and self-serving politicking of the churchmen is to the deliberations that precede the hostilities with France what the discreditable conduct of a few of the king's soldiers is to the heroism of Agincourt. They impinge on Henry, they are part of the nation he must lead to glory, but he is not tarnished by them. There are politicians among the clergy, traitors among the nobles, and shabby characters among the soldiers, but the king employs or disposes of these as he must, moving about them without losing his independence and national regard. There are, moreover, two nations involved in these negotiations. The answer which the French embassy brings in act 1 is not from the king of France but from the dauphin, and it is an insult, which therefore renders further diplomatic negotiations impossible. National honor is a concept which our times have made to seem shabby, but it is nevertheless still true that in diplomacy a public insult from a weak nation is easier to disregard than from an equal. In the setting of the play, the uncompromising reply and the dauphin's contemptuous gift of tennis balls allows a choice only between humiliation and war. Act 1 is thus a dramatization of the crosscurrents of debate, negotiation, and diplomacy which precede and in their mixed and sometimes irrelevant way combine to bring nations to war.

The second act encompasses the events between the breakdown of diplomatic missions and the actual fighting, in a loose sequence of events. The chorus tells of the contagious excitement that makes youth eager to take part in the national adventure:

> Now all the youth of England are on fire,
> And silken dalliance in the wardrobe lies;
> Now thrive the armorers, and honor's thought
> Reigns solely in the breast of every man.
> They sell the pasture now to buy the horse,
> Following the mirror of all Christian kings
> With winged heels, as English Mercuries.
>
> (1–7)

The play, however, shows us none of this. The odd assortment of characters from the tavern at Eastcheap are all we actually see responding to the war fever, and they are about to join Henry's forces for sordid reasons. In Pistol's inelegant but vivid language, "Let us to France, like horse-leeches, my boys, / To suck, to suck, the very blood to suck" (2.3.56–57). They threaten the lofty tone, like the practical politics of the bishops. We do not see the Gowers and Fluellens, the Williamses and the Courts being moved by the spirit of the moment to join the troops, though they are there at Harfleur and at Agincourt to carry the honor of their country while the Pistols and Bardolphs come to a bad end. The second major episode of act 2, clearly anticipated with appropriate comment by the chorus, is the discovery of the traitors. The final scene is in the French court, and while the picture suggested by the chorus, of the French quaking with fear and pale policy, is not borne out by the dramatization of the episode, the king of France warns the arrogant dauphin not to underestimate the English, and even the dauphin agrees to prudent preparations. The scene ends with the arrival of Exeter bringing an English ultimatum which is dismissed by the French with defiance. In the midst of these miscellaneous scenes, only Henry's confident words after he has dismissed the traitors match the high promise of the opening lines of the chorus:

> We doubt not now
> But every rub is smoothed on our way.
> Then forth, dear countrymen. Let us deliver
> Our puissance into the hand of God,
> Putting it straight in expedition.

Cheerly to sea; the signs of war advance:
No king of England, if not king of France!

(2.2.187–93)

The next two acts depict the war itself. Act 3 presents two phases of it. The act opens with the siege of Harfleur, the kind of early victory, deceptively easy, which falls to an eager army against a foe not yet prepared to take the invasion seriously. The talk of Henry before Harfleur is in this spirit: "Once more unto the breach, dear friends, once more; / Or close the wall up with our English dead!" (3.1.1–2). It is easy enough to talk about closing the wall up with English dead when casualties are still few and the army still fresh. Even the cowardly buffoonery of Pistol, Nym, and Bardolph is not enough to sully the occasion, since it is balanced by the solid character of the professionals, Gower, Jamie, Macmorris, and Fluellen. The comedy of the latter group, arising as it does out of their shop talk and their temperamental and national differences, does not diminish them as capable trained officers. The concluding portion of the third act brings us, with considerable foreshortening of time, to a later and more sober stage in the war, when sickness, lack of supplies, and war-weariness have taken their toll and the once spirited forces before Harfleur, now badly reduced, face an aroused and prepared enemy. At this stage there is no patience with the comic parody of soldiering provided by the Eastcheap gang, and the darkening of the situation is marked by Pistol's inability to get a reprieve for Bardolph, who must hang for not observing the king's stern orders against theft.

The fourth act carries the war portion to its climax at Agincourt. It opens with a series of episodes which show the king meeting with various parts of his army to assess their spirit, a device that provides a view of all the diverse groups that combined to make up his expeditionary force. These opening episodes prepare the mood for the battle, and for Henry's speech to the camp—a very different oration from the one before Harfleur. There is no talk of imitating the action of the tiger, no battle cries of "Harry, England, and St. George." The confidence expressed in this instance comes from the knowledge that this small, beleagured army is united in waiting to face a common danger with courage. "We band of brothers," Henry calls them, "For he today that sheds his blood with me / Shall be my brother" (4.3.60–62).

The decisive victory at Agincourt is followed in the next act by the negotiations that conclude the peace. Burgundy is the go-between:

> I have labored
> With all my wits, my pains, and strong endeavors
> To bring your most imperial majesties
> Unto this bar and royal interview.
>
> (5.2.24–27)

And he prefaces the negotiations with an eloquent plea for peace, the "dear nurse of arts, plenties, and joyful births" (5.2.35). Henry, with all the advantages on his side, proves a firm negotiator—"You must buy that peace / With full accord to all our just demands" (5.2.70–71). His victory is total: his demands are met, he wins the princess Katherine for his wife, and the two erstwhile enemies seal the bargain with hopes for future amity. There is some justice in the common criticism that the last act is dramatically a letdown, but it is certainly a fitting completion of the design called for by the general idea which governs the play.

The structure of the play is straightforward and simple, and it makes clear the controlling idea. We begin with the debates and diplomatic mission that lead to war, and end with the negotiations that lead to peace. These two acts frame the portions of the action which involve the preparations preliminary to the war, and which deal with the war itself, from its buoyant beginning to the dark moment of danger, and then to its splendid victory.[9] Everything in *Henry V* is accommodated to this design. Battles and fighting occur in all the other history plays, but in none of the others is war so exclusively the setting and the subject. There is a great deal more about such details as preparations for battle, sieges, defenses, and the like than in the other plays, and for the first time we are aware of professionals versed in the art and technique of war, represented by Gower, Jamie, Macmorris, Fluellen, as a class distinct from nobles and knights trained in the chivalric tradition. We are also aware for the first time, except for Falstaff's sadly comic charges, of the ordinary soldier. Moreover, it is primarily as a soldier that we see the king, and hence the potentialities inherent in the character that Shakespeare has been developing for two plays are considerably reduced. "I am a soldier," he says before Harfleur, "A name that in my thoughts becomes me best" (3.3.5–6). And it is as a blunt soldier that he courts Katherine: "take me, take a soldier; take a soldier, take a king" (5.2.170–72). "In his portrait of Henry V as general," writes Paul Jorgensen,

> Shakespeare demonstrated that whatever deficiencies the play might have in representing army life were not due to lack of pains. In no other military portrait—Falstaff excepted—can we say with more assurance that here the dramatist made a careful study of military theory, and sketched character with the theory constantly in mind.[10]

Most of the comedy is also accommodated to the military environment. One strain is provided by the familiar group from Eastcheap. Their first scenes recall the comedy of 2 *Henry IV*, but once the action moves to France, these characters become absorbed into the environment of the camp and battle, which then controls their comic uses. At Harfleur they are the braggarts who shout, "On, on, on, on, on to the breach" (3.2.1), and then hang back, like the policemen in *The Pirates of Penzance*. Pistol, with his wonderful private language, alone survives from the group to play the ridiculous scene of capturing the cowardly French soldier (part of the chauvinism? even Pistol looks good in the face of a cowardly French soldier), and to be beaten by Fluellen in revenge for a fleer at the Welsh. The practical joke played by the king on Williams also has some of the rough and tumble of an army camp, but this is a minor detail and Williams is not a comic character. The principal new strain in the comedy is introduced by the group of professionals. Some of it comes to little more than the exploitation of local accents, a low but perennial form of stage humor. Some of it plays with local sensibilities. When Fluellen begins, "Captain Macmorris, . . . there is not many of your nation," Macmorris, who at once expects the inevitable fleers and insults at the Irish, breaks in: "Of my nation! What ish my nation? Ish a villain, and a bastard, and a knave, and a rascal. What ish my nation? Who talks of my nation?" (3.2.123–27). The principal line of humor, however, grows out of the military setting, and it centers in Fluellen with his pedantic passion for "the disciplines of war, the Roman wars" (3.2.99–100).

The chauvinism encouraged by war is at times as blatant in *Henry V* as in *1 Henry VI*. The French warriors are arrogant and self-assured, and Henry for his part speaks to Mountjoy with equal contempt of the French as soldiers. The dauphin, as the nominal leader of the French forces, suggests comparison with Henry, not without some heavy exaggeration, for the dauphin's boasting about his horse and armor while awaiting battle is ludicrous and something of a joke even to his own companions. The important comparison, however, is that implied between the two armies. Before the battle, Henry is shown visiting every echelon of his army, from the highest to the lowest. All we see of the French is the elegant nobles impatiently waiting for the morning to destroy the English. We learn later that the French use mercenaries. The English are a national army, fighting for a national cause; the French still look on war as the sport of princes and nobles. Whereas the war exacerbates the differences between the rival countries, it is shown to resolve traditional rivalries within the British Isles. Scotsmen, Irishmen, and Welshmen retain their local pride and sensitivity along with their local accents, but they are united in their common dedication to the professional side of army life and in their admiration for Henry.

Of Diplomacy, War, and Peace

We witness none of the horrors of war, though they are spoken of often enough, for example, in Henry's warning to the governor of Harfleur of what will happen if the city does not surrender and becomes instead the victim of an army unleashed for total victory (3.3.7 ff.), in Exeter's warning to the French king of the horrors that will ensue if war is permitted to break out (2.4.103 ff.), and in the brief description by Williams of men dying in battle—"some swearing, some crying for a surgeon, some upon their wives left poor behind them, some upon debts they owe, some upon their children rawly left" (4.1.140–44). Appropriately, too, Burgundy speaks in his noble plea for peace of the devastation brought on by war upon the countryside, and the decline of civility and civilized life (5.2.38 ff.). Nowhere, however, is there any direct impression of the savagery of war such as we get in *Henry VI*, with Clifford seeking vengeance for his father's death, the killings of Rutland and Prince Edward, and the humiliation and killing of York, nor is there anything like the feeling of pathos found in King Henry's reflections as, alone, he watches the pageant of the son who killed his father and the father who killed his son. But the wars in *Henry VI* are civil wars, and then as now civil wars were looked upon as the ultimate national disaster, whereas occasional foreign wars were regarded by many as healthful.[11] One of the reasons urged on Henry to undertake the war is that some such kingly enterprise is expected of him:

> *Exeter.* Your brother kings and monarchs of the earth
> Do all expect that you should rouse yourself,
> As did the former lions of your blood.
> *Westmoreland.* They know your grace hath cause
> and means and might.
> (1.2.122–25)

A war nobly fought is regarded as a sign of a nation's greatness. Canterbury, invoking the spirit of Edward III and Edward the Black Prince, urges the king to unwind his bloody flag, and Ely reminds him that he is heir not only to the throne of his great predecessors but to their prowess in arms:

> Awake remembrance of the valiant dead
> And with your puissant arm renew their feats.
> You are their heir, you sit upon their throne;
> The blood and courage that renowned them
> Runs in your veins.
>
> (1.2.115–19)

The general impression of the war with France is one of national unity and purpose, and of war generally as an enterprise which, under proper circumstances and inspired leadership, tests the individual and national virtues and brings them out.

It is not, however, the battle scenes which contribute to this impression. Harfleur is principally a piece of showy rhetoric on the part of the king, with a not terribly inspired bit of comedy following. And the dramatization of the great battle of Agincourt itself is certainly curious and not a little disappointing. Four scenes are given to the actual battle itself. The first of these (4.4) is the comic scene of Pistol capturing the French soldier. The next is a brief scene showing the consternation of the French nobles at the disaster that has struck their army. The next consists largely of a report by Exeter to the king of the death of Suffolk and York, reminiscent of the touching death scene of Talbot and his son in *1 Henry VI*, and ends with the king's order to kill the prisoners. The next opens with Fluellen's indignation at the news that the French have killed the boys who had been left behind to guard the luggage (" 'Tis expressly against the law of arms" [4.7.1–2]), but most of this part of the scene is between Gower and Fluellen with Fluellen's long ramble about Alexander the Great in support of his admiration of Henry. The king then appears, angered at the conduct of the French and threatening to give no quarter, when Montjoy enters to tell Henry that the English have won the field. That is all. The lack of stage fighting is not of itself a serious matter, and it might well have been a step in the right direction.

It is simply that an obvious comic scene, a scene of drollery, a sentimental report of the death of two exemplary soldiers in the chivalric mode, and a few glimpses of the king in various moods should be all that stands for the climax toward which the play has been moving. Only the brief moment in which Montjoy submits to the king brings with it any of the human drama of men who had taken the destiny of themselves and their country into their hands. And what follows this moment is not the concluding episode of the act—in which the herald reports on the miraculously small English losses, and Henry gives praise to God and commands the singing of "Non nobis" and "Te Deum" and charitable burial of the dead—but the scene in which the king prepares Fluellen for the practical joke on Williams, followed by the next scene in which the joke is played out.

The serious high point of the military portion is not the battle but the sequence of vignettes preceding Agincourt itself. These episodes evoke the sights and sounds which surround the two armies preparing through the night for the battle, and express the thoughts and moods of the men who must fight it when the morning comes. As the king makes the tour of his forces, we observe the dignified, quiet resolve of his general officers, and the busy preparations of the professionals with their shop talk. Even Pistol has his moment and does not make too ludicrous a showing. Finally, in the longest of these episodes, we see the common soldiers, huddled together, waiting for the dawn, wondering what they are doing here far from home, about to face death for a cause they do not understand. It is one of the extraordinary features of this play that Shakespeare makes no comic use of the common soldier. In the incident of the practical joke on Williams, Williams comes off with greater dignity and credit than the king. It is Williams, Bates, and Court who raise the most serious questions about the war, and it is after the talk with them that Henry reflects on the responsibilities and cares of kingship and prays that God will not hold his army to account for Bolingbroke's sin. When the disguised king comes on the group they are less than enthusiastic about the coming business. They would as soon see the king ransomed or facing the French alone. When Henry says, "Methinks I could not die anywhere so contented as in the King's company, his cause being just and his quarrel honorable," Williams replies curtly, "That's more than we know" (4.1.127–30), and his reply has echoed over the years in many a camp and in many a novel and play and film about war. Bates is less disposed to trouble about such questions at this hour: "Ay, or more than we should seek after," he tells Williams, "for we know enough if we are the King's subjects; if his cause be wrong, our obedience to the King wipes the crime of it out of us" (4.1.131–35). Williams does not let the argument rest there, but even he does not deny that a soldier's duty is to obey the king. His concern is that "few will die well that die in battle; for how can they charitably dispose of anything when blood is their argument" (4.1.144–46), and he wonders what reckoning a king can make for all those soldiers that die badly in a cause that might not be good. Henry himself had warned the archbishop of this:

> We charge you in the name of God take heed,
> For never two such kingdoms did contend
> Without much fall of blood, whose guiltless drops
> Are every one a woe, a sore complaint
> 'Gainst him whose wrongs give edge unto the swords
> That makes such waste in brief mortality.
>
> (1.2.23–28)

The argument now takes a direction more suited to engage the feelings of the sixteenth century than our own: the king's cause may be spotless, Henry argues, but there is no army of unspotted soldiers, and since war is God's beadle and vengeance, it punishes men for crimes committed before the battle. "Every man's duty is the king's; but every subject's soul is his own" (4.1.182–84). And this conclusion even Williams accepts. The king has been accused of evading the issue of the injustice of his war by shifting the discussion to another ground, but this amounts to asking that the question which would be of paramount interest to us if the play were written today should have been the one to disturb Harry's soldiers. The king does not, in fact, shift the argument. On the eve of battle the soldiers are worried less about war aims and causes than about dying well. Williams is troubled about whether the king's cause is good or bad because if it is bad then how can a soldier die well? This is the argument the king tries to answer.[12] What stays in the memory about Agincourt in *Henry V* is not the battle itself but the vivid sense of what it feels like for an army in a tight spot to wait out the long night before a battle. There are no conspicuous individual acts of courage or chivalry in the dramatization of Agincourt. The moment of heroic dedication is reached in Henry's oration to his men, after which the battle itself is an odd anticlimax, until the once confident Montjoy comes to admit defeat and to ask permission to remove their dead.

Some such view of the play is possible if *Henry V* is separated from its predecessors and approached as an independent play. What emerges from this approach is a work that would lend itself to a strong, coherent production without leaving out a single scene or putting a single line to the rack. It is, moreover, the play that has led many critics to call *Henry V* an epic and to think of the *Aeneid* as the closest parallel, not only because it is a play about war and heroic conduct but because it depicts a nation displaying its virtues in a time of danger and through this experience realizing itself. It can be objected that the *Henry V* of this discussion not only is separated from its links with the other histories but is isolated moreover from the large body of incisive critical attacks that have grown around it, and that in consequence it is a sanitized and whitewashed *Henry V* which has been substituted for the complex and controversial play with which most modern students are familiar. This is a fairly reasonable objection. More to the point, the view of the play proposed here is not without puzzles of its own, and even for many who accept a straightforward heroic conception of the play, *Henry V* leaves a sense of disappointment and its hero fails to charm. In the present critical context, however, the essential play has been submerged in the debates. It is necessary, first of all, to get around the criticism and try to restore the main if simplified outlines of the play that was once there.

XV

Two Political Myths:
i. Richard III

Richard III and *Henry V* bear a special relation to each other. Each comes as the concluding play in a tetralogy and completes the narrative line which the first play in the series initiates. The first tetralogy begins with the death of Henry V and ends with the death of Richard III and the establishment of the new Tudor dynasty. The second begins with the abdication of Richard II and ends with the successful reign of Henry V and his triumph at Agincourt. However, *Richard III* is also the first of a series of five plays each of which treats a particular aspect of political sovereignty and power, with *Richard III* and the last play, *Henry V*, representing the two political polar extremes, that of the tyrant and of the good and successful king. These were well-recognized opposite types, which Erasmus distinguished succinctly as follows:

> The main object of a tyrant is to follow his own caprices, but a king follows the path of right and honor. . . . The tyrant's role is marked by fear, deceit, and machinations of evil. The king governs through wisdom, integrity, and beneficence. The tyrant uses his imperial power for himself, the king for the state.[1]

Richard III is the only unmistakable instance of a tyrant in the entire series; Henry V can say of himself, without fear of contradiction, "We are no tyrant but a Christian king" (1.2.241). In the dramatic treatment of the materials the plays have certain qualities in common. In each, the protagonist dominates the play. Richard appears in fourteen of twenty-four scenes, and is the topic of discussion when he does not appear. In *Henry V*, the comic scenes and the scenes in the French court serve to diversify the interest, but not enough to take the central position away from Henry. He appears in ten of the twenty-three scenes, and he completely dominates the first act, the fourth, which is taken up with the battle of Agincourt, and the fifth, the negotiations for peace. Moreover, in these two plays, as not in the others, the providential disposition of events is strongly suggested: the retributive justice of God seems to operate in *Richard III*, and in *Henry V* a worthy vicegerent of God relies, with complete success, on divine support. Finally, and perhaps most important of all, the way in which the two protagonists are conceived distinguishes these two plays from the others. Each seems to lie outside the scale by which the characters and achievement of the other men and women in the history plays are measured. Distinct from the remarkable gallery of men and women who find themselves swept up in affairs of state, Richard and Henry seem of mythic proportions, not drawn within the normal human scale.

Shakespeare found the outlines of this larger-than-life treatment in his sources. Tillyard remarks of Hall that "two entire reigns he does dramatise in an unusual way, so that they stick out from the whole structure: the reigns of Henry V and Richard III. For Hall, these two are not so much historical personages as Good King and Bad King respectively."[2] Hall was not unique in this respect. In any of the histories which Shakespeare might have consulted he would have found these two depicted as representatives, respectively, of kingly vices and virtues.

The accepted idea of Richard for the sixteenth century was

fixed by a writer of genuis, Thomas More, in his incomplete *History of Richard III*.[3] The other principal source for Richard's reign was Polydore Vergil's *Anglicae Historiae*. The two accounts are somewhat different in emphasis and style, but they are sufficiently compatible so that Hall and Holinshed were able to make up their accounts of Richard in large part by basing their work on More and relying on Vergil for the portions not covered by him. Holinshed used Rastell's edition of More, and so Shakespeare had a good text of More's account though modified by occasional moralizing interpolations.[4] The vividness of More's biography left its mark on Shakespeare. Here is More's account of Richard's appearance and birth:

> Richard the third son [of the Duke of York] was in wit and courage equal with either of them, in body and prowess far under them both, little of stature, ill featured of limbs, crook backed, his left shoulder much higher than his right, hard favored of visage, and such as is in states called warlie [warlike], in other men otherwise, he was malicious, wrathful, envious, and from afore his birth ever froward. It is for truth reported, that the duchess his mother had so much ado in her travail, that she could not be delivered of him uncut; and that he came into the world with the feet forward, as men be born outward, and (as the fame runneth) also not untoothed, whether men of hatred report above the truth, or else that nature changed her course in his beginning, which in the course of his life many things unnaturally committed. [So that the full confluence of these qualities, with the defects of favor and amiable proportion, gave proof to this rule of physiognomy: Distortum vultum sequitor distortio morum.] None evil captain was he in the war, as to which his disposition was more meetly than for peace.[5]

Every detail of this finds a place somewhere in Shakespeare's play. Of his character More writes:

> He was close and secret, a deep dissembler, lowly of countenance, arrogant of heart, outwardly companionable where he inwardly hated, not letting to kiss whom he thought to

kill: despiteous and cruel, not for evil will alway, but ofter for ambition, and either for the surety or increase of his estate. Friend and foe was much what indifferent, where his advantage grew, he spared no man's death whose life withstood his purpose. He slew with his own hands King Henry the sixth, being prisoner in the Tower, as men constantly said, and that without commandment or knowledge of the king, which would undoubtedly (if he had intended that thing) have appointed that butcherly office to some other, than his own brother. Some wise men also ween, that his drift covertly conveyed, lacked not in helping forth his brother Clarence to his death: which he resisted openly, howbeit somewhat (as men deemed) more faintly than he that were heartily minded to his wealth.[6]

It may be noted that there is a slight but nevertheless significant difference here between More and Shakespeare. More does not positively accuse Richard of responsibility for the killing of Henry VI, and in reviewing the theory that Richard wished Clarence's death in order to succeed Edward if the latter's children were still young, More adds: "But of all this point, there is no certainty, and whoso divineth upon conjecture, may as well shoot too far as too short."[7] Shakespeare resists these qualifications: Richard's complicity in the murder of Clarence is one of the memorable things in the play. It is, in fact, characteristic of Shakespeare's treatment of his sources in this play that any opportunity they offer for mitigation or for rounding out the portrait he rejects. For instance, Holinshed notes that to the lords who attended his coronation "he gave straight charge and commandment, to see their countries well ordered, and that no wrong nor extortion be done to his subjects," and that when certain "Northernmen" took advantage of his favor to behave ruthlessly, "the king was fair to ride thither in his first year, and to put some in execution, and stay the country, or else no small mischief would have ensued."[8] There is no hint of this, or of any other instance of Richard's acts in the public interest, or of his administrative accomplishments in Shakespeare. In the account derived by Holinshed from Hall, Morton, in speaking

to Buckingham, contrasts the "good qualities of the late protector, now called king, so violated and subverted by tyranny,
so changed and altered by usurped authority, so clouded and
shadowed by blind and insatiable ambition: yea and so suddenly
(in manner by a metamorphosis) transformed from politic civility to detestable tyranny."[9] Shakespeare's Richard experiences
no change under the influence of power. The essential Richard
is there from the first lines he utters in 2 *Henry VI*. Shakespeare
found the myth of Richard III in the histories, but he bettered
the instruction. His treatment of his sources makes clear that
what he was trying to do in this play required a rigorous and
deliberate exclusion of anything that would lessen the malignity
of the portrait.[10]

The result is a consistently logical, if somewhat circumscribed, presentation of Richard and his rise to power. J. Dover
Wilson finds it a cause for regret that two such versatile and
deeply humane men of genius as More and Shakespeare should
have converged to produce this brilliant monster: "it is strange,
to some extent exasperating, that this of all plays should be the
joint product of the two greatest minds of the Tudor age, since
it afforded little or no scope for the humanity, tenderness, and
spiritual depth which characterizes them both."[11] It is an interesting and disquieting thought, but the fierce and brilliant con-
centration in both works bespeaks an intensity of intellectual as
well as artistic purpose. What More was probably about is described by his most recent editor in attempting to explain why
the *History of Richard III* was left unfinished:

> The history was an exemplum but, as More must have come
> to see, it was also a handbook. The potentially good mon-
> arch would profit from its powerful depiction of monstrous
> injustice, but it could also teach the potential tyrant much
> about the subtle policy which the later sixteenth century
> would identify as 'Machiavellian'. In 1518, More was per-
> haps no longer sure which lesson Henry VIII might read
> in its pages.[12]

The underlying conception of Shakespeare's *Richard III* was essentially the same as that of More's biography, and it is understandable that the art of More would have left a deep impression. At the center of *Richard III* is the idea of politics divorced from all considerations of humanity or law or conscience, grounded on principles and rules which can be learned like the principles and rules of engineering and then applied without reference to any particular moral, social, or political ends. What gives the play the quality of a myth rather than of a history is that Shakespeare has created an impressive character to fit this conception in every detail and has followed the logic of his premises without deviation or qualification. Shakespeare's play is more uncompromisingly shaped by the controlling idea than is More's biography because, unlike More, he was not under the necessity of bending occasionally to the scruples and critical doubts of a historian.

Beyond the historical materials, Shakespeare was indebted to a number of other influences, and although for some of these Shakespeare provides direct clues and for the others the evidence of their influence lies close to the surface, none of the borrowings remained unmodified and all were brought under the discipline of the central conception. The principal influences besides More's biography were Marlowe's *Tamburlaine*, the medieval morality play character of the Vice, Seneca and the Senecan tyrant, and the popular current notions about Machiavelli.[13] The Marlovian influence, which has been cited for the idea of an imposing, powerful figure who sustains the play and around whom the other characters revolve, is discernible in unmistakable verbal echoes in a speech of Richard's in *3 Henry VI*, urging his father to break his oath and seize the crown by force:

> And, father, do but think
> How sweet a thing it is to wear a crown,
> Within whose circuit is Elysium
> And all that poets feign of bliss and joy.
>
> (1.2.28–31)

These lines recall two celebrated speeches in *Tamburlaine*—
Tamburlaine's speech to Cosroe beginning "The thirst of reign
and sweetness of a crown" and ending "That perfect bliss and
sole felicity, / The sweet fruition of an earthly crown," and his
apostrophe to beauty and Zenocrate, beginning "If all the pens
that ever poets held." By the time Richard appears for his opening soliloquy in *Richard III*, however, this hint of godlike aspiration is lost. It has, in fact, already disappeared in *3 Henry VI*,
for the exaltation in the quest for empire suggested in Richard's
speech to his father is, two acts later, changed to torment:

> And I,—like one lost in a thorny wood,
> That rents the thorns and is rent with the thorns,
> Seeking a way, and straying from the way;
> Not knowing how to find the open air,
> But toiling desperately to find it out—
> Torment myself to catch the English crown:
> And from that torment I will free myself,
> Or hew my way out with a bloody axe.
>
> (3.2.174–81)

Just about everything, in fact, that is essential to the idea of
Tamburlaine's character is reversed in Richard. Tamburlaine
amazes with his majesty: Theridamas yields himself and his
men to him because at first sight he recognizes Tamburlaine to
be a man embellished with "nature's pride and richest furni-
ture," capable of daring the gods themselves. The aspiration
which drives Tamburlaine is something which he shares with
Jove who overthrew his father Ops, and the thirst for empire is
thus wholly natural:

> Nature that framed us of four elements
> Warring within our breasts for regiment,
> Doth teach us all to have aspiring minds.

Even if it eventually means butchering the vigins of Zenocrate's
native city, the impulse to seize power is no different, he suggests, from that which moves the mind to "measure every wan-
dering planet's course" or climb "after knowledge infinite."

The idea underlying Richard's character is the opposite of this. The impulse that drives Richard to the crown against all social, moral, and humane restraints is depicted as unmistakably unnatural, and whereas the images which enhance Tamburlaine are derived from pagan deities and the starry heavens, those associated with Richard are satanic and ugly—"hell's black intelligencer," "bottled spider," and the like.[14] The fascination which Tamburlaine exercises over Theridamas is majestic, that by which Richard wins over poor Anne is the fascination of a serpent; and whereas Tamburlaine presents himself as he is to Theridamas, Richard's performance before Anne is deceitful, underhanded, and sly. Tamburlaine triumphs by the force of his arms and the attractive power of his will; Richard employs the devious, deceitful wiles of an unscrupulous politician. And while Tamburlaine is publicly indifferent to laws and traditions of state which stand in his way, Richard pretends to respect these in order to defraud those who still entertain some respect for them. What the two have in common—the element which Shakespeare probably owed to Marlowe—is that they are both driven by a lust for power, and tower above the others in the world in which they have their being. But in *Richard III* Shakespeare divested the demonic aspiration for power of all its glamor.

The association of Richard with guile and Satanic images represents a tie with another and totally different dramatic tradition, the late medieval morality play. For this element, Shakespeare provides the clue in Richard's aside during the scene in which he is trying to circumvent the suspicion and curiosity of the prince: "Thus like the formal Vice, Iniquity, / I moralize two meanings in one word" (3.1.82–83). Some aspects of Richard's behavior show a marked similarity with this old native theatrical tradition of the Vice, notably his continual shifting to suit the occasion and the victim, and his gloating self-revelations as though inviting the audience to share with him his delight in his cunning practice.[15] Moreover, Richard has in common with the Vice an irrepressible comic vein and a taste for irony. There are two important differences, however, both of them the consequence of bending an old dramatic convention to the central idea about Richard. The Vice, unlike the personifications of particular vices which may be represented among the characters in a morality play, is generalized, undifferentiated evil, and thus a free-lance figure among the other characters. Having no special vocation, he simply takes delight in tempting and ruining as a pleasant activity for its own sake. Richard also shows evident pleasure in tricking his victims, but his attack on them is guided by a settled purpose.[16] Though there is an ebullience about his style, he does not usually waste any effort or indulge in useless intrigue. Hence, his vice is not undifferentiated. His goal is power and empire and his genuis is political, and the form of the malignity he visits on his kingdom is therefore political.

The literary antecedent most closely associated with the political aspect of *Richard III* is Seneca, whose plays were the classic source of the tyrant figure in the drama. It is not an accident that there are more traces of the Senecan idiom and manner in *Richard III* than in any of the other history plays.[17] As far as the character of Richard is concerned, however, the Senecan tyrant was submerged by an important influence to which Shakespeare gives us the clue in *3 Henry VI* when, at the triumphant climax to his long and tortured monologue, Richard boasts that he can "set the murderous Machiavel to school" (3.2.193).

It was well-nigh inevitable that somewhere in his comprehensive gallery of political figures Shakespeare would have produced a full-length portrait of the Machiavellian virtuoso. Whether he knew *The Prince* at first hand is beyond reasonable conjecture, and is in any case not significant for the matter under discussion. Neither the author's name nor what he stood for could well be avoided during Shakespeare's day. The political activity within and between states during the sixteenth century was of an intensity and ruthlessness to which the label Machiavellian was often attached, and certain statesmen and political opportunists of the age who gained notoriety for their cunning and presumed lack of Christian scruple were believed to have gained their art from studying *The Prince*. Such types are alluded to in the prologue to *The Jew of Malta*, spoken by Machiavelli:

> Admired I am by those that hate me most:
> Though some speak openly against my books,
> Yet still they read me, and thereby gain
> To Peter's chair.

The pious hypocrisy attributed to these politicians in Marlowe's lines was a common feature of the Machiavellian villain who was becoming a stock figure in the drama.

The popular idea of Machiavelli was in many respects a misconstruction, often approaching parody and not based on knowledge of the original work itself. Machiavelli, a product as well as a victim of the complicated early-sixteenth-century struggle for power between the Italian cities and their predatory allies, France and Spain, attempted to reduce his experiences to a system of how power is acquired and managed, and did this so dispassionately that he earned the praise of Bacon for having described men not as they ought to be but as they are. It enhanced the notoriety of *The Prince* that it was written with detachment and in an aphoristic, quotable (and misquotable) style that makes it fascinating even today—it has something of the appeal of La Rochefoucauld's maxims. Machiavelli had formulated the rules of political practice as an instrument to be used for the good of the state, especially for the political salvation of his native Florence. He did not recommend *Schreklichkeit*, and indeed he repudiated everything that popular Machiavellianism was later to identify with his name. Commenting on the career of Agathocles, he wrote, "Yet it cannot be called true prowess to kill his fellow citizens, to betray his friends, to be without faith, without pity, without religion; such courses enable one to gain dominion, but not glory." [18] *The Prince*, however, does not aim to provide the means for achieving glory, but dominion. It prescribes how to acquire power and exercise it. Like any science, it can propound principles and instruct in their use, but it cannot prescribe proper ends except by way of admonition, which anyone is free to disregard if he wishes. *The Prince* taught how power may be gained over other men without regard to humanitarian and ethical considerations. It did not specify that only a political figure who aimed to be head of state with the purpose of governing wisely and well is to make use of these teachings; indeed, it could not do so. The popularizers instinctively grasped this feature of *The Prince*, whether they had read it or not. They created a grotesque image of the original, but underlying it was the important realization that such a science can be used by anyone, that it provides means without prescribing ways of limiting them to good ends alone, and that in any case even with the noblest ends in view it calmly proposes the use of means that violate the requirements of the individual moral life.[19]

The popular idea of the Machiavellian figure is embodied in the colorful sketch which concludes Richard's long soliloquy in *3 Henry VI*:

> Why, I can smile, and murder whiles I smile,
> And cry "Content" to that which grieves my heart,
> And wet my cheeks with artificial tears,
> And frame my face to all occasions.
> I'll drown more sailors than the mermaid shall;
> I'll slay more gazers than the basilisk;
> I'll play the orator as well as Nestor,
> Deceive more slily than Ulysses could,
> And, like another Sinon, take another Troy.
> I can add colors to the chameleon,
> Change shapes with Proteus for advantages,
> And set the murderous Machiavel to school.
> Can I do this, and cannot get a crown?
> Tut, were it farther off, I'd pluck it down.
>   (3.2.182–95)

The comparable passage in *Richard III* is less flamboyant, more calculated, precise, and professional:

> I do the wrong, and first begin to brawl.
> The secret mischiefs that I set abroach
> I lay unto the grievous charge of others.

Clarence, who I indeed have cast in darkness,
I do beweep to many simple gulls,
Namely to Derby, Hastings, Buckingham,
And tell them 'tis the Queen and her allies
That stir the King against the duke my brother.
Now they believe it, and withal whet me
To be revenged on Rivers, Dorset, Grey.
But then I sigh, and, with a piece of Scripture,
Tell them that God bids us do good for evil;
And thus I clothe my naked villainy
With odd old ends stolen forth of holy writ,
And seem a saint when most I play the devil.

(1.3.324–38)

Richard is associated with a few other marks of the popular idea of a Machiavellian villain. He is said to rule by fear, a charge made against him by Richmond: "He hath no friends but what are friends for fear, / Which in his dearest need will fly from him" (5.2.20–21). Richmond also accuses him of the practice of using and then destroying his agents: "One that made means to come by what he hath / And slaughtered those that were the means to help him" (5.3.249–50). However, Richard's character is not simply built up out of such familiar bits and pieces of the conventional image and stage bogey of the Machiavel. In the very opening soliloquy Shakespeare exposes the deformities and deep-seated resentments which might serve as the driving force behind so prodigious a career. Shakespeare's Richard is the realization in human form of the implications of political Machiavellianism. He is the embodiment of political genius with a lust for power, mastery of the calculus by which men are manipulated and power is gained, and total disregard of humanitarian and ethical considerations.[20]

What would such a man be like? Richard provides one important clue in the two soliloquies quoted above. He would have to be a chronic hypocrite, since his chief political resource must be a talent for deception. To reveal himself in his true colors would be to expose his secret plans and interfere with his method of using others as unwitting agents of his purpose. And so he never reveals his character; he projects an image, and usually an image that is of necessity at odds with the true nature beneath.[21] Richard's self-characterizations in both *3 Henry VI* and *Richard III* make a virtue of these qualities. Because the Machiavel must have a gift for dissimulation, Shakespeare makes Richard a talented actor: witness his pretense of friendship to Clarence—"But what's the matter, Clarence? May I know?" (1.1.51); his pose of bluff candor and honesty—"Cannot a plain man live and think no harm / But thus his simple truth must be abused . . . ?" (1.3.51–52); the charade of piety with the priests (3.7.92 ff.); and the extraordinary performance at the council scene in which he fools Hastings with the disarming request to the bishop for strawberries and then suddenly changes to accusations of witchcraft and treason which send Hastings to his death (3.4). Even when he is being forthright he is dissembling. He does not conceal his unfriendliness from the queen and her relatives, because in this way he manages to keep alive the old quarrels among the nobles and to disturb the peace arranged by the dying Edward. But even here he is playing a role. He stands against the Woodvilles as the injured party, as the man who was the packhorse in Edward's great affairs and is now being discarded by that ambitious clan: " 'Tis time to speak; my pains are quite forgot" (1.3.117). He attacks them in the guise of a blunt, honest fellow trying to protect himself against shrewd, unscrupulous people, and in this role can even play the penitent before old Queen Margaret whom he, among the rest, had wronged (1.3.306 ff.).[22]

Before what appreciative audience can such a talented actor perform? Richard II could monarchize before his entire nation; Richard III can perform only for himself. Even from Buckingham, the man who becomes for a time his close collaborator, he cannot earn the full measure of applause for his performances, because he allows Buckingham to think of himself as the initial mover:

> My other self, my counsel's consistory,
> My oracle, my prophet, my dear cousin;
> I, as a child, will go by thy direction.
>
> (2.2.151–53)

So he must be his own best audience and applaud himself. He gloats over his success with Anne, and when the deceived Clarence goes on to prison, and to death, he says to himself,

> Simple, plain Clarence; I do love thee so
> That I will shortly send thy soul to heaven,
> If heaven will take the present at our hands.
>
> (1.1.118–20)

Irony is one of the ways in which he expresses his appreciation of his talents. In More's biography, the irony is in More; in *Richard III*, it is in Richard. And it finds expression not simply in his self-indulgent asides but in those innocent-seeming speeches in which the surface meaning conceals a sinister private meaning, as in his friendly reassurance to Clarence:

> Well, your imprisonment shall not be long;
> I will deliver you, or else lie for you.
> Meantime, have patience.
>
> (1.1.114–16)

The soliloquy and the aside are from the beginning a principal dramatic device for displaying the character. Since Richard is a dissimulator, these conventional devices are useful in making his actions and motives apparent to the audience, but simple exposition is never their sole effect. "I do the wrong, and first begin to brawl" (1.3.24), he begins simply enough, but as he continues in the exposition of his plans and methods, the tone becomes more zestful: "But then I sigh, and, with a piece of Scripture / Tell them that God bids us do good for evil" (1.3.334–35). It sounds like an actor explaining the staging of one of his favorite scenes. The soliloquies and asides are not deeply introspective, but they nevertheless reveal the man, his contempt for his victims, his sense of style and his delight in success—"Was ever woman in this humor wooed? / Was ever woman in this humor won?" (1.2.228–29).[23]

Richard could enjoy no other adulation as much as his own, because implicit in his delight is a mocking scorn of others. It was Shakespeare's brilliant insight into the Machiavellian idea that a solemn practitioner of the art of *Realpolitik* is fit only for commonplace theatrical intrigues and melodramatic mugging, and that to realize imaginatively the complete Machiavel on the grand scale there must be included a sense of comedy, if only because such a titan of intrigue and dissimulation will always perceive the grotesque disproportion between the puny victim's view of the situation and the intriguer's true estimate of it.[24] The Machiavel can entertain at best a mean view of human nature, for since his success depends on his ability to manipulate others to suit his designs, he can never consider them as anything but inferior objects whose own purposes and feelings cannot matter. He is therefore free of those involvements of sentiment which interfere with a comic response. If a good man perceives that all decent people, and even those who have some limit on their capacity for evil, are fools among knaves, he must, like Swift, express his feelings through pity or indignation, and if his response takes the form of humor the result will be savage satire. But one who capitalizes on this knowledge to make himself the king of knaves will regard others as the dupes of his plans, the objects of his scorn and wit. Seldom does Richard indulge in a display of his talents for the sheer delight of it, but in the first scene Shakespeare introduces such a moment, perhaps to give the audience an open demonstration of the talents that his hero will put to more serious and covert uses later. Brakenbury, conveying Clarence to the Tower under instructions not to permit anyone to talk with the prisoner, is nervous about Gloucester's conversation and the direction the talk is taking, and he objects in some embarrassment. Richard pretends to be considerate of Brakenbury's predicament and protests the innocence of their remarks:

Richard. Even so? An't please your worship, Brakenbury,
You may partake of anything we say.
We speak no treason, man; we say the King
Is wise and virtuous, and his noble queen
Well struck in years, fair, and not jealous;
We say that Shore's wife hath a pretty foot,
A cherry lip, a bonny eye, a passing pleasing tongue;
And that the Queen's kindred are made gentlefolks.
How say you, sir? Can you deny all this?

Brakenbury. With this, my lord, myself have nought to do.

Richard. Naught to do with Mistress Shore? I tell thee,
    fellow,
He that hath naught to do with her, excepting one,
Were best to do it secretly alone.

Brakenbury. What one, my lord?

Richard. Her husband, knave. Wouldst thou betray me?
                         (1.1.88–102)

It is a fine performance, but in one sense not a characteristic one, for Richard does not usually waste his talents in demonstrations of his virtuosity, and here the victim is made aware that he is being played with. The true victim must be deceived, and will learn what is going on, if he ever does, only when he discovers the grim joke that has been played on him.

There is, in fact, something of the practical joker and confidence man about Richard—and indeed the confidence man is one who makes a profitable profession out of a grim species of practical joke. This is one source of Richard's ironic humor—"poor, simple Clarence." For what is the fate of Clarence but to be the victim of a cruel jest engineered by Richard? Or that of Hastings, lulled into a state of happy security, only to have the thunder fall on him with, "Off with his head"? And what is that elaborate job which Richard and Buckingham pull on the Lord Mayor except a fraudulent sale to a simple-minded man who seems eager to be taken in by such impressive and plausible salesmen? Like a successful con man, Richard works not merely on the simplicity of his victims, but on their willingness to become involved in something shifty because of their own interests.[25] One of the reasons that the machinations do not at once offend our moral sense is that, with the exception of Anne and the princes, there is something discreditable or self-seeking about those he succeeds in using and destroying.[26] Indeed, the totality of his commitment to amoral politics gives him an inverse kind of moral superiority over those who, like Clarence, Hastings, Buckingham, and the Woodvilles, enter the arena of unscrupulous power politics with a few residual ethical reservations. But even as we concede the presence of a kind of perverse justice in the fate of some silly, avaricious victim of a con man, or are amused in spite of ourselves at the plight of the victim of a cleverly engineered practical joke, we cannot be completely comfortable knowing that human nature has been cruelly exposed if not wronged. And in Richard's case we recognize the whole bizarre performance as one which is being played for the most sinister political ends. "The most terrifying kind of tyrant," writes Ian Kott, "is he who has recognized himself as a clown, and the world as a gigantic buffoonery. . . . But buffoonery is not just a set of gestures. Buffoonery is a philosophy, and the highest form of contempt: absolute contempt."[27]

Given this contempt for others, Richard's bid for power can have no other than a selfish purpose, and the possession of the crown is an end in itself. This is an important detail, since it enables Shakespeare to pursue the implications of the Machiavel to its furthest limits. Machiavelli would reject such a goal—the whole immediate purpose of *The Prince* was to show the future ruler of Florence how to acquire the power necessary to deliver the city from political chaos. But, as Bacon observes in "Of Great Place," though "power to do good is the true and lawful end of aspiring," it is also true that "in place there is license to do good and evil." The desire to use power to do good implies a social impulse, a care and concern for others which is at odds with the total contempt which Richard feels for the rest of mankind and which, Shakespeare implies, is inherent in the assumptions underlying the Machiavellian idea of power. The eternal argument about the use of questionable means to gain noble and humane ends, often invoked by political reformers and revolutionaries, can have no meaning for Richard, for unlike these he has no desire to alter the prevailing order except insofar as it stands in his way. As a technician of power, he uses the political forms, myths, and pieties as his steps to the crown, though in the process he violates them all in spirit. This sense of superiority over others and indifference to their welfare frees Richard from any scruple. The best expression of this attitude is in the soliloquy which follows the murder of Henry VI in *3 Henry VI*:

> I have no brother, I am like no brother;
> And this word "love," which graybeards call divine,
> Be resident in men like one another
> And not in me: I am myself alone.
>
> (5.6.80–83)

Tyranny is implicit in the idea "I am myself alone" when it is accompanied by the conviction that others are enfeebled by their humanity and are therefore fit only to be used.

It is an attitude, however, which leads to isolation. A man like Richard cannot have friends. He needs only instruments—even Richard cannot dispense with these and must depend in part on Buckingham and Catesby. If he does confide in anyone, it must be in someone whose capacity to be corrupted he has guessed or who has qualities like his own in an inferior degree. Such a man is Buckingham. As soon as Edward is dead, he seems to sense at once the direction Richard will go (2.2), and he cooperates so well that Richard can say to him, "Thus high by thy advice / And thy assistance, is King Richard seated" (4.2.3–4). Buckingham also has a trace of Richard's wit and his flair for putting on an act, and in that grotesque performance after Hastings' death when they appear "in rotten armor, marvellous ill-favored" to impress on the Mayor the danger they have just survived, he can reassure Richard of his talents in words that the master himself might have uttered:

> Tut, I can counterfeit the deep tragedian,
> Speak and look back, and pry on every side,
> Tremble and start at wagging of a straw,
> Intending deep suspicion: ghastly looks
> Are at my service, like enforced smiles;
> And both are ready in their offices,
> At any time to grace my stratagems.
>
> $(3.5.5-11)$

Buckingham seems another Richard—but not quite. The small trace of the milk of human kindness that Richard detects when Buckingham hesitates at taking part in the murder of the princes is all he needs to discard him:

> none are for me
> That look into me with considerate eyes:
> High reaching Buckingham grows circumspect.
> . . . .
> The deep-revolving witty Buckingham
> No more shall be the neighbor to my counsels:
> Hath he so long held out with me untired
> And stops he now for breath? Well, be it so.
>
> $(4.2.29-31, 42-45)$

There is a splendid logic about the way the parts all fit together in the figure of Richard, all of them inherent in the central conception which controls the play. But it is characteristic of Shakespeare that he goes behind this consistency to suggest how such a monstrous figure could have come into being. Shakespeare has already suggested in the opening soliloquy the psychological basis for Richard's unnatural drives, but what emerges from the three plays is that Richard is a product not only of nature but of the times, that for a Richard to come into being and flourish both must cooperate, and that the deformities which he owed to his prodigious birth were shaped and disciplined for his evil mission by the vicious and fiercely cruel world of strife into which he was born. It is remarkable how, after a mere one or two preliminary strokes on Richard's first appearance in 2 *Henry VI*, Shakespeare realizes in every phrase the full implications of the character who grows in importance until he takes over completely in *Richard III*. It is as though the age of Winchesters and Suffolks, Cliffords and Margarets, Yorks and Warwicks, has suddenly spawned its true genius.

This is the substance of the soliloquy that opens *Richard III*. The delights of peace are not for him; his proper environment is the bruised arms, stern alarums, and dreadful marches of grim-visaged war in which he grew up. That was a world in which his deformities of mind and body were no handicap; in the present one he lacks a vocation:

> Why, I, in this weak piping time of peace,
> Have no delight to pass away the time,
> Unless to spy my shadow in the sun
> And descant on mine own deformity.
> And therefore, since I cannot prove a lover
> To entertain these fair well-spoken days,
> I am determined to prove a villain
> And hate the idle pleasures of these days.
>
> (1.1.24–31)

The opening scenes continually evoke the past like some fearsome inheritance that cannot be shaken off. In the second scene, with Anne, the violent past intrudes physically with the body of the murdered Henry VI; and the appearance of Queen Margaret in the next scene, thrusting herself among the quarreling court factions, brings to the surface the unresolved passions of the Wars of the Roses. All the characters in the first act behave as though the sun of York has not yet dispelled the former ills. They are still living in the shadow of an ugly past, and they all come to recognize in Richard the evil genius that will perpetuate it. Each entry of Richard is a dramatic assertion of his unwillingness to let the legacy of the past die: "Stay, you that bear the corse, and set it down" (1.2.33); "They do me wrong, and I will not endure it! / Who is it that complains unto the King . . . ?" (1.3.42–43); and most startling of all, the con-

trast between the false genial greeting of his entrance to the
gathering at dying Edward's bedside—"Good morrow to my
sovereign king and queen; / And, princely peers, a happy time
of day!" (2.1.46–47)—and the shattering effect of his time bomb,

> Why, madam, have I offered love for this,
> To be so flouted in this royal presence?
> Who knows not that the gentle duke is dead?
> (2.1.77–79)

This impression of a past no one can escape because of Richard
is daringly introduced in the confrontation and courtship of
Anne by Richard, for she, who has supped full with horrors,
behaves like one experiencing a recurrent nightmare in which
such a shocking courtship has come to seem part of the normal
order of things.[28] The same sense of a terrible past that will not
end is summed up by the duchess of York when the news comes
that Richard has taken custody of the princes and sent Rivers,
Grey, and Vaughn to prison:

> Accursed and unquiet wrangling days,
> How many of you have mine eyes beheld!
> My husband lost his life to get the crown,
> And often up and down my sons were tossed,
> For me to joy and weep their gain and loss;
> And being seated, and domestic broils
> Clean overblown, themselves the conquerors,
> Make war upon themselves, brother to brother,
> Blood to blood, self against self. O preposterous
> And frantic outrage, end thy damned spleen,
> Or let me die, to look on death no more!
> (2.4.55–65)

Richard is the most enduring legacy of this past, its purest dis-
tillation. All the others who have been an active part of it are
explicable in terms of simple if reprehensible human drives—
envy, ambition, a sense of being wronged, vengeance. In Richard these, though applicable, seem an inadequate explanation.

He is the thing itself, created by nature to fit these times and refined and disciplined by them so that he can thrive in no other setting.

The unquiet and wrangling days of which Richard is now the *primum mobile* do have an end, however, because what Richard is cannot long survive. Deceit and dissimulation are as essential to him as breathing, but whom, really, does he deceive? Clarence accepts Richard's insincere offer of help and friendship (though a hidden fear of Richard haunts his dream), but his case is desperate and Richard speaks the truth when he puts the initial blame for the arrest on Edward. Hastings is deceived, chiefly because he is so delighted that Richard has destroyed his enemies that he assumes Richard is therefore his friend. And there is the simple overawed Lord Mayor who seems eager to be taken in. As for the rest, Richard is already known from his past as the one who killed Prince Edward, Henry VI's heir, and then murdered Henry in the Tower. The Woodvilles know him as their enemy. His mother, the duchess of York, can no longer believe any good of him. And the princes, young, unspoiled, and sensitive, mistrust and fear him from the start (3.1). The man in the street is not deceived. "O, full of danger is the Duke of Gloucester," says the Third Citizen on the news of Edward's death (2.3.27), and the Scrivener readily sees through the deceit of the indictment of Hastings—"Who is so gross / That cannot see this palpable device?" (3.6.10–11). Dissimulation is his favorite method, and sometimes it works, but Richard commands not because his political cleverness fools everyone all of the time, but largely because he has created an atmosphere of fear. His success is enormous. The almost insuperable barriers between him and the crown which he lists in his soliloquy in *3 Henry VI* give way with an ease that seems to prove the rightness of his methods. But there is one difficulty not dreamt of in his philosophy: the rewards of the goal which consumes him and which calls forth the exercise of all of his great powers are self-limiting. Getting the crown was his great aim, but the use which he could make of his power seemed not to interest

him at all. What, then, is there for Richard to do once he has
the crown? His occupation is gone, and something in Richard
goes with it.

Beginning with the scene after the coronation, the tone
changes. He meets his first reversal—Buckingham does not agree
to undertake the murder of the princes—and his tone becomes
irritable and truculent.[29] The engaging, zestful, witty Richard
belongs to the first half of the play. What now remains for him
to do is to preserve his hold on the throne, and in comparison
with the getting of it, this becomes a futile and joyless vocation.
Compare the gleeful anticipation in the first outline of his
plots (1.1.32–41) with the jaded note in his review of the plan
he proposes to follow after Buckingham hesitates and Stanley
informs him that Dorset has fled to Richmond:

> I must be married to my brother's daughter,
> Or else my kingdom stands on brittle glass.
> Murder her brothers and then marry her!
> Uncertain way of gain! But I am in
> So far in blood that sin will pluck on sin.
> Tear-falling pity dwells not in this eye.
>
> (4.2.60–65)

The word "sin" has an odd sound coming from Richard, yet
this does not seem like the speech of a man satiated with crime,
but one facing boredom. There is a touch of the old Richard
when, cheered by the news of the death of the princes and of
Anne, he goes to ask Elizabeth for her daughter's hand as "a
jolly thriving wooer" (4.3.43), but one has only to recall the
scene of the wooing of Anne to see how lacking in brilliance
this performance is in comparison. As the news of opposition
to him increases he gets confused about orders he has given
and strikes a messenger without waiting to learn that this time
the news is good (4.4.509 ff.). On the eve of battle he remarks,
"Here will I lie tonight; / But where tomorrow? Well, all's one
for that" (5.3.7–8). He asks for wine, and adds, "I have not that
alacrity of spirit / Nor cheer of mind that I was wont to have"

(5.3.74–75). The audacious genius of the opening scenes is scarcely recognizable.

The later portions expose the fallacy in Richard's conviction that he could successfully and permanently separate himself from all other men by virtue of his superiority, his command of the art of gaining power through managing the weaknesses of others, and his freedom from all moral scruple. Ordinary human impulses which he despises act to detach people from him, and though he rules by fear as much as guile, fear is apparently not enough to discourage men from joining in an effort to expel an unnatural monster from their midst. What is even more important, his philosophy of total individualism, "I am myself alone," contains an illusion about himself. After he has gained the crown and the tide slowly begins to turn against him, Richard reveals human limitations such as he has mocked and played with in others. He too can be indecisive, lose his temper, brood, and ask questions. And is it possible that there is a fleeting trace of gentleness, considerateness, and simple courtesy in his behavior on the eve of battle? "Good Norfolk, hie thee to thy charge; / Use careful watch, choose trusty sentinels" (5.3.54–55). There is the merest echo here of Richmond's style with his men, a few lines earlier:

> Good night, good Captain Blunt. Come gentlemen,
> Let us consult upon tomorrow's business.
> Into my tent; the dew is raw and cold.
>
> (5.3.44–46)

Shakespeare seems to be preparing us for the most surprising revelation of all, that, buried deep within him, Richard has the capacity to experience guilt and fear. His unexpected use of the word "sin" was a sign, but it is only when his consciousness is at rest that he discovers himself harboring weaknesses like other men. He awakens from a sleep disturbed by the ghosts of those he has slaughtered, crying,

> Give me another horse! Bind up my wounds!
> Have mercy, Jesu! Soft! I did but dream.
> O coward conscience, how dost thou afflict me!
> (5.3.178–80)

The most astonishing betrayal is the cry, "Have mercy, Jesu," but even in his semiconscious perturbed state, he rushes instinctively to his own defense—"I did but dream," "coward conscience." Nevertheless, the experience impels him to look into himself. The soliloquies which follow, unlike the others, which are largely zestful projections of plots and schemes and expressions of contempt for others, reveal through the stilted rhetoric of the dialogue with himself a despondent confrontation between conscience and the doctrine, "I am myself alone":

> What do I fear? Myself? There's none else by,
> Richard loves Richard.
> . . . .
> Alack, I love myself. Wherefore? For any good
> That I myself have done unto myself?
> O, no! Alas, I rather hate myself
> For hateful deeds committed by myself.
> (5.3.183–84, 188–91)

The thought of all his perjuries, villainies, and murders overwhelms him with a sense of total isolation, for this too is an aspect of being oneself alone:

> I shall despair. There is no creature loves me;
> And if I die, no soul will pity me.
> Nay, wherefore should they, since that I myself
> Find in myself no pity to myself.
> (5.3.201–4)

This extraordinary internal debate is not a prelude to repentance and change. Richard can be betrayed by his dreams to a terrified glimpse into his lower depths and a confession of fears and moral apprehensions which he has in common with other men, but he is incapable of introspection and can therefore always return to himself.[30] With the approach of battle the old audacity returns—here at last is something to do, to give all his mind and spirit to again. The apprehensions following his bad dreams and the flash back of his crimes in the appearance of the ghosts disappear, and as though in defiance of what he has been through he confidently and for the first time publicly proclaims his amoral philosophy of power:

> Go, gentlemen, every man unto his charge.
> Let not our babbling dreams affright our souls;
> Conscience is but a word that cowards use,
> Devised at first to keep the strong in awe.
> Our strong arms be our conscience, swords our law.
> (5.3.308–12)

The dreams which troubled and the conscience which afflicted him are rebutted by being incorporated into his philosophy of uncompromising *Realpolitik*. His address to his soldiers has a good deal of the old animation in its vigorous rhetoric, splendid contempt for the enemy, and rousing call to arms:

> Fight, gentlemen of England! Fight, bold yeomen!
> Draw archers, draw your arrows to the head!
> Spur your proud horses hard, and ride in blood!
> Amaze the welkin with your broken staves!
> (5.3.339–42)

Cowardice in the face of danger would not be consistent with the premises on which the character is drawn, and the same restlessness that drove him to the throne drives him to fearless encounter in battle: "A thousand hearts are great within my bosom" (5.3.348), he exclaims as they move to action. But the one brief scene of battle shows a man not fighting to achieve an overriding aim, but expending himself in an almost purposeless gamble with death. What could success in battle bring him now except continued possession of the crown, to the purposes of which he has always been indifferent? When Catesby comes in for a rescue and offers to help him to a horse, Richard exclaims:

"Slave, I have set my life upon a cast / And I will stand the hazard of the die" (5.4.9–10). His final outcry, "A horse, a horse! My kingdom for a horse" (5.4.13), strikes a note of desperate courage, but somehow also of isolation as well—a king, refusing succor, without a mount, rushing back into the fray with nothing to sustain him except his perverse greatness of spirit.

Shakespeare does not arrange an ending that will allow a conventional response of moral superiority over a bad man, or sentimental gratification over a penitent sinner. It is significant in this connection that Shakespeare makes no use of the confession of guilt and expression of contrition which Holinshed includes in Richard's oration to his "chieftains" before Bosworth Field, in which, after reminding them of their assistance in gaining the crown and assuring them that he has "omitted nothing appertaining to the office of a wise prince," Holinshed's Richard continues:

> And although in the adeption and obtaining of the garland, I being seduced, and provoked by sinister counsel, and diabolical temptation, did commit a wicked and detestable act: yet I have with strict penance and salt tears (as I trust) expiated and clearly purged the same offense: which abominable crime I require you of friendship as clearly to forget, as I daily remember to deplore and lament the same.[31]

The moment of transient fear and remorse in Shakespeare's Richard calls attention to something in what Richard stands for that makes him abnormal and is self-defeating, and it also reveals the chasm that separates the essential Richard from ordinary wicked humanity. Every detail about Richard is believable as having its counterpart in human experience, but what makes him fascinating is that he combines these qualities and capacities in a degree of consistency and magnitude that places him outside the usual human scale of measure and judgment. Richard is Machiavellianism raised to the nth power, but the nth power is realizable only in the imagination. He resembles certain conditions of nature which can be theoretically derived but elude discovery in their perfect form, some absolute zero which nature seems to be approaching as a limit but which escapes realization except in the mind of the scientist. To push the conception of the virtuoso of power to its limits is one way of revealing its full possibilities and discovering its true nature. It is the method by which Shakespeare translates a historical Richard into a political myth. The result is a brilliant tour de force which pictures the fall of its towering figure as something other than tragedy. Richard himself speaks his own epitaph as a tragic hero: "If I die, no one will pity me."

It is an indication of the consistency of the art of *Richard III* that the man who emerges in the last act to destroy Richard is made into an ideal antagonist to fit the mode of the play. The Richmond who emerges briefly in *Richard III* is built up from a few hints derived from his oration before the battle as reported by Holinshed, but he bears only a faint resemblance to the historical Richmond—a man who was cold and distant, who deferred the marriage to Yorkist Elizabeth until he had gained full control and was his own master, who did not have her crowned queen for two years, and who as a master of politics could have set the more flamboyant Richard to school. He had a deserved reputation for moral probity and was attentive to the needs of his nation, but considerable liberties with the full record were necessary to produce the gallant, pious arm of God's justice who is brought in in act 5 to triumph over Richard. The polar opposition between the two is dramatically stated in the scene of the ghosts, as each victim of Richard first haunts the evil genius who took his life, and then blesses the sleeping figure who has come to defeat Richard and save his country. The nemesis of the perfect Machiavellian virtuoso of power is a highly idealized figure, who in a few brief scenes foreshadows the mirror of all Christian kings.

XVI

Two Political Myths:
ii. Henry V

"It is one of the curiosities of literature," writes L. C. Knights, "that *Henry V* should have been seen so often as a simple glorification of the hero-king."[1] It is also one of the curiosities of literature that the heroic view of the play can in our day be undercut with the air of an uncontroversial judgment. Diversity of critical opinion is, certainly, a sign that the plays are very much alive; but in the case of *Henry V* the problem much of the time is to find the same play beneath those criticisms which admire Henry as the image of a great and noble warrior king, and those which condemn him as a cunning and reprehensible politician, an unlikeable character for whom such epithets as "prig" and "cad" are not too strong.[2] The critical debate over Prince Hal and Henry V has acquired an independent fascination of its own, and to the extent that it has done so it stands as a barrier between the serious student of the histories and the play. Coming to terms with the criticism can be a useful step toward coming to terms with *Henry V*.

It has been noted that *Henry V* is unusually susceptible to the fluctuations of taste that affect the fortunes of works of art in popular favor and to differences in temperament which determine individual preferences. It is with this theme that J. Dover Wilson begins his critical introduction to the Cambridge edition of the play: "*Henry V* is a play which men of action have been wont silently to admire, and literary men, at any rate during the last hundred and thirty years, volubly to condemn." Wilson's own appreciation of the play was gained through personal experience with *Henry V* in two great wars. It was at a performance in September, 1914, he tells us, that he "discovered for the first time what it was about. The epic drama of Agincourt matched the temper of the moment."[3] Wilson's edition of *Henry V* appeared in 1947, shortly after England had come through a second and more severe test of its capacity to fight and survive, and the edition bears many marks of this association. It is dedicated "To Field-Marshall Wavell, 'Star of England' in her darkest night"; the speech of Henry at Agincourt is likened to that of Churchill after the Battle of Britain; the similarity in spirit with "The Battle of Malden" and Raleigh's "The Fight of the Revenge" is noted; and there is a reference to the popularity of Olivier's film version, which had appeared in November, 1944. Because of his sympathetic view of the play, Wilson has been able to write persuasively of its merits and in support of a favorable impression of its hero. However, the idea of war as a heroic episode in a nation's history has had a bad time of it since the late nineteenth century, and in the aftermath of each of the world wars in the twentieth the reaction against war has been unusually severe. In these moods, Euripides' *Trojan Women* is more likely to strike a responsive chord than *Henry V*. "Our attitude toward war has changed," writes Michael Quinn, editor of a recent collection of essays about the play. "The experience of two world wars and innumerable other wars, involving innocent civilians as well as fighting men, has made us less nationalistic and even less patriotic, and certainly more pacifist and far less inclined to be enthusiastic about wars of aggression."[4] Such observations are not without value. It does tell us something about *Henry V*, after all, that it is so readily vulnerable to the political climate.[5] There are no special seasons for *Hamlet* or *Richard III*, or for that great epic of war, the *Iliad*. But once we have determined the personal biases of the critic or the political climate of the age, we are left with a kind of *ad hominem* resolution which does not define precisely the critical problem of the play. If a work arouses admiration in some and hostility in others, it cannot be said that the reason lies entirely in the viewer. Making all allowances for the normal amount of eccentricity and critical perversity, such a sharp division of responses among serious critics to an important play cannot be independent of something in the work which produces them.

Those who support the heroic view of *Henry V* have on the whole a simpler time of it. They have the advantage of a straightforward, common-sense approach, and they can either disregard the persistent lack of sympathy on the part of many students of Shakespeare toward the hero, or they can find in the text of the plays sufficient material for a reasonable defense of him against the usual charges. The unsympathetic critics face a more formidable problem. They must demonstrate that a play which on the surface appears to represent its main character as admirable and his conduct as heroic is in fact disapproving of the explicit sentiments and highly critical of the leading character. One ingenious solution, that of Harold Goddard, separates out two levels of meaning and associates each with a different portion of the text: "Through the Choruses, the playwright gives us the popular idea of his hero. In the play, the poet tells the truth about him."[6] This solution actually intensifies the problem, for our normal theatrical expectations are that choruses provide a clue to the "truth" about a play.[7] Goddard's particular resolution of the difficulty, which in any event has not been generally adopted, has however the merit of calling explicit attention to a feature of the critical method common to many unsympathetic discussions of *Henry V*—the necessity of seeking below the surface meaning of the text to discover a "truer" one, which is at odds with it. "In every word of the first scene," writes Henry Howarth in a characteristic vein,

> there is, if we listen, a subtle urgency. Shakespeare tells us that the King's war against France is unjust and unscrupulous. We recollect the second part of *Henry IV*, and we know that Hal . . . has taken on his father's scepter and his father's guile with it. He is acting without delay on the old fox's dying counsel to concoct a war with France and so solidify the nation behind him.[8]

We are thus required to regard *Henry V* as a work of sustained irony, with the inevitable result that the idea of Henry as "the mirror of all Christian kings" appears to be a gigantic put-on which, in its own day, presumably only Shakespeare could have been on to: "What fun," says Goddard of the Salic law speech, "Shakespeare must have had making such a fool of this Archbishop, knowing all the while that his audience would swallow his utterances as grave political wisdom."[9] The clues to such an ironic reading of *Henry V* are not, however, to be found within that play, which manifests none of the usual signs of satirical intention. They are sought for in the two parts of *Henry IV*, which then becomes the guide to the inner meaning of the later play. Howarth asks us to recollect *Henry IV*, and Honor Matthews is even more explicit on this point:

> When *Henry V* is performed by itself it is possible to interpret Henry as sincerely anxious to establish his rightful title to the French crown before declaring war and as genuinely convinced by the archbishop's deliberately tendentious reasoning. But when the earlier play is remembered his motives may be suspect.[10]

Suspect indeed! "Like his father, like Claudius, like Macbeth even, Henry V succeeded in establishing a temporary order on an unsound foundation, but in spite of its glamour it was . . . a mere mockery of the god-given order which had been violated."[11] Once we retrace our steps to the earlier plays, we can arrive at a reductive equation: Henry IV = Henry V = Claudius = Macbeth.

We come inevitably to Richard III or what he stands for: "Hal admits in words his bond to God, but like other 'machiavels' he cultivates deliberate 'non-attachment' to humanity and Shakespeare reveals this both in his words and behaviour."[12] According to John Danby, Henry, as one of Shakespeare's delineations of the realistic successful "new man," is essentially a machiavel:

> In Hal the figure of the machiavel undergoes a further and most surprising development. The full machiavel strategy is retained, but it is machiavelism turned inside out. Hal is the sheep in wolf's clothing, a machiavel of goodness. . . . This is a bold attempt to enlist the machiavel in the ranks of virtue. But virtue itself wilts when it is made the object of machiavellian strategy. It sinks to reputation, and that to the acclamation of one's dupes. The externals have again replaced the internals. To the pseudo-good-fellowship in Hal must be added pseudo-morality.[13]

Danby distinguishes Richard III from Henry by the former's diabolism. Unless, however, we can grant a fundamental distinction between the two on the basis of public spirit and sincerity in public utterance, the difference in their political behavior becomes only one of style. Like Henry, Richard also makes public displays of piety—the scene with the priests, and "O, do not swear, my lord of Buckingham"; like Henry's "I will weep for thee" at the condemnation of Lord Scroop, Richard says of Hastings, whom he has had beheaded, "So dear I loved the man that I must weep"; like Henry, Richard protests that he would not go "against the form of law"; and, like Henry, he proclaims his virtues as a Christian—"Think you we are Turks or infidels?" "Else wherefore breathe I in a Christian land?" (compare Henry's "We are no tyrant but a Christian king"). If we cannot grant Henry sincerity and good will, then all his expressions of piety and social conscience become suspect, and he is only a more urbane and sophisticated—and hence more distasteful—Richard. If on the other hand a fundamental difference does exist, then we cannot describe the universal approbation for him expressed in *Henry V* as "the acclamation of one's dupes." Confronted with such dilemmas, there are critics who ask for a double meaning. John Palmer, for example, thinks of *Henry V* as providing two simultaneous orders of response,

> at once the glorification of a patriot king and an exposure of the wicked futility of his enterprise. . . . Henry is prompted by a subtle father and fortified by the complicity of a politic priest to invade France to save his dynasty. But all is forgotten on the field of Agincourt, where an English king is identified with the valour of simple men whose loyalty consecrates his leadership.[14]

Not quite all is forgotten—the critics seem to remember. And it is, indeed, not easy to think of a "patriot king" as one who knowingly leads his nation to a wicked and futile war, or to believe that the cynical warmonger son of a sly father is the kind of man who could earn the devotion of his country and inspire the kind of loyalty which can win a historic victory over impossible odds. We have not gotten away completely from the ironic *Henry V* with its irreconcilable contradictions.

The crux of the problem is, as these examples illustrate, the relationship of *Henry V* to the two parts of *Henry IV*, since invariably the earlier plays are referred to in support of an attack on the hero of Agincourt. This reliance on the earlier plays is not entirely without justification. In the two *Henry IV* plays Shakespeare has given close attention to the prince, and from these plays there emerges a character that has been growing in interest and complexity, about whose charms and virtues we are not wholly certain, and who is not yet fully enough realized to enable us to enter into all his actions with understanding and sympathy. At the conclusion of Part 2, in his speech to the Chief Justice, he dedicates himself to his high office and resolves to become, with the help of others, the leader of "the best-governed nation." We can begin to feel that we are on the threshold of the fulfillment of a painstaking and potentially exciting dramatic development, and that the play to follow, announced in the epilogue, will be the capstone to this remarkable series and will reveal the completed and fully rounded characterization of the prince now a king and grown to mature manhood. For many admirers of Shakespeare these expectations are not fulfilled, and they turn to the *Henry IV* plays for clues to a consistent understanding of the character of the king. When this approach is zealously applied, *Henry V* emerges as a deliberate undermining of a popular national myth and a devastating criticism of political man, and the best that can be said of its hero king is that he is a political genius whose Machiavellianism is so refined that he can delude a nation into accepting cynical power politics as a benevolent and humane administration of sovereignty. The play thus conceived is one which would defy realization in the theatre. Shakespeare provides no clear signs that he is subverting the image of Henry enshrined by the historians and national tradition, and he is explicit about the model on which he constructs the character of the king. Moreover, Shakespeare's dramatic strategy seems pointedly to suggest that most of what has been painstakingly built up in the characterization of the prince is set aside in *Henry V* in favor of the idol of the histories whose reformation and military success had become legendary. The grounds of our disappointment or admiration must be sought within *Henry V* itself.

Henry V emerges from the pages of the early historians of his reign as a heroic figure without blemish. The note of almost pious admiration reaches a high pitch with Hall:

> This prince was almost the Arabical Phoenix, and amongst his predecessors a very Paragon: for that he amongst all governors, chiefly did remember that a king ought to be a ruler with wit, gravity, circumspection, diligence and constancy, and for that cause to have a rule to him committed, not for an honor, but for an onorarious charge and daily

burden, and not to look so much on other men's livings, as to consider and remember his own doings and proper acts. For which cause, he not too much trusting to the readiness of his own wit, nor to the judgments of his own wavering will, called to his counsel such prudent and politique personages, the which should not only help to ease his charge and pain in supporting the burden of his realm and empire, but also incense and instruct him with such good reasons and fruitful persuasions, that he might shew himself a singular mirror and manifest example of moral virtues and good qualities to his common people and loving subjects.[15]

After a final panegyrical summary of the king's qualifications and virtues he concludes, as though at a loss for words: "What should I say, he was the blazing comet and apparent lantern in his days, he was the mirror of Christendom and the glory of his country, he was the flower of kings past, and a glass to them that would succeed."[16] This left Holinshed with a mark too high to surpass, but he met the challenge with honor:

This Henry was a king, of life without a spot, a prince whom all men loved, and of none disdained, a captain against whom fortune never frowned, nor mischance once spurned, whose people him so severe a justicer both loved and obeyed (and so humane withal) that he left no offense unpunished, nor friendship unrewarded; a terror to rebels, and suppressor of sedition, his virtues notable, his qualities most praiseworthy. . . . For conclusion, a majesty was he that both lived and died a pattern in princehood, a lodestar in honor, and mirror of magnificence: the more highly exalted in his life, the more deeply lamented at his death, and famous to the world alway.[17]

This is not how histories are written, but it is the stuff out of which national heroes are made.

The historical Henry was the kind of man to encourage legend-makers, for even his enemies acknowledged his prowess and his sense of justice. Modern historians, too, can be extravagant in their praises:

> Thus in the reign of Henry V [writes R. B. Mowat], in ten
> short years, England was raised, from almost its lowest point
> to the height of its medieval fame. This was done by a king,
> who came to the throne at the age of twenty-five, and gave
> a jaded, disappointed nation the ideals of peace and order
> at home, of adventure, government and justice abroad. He
> educated the whole nation, and infused it with the spirit of
> his own youth and energy. Like Alexander of Macedon he
> died young, having astonished the world. He left an empire
> that would crumble, but he left an ideal that could never
> die. He permanently raised a whole people to another plane
> of life.[18]

This encomium would have almost satisfied Hall. Most modern
historians, however, have some serious reservations. Charles
Kingsford can write of Henry with admiration, but is nevertheless critical of his aims: "Henry had a fine conception of his duty
as king, but we cannot regret that his dream of a united Christendom and a new Crusade should have failed. The modern order
was not to spring from any restoration of ancient ideals."[19]
Others are more uncompromising: "He did nothing for the
good of England, and the legacy he left her was almost wholly
evil."[20] The sixteenth century can hardly be blamed for lacking the perspective from which it could perceive or understand
such judgments, if only because Henry, fortunate in so many
things, was fortunate also in his early death. He reigned for just
under ten years, more than half of them spent away from England, successfully dividing the French and winning battles and
grim sieges; he died at the age of thirty-five, before it could
become apparent during his own lifetime that his grandiose
plans for a great Christian power were anachronistic, ruinous to
the wealth and manpower of his country, and a legacy of disaster to his heir. The historians were not unmindful of the
disaster which followed, but they could explain it away as de-
layed punishment for the guilt of Henry IV and thus avoid a
serious political evaluation of Henry V's policies and actions.
What the sixteenth century could see was that Henry stood well

above any of the continental rulers and military leaders of his day, that he was admired as well as feared by his foes, and that his exploits were brilliantly executed and heroic. Against this view there were no dissenting voices.

That nothing should be lacking to give the sixteenth-century view of Henry V the authentic legendary touch, all accounts include some mention of the riotous youth of the prince and the remarkable change which came over him when he became king. Modern historians agree that as a young man the prince was not beyond reproach, that he had some differences with his father, and that he impressed everyone with the change he underwent after the death of his father.[21] The more picturesque stories went well beyond the truth and contained a good deal of fabrication. These stories were not used in such a way as to leave the impression that this great man was human after all, but rather to set in striking relief the more than human virtues of the paragon king. This effect was secured by insisting on the suddenness and even the improbability of the change. Hall thus describes the transformation:

> This king, this man was he, which (according to the old proverb) declared and shewed that honors ought to change manners, for incontinent after he was installed in the seige royal, and had received the crown and scepter of the famous and fortunate region, determined with himself to put on the shape of a new man and to use another sort of living, turning insolence and wildness into gravity and soberness, and wavering vice into constant virtue.[22]

The phrase "new man" becomes the motif. Holinshed writes that "he determined to put on him the shape of a new man,"[23] and the phrase appears in Hardynge and Fabyan.[24] In the pre-Shakespearean play, *The Famous Victories of Henry the Fifth*, the prince, suddenly repentant after appearing before his father with a dagger, proclaims, "Even this day, I am born again," and the change in style, tone, and content immediately after this line is so great as to make what follows seem like a different play. The associations of "new man" and "born again" are such as to suggest something approaching a religious and spiritual transformation. The first echoes a familiar passage in Ephesians 4:22–24: "put off concerning the former conversation the old man, which is corrupt according to the deceitful lusts; and be renewed in the spirit of your mind; and that ye put on the new man, which after God is created in righteousness and true holiness." The phrase used in *The Famous Victories* recalls John 3:6–7: "That which is born of the flesh is flesh; and that which is born of the Spirit is spirit. Marvel not that I said unto thee, Ye must be born again." The historians' idea of the new man, of rebirth, marks a separation of the king from his past in such a way as almost to set him up beyond human imperfections. The king was not someone that the prince had grown into by a process of development, through experience and trial which bring wisdom and knowledge, and maturity; what happened to him as a prince becomes no longer relevant to an understanding of him as king. This is why the youthful exploits of the prince could be painted in any colors, for the king in putting on the new man had repudiated his past and had no more connection with it than Paul after the experience on the road to Damascus.

This is the traditional story that Shakespeare inherited, and which in this particular among others he followed, but he did so with a notable difference. In the two *Henry IV* plays the wild prince aspect becomes an unusual and original account of the prince's growth; but in *Henry V* it becomes, as in the sources, the measure of his sudden transformation, and serves to set in relief the emergence of the perfect king which surprised and astonished the nation. Before the king appears in the play, the story of his reformation is the topic of an admiring speech by the archbishop of Canterbury:

> The courses of his youth promised it not.
> The breath no sooner left his father's body
> But that his wildness, mortified in him,
> Seemed to die too; yea, at that very moment

> Consideration like an angel came
> And whipped th' offending Adam out of him,
> Leaving his body as a Paradise
> T' envelop and contain celestial spirits.
>
> (1.1.24–31)

Such words and phrases as "consideration" (repentance), driving out the "offending Adam," and leaving the "body as a Paradise" echo the Bible and the Book of Common Prayer, and convey essentially the same sense of spiritual conversion as "new man" and "born again." [25] The archbishop of Ely suggests an analogy from nature:

> The strawberry grows underneath the nettle,
> And wholesome berries thrive and ripen best
> Neighbored by fruit of baser quality;
> And so the Prince obscured his contemplation
> Under the veil of wildness, which, no doubt,
> Grew like the summer grass, fastest by night,
> Unseen yet crescive in his faculty.
>
> (1.1.60–66)

Canterbury, with some apparent reluctance, accepts this explanation of how the change might have come about:

> It must be so, for miracles have ceased;
> And therefore we must needs admit the means
> How things are perfected.
>
> (1.1.67–69)

The statements are not in any real contradiction to one another. The change that Canterbury describes is presumed possible for any believing man, and is urged by the New Testament. Ely comments on how the preparation for it may have taken place under unlikely but propitious conditions. Both agree on the suddenness and completeness of the change, and, as Canterbury's admiring description of Henry's kingly perfections indicates, the unanticipated emergence of such attributes and virtues is seen as astonishing. The king is effectively separated from the prince just as he is in the historical accounts. For the historians, the transformation of the gay, dissolute prince into the model king created no serious political or narrative consequences; the story of the prince's youthful indiscretions was a mere embellishment on the main legend. For Shakespeare, however, the consequences were drastic. In *1* and *2 Henry IV* the wild youth legend was no mere flourish, but the germ of a major development in the action and in characterization, so that in accepting the idea of a sudden and almost inexplicable transformation to the new man in *Henry V*, he was setting aside the whole conception of the growth of the prince, of how Hal became Henry V, which he had labored in two plays to create. Critics, accustomed to tracing a continuous characterization from play to play, as in the case of Richard III and of Bolingbroke-Henry IV, have generally failed to take notice of the change in dramatic strategy, though it did not escape Tillyard:

> The whole point of the Prince's character was that his con-version was not sudden and that he had been preparing with much deliberation for the coming burden. . . . Shake-speare came to terms with this hopeless situation by jetti-soning the character he had created and substituting one which, though lacking all consistency, satisfied the require-ments both of the chroniclers and of popular tradition.[26]

The character who becomes Henry V on the death of his father in *2 Henry IV* undergoes a fundamental change before appear-ing in *Henry V* as the legendary hero of Agincourt. And there is a commensurate change in dramatic conception: the candidly political and worldly conflicts of *Henry IV* are replaced by a series of stately pageants celebrating the hero of a national myth.

The model on which Shakespeare formed his portrayal of Henry is clearly announced in the chorus to act 2, where Henry is referred to as "the mirror of all Christian kings." The phrase calls to mind the extensive body of writings delineating the qualities of a good king and offering advice for his proper con-duct. What, if any, specific work might have influenced Shakespeare in shaping the character of Henry V is not of itself important; the treatises on the ideal ruler tend to repeat each other, and the common elements of the type could be derived from almost any one of them. J. H. Walter, in his introduction to the Arden edition of the play, has demonstrated how closely Shakespeare based his Henry V on such models in a point-by-point comparison between the qualities demanded by Erasmus and Chelidonius and Henry's principal characteristics as king.[27] Henry is a good Christian and a religious man. He listens to his counselors, whom he has chosen for their learning and wisdom. He is just, and if necessary sternly so. But he can also be merciful. He knows the vanity of ceremony and pomp. His position is lonely and demanding, for though the Christian king should have a human capacity to know his people, he should not demean himself by associating with common persons or run the danger of being abused by flatterers. War is a grave matter and a great evil, and should not be lightly entered upon; Henry warns Canterbury of this and wants to make sure that his cause is just. These are the principal items. The correctness of Henry's conduct can also be supported by other, more secular, treatises of advice for kings. Henry's conduct in the first act conforms to Claude de Seysell's advice that before deciding on hostilities there should be serious consultation and debate concerning the reason for the war, the right to the territories to be claimed, and the justice of the cause, as well as meditation on God's justice against wrongdoers.[28] When victory has been won, Henry, in a manner approved not only by Erasmus but by the best military manuals, attributes the victory to God and orders appropriate religious observances.[29]

From the beginning of the play, Shakespeare points out the direction which his treatment of the story is to take. The opening invocation announces a play on a warlike theme. Canterbury's speech isolates the king from the prince and briefly sets forth the image of the national hero which the historians had established. The reference in the chorus to "the mirror of all Christian kings" points to the ideal qualities with which the monarch was to be endowed as a model king and warrior. It is a clearly defined conception which called for a different kind of play from any that had preceded.

In the first lines of the prologue, Shakespeare makes it clear that he had in mind a work lofty in tone and majestic in scope, for these lines do not derive from the idiom of theatrical prologues but have the unmistakable ring of an invocation to an epic: "O for a Muse of fire, that would ascend / The brightest heaven of invention" (Prologue 1–2). The theme he announces in the prologue is epic in character—a warrior king with "the port of Mars," who is to lead his nation to a victory whose very name has become a legend. The invocation shifts rapidly to apology, as though to concede that the theatre is not a proper frame for an epic action and an epic theme. The choruses which follow are certainly unnecessary as summaries of the action, since this of all plays requires no aid to follow the plot; but they manage to report what is going to happen in a style which is often lively but elevated in manner, as though to provide a handsome pedestal for the ensuing scenes. Some of these choruses read, in fact, like portions of a blank verse epic on Henry V, encouraging vain reflections on the kind of heroic poem Shakespeare might have written instead of the play which has been a disappointment to so many.

The aims set forth in these clues presented formidable difficulties. As the Arden editor puts it:

> Shakespeare's task was not merely to extract material for a play from an epic story, but within the physical limits of the stage and within the admittedly inadequate dramatic convention to give the illusion of an epic whole. In consequence *Henry V* is daringly novel, nothing quite like it had been seen on the stage before.[30]

This general problem had several aspects. Shakespeare was never seriously inhibited by his sources or dramatic models, but a comparison of the materials out of which *Richard III*, a parallel case, was developed with those which formed the starting point for *Henry V* will indicate the advantages of the former. For *Richard III* Shakespeare drew from the most brilliant piece of sixteenth-century English historical writing; he took over and adapted to his purpose certain features of established dramatic traditions, and found inspiration in the innovations of his most brilliant young contemporary, Christopher Marlowe; and he incorporated into the play and the leading character an idea of political power so influential in its day, and ever since, that it has added a word to the language. By way of contrast, the historical accounts which he used for *Henry V* were written in so much awe of the subject as to take on the air of hagiography. The political idea which gave direction to the shaping of the main character was derived from a tradition of earnest treatises on how a good king should conduct himself which even the genius of Erasmus does not enliven for us today. And, finally, he had no dramatic models which he could bend to his purposes and, as the apologetic choruses suggest, no absolute conviction that what the subject required could be accomplished within the conventions of the drama. It is not primarily the physical limitations of the theatre which were troublesome, though Shakespeare refers to these:

> may we cram
> Within this wooden O the very casques
> That did affright the air at Agincourt?
> (Prologue 12–14)

Dramatic magnitude does not depend significantly on grand spectacle, and the point has frequently been made that the wooden O which could contain *King Lear* needs no apology. A more serious problem lay in creating a drama around an image of perfection.

How does one dramatize a model hero who has become a national myth of royal greatness? Swift's observations on why satire comes more easily to a writer than encomium touch indirectly on this problem:

The materials of panegyric being very few in number, have been long since exhausted. For, as health is but one thing and has always been the same, whereas diseases are by thousands, besides new and daily additions; so all the virtues that have been ever in mankind are to be counted upon a few fingers; but their follies and vices are innumerable, and time adds hourly to the heap.[31]

In a dramatic action, interest arises in large part from our becoming involved in how a character will meet a new situation, knowing that, being himself, he must respond in a particular way, but also that in making a choice he is in danger of making one that may lead to failure. A model character that meets each situation in a serious action by exercising exactly the right virtue to insure success and approbation is not responding to challenges with his total imperfect nature, but reacting predictably to opportunities. Narrative interest can be sustained by depicting the progress of such a character through a series of events, and interest in the character can be sustained by arranging a sequence of episodes to illustrate a number of distinctive qualities which together constitute the ideal he exemplifies. The method is not entirely suited to the drama, for while certain traits common to an ideal conception, such as a model king or courtier or man of learning, will all find a proper place in a single book on the subject, it does not follow that they can for that reason be convincingly associated with a single individual as a living man or a believable character. The character of Henry V is a composite.[32]

In our first view of the king, we see him deciding the issue of the French war with his council and with the French ambassadors. In this setting, which is the only time we see him in his native land except for the scene before his departure, he exemplifies the ruler who has chosen grave counselors whose advice he listens to courteously and carefully, the just king who wants to be sure his procedure is lawful, and the patriot king who upholds the honor of his country against foreign insult. Where his rights and national honor are concerned he displays an unsentimental toughness and a disinclination to compromise: "France being ours, we'll bend it to our awe, / Or break it all to pieces" (1.2.224–25). His clergy are shown to be politic, but he conspicuously is not. In this entire scene he is a model of correctness. Just before he leaves for France, Henry displays his sense of firm justice when the conspiracy is discovered and he has to condemn the three men to death, though all are well known to him and Scroop was a close friend and companion. Our next view of him is before Harfleur, urging his troops on with rousing martial rhetoric, and using the same rhetorical skill to threaten the city with all the brutal savagery and awful horrors of total war if it does not surrender peacefully. The tone of this is fiercely unchristian—it has a trace of Tamburlaine's threats before he sets up his black tents, and modern critics are reluctant to forgive the king.[33] But his strategy succeeds, and he accepts the surrender of the city in all mildness: "Use mercy to them all," he proclaims (3.3.54). Shakespeare shows Henry to better advantage here than he appears in Holinshed's account, where the city is sacked and Holinshed describes "the distress whereto the people, then expelled out of their habitations were driven: Inasmuch as parents with their children, young maids and old folk went out of the town gates with heavy hearts (God wot) as put to the present shifts to seek them a new abode."[34] Shakespeare has taken pains here not to damage the impression of the Christian king as a warrior. He is similarly protective of our sensibilities in the matter of the later order to kill the French prisoners. We are not permitted to view, or even to reflect on, any of the unpleasant consequences to the French, whereas in Holinshed we are told of their agony:

> When this dolorous decree, and pitiful proclamation was pronounced, pity it was to see how some Frenchmen were suddenly sticked with daggers, some were brained with poleaxes, some slain with mails, other had their throats cut, and some their bellies paunched, so that in effect, having respect to the great number, few prisoners were saved.[35]

ii. *Henry V*

In the scenes from Harfleur to Agincourt, Shakespeare pictures Henry as a tough and knowledgeable but thoroughly honorable soldier.[36] And in the closing scene following Agincourt, he is shown as a religious and pious man.

With the fifth act, we meet Henry in still another guise. He opens the negotiations for peace in a speech of firmness and dignity, but when he is left alone with Katharine and begins to act the royal wooer, something surprising happens, and if there was any doubt that Shakespeare had left Prince Hal behind, this scene should dispel it. Johnson was puzzled: "I know not why Shakespeare now gives the King nearly such a character as made him formerly ridicule in Percy."[37] Quite unexpectedly, inexplicably, Henry becomes an awkward, blunt fellow—"thou wouldst think I had sold my farm to buy my crown" (5.2.125–26). Even taken at his word he puzzles us in this scene, for the speech in which he protests that he is neither a poet nor a talker runs to some forty lines of coy prose. It does not matter whether one finds this scene charming or a bore. What is significant is that one cannot find the basis for this Henry anywhere in the play. This cannot be the Henry who replies smartly to the French ambassadors:

> We are glad the Dauphin is so pleasant with us;
> His present, and your pains, we thank you for.
> When we have matched our rackets to these balls,
> We will in France, by God's grace, play a set
> Shall strike his father's crown into the hazard.
> (1.2.259–63)

And we have certainly lost the Henry of the oration before Agincourt, whose splendid rhetoric might move one to lament that this play never quite soared into poetry. If we ask where this notion of an unhandsome, tongue-tied king comes from, the answer seems to be that he came directly out of contemporary accounts of the disabilities of soldiers as lovers, lacking in good looks and having no skill in words.[38]

329

It may be said of this, as of the other attitudes Henry assumes, that it is a virtue in a talented and versatile hero to know what the proper line is under any circumstance, but such an interpretation sounds the note of politic expediency which leads to the ironic undermining of the heroic Christian king, even though the latter is the image indicated by all the signs in the play. It is possible to discern certain common elements in the several Henrys, but these are not enough to bind the character into a whole. There are characters in Shakespeare who utter a scant dozen lines and leave their mark on us, and his greatest characters sometimes speak lines which take us by surprise yet help to illuminate everything they have said or done. Henry does not act on us in that way. It is not the whole man we hear at any given moment, but some particular manifestation of an *exemplum*.

The king's actions sometimes produce offense rather than the reaction apparently intended, precisely because we have no deep insight into his character and cannot therefore enter sympathetically into his trials and dilemmas. To suggest a contrast, we do not hear or see Othello agonize over his decision to dismiss Cassio, but we have already been allowed to see enough into his character to understand what this act means to him and why he can do nothing else. We experience no such immediate response with, for example, Henry's order to kill the prisoners, or his refusal to intercede for Bardolph, or his trapping of the traitors, and therefore many readers entertain ill thoughts about the lack of Christian charity and plain humanity on the part of this much-heralded model of perfection. We see the gesture by which an act is accomplished but not the man behind it, and where it is possible to read an act in either of two ways it is more satisfying to see it as a manifestation of human imperfection. The very effortlessness of the king's actions arouses mistrust. Everything comes so easily and readily to this fortunate young man. We do not see him struggle against the dangers of great place, and when he calls for an earnest debate on the justice of his cause, it comes over like a ceremony required by his office. We do not see him tried by the dilemmas which great place imposes on the private man, and so when late in the play he soliloquizes on kingly burdens and the vanity of ceremony, the speech has the effect of an aria on an obligatory theme. It is well within the character of the two parts of *Henry IV* to observe that Prince Hal "carried on Shakespeare's conscious intent to come to terms with contemporary social reality," [39] but it would be entirely inappropriate to apply the same observation to *Henry V* and its hero king. The defect of Henry V as a character in a political play is that he acts as though he has never personally known political sin, never been threatened, or sullied, or even seriously tempted by the evils of sovereign power. Where he must perform an act that might be thought to challenge his right to the title "the mirror of all Christian kings," it can always be shown that he has acted correctly according to the best authorities. The misleading notion of a sly Machiavellian Henry V growing out of *Henry IV* is an understandable product of unsympathetic critics attempting to find a consistent center for this character. Since it is hard to believe in the paragon, it seems sensible to look for the smart operator. There is, one might more properly contend, too little of Prince Hal and his father in the character. All the rich if sometimes contradictory and even unpleasant possibilities which have been built up over two plays are largely set aside in the interest of the hero of Agincourt and the myth of the spotless Christian king who upon his coronation was made new. The reader is not so completely persuaded of the miraculous change as the bishops, and in consequence Henry V turns off more people than does his father, the political man who knew himself for what he was.

It is one consequence of the central conception and the character which develops out of it that the play leaves the impression of a series of notable episodes and moments. Each act is a pageant illustrating one of the major episodes related to the hero's progress as a warrior king. The big scenes seem staged, and the effect is therefore sometimes one of calculation. The episode, for instance, of the uncovering of the traitors allows

Henry the opportunity for a virtuoso performance, but the incident can be turned to his disfavor—and has been—because the management of the proceedings leaves the impression that the king manipulated the situation to entrap the three conspirators into denying mercy for themselves, and hence the king's lament for his friend Scroop seems part of a public occasion, its pathos suspect:

> I will weep for thee;
> For this revolt of thine, methinks, is like
> Another fall of man.
>
> (2.2.140–42)

When this big scene ends, we move on at once, with no residual effect, to the next business—"Now, lords, for France" (2.2.182).

Many of the big speeches, though related to the main theme in one or another way, have the air of set recitations. The occasion for the discourse on order delivered by Exeter and Canterbury (1.2.180–213), often cited in illustration of Shakespeare's belief in the principle of degree, is the need to provide forces at home in order to meet a possible threat from Scotland, yet not only is this long theoretical discourse developed quite independently of any precise application to its occasion, but when, after enlarging on the conventional analogies with music and the beehive, Canterbury concludes, "Therefore to France, my liege!" (1.2.213), the effect is that of a *non sequitur*. The long soliloquy by Henry on the woes of kings and the vanity of ceremony which comes after the talk with the soldiers (4.1.236–90) is on a theme which might reasonably be thought to have been suggested by the occasion, and it is eloquently expressed—fuller and handsomer and more strikingly phrased than the two similar speeches in 2 *Henry IV*: "the tide of pomp / That beats upon the high shore of this world"; the lackey who "Sweats in eye of Phoebus; and all night / Sleeps in Elysium"; "horrid night, the child of hell." Yet the earlier soliloquies on this theme relate the sentiments in a more direct human way to the men who speak them, while the very fullness and rhetorical elegance of this statement intrudes a long, stiff, formal note between the simple humanity of the unusual scene which has just been completed and the more direct and touching response to it in the king's prayer, that his soldiers not be possessed with fear and that the sin of his father not be remembered in this hour of peril. The images are often striking but in a disturbing way:

> Turn him to any cause of policy,
> The Gordian knot of it he will unloose,
> Familiar as his garter.
>
> (1.1.45–47)

The impression of amazed respect breaks down—"garter" reduces "cause of policy" to triviality. It is as if a breach of taste had been committed.[40]

The features of the play which arouse the critical intelligence do not, apparently, stand in the way of a theatrically effective production, and this is a consideration which has been raised against the unsympathetic critics:

> It has been severely criticized by devoted Shakespeareans.
> . . . But it has been a favorite in the theatre. . . . The best
> way to enjoy it is to see it on the stage. . . . His theatre
> magic and his grasp of popular psychology is so sure in
> *Henry V* that a good production can move us too in the
> theatre, where the play belongs.[41]

Can it be said any longer that a play of Shakespeare's belongs *only* in the theatre? The argument from the theatre against the critics of *Henry V* seems at times to be applied with unnecessary force: "The immediate effect in the theatre concerned him [Shakespeare] the most." "No play of Shakespeare's has such a simple unvarying effect. It is absolute proof against the perversity of directors."[42] "Perversity" seems the right word for the comic treatment of the bishops in the second scene of Olivier's handsome and successful film production. In the theatre, there are all those coronation scenes and processions by which producers sought for more than a century to enhance the effect in the theatre by taking advantage of the opportunity the play affords for spectacle. Such embellishments are merely accessories to the essential play. *Henry V* has all the ingredients which in a lively performance can subdue the critical intelligence and appeal to simple emotions which a spectator may discover have been touched, even against his will, particularly when the climate is favorable. And there are eloquent speeches and splendid gestures to provide an attractive actor the opportunity to project a commanding stage presence and create through his own impersonation the image of a coherent character and an impressive action. It is not necessary to argue that a dramatic realization of this play as a heroic epic action can be an effective theatrical experience.[43]

Our experience with Shakespeare, however, is that reading one of his plays or witnessing a performance of it leaves the kind of impression that encourages reflection, and those of his plays which we most admire always seem to reward our efforts to know them better and in the process enlarge our esteem. In the case of *Henry V*, second thoughts are likely to be damaging. Yet even when we think that we have discovered after reflection the possible grounds for our reservations and misgivings, there still remains something puzzling about *Henry V*, a work written during a period of high achievement and designed to bring to completion a remarkable sequence of plays.

Henry V was the concluding play in the cycle of histories in more than one sense. It rounded out the series initiated by *Richard III* by presenting the picture of a successful and popular king, and it also completed the chronological historical pattern and thus brought the entire series back to the opening line of the first play which begins by announcing the death of the great hero king. Irrespective of when or how the series began to take its ultimate shape, the writing of this play became virtually inescapable, and Shakespeare took the unusual step of announcing its forthcoming appearance at the end of *2 Henry IV*. The requirement of Shakespeare's now almost complete design and the claims of a popular historical tradition coincided,

ii. *Henry V*

and it became necessary to dramatize the career of a national heroic myth. The technical difficulties of creating a suitable vehicle for such a character and such an action, pointedly alluded to in the choruses, should not be underestimated, but these, it may be said, were met with fair success. The most serious difficulties were not of a technical nature, but lay well below the surface; and though we can only speculate about them, there are a few clues, and they point to the possibility that by the time he came to write *Henry V* Shakespeare had become impatient with the myth itself.

The making of heroic myths out of a nation's past usually serves the purpose, not simply of glorifying high moments in the nation's history and extolling its traditions, but of embodying in the hero virtues which are believed to be valuable and needful for later times. For sixteenth-century England, hereditary monarchy appeared to be the only reasonable and workable form of government. History, however, provided abundant evidence that, as a way of centralizing and coordinating the authority of the state, it was fraught with difficulties and paradoxes, and this impression was sharpened by the growing power of the king, which was one of the realities of contemporary statecraft. Thanks to her unusual gifts and the special circumstances of her reign, Elizabeth became quite early in her own time the object of legend-making to which the poets contributed. No living person, however, can support a myth about himself over a long lifetime while continually having to meet the daily crises and adversities of a nation and the growing disabilities of age, and indeed the myth can become a serious political burden and a liability to a living statesman. Altogether more useful and viable is a myth which is created upon a historical figure but which speaks to the ideals and emotions of a later day. The making of the Henry V legend began almost immediately after his death, for his brief career lent itself to eulogy and embellishment; but the persistence of the myth was owing to the fact that subsequent events enhanced its appeal. To any later historian looking at the hundred-odd disordered years between the reign of Richard II

335

and the coming of the Tudors, Henry would have appeared as Hall described him, a blazing comet; for during his brief and meteoric career, Henry V provided the one brilliant exemplification of the monarchical idea, a historic demonstration that, given even a dubious title with some popular support, a king who combined genius for rule, courage, love of justice, and the capacity to inspire loyalty could make the monarchical idea work and bring glory to his country.[44] There are several clear signs early in *Henry V* that this is the idea which was to give direction to Shakespeare's dramatization of Henry's reign. Such a treatment of the legend would be consistent with the admiration for Henry as a king which runs through the *Henry VI* trilogy, at the very beginning of the cycle. However, by the time Shakespeare in the course of writing the histories, had come to dramatize the reign of the hero king, he had already produced eight plays (including *King John*) in which political man and the world of power are presented from many angles with a thoroughness and imaginative vividness without parallel in the world's literature. In all these plays, the hard light of Shakespeare's political intelligence illumines every corner. And just ahead lay *Julius Caesar*. At this moment, the notion of an ideal king who had become a national symbol of monarchical perfection and success must have seemed to Shakespeare unreal and lacking in substance.

Shakespeare's sense of historical reality and political truth has little place in this celebration of the national myth of kingship, but it does intrude now and then; for instance, in the politicking of the bishops, the doings of Pistol and his companions who join Henry's expeditionary forces not out of patriotic fervor but to make a dishonest penny out of the opportunity, and in the treachery of the small group of nobles. Shakespeare manages for the most part to keep the king above and thus unsullied by these contaminating elements, though not so unequivocally in the matter of the bishops' offer of money for a war with France to avoid a shock at the very outset from which some readers do not recover. There are, however, two features of the play which in a subtle way have the effect of undermining and questioning the myth itself. The first of these is the references to Falstaff. Most allusions to Hal's riotous youth serve to emphasize the complete separation of the king from the prince, and this could be said even of the death of Falstaff: "Of Falstaff we read only concerning his death. It is a dramatic touch. The King's old life is dead in the person of his boon companion." [45] But the reports of Falstaff's death are not to be so simply disposed of. They introduce, just before the king's departure for France, a haunting note—"The King has killed his heart" (2.1.88). Even the inspired malapropism of the Hostess, "he's in Arthur's bosom" (2.3.9–10), adds a wry pathos to her account of how Falstaff died. And this is not the end of the matter. Falstaff is referred to once again in the midst of the battle of Agincourt. Fluellen, in a laborious comparison between Alexander and Henry, explains to Gower that whereas Alexander the Great killed his friend Cleitus "in his ales and angers," in contrast, "Harry Monmouth, being in his right wits and his good judgments, turned away the fat knight with the great-belly doublet' (4.7.35–50). The battle of Agincourt, where Henry is light-years away from his past and at his heroic best, is certainly an odd place to introduce a defense of Henry's rejection of Falstaff. Though Fluellen speaks it in praise of the king, it is nevertheless just one more pointed reminder, at the very moment of the king's greatest triumph, of the harsh personal act that was demanded by the hero's accession to power. The effect of these allusions to the past, both in a comic context, both set within a picture of royal greatness, is difficult to describe and evaluate, but they do run counter to the dramatic strategy by which the king is separated from the prince. In both instances, the reference is finally turned to Henry's advantage ("The King is a good king," observes Nym [2.1.125]); nevertheless, a shadow is allowed to pass over this model of royal perfection by the pointed recall of the *Henry IV* plays and a humanly disturbing consequence of that misspent youth which was so miraculously set aside and so should now have been forgotten.

337

In the concluding scene another and different sort of implied contrast turns the very glow of optimism and joyful success of the finale into an ironic comment on the myth itself. During the courtship of Katharine, Henry says, "Shall not thou and I, between Saint Dennis and Saint George, compound a boy, half French, half English, that shall go to Constantinople, and take the Turk by the beard?" (5.2.215–18). With the marriage and the other terms agreed upon, the queen of France, just before Henry's final speech which concludes the play, pronounces a benediction on these doings:

> God, the best maker of all marriages,
> Combine your hearts in one, your realms in one!
> As man and wife, being two, are one in love;
> So be there 'twixt your kingdoms such a spousal
> That never may ill office, or fell jealousy,
> Which troubles oft the bed of blessed marriage,
> Thrust in between the paction of these kingdoms
> To make divorce of their incorporate league;
> That English may as French, French Englishmen,
> Receive each other! God speak this Amen!
> (5.2.377–86)

And all join in crying "Amen!" In tone and sentiments this recalls Richmond's final speech in *Richard III*, which also concludes, "God say Amen" and casts a prophetic glow over the coming of the Tudor dynasty. Only, of course, Richmond's benediction on the future, idealized though it is, has support from history, whereas none of the things hopefully anticipated by Henry and fervently prayed for by the queen ever happened, and anyone who had read history or had been attending plays at the Globe knew it. The son was feeble and a pathetic failure, and the two countries wore each other out in bitter and useless fighting. Some recent commentators find in these unhistoric details ironic reference to the curse which the original crime of Bolingbroke had placed on England and which had to be expiated in the fullness of time.[46] This seems an unlikely inference for, as the immediately preceding plays imply, Shakespeare had

338

long since finished with this particular aspect of the providential theme. In the epilogue, in explanation of how Henry's great achievements were erased and wasted away, he calls attention to the infancy of the next king and the many who had the managing of the state. As history, therefore, the happy optimism of the ending is totally unfounded and absurd.

If, however, for one moment, we set history aside and think of the play simply as a dramatic spectacle, we can recognize that, poetically speaking, such an ending is inevitable and dictated by the progress of the fable. If poetry can be considered to be, as the common phrase had it, more philosophical than history, and if, as Bacon put it, poesy "raises the mind and carries it aloft, accommodating the shows of things to the desires of the mind, not (like reason and history) buckling and bowing down the mind to the nature of things,"[47] then a happy and untroubled ending was called for by the logic of the play. A legendary king, endowed by nature and favored by God, conquers a foreign land which he claims as his own, marries the beautiful princess of that realm, and makes an honorable peace with his foes; surely we must therefore grant that he lived happily ever after. That is what this heroic fairy tale imperatively calls for, and with a little help from our imagination we allow the dramatic myth to take us to its proper conclusion. But if we have permitted ourselves to be thus carried away, the epilogue is there to bring us back to earth and reality:

> Thus far, with rough and all-unable pen,
> Our bending author hath pursued the story,
> In little room confining mighty men,
> Mangling by starts the full course of their glory.
> Small time, but in that small, most greatly lived
> This star of England. Fortune made his sword;
> By which, the world's best garden he achieved;
> And of it left his son imperial lord.
> Henry the Sixth, in infant bands crowned King
> Of France and England, did this king succeed;

Whose state so many had the managing,
    That they lost France, and made his England bleed:
Which oft our stage hath shown; and, for their sake,
In your fair minds let this acceptance take.

That is the way things really turned out; the king's buoyant
hopes for his future son, the queen's blessings on the peace and
the marriage which was to seal it, and her prayers for the future
are fit accompaniments for this heroic patriotic spectacle, but are
inconsistent with reality. What we had been seeing was an insub-
stantial pageant. The strongest effects and the most moving moments in *Henry V* are those which arise from its preoccupation
with war, and the subsequent need for peace, but it is not serious
as dramatized history or as an image of the political world. Even
the epilogue deceives us a little, for at his death Henry had by
no means achieved the world's best garden, and what he left his
infant son was an inconclusive war.

   There is to be noted in some commentators on Shakespeare an
uneasy sense of disappointment with the history cycle—a note
struck, for example, by John Danby in his allusion to "the false
conflicts and false solutions of the later histories."[48] If we may
draw an inference from the critical debate over *Henry V*, this
disappointment may in part be attributed to the failure of the
final play in the series to fulfill the sense of promise which its
subject and its position in the series holds out. *2 Henry IV* ends
on a note of muted triumph and expectant hope—Henry IV
manages to retain his crown and pass on the succession to his
son, and in the closing scene the conduct of the prince is exemplary; but the two *Henry IV* plays do not encourage illusions,
and the confidence of the prince at the end does not fully put
to rest questions about the demands of regal authority and the
exercise of power by which he is still to be tested. The success
of the hero of Agincourt, however, does not so much resolve
such questions as evade them. *Henry V* fails us because whereas
the preceding plays are permeated with the ambiguities and
harsh dissonances of the political world, the king in this one is

separated from them and is presented as politically uncontaminated. And, although there is created under the king's leadership a national order and a strong sense of unity, the accomplishment is momentary and holds no promise for the daily struggle of a nation to achieve peace and justice, for this order and unity are achieved in a patriotic war and reach fulfillment on the occasion of a desperate battle. A heroic military victory is one act of state that binds men together though they may have but little in common, and that does not impose any need for repentance and regret on its leader though men must die for it. It calls for the power of a nation in its most uncompromising and violent form, but as an isolated event, a spectacular victory on the field of battle against great odds is, paradoxically, like a momentary return to a state of political innocence. Hence the fairy-tale optimism of *Henry V* does not eclipse or resolve the issues raised by the spectacles of national disorder which preceded it. Above all it does not answer the disquieting and near tragic implications of Henry IV's dilemma, and for that reason *Henry IV* may be regarded as the last serious study of kingship in the cycle.

Richard III is also the dramatic re-creation of a myth and a political idea, but it has its foundations in the realities of power, and its hero, monstrous as he is, represents a danger that continually threatens to come into being and calls to mind historic parallels too actual for comfort. *Henry V* derives from a different kind of myth. It celebrates in its hero a national ideal that bends the facts of history to the services of a concept which is out of touch with the realities of power and which in consequence evades experience and eludes expectation. In the perspective of the plays which preceded it, *Henry V* appears as a theatrically handsome fulfillment of an obligation, performed with skill but without deep conviction.[49]

Notes

Abbreviation of names of periodicals in the notes are those which have become standard in the notes and bibliographies of a number of journals of literary scholarship and criticism (for example, *Shakespeare Quarterly*). For a few frequently cited works, the following abbreviations are used in the notes:

Union. Edward Hall, *The Union of the Two Noble and Illustrate Famelies of Lancastre and Yorke* (London, 1548). The section on Henry VIII after 1532 was completed by Richard Grafton on the basis of Hall's notes. Modern editions are those of Henry Ellis (London, 1809) and Charles Whibley (London, 1904). References in the notes are to the 1550 edition (the title in this edition has Illustre for Illustrate).

Chronicles. Raphael Holinshed, *Chronicles of England, Scotland, and Ireland*, 2 vols. (London, 1577); 3 vols. (London, 1587). The second edition included the work of several collaborators. References in the notes are to the edition of Henry Ellis, 6 vols. (London, 1807–8).

Homilies. Certayne Sermons, or Homelies (London, 1547). Frequently reprinted. In 1571 was added the important "Homilie against Disobedience and Wylfull Rebellion." The text followed here is *Certain Sermons or Homilies Appointed To Be Read in Churches in the Time of Queen Elizabeth of Famous Memory* (London, 1766).

Mirror. A Mirror for Magistrates, compiled and edited by James Baldwin (London, 1559). It was reprinted, with additions in each case, in 1563, 1578, and 1587. The edition used here is that of Lily B. Campbell (Cambridge, 1938), which gives a full account of the growth of the collection and the numerous re-printings.

Line numberings for quotations from Shakespeare's plays are to the Arden Shakespeare in the revised edition, except for *Richard III*, which has not yet appeared in revised form and for which the original edition is used. Quotations do not always follow the Arden text in every detail. The abbreviation, Arden ed., is used throughout the notes in referring to any of the following:

1 Henry VI, ed. Andrew S. Cairncross (London and Cambridge, Mass., 1962).
2 Henry VI, ed. Andrew S. Cairncross (London and Cambridge, Mass., 1957; reprinted with minor corrections, 1962).
3 Henry VI, ed. Andrew S. Cairncross (London and Cambridge, Mass., 1964).
Richard III, ed. A Hamilton Thompson (London, 1907).
Richard II, ed. Peter Ure (London and Cambridge, Mass., 1956).
1 Henry IV, ed. A. R. Humphreys (London and Cambridge, Mass., 1960; reprinted with minor corrections, 1961).
2 Henry IV, ed. A. R. Humphreys (London and Cambridge, Mass., 1966).
Henry V, ed. J. H. Walter (London and Cambridge, Mass., 1954).

The spelling in quotations from sixteenth-century texts has been modernized, except for titles of books.

Preface

1. Quoted in Paul Van Tieghem, *La Découverte de Shakespeare sur le continent* (Paris, 1947), p. 78.

Acknowledgments

1. There is a valuable and judicious review of the scholarship and criticism of the history plays during the first half of the twentieth century by Harold Jenkins, "Shakespeare's History Plays: 1900–1951," *Shakespeare Survey*, VI (Cambridge, 1953), 1–15.

2. Between 1970 and 1972 six books appeared devoted entirely or in large part to the history plays. They are Henry Kelly, *Divine*

Providence in the England of Shakespeare's Histories (Cambridge, Mass., 1970); David Riggs, *Shakespeare's Heroical Histories: "Henry VI" and Its Literary Tradition* (Cambridge, Mass., 1971); Robert Pierce, *Shakespeare's History Plays: The Family and the State* (Columbus, O. 1971); Theodore Weiss, *The Breath of Clowns and Kings* (New York, 1971); John Bromley, *The Shakespearean Kings* (Boulder, Colo., 1971); and Robert Ornstein, *A Kingdom for a Stage* (Cambridge, Mass., 1972). An entire issue of *Studies in the Literary Imagination*, V (1972), 1–162, is devoted to essays on the history plays and contains a review article by Raymond Utterback on all but the last of the books named above. Announced but unavailable at the time the present study was ready for press is a book by Michael Manheim, *The Weak King Dilemma in the Shakespearean History Plays* (Syracuse, N.Y., 1973).

Chapter I

1. *King Lear* and *Macbeth* are in large part based on materials to be found in Holinshed's *Chronicles*, but they are not regarded as English "history" plays. Their stories belong to a legendary past, and though the action involves politics, they are not in the proper sense political plays and are not normally thought of as such. "We do not think of *King Lear* as political," writes F. P. Wilson. "It has a political interest, but it is there only to make possible the human interest" ("The English History Play," *Shakespearian and Other Studies*, ed. Helen Gardner [Oxford, 1969], p. 4).

2. R. A. Law, "Links between Shakespeare's History Plays," *SP*, L (1953), 168–87. E. M. W. Tillyard discusses this article in "Shakespeare's Historical Cycle: Organism or Compilation?" *SP*, LI (1954), 34–39, and there is a rejoinder by Law, *ibid.*, 40–41.

3. Wolfgang Keller, "Shakespeares Königsdramen," *Jahr.*, LXIII (1927), 35. The idea seems to have originated with A. W. Schlegel: "It is, as it were, an historical heroic poem in dramatic form" (*Dramatic Art and Literature*, trans. John Black [London, 1846], p. 419).

4. "In none of the plays is there a hero; and one of the reasons is that there is an unnamed protagonist dominating all four [of the first group]. It is England, or in Morality terms Respublica. . . . England, though she is quite excluded as a character, is the true hero of Shakespeare's first tetralogy" (E. M. W. Tillyard, *Shakespeare's History Plays* [London, 1948], p. 160). H. B. Charlton writes, "The real hero of the English history-play is England" (*Shakespeare, Politics, and Politicians*, English Association, Pamphlet 72 [Oxford, 1929], p. 11).

5. Una Ellis-Fermor, *Frontiers of Drama* (London, 1946), p. 36.

6. Beverley Warner, *English History in Shakespeare's Plays* (New York and London, 1894), p. 7. Almost certainly adapted from Schlegel, *Dramatic Art*, p. 422.

7. S. C. Sen Gupta, *Shakespeare's Historical Plays* (Oxford, 1964), p. 6. See also Joseph Kohler, "Die Staatsidee Shakespeares in *Richard II*," *Jahr.*, LIII (1917), 12.

8. Alvin Kernan, "*The Henriad*: Shakespeare's History Plays," *Modern Shakespearean Criticism* (New York, 1970), p. 245. Kernan observes other parallel transitions: "In political and social terms it is a movement from feudalism and hierarchy to the national state and individualism. In psychological terms it is a passage from a situation in which man knows with certainty who he is to an existential condition in which any identity is only a temporary role. In spatial and temporal terms it is a movement from a closed world to an infinite universe. In mythical terms the passage is from a garden world to a fallen world. In the most summary terms it is a movement from ceremony and ritual to history" (pp. 245–46). Compare, however, Walter Pater: "It is no *Henriade*, no history of the English people, but the sad fortunes of some English kings as conspicuous examples of the ordinary human condition" (*Appreciations* [London, 1927], p. 186).

9. This theme is developed fully by Richard Moulton, *Shakespeare as a Dramatic Artist* (Oxford, 1906).

10. This view of the history plays is associated with Tillyard's influential book, *Shakespeare's History Plays,* and with Lily B. Campbell's *Shakespeare's "Histories": Mirrors of Elizabethan Policy* (San Marino, Calif., 1947). Geoffrey Bullough summarizes the views about the plays which this approach has established and made well known: "If we read the main corpus of the English Histories not in the order in which Shakespeare wrote them but according to their historical chronology, it is easy to agree with Dr. Tillyard and Professor L. B. Campbell that they make a great pageant of moral and political cause and effect beginning with the conflict between Richard II and Bolingbroke and ending with the conflict between Richard III and Henry Richmond" (*Narrative and Dramatic Sources of Shakespeare*; 6 vols. [New York and London, 1957–73], III, 355).

11. The idea of the history plays as political is now fairly commonplace. "The chief interest in a history play," writes F. P. Wilson matter-of-factly, "is political or, with Shakespeare, in character revealing itself in politics" ("English History Play," p. 4). There was

a time not too long ago when this notion would not have been sympathetically received. John Palmer regarded the political content as an accidental consequence of Shakespeare's following public taste: "The Elizabethans expected to find upon the stage kings, princes and generals. The dramatist must therefore fill his scene with political figures. . . . But his [Shakespeare's] characters interested him first and foremost as men; it is an accident that they should be men in public affairs or hoping to be so" (*Political Characters in Shakespeare* [London, 1945], p. vii). In 1949 Brents Stirling thought it necessary to provide a rebuttal for what he assumed to be the current view that if a critic chose "to approach the many sided dramatist from a political point of view, he is likely to be asked whether he thinks of Shakespeare as a pamphleteer" (*The Populace in Shakespeare* [New York, 1949], p. 3). Today he would not have needed to make the point.

12. *Studies in Spenser's Historical Allegory* (Baltimore, Md., 1932), p. 7; see also pp. 83–84. The matter was considerably more involved than it appears in Greenlaw's statement, as Josephine Bennett makes clear in *The Evolution of "The Faerie Queene"* (Chicago, 1942), pp. 61–79.

13. Identification of specific persons and incidents invites ingenuity and speculation, and it does not end in certainty. The pioneer study, and still useful, is that of Richard Simpson in two extensive essays, "The Political Use of the Stage in Shakespeare's Times" and "The Politics of Shakespeare's History Plays," which appeared in *New Shakespeare Society Transactions* (1874). The best of modern studies is Lily Campbell's *Shakespeare's "Histories,"* the interest of which is not confined to its concern for specific identifications. David Bevington, in *Tudor Drama and Politics: A Critical Approach to Topical Meaning* (Cambridge, Mass., 1968), relates English historical drama, including that of Shakespeare, to a more general topicality, involving, for example, political relations with Spain, Catholic intrigues centering on Mary Stuart, and the like.

14. H. M. Richmond, *Shakespeare's Political Plays* (New York, 1967), p. 13.

15. "Shakespeare's political plays are creative explorations of conceptions such as power, authority, honour, order, and freedom, which too easily become objects of idolatory. Their real meaning is only revealed when political life is seen, as Shakespeare makes us see it, in terms of the realities of human life and human relationships" (L. C. Knights, *Further Explorations* [London, 1965], p. 32).

347

Chapter II

1. The references to historiography in this note have been selected with the student of Shakespeare's history plays in mind. General discussions of historiography: Eduard Fueter, *Histoire de l'historiographie moderne*, trans. Emile Jeanmaire (Paris, 1914); J. W. Thompson, *A History of Historical Writing* (New York, 1942); R. G. Collingwood, *The Idea of History* (Oxford, 1946); C. A. Patrides, *The Phoenix and the Ladder: The Rise and Decline of the Christian View of History* (Berkeley, Calif., 1964). Specialized studies: Leonard F. Dean, "Tudor Theories of History Writing," *University of Michigan Contributions to Modern Philology*, no. 1 (1941), pp. 1–24, and "Sir Francis Bacon's Theory of Civil History-Writing," *ELH*, VIII (1941), 161–83; R. Mark Benbow, "The Providential Theory of Historical Causation in Holinshed's *Chronicles: 1577* and *1587*, " *University of Texas Studies in Literature and Language*, I (1959), 264–76; Walter Staton, Jr., "Roger Ascham's Theory of History Writing," *SP*, LVI (1959), 125–37; F. Smith Fussner, *The Historical Revolution: English Historical Thought 1580–1640* (London, 1962); Myron P. Gilmore, *Humanists and Jurists* (Cambridge, Mass., 1963), chs. 1 and 2; Felix Gilbert, *Machiavelli and Guicciardini* (Princeton, N. J., 1965), pp. 203–301; Sidney Alexander, Introduction to his translation of Francesco Guicciardini, *The History of Italy* (New York and London, 1969). Historiography in relation to Shakespeare: Lily B. Campbell, *Shakespeare's "Histories"* (San Marino, Calif., 1947); E. M. W. Tillyard, *Shakespeare's History Plays* (London, 1944); Michael Quinn, "Providence in Shakespeare's Yorkist Plays," *SQ*, X (1959), 44–52; Tom F. Driver, *The Sense of History in Greek and Shakespearean Drama* (New York, 1967); Irving Ribner, *The English History Play*, rev. ed. (London, 1965); Wilbur Sanders, *The Dramatist and the Received Idea* (Cambridge, 1968), pp. 72–120; Henry Kelly, *Divine Providence in the England of Shakespeare's Histories* (Cambridge, Mass., 1970); David Riggs, *Shakespeare's Heroical Histories: "Henry VI" and Its Literary Tradition* (Cambridge, Mass., 1971). For a brief review of the development of the idea of the "Tudor myth" see Robert Ornstein, *A Kingdom for a Stage* (Cambridge, Mass., 1972), pp. 14–16.

2. *Shakespeare's History Plays* (London, 1948), pp. 200–201.

3. *Ibid.*, p. 165.

4. *Ibid.*, p. 291.

5. Ribner says of the limitations of Tillyard's study, "There were other schools of historiography in Elizabethan England. The providential history of Hall, in fact, represents a tradition which, when

Shakespeare was writing, was already in decline" (*English History Play*, p. 10). Benbow notes that the chroniclers generally limited the scope of their providentialism: "While we can find examples of retributive justice throughout the earlier histories, we do not so often discover the concept of a teleological providence" (*Texas Studies in Lit. and Lang.*, I [1959], 272). The most recent studies tend to play down the providential implications of sixteenth-century English historians. Kelly, *Divine Providence*, p. 160: "Neither Vergil nor Holinshed regards the troubles of the Wars of the Roses as punishment sent by God upon England; nor do they regard the advent of Henry Tudor as reflecting a decision on God's part to bring an end to the punishment he had been dealing out to England." Ornstein, *Kingdom for a Stage*, p. 16: "There is very good reason to doubt that Shakespeare wrote his tetralogies to set forth what Tillyard calls the Tudor myth of history. There is reason also to question whether the view of history which Tillyard sets forth as the Tudor myth was in fact the Tudor myth and can be attributed as such to Hall." Riggs questions the susceptibility of the dramatists to the providential theory: "A humanistic approach to history came intuitively to the Elizabethan dramatists, while the providentialism of the chroniclers, with its tendency to minimize the possibility of individual achievement, was more the exception than the rule" (*Shakespeare's Heroical Histories*, p. 33).

6. For the widespread diffusion of the classical idea of history during the sixteenth century, see Campbell, *Shakespeare's "Histories,"* pp. 18–84. Riggs, *Shakespeare's Heroical Histories*, traces the humanistic idea of history which underlies Elizabethan historical plays to the study of rhetoric and the use of commonplace books, "in the rhetorical topics and styles used to define and express the attributes of great men" (p. 23). The artistic development, according to Riggs, begins with Marlowe (p. 36).

7. "From classical time truthfulness has been acclaimed as the 'first law of history,' but by writers with such diverse basic philosophies that they virtually contradict each other. . . . During the Renaissance the meaning of historical truthfulness was progressively particularized. Not only were religious and secular 'truth' separated, but there were formulated, following the classics, increasingly explicit directions for the achievement of secular truthfulness" (Dean, *ELH*, VIII [1941], 166).

8. Since More's biography of Richard III is unfinished there is no way of knowing whether he would have attributed the victory of Richmond and his marriage with Edward IV's daughter to God's providence, as do all other accounts.

9. *Union*, section on Henry IV, fol. ix verso. A striking example of Hall's momentary desertion of the providential view is his com-

ment on Henry V's sense of security after the execution of the three conspirators against his life: "The king thought surely in his conceit all sedition to be drowned and utterly extinct. But if he had cast his eye to the fire that was newly kindled, he should have surely seen an horrible flame incensed against the walls of his own house and family by the which in conclusion his line and stock was clean destroyed and consumed to ashes, which fire at that very time peradventure might have been quenched and put out . . . which thing, if King Henry had foreseen I doubt whether ever that line [of York] should have either claimed the garland or gained the game" (fol. xii verso).

10. *Ibid.*, section on Richard III, fol i.

11. *Three Books of Polydore Vergil's English History*, from an early translation, ed. Henry Ellis, Camden Society, XXIX (London, 1844), 83.

12. Guicciardini, *History of Italy*, p. 3.

13. *Ibid.*, p. 83.

14. *Ibid.*, p. 56.

15. *Ibid.*, pp. 329–31.

16. *Ibid.*, p. 385.

17. Niccolo Machiavelli, *Florentine History*, trans. W. K. Marriott (London and New York, 1912), p. 339.

18. Philippe de Comines, *Memoirs*, trans. Andrew Scoble (London, 1911), bk. 5, ch. 18.

19. *Ibid.*

20. *Ibid.*, bk. 5, ch. 20.

21. *Ibid.*, bk. 7, ch. 1.

22. Comines' most recent French editor writes: "Il nous donne . . . la sensation exacte du croisement incessant de ces 'marches', de ces 'besongnes' dont se tisse la trame de la politique quattrocentiste, aussi bien au pays de Commynes qu'au pays de Machiavel. Les sentences morales, voire pieuses, dont l'auteur des *Mémoires* aime à parsemer son développement, n'y contradisent point" (*Mémoires*, ed. Joseph Calmette [Paris, 1924], I, xvi-xvii).

23. *Idea of History*, p. 48.

24. *History of Italy*, p. 56.

25. *Ibid.*, pp. 101–2. On Guicciardini's views on fortune and reason in history see Alexander, Introduction to *History of Italy*, pp. xvii–xviii, and Mario Domandi, Introduction to his translation of Guicciardini's *History of Florence* (New York, 1970). On Machiavelli see Allan Gilbert, *Machiavelli's Prince and Its Forerunners* (Durham, N.C., 1938), pp. 204–21.

26. It is usual to associate the idea of providence in history with medieval and certain Renaissance historians. However, as a philosophical concept it continued to be useful to later writers. Alexis de Tocqueville, looking back from the establishment of democracy in America to the gradual enlargement of the "equality of condition" during some seven hundred years of European history, can find no other explanation for the persistence of this phenomenon against so many impediments to success: "Whithersoever we turn our eyes, we shall witness the same continual revolution throughout the whole of Christendom. The various occurrences of national existence have everywhere turned to the advantage of democracy; all men have aided it by their exertions: those who have intentionally labored in its cause, and those who have served it unwittingly; those who have fought for it, and those who have declared themselves its opponents, have all been driven along the same track, have all labored to one end, some ignorantly and some unwillingly; all have been blind instruments in the hands of God. The gradual development of the equality of conditions is therefore a providential fact, and it possesses all the chief characteristics of a Divine decree: it is universal, it is durable, it constantly eludes all human interference, and all events as well as all men contribute to its progress." The whole book, he tells us, was "written under the impression of a kind of religious dread produced in the author's mind by the contemplation of so irresistible a revolution, which has advanced for centuries in spite of such amazing obstacles, and which is still proceeding in the midst of the ruins it has made." Nations that resisted this change would be resisting the will of God, and "would then be constrained to make the best of the social lot awarded them by Providence" (*Democracy in America*, trans. Henry Reeve [New York, 1899], pp. xxxii–xxxiv). De Tocqueville's providential sentiments can hardly be accounted for by the familiar notion that they represent an unthinking survival of medieval ways of thought and feeling of which the later age had not yet purged itself.

27. *Union*, section on Edward IV, fols. xxi–xxi verso.

28. *Ibid.*, fol. xxxiv verso. Polydore Vergil reminds the reader of Henry's heavenly joys: "Such was the pleasure of God, that King Henry, a most holy man, should by so many calamities, wherewithal he was continually afflicted, be deprived of this earthly kingdom to

enjoy forthwith the everlasting: for a good man can never be but good, though he suffer a thousand afflictions" (*English History*, p. 108).

29. *History of Italy*, p. 166.

30. Vergil, *English History*, pp. 189–90; Hall, *Union*, section on Richard III, fol. v; Holinshed, *Chronicles*, III, 477–78.

31. *Works*, ed. Ellis, Spedding, and Heath (Boston, 1860–64), XI, 444–45.

32. *Ibid.*, XI, 453.

33. *Ibid.*, XI, 45.

34. *English History*, for example, pp. 135, 197, 214.

35. Ed. John Bruce (London, 1838), pp. 13, 1. Henry Kelly points out that in early histories of England the way in which providence is shown to manifest itself is determined by one of three biases—the Lancastrian myth, the Yorkist myth, and the Tudor myth (*Divine Providence*, pp. 9–81).

36. *The History of the World* (Edinburgh, 1820), I, xxiv–xv. Raleigh's history, written in prison, is as much his consolation of philosophy as his political testament. The preface, ostensibly a review of commonplaces about the nature and uses of history, is a moving personal statement of one who faces "the shipwreck of worldly things, where all sinks but the sorrow" (I, xl).

37. *The Idea of Perfect History* (Urbana, Ill., 1970), pp. 170–80, 210–12.

38. *Idea of History*, pp. 55–56.

39. P. 1.

40. William Camden, *The History of the Most Renowned and Victorious Princess Elizabeth, Late Queen of England*, 3d ed. (London, 1675), sg. b2.

41. In *The Complete Works of St. Thomas More*, ed. Richard Sylvester (New Haven, Conn., and London, 1963), II, 91.

42. *Mirror*, p. 198.

43. *Ibid.*, p. 178.

44. *Ibid.*, p. 65.

45. *Ibid.*, p. 64.

46. *Ibid.*, pp. 65–66.

47. *Union*, section Edward IV, fol. vi.

48. Tillyard, *Shakespeare's History Plays*, p. 146.

Chapter III

1. There is increasing skepticism concerning the validity of the providential idea as a significant feature of the *Henry VI* trilogy. J. P. Brockbank: "The plays of *Henry VI* are not, as it were, haunted by the ghost of Richard II, and the catastrophes of the civil wars are not laid to Bolingbroke's charge; the catastrophic virtue of Henry and the catastrophic evil of Richard are not an inescapable inheritance from the distant past but are generated by the happenings we are made to witness" ("The Frame of Disorder: *Henry VI*," *Early Shakespeare* [London, 1961], p. 98). A. L. French: "I now suggest that there is no evidence whatever for the belief that, in the whole tetralogy, Shakespeare meant to present the Wars of the Roses as the outcome of Bolingbroke's 'original sin' " ("*Henry VI* and the Ghost of Richard II," *English Studies*, L [1969], xxxvii). See also his attack on the idea of Joan of Arc as the scourge of God in "Joan of Arc and *Henry VI*," *English Studies*, XLIV [1968], 425–29). H. M. Richmond: "the scenes of Gloucester's fall show the secularization of the drama, in that Henry's faith in the realization of God's justice on earth has proven to be shockingly at odds with the truth of particular situations" (*Shakespeare's Political Plays* [New York, 1967], p. 45). James Winny: "Setting aside the fact that all Shakespeare's history plays are concerned with political disorder, there is no evidence in *Henry VI* that at that time Shakespeare recognized any special significance in Bolingbroke's crime. Throughout the first history-play the deposition of Richard is spoken of simply as a political event, whose importance lies in its bearing upon the claims and counterclaims of the Yorkist struggle" (*The Player King* [London, 1968], p. 20). A similar view is developed in Henry Kelly, *Divine Providence in the England of Shakespeare's Histories* (Cambridge, Mass., 1970), pp. 246–76, 160.

2. Shakespeare disregards the providential interpretation of the consequences of the marriage as given in Holinshed: "But most of all it should seem, that God was displeased with this marriage," he writes, and in confirmation summarizes all the disasters which followed (*Chronicles*, III, 208).

3. R. Mark Benbow, "The Providential Theory of Historical Causation in *Holinshed's Chronicles:* 1577 and 1587," *Texas Studies in Literature and Language,* I (1959), 275. Other representative statements: "God may and often does make use of an evil instrument in the execution of his divine vengeance, and Richard, like Tamburlaine, functions as the scourge of God" (Lily B. Campbell, *Shakespeare's "Histories"* [San Marino, Calif., 1947], p. 313). "*Richard III* is cast according to the pattern of the traditional Christian conception of history in which at the proper time, decisive and redemptive action is taken" (Tom F. Driver, *The Sense of History in Greek and Shakespearean Drama* [New York, 1967], p. 103).

4. "It is impossible," writes Wolfgang Clemen, "to find an answer to the vexed question of what the author himself felt about the various arguments on law and justice raised in the sequence, since, far from pursuing a particular line of argument, Shakespeare chooses here to present several points of view, examining the ethics of the situation from different angles" (*A Commentary on Shakespeare's Richard III,* trans. Jean Boheim [London, 1968], p. 88). Shakespeare's attitude is implied to the extent, however, that he succeeds in questioning the commonplaces. This point is also brought out in an analysis of this scene, with a somewhat different emphasis, by Wilbur Sanders, *The Dramatist and the Received Idea* (Cambridge, 1968), pp. 76–79. Sanders sums up his discussion: "What answers there are, are paradoxical: Clarence has no right to live, the Murderers none to kill. One may punish justly and be justly punished for it. What is true in one man's mouth is false in another's" (p. 79). Brockbank also sees this scene as well as Margaret's curses as questioning the view of the chronicles: "It is in *Richard III* that Shakespeare's questioning of the chronicle providence is most telling, when Margaret, disengaged from the action but brought to the court in the teeth of historical fact, is made the malignant prophetess of God's displeasure, and Clarence is allowed to protest with humane eloquence against the theology of his murderers" (*Early Shakespeare,* p. 8).

5. "Throughout this scene, the invocation of divine sanctions is so deeply intertwined with personal malice and unappeased rancour that it is dangerous to take any of it at face value. This is especially true of Margaret, the chief exponent of the philosophy of Providence in the play" (Sanders, *Dramatist and the Received Idea,* p. 94).

6. *Shakespeare's "Histories,"* pp. 223–24.

7. E. M. W. Tillyard, *Shakespeare's History Plays* (London, 1948), p. 208.

8. Anne thinks that she has unwittingly cursed herself when she wished that whoever became Richard's wife would be more miser-

able than Richard had made her (4.1.65–86). It is, I believe, a mistake to regard her case as identical with that of Buckingham, as, for example, does Campbell: "Anne calls down the wrath of God upon the wife of Richard III and thereby curses her future self. Buckingham calls upon God to take vengeance if he be not true to England's queen and so curses himself" (*Shakespeare's "Histories,"* p. 224). Buckingham made an oath with the cynical intention of not preserving the peace. Anne's speech calls attention to the grim irony of her initial encounter with Richard and her capitulation; her wretched fate calls for pity. It belies the complexity and ambiguity of this issue in the play to equate these two as identical cases in the operation of God's moral system in *Richard III*.

9. There is some truth to Sanders' contention that Richmond's speech sounds tagged on: "Richmond's speech is almost as tenuously integrated with *Richard III* as is the Bastard's analogous curtain speech with the play *King John*. In both cases, the kind of human/critical awareness which Shakespeare has set in motion in the course of the play makes short work of the platitude with which he tries to wind it up" (*Dramatist and the Received Idea*, p. 73). I am entirely in sympathy with Sanders' rejection of the providentialism of the historians as the key to this play, but I do not think we can so readily detach Richmond's concluding role and sentiments from any comprehensive interpretation of the play. I have a somewhat similar objection to A. L. French's view of Richmond: " 'God' in *Richard III* is a highly jealous Old Testament figure whose main function is to bring curses to fruition. It is in this spirit that Queen Margaret invokes him. But since 'God' is taken in vain so consistently, we cannot help feeling the strongest dubiety when, in Act V, Richmond interlards his exhortations with pious ejaculations" ("The World of *Richard III*," *Shakespeare Studies* IV [1968], 33). If we have to construe Richmond's speeches as ironic expressions of platitudes which at this point in the play we are in a mood to reject as hypocritical political expediency, then the scene of the ghosts has to be played as absurdly comic camp or high parody.

10. I must qualify my general approval of Sanders' critical attitude toward the providentialist interpretation of *Richard III* on one further point: in his opinion, "the overtly 'providential' element in *Richard III* is disappointing. It simply asserts something which is, quite literally, *reçu*, something for which Shakespeare had not had to fight, and it ignores the fairly obvious objections to which the *idée* was, and still is open. . . . It is not surprising that an imagination as alive as Shakespeare's to the complexity of human affairs ran into difficulties when he tried to dramatize this view of history; not surprising, either, that once he had outgrown it he never returned to it" (*Dramatist and the Received Idea*, p. 111). It is my view that Shake-

speare did not accept the idea as he found it in his sources, but that he subjected it to dramatic exploration which is at times shattering in exposing the absurdities of the idea as it is used in the chronicles. He had, moreover, already "outgrown" it in *Henry VI*, though he was compelled, because of the persistence of the "received opinion" in his sources, to return to the problem in *Henry V*.

Chapter IV

1. The expedient character of the *Henry IV* plays is dealt with in John Danby, *Shakespeare's Doctrine of Nature* (London, 1949), pp. 81–101; and also A. R. Humphreys, Introduction, *1 Henry IV*, Arden ed., pp. l–li.

2. The notion that war was necessary therapy for the ills produced by long peace was frequently expressed in imagery of disease with war as curative bloodletting, and the like. The archbishop's speech cited earlier embodies this idea in the reference to "our surfeiting and wanton hours" (*2 Henry IV*: 4.1.55). See Paul Jorgensen, *Shakespeare's Military World* (Berkeley and Los Angeles, 1956), pp. 187–90.

3. On the theme of time, see also an interesting discussion with a somewhat different emphasis by L. C. Knights, "Times Subjects: The Sonnets and *King Henry IV Part II*," *Some Shakespearian Themes* (London, 1964), pp. 45–64.

4. There is a comparable moment in *Richard III* before Bosworth Field:

> *Richard.* Tell the clock there. Give me a calendar.
> Who saw the sun today?
> *Ratcliffe.* Not I, my lord.
> *Richard.* Then he disdains to shine; for by the book
> He should have braved the east an hour ago.
> A black day will it be to somebody.
> Ratcliffe!
> *Ratcliffe.* My lord?
> *Richard.* The sun will not be seen today;
> The sky doth frown and lour upon our army.
> I would these dewy tears were from the ground.
> Not shine today! Why, what is that to me
> More than to Richmond? For the selfsame heaven
> That frowns on me looks sadly upon him.
> (5.3.277–88)

There is a notable difference in spirit. Richard repeats himself nervously and seems to be trying to buoy up his spirits with the final sentiment. Henry IV speaks as a realist, and a fairly confident one.

5. Humphreys, in his note to this passage in the Arden edition, states that there is no historical record of this prophecy and calls attention to instances of parallel prophecies in the case of other men. There are numerous instances of such riddling prophecies in the history of this period. J. R. Lander cites several instances in *The Wars of the Roses* (London, 1965). Gloucester, on receiving a summons to Parliament at Bury, from a mid-fifteenth-century chronicle: "And then the duke asked a poor man that dwelt in the same lane, 'What call men this lane?' The poor man answered and said, 'For sooth my lord, it is called the Dead Lane.' And then the good duke remembered him of an old prophecy that he had read many a day before and said, 'As our Lord will, be it all'" (p. 48). Suffolk, after being taken by a ship called *Nicholas of the Tower*, from the Paston Letters: "Also he asked the name of the ship, and when he knew it, he remembered Stacey that said, if he might escape the danger of the Tower he should be safe; and then his heart failed him, for he thought he was deceived" (p. 56). Richard III's vain preparations to meet Richmond at the wrong harbor, from the Croyland Chronicle: "Some persons endowed, as it were, with a spirit of prophecy, these predicted that those men would land at the harbour of Milford, and were in the habit of looking for the fulfilment of their prophecies to that effect, not at the most famous place, but most commonly at the other one which bore the same name. . . . But it was all in vain: for, on the first day of August the enemy landed with a fair wind and without opposition, at the most celebrated harbour, Milford Haven, near Pembroke" (pp. 256–57). C. L. Kingsford, in *Henry V: The Typical Medieval Hero* (New York and London, 1901), reports one relating to Hotspur: "There he proposed to give battle, and calling for his favorite sword learnt that it had been left at the village of Berwick where he had lodged the previous night. On hearing the name Percy grew pale: 'We have ploughed our last furrow,' he said, 'for a wizard in mine own country foretold that I should die at Berwick'" (p. 43). There are two such riddling prophecies in *Richard III*, Clarence's imprisonment over the letter G (1.1.52 ff.) and Richard's worry over a prophecy that involves the words Rugemont and Richmond (4.2.102 ff.). These fit into the general atmosphere of *Richard III* and have something of the effect of the deceiving prophecies of the "juggling fiends" in *Macbeth*. In introducing the unhistorical quibbling prophecy in *2 Henry IV*, Shakespeare secured an effect of irony, but this one instance is hardly sufficient to alter the essentially secular tone of the play.

6. Henry admits to fear in his talk with the soldiers, but explains that "no man should possess him with any appearance of fear, lest

357

he, by showing it, should dishearten his army" (4.1.111–13). See Jorgensen, *Shakespeare's Military World*, pp. 91–93.

7. *Chronicles*, III, 79.

8. *Ibid.*

9. *Union*, section on Henry V, fols. xvi verso–xvii.

Chapter V

1. Detailed discussions of the general issues dealt with in this chapter will be found in the following works: J. W. Allen, *A History of Political Thought in the Sixteenth Century* (London, 1928); Franklin Baumer, *The Early Tudor Theory of Kingship* (New Haven, Conn., 1940); S. B. Chrimes, *English Constitutional History* (London, 1956); William Dunning, *A History of Political Theories from Luther to Montesquieu* (New York, 1947); John Figgis, *The Divine Right of Kings* (Cambridge, 1922); Christopher Morris, *Political Thought in England: Tyndale to Hooker* (London, 1953); Felix Raab, *The English Face of Machiavelli* (London and Toronto, 1964); William Stubbs, *The Constitutional History of England*, 3 vols. (Oxford, 1874–78, and later eds.); Gordon Zeeveld, *Foundations of Tudor Policy* (Cambridge, Mass., 1948).

2. The complexity of this phenomenon is indicated by recent challenges to the widely held notion of the "new monarchies" and the nationalistic state in the Renaissance. For a brief criticism of the established view see J. Russell Major, "The Renaissance Monarchy as Seen by Erasmus, More, Seyssel and Machiavelli," *Action and Conviction in Early Modern Europe*, ed. T. K. Rabb and J. E. Seigel (Princeton, N.J., 1969), pp. 17–31. Many of Russell's reservations are well taken, and are in fact in accord with the general drift of the present discussion on a number of essential matters. However, the wish to demonstrate that "the typical Renaissance monarchy . . . was dynastic, not national; decentralized, not centralized; and constitutional, not absolute, in that there were laws, customs, and institutions which checked the authority of the ruler" (p. 17) obscures the strong drift toward national organization and especially the aspiration toward great monarchical power as expressed in contemporary statements about the divine sanction of the king's authority and the sinfulness of disobedience.

3. For the debate over Vergil's rejection of the Arthurian myth see Edwin Greenlaw, *Studies in Spenser's Historical Allegory* (Baltimore, Md., 1932), pp. 1–58.

4. *The Anglia Historia of Polydore Vergil A. D. 1485–1537,* ed. and trans. Denys Hay, Camden Society, 3rd ser., LXXIV (London, 1950), 7.

5. This aspect of Henry's patronage of letters is made clear in Zeeveld's *Foundations of Tudor Policy.* Of Henry VII William Nelson writes, "Scholars followed the humanistic discipline because they hoped for employment at court. And the king fostered and encouraged the humanists because they were needed in the affairs of the nation" (*John Skelton Laureate* [New York, 1939], pp. 7–8).

6. "Large numbers of men," writes Figgis, "may embrace a belief without good reason, but assuredly they will not do so without adequate cause" (*Divine Right of Kings,* p. 2).

7. *The Obedience of a Christian Man* (1528), fol. xxxii.

8. *Ibid.,* fol. xxxi verso.

9. *Mirror,* p. 178.

10. V, ii, 41.

11. V, Intr. 10.

12. P. 419. "It appears that Kingship has ever been regarded as in some especial way protected by a divine authority; that the influence of Christianity has in all ages been held to support this view; that the English Kingship from being elective in a single family had become purely hereditary by the fourteenth century; that coronation had ceased to be regarded as necessary to the making of a king; and that in the systematic presentment of English law in the thirteenth century there were ample materials for men in a later age, devoid of the historical sense and imbued with the theory of sovereignty, to suppose that the English Kingship towards the close of the Middle Ages was strictly hereditary and unconditioned by constitutional restraints" (Figgis, *Divine Right of Kings,* pp. 36–37).

13. *Ecclesiastical Polity,* bk. 8, ch. 2.

14. *England in the Reign of Henry the Eighth: A Dialogue between Cardinal Pole and Thomas Lupset,* ed. J. M. Cowper (London, 1871). Early English Text Society, ex. ser. XII, 167–68. Written about 1538, published for the first time in this edition.

15. For a summary of Doleman's arguments and replies to them see Lily B. Campbell, *Shakespeare's "Histories"* (San Marino, Calif., 1947), pp. 174–87. The effect of religious convictions on the attitude toward nonresistance is presented in separate chapters on "The

Catholic Protest" and "The Protestant Protest" by Morris, *Political Thought in England.* See also Zeeveld, *Foundations of Tudor Policy.* Morris' view that the argument from the law of nature was characteristic of Catholic thought rather than of Protestant must be qualified. It does not account for Starkey, nor Ponet, nor for that bastion of Anglican thought, Thomas Hooker.

16. William Stubbs, *Constitutional History of England,* is a storehouse of information on the succession, though nowhere is the entire issue discussed comprehensively. Useful discussions of the succession will be found in John Figgis, *Divine Right of Kings,* pp. 82–90; Frederick Marcham, *A Constitutional History of Modern England* (New York, 1960), pp. 10–14; Morris, *Political Thought in England,* pp. 126–42; C. W. Prosser and Margaret Sharp, *A Short Constitutional History of England* (London, 1938), pp. 6, 27–28, 88–89, 110–12.

17. The arguments for this position are developed in chs. 4, 5, and 6 of Ponet's *A Short Treatise of Politike Power* (1556).

18. *The Appellation of John Knox, Works,* ed. David Laing (Edinburgh, 1855), IV, 496.

19. *England in the Reign of Henry the Eighth,* EETS, ex. ser. XII, 167–68.

20. *Ecclesiastical Polity,* bk. 1, ch. 9, par. 5.

21. *De Republica Anglorum: A Discourse on the Commonwealth of England,* ed. L. Alston (Cambridge, 1906), p. 19 (bk. 1, ch. 9).

22. *Ibid.,* p. 28 (bk. 1, ch. 15).

23. *The Boke Named the Governour,* bk. 1, ch. 2.

24. *De Republica Anglorum,* p. 48 (bk. 2, ch. 1).

25. *Ibid.* Hooker relies on this view of Parliament to support the position of the Anglican church as a national institution: "There are which wonder that we should count any statute a law, which the high court of parliament in England hath established about the matter of church regiment. . . . The parliament of England together with the convocation annexed thereunto, is that whereupon the very essence of all government within this kingdom doth depend; it is even the body of the whole realm; it consisteth of the king, and of all that within the land are subject unto him: for they all are there present, either in person or by such as they voluntarily have derived their very personal right unto. . . . Touching the supremacy of power which

our kings have in this case of making laws, it resteth principally in the strength of a negative voice; which not to give them, were to deny them that without which they were but kings by mere title, and not in exercise of dominion" (*Ecclesiastical Polity*, bk. 8, ch. 6. Book 8 was not published during Hooker's lifetime).

26. On the role of Parliament during the fifteenth and sixteenth centuries and the idea of the king in Parliament see Chrimes, *English Constitutional History*, pp. 128–36, and Baumer, *Early Tudor Theory of Kingship*, pp. 120–91. Henry VIII, who found it convenient to use Parliament as the instrument of his revolution, declared to representatives of Parliament in 1543: "We be informed by our judges that we at no time stand so highly in our estate royal as in time of Parliament, wherein we as head and you as members are conjoined and knit together in one body politic" (quoted by Chrimes, p. 132).

27. *Obedience of a Christian Man*, fols. lxxviii verso–lxxix.

28. *The Governance of England*, ed. Charles Plummer (London, 1885), p. 117. The idea is developed in the first two chapters.

29. *Ecclesiastical Polity*, bk. 8, ch. 2.

30. Of the problem of kingly authority and law, J. H. Hexter writes: "Lack of governance, weakness at the center, had prevailed in the era that preceded [More, Machiavelli, Seyssel], and having tasted its bitter fruits, men in the politically advanced lands of Europe wanted an end to it. They wanted to be ruled, and if they were to have what they wanted, they must allow their rulers the power needed to govern. If the prince were really to rule, his will must be effective, and to be effective, it had to be law or something very like law. But in the common opinion law ought never to be the mere expression of any mortal mere will; it ought to be inextricably bound into the complex pattern of perdurable relations in which justice, reason, experience, custom, nature, and virtue were indispensable terms. The pressing problem was how to keep law bound into that pattern of relations and at the same time allow rulers the power to rule, which meant in effect the power to make rules with the force of law" ("Claude de Seyssel and Normal Politics in the Age of Machiavelli," *Art, Science, and History in the Renaissance*, ed. Charles Singleton [Baltimore, Md., 1967], pp. 408–9).

31. *Mirror*, pp. 199–200, 202.

32. William Camden, *The History of the Most Renowned and Victorious Princess Elizabeth, Late Queen of England*, 3d ed. (London, 1675), p. 556.

33. See David Bevington, *Tudor Drama and Politics* (Cambridge, Mass., 1968), pp. 234–57. Of the circumstances which provided occasion for this drama Bevington writes: "Drama of civil rebellion did not gain currency until the Armada years. It was, like war drama, occasioned by renewed anxieties over the regal succession, Catholic plotting in the 1580's, dissension over the fate of Mary Stuart, and lower-class restiveness" (p. 234).

Chapter VI

1. *Policraticus*, trans. John Dickinson under the title *The Statesman's Book of John of Salisbury* (New York, 1927), bk. 5, ch. 7. On the constitutional issues as they relate to the question of the succession in the plays, see George Keeton, *Shakespeare's Legal and Political Background* (London, 1967), pp. 248–63.

2. In the earlier scene in which he claimed the title by descent, Cade proposes a compromise to Stafford in the name of Henry V: "Go to sirrah, tell the King from me that, for his father's sake, Henry the Fifth, in whose time boys went to span-counter for French crowns, I am content he shall reign; but I'll be Protector over him" (4.2.149–52).

Chapter VII

1. For a review of the important texts dealing with tyranny from antiquity to the beginning of the sixteenth century, see Alfred Colville, *Jean Petit: La Question du tyrannicide au commencement du XVe siècle* (Paris, 1932).

2. Book 8 is devoted to the subject of tyranny, and the account given here is a concise summary of the argument in that book. Quotations are from the (incomplete) translation of *Policraticus* by John Dickinson, in *The Statesman's Book of John of Salisbury* (New York, 1927). Dickinson's Introduction is valuable for the analysis not only of John's thought but also of the general issue of tyranny and tyrannicide, especially pp. lxvi–lxxii.

3. The title of Aquinas' work was *De regno: Ad regem Cypri*. I. T. Eschmann distinguishes between this genuine text, which is incomplete, and *De regimini principium* which incorporated Aquinas' text and passed under his name for years, in the Introduction to the English translation of *De regno*, *On Kingship: To the King of Cyprus*, trans. G. B. Phelan (Toronto, 1949). All quotations are from this translation.

4. *Ibid.*, p. 8.

5. *Ibid.*, pp. 24–29.

6. Quoted from the English translation of *De tyranno* by Ephraim Emerton, in his *Humanism and Tyranny: Studies in the Italian Trecento* (Cambridge, Mass., 1925), p. 78.

7. *Ibid.*, p. 85.

8. *Ibid.*, pp. 92–93.

9. *Ibid.*, p. 86.

10. *Ibid.*, pp. 100–108. On the political setting of Salutati's argument, see Eric Voeglin, "Machiavelli's Prince: Background and Formation," *Review of Politics*, XIII (1951), 150.

11. For a detailed account of this episode, see Colville, *Jean Petit.*

12. *De Republica Anglorum*, ed. L. Alston (Cambridge, 1906), p. 13 (bk. 1, ch. 5).

13. For a review of the English idea of tyranny during this period from a slightly different perspective see W. A. Armstrong, "The Elizabethan Conception of the Tyrant," *RES*, XXII (1946), 161–81; and "The Influence of Seneca and Machiavelli on the Elizabethan Tyrant," *RES*, XXIV (1948), 19–41. I have a serious reservation about one aspect of Armstrong's argument. According to Armstrong, "though Elizabethans were admonished to endure a tyrant who had succeeded lawfully to his throne, they were counselled not to tolerate any usurper who might seize the crown" (*RES*, XXII, 166). What does "not tolerate" cover? Does it include assasination? civil war? It is difficult to find texts which explicitly make the distinction as Armstrong makes it. The *Homilies* do not do so. Moreover, of those whom certain political dissidents condemned as tyrants—Mary Stuart, Mary Tudor, Elizabeth—all were lawfully crowned, yet their removal was urged by their opponents. The *Homilies* may seem to be implying a distinction when, for example, they urge that "ye shall not find that God ever prospered any Rebellion against their natural and Lawful princes" (*Homilies*, p. 357). The words "natural and lawful" are part of the rhetoric, and do not imply a distinction between rebellions against lawful and those against unlawful tyrants. The argument of the 1571 homily is a fortiori: if we are commanded to obey the worst princes, what shall we say of those who wish to urge rebellion against the present lawful and just ruler, "who, if God for their wickedness had given them a heathen tyrant to reign over them, were by God's word bound to obey him, and to pray for him" (*ibid.*, p. 342). The stress throughout is on the evils of rebellion: "A rebel is

worse than the worst princes, and rebellion worse than the worst prince that hitherto hath been. . . . God placeth as well evil princes as good." It is difficult to squeeze Armstrong's distinction from the *Homilies*. The only tyrant mentioned in the 1571 homily is the pope, and the only tyranny that of the church of Rome.

14. *England in the Reign of Henry the Eighth*, Early English Text Society, ex. ser. XII, 107, 103.

15. Both quotations are from Armstrong, *RES*, XXIV, 22.

16. On the general influence of Seneca see the Introduction to *The Poetical Works of Sir William Alexander*, ed. L. E. Kastner and H. B. Charlton (Manchester, 1921). On Seneca as a possible source of political aphorisms and maxims see Marvin Herrick, "Senecan Influence in *Gorboduc*," *Studies in Speech and Drama in Honor of Alexander M. Drummond* (New York, 1968), pp. 78–104. Herrick takes account of other than Senecan sources for *Gorboduc* (pp. 98–100). The conventional tyrant became associated with rant. Bottom, it will be recalled, had the humor for a tyrant's role "or a part to tear a cat in," and after delivering a few samples observes, "This is Ercles' vein, a tyrant's vein."

17. See David Bevington, *Tudor Drama and Politics* (Cambridge, Mass., 1968), pp. 157–67. Bevington associates the emergence of the theme of tyranny during these years to such circumstances as Knox's attack on Mary Stuart and her dethronement in 1567, the Northern Rising against Elizabeth in 1569, and her excommunication in 1570. He views these plays collectively as "an early Elizabethan debate on the limits of obedience to a potentially corrupt civil authority" (p. 165).

18. The Senecan characteristics of Legge's play in general and in detail, as well as the association of Richard with the Senecan tyrant, are fully dealt with in an extended discussion of Legge's play by George Churchill, *Richard the Third up to Shakespeare* (Berlin, 1900), pp. 265–396. John Harrington's *Apologie of Poetry* (1591) suggests the idea conveyed by Legge's play: "For tragedies, to omit other famous tragedies, that which was played at St. John's in Cambridge, of Richard III, would move, I think, Phalaris the tyrant, and terrify all tyrannous minded men" (quoted in Churchill, p. 265).

19. *Mirror*, p. 360.

20. *Ibid.*, p. 370.

21. *Ibid.*

22. *Ibid.*, p. 360.

23. Polydore Vergil thus explains the shocking murder of the two princes: "Who, if we have regard unto such noble children thus shamefully murdered, will not tremble and quake, seeing that such matters often happen for the offense of our ancestors, whose faults redound to the posterity? That fortuned peradventure to those two innocent imps because Edward their father committed the offense of perjury, by reason of that most solemn oath which . . . he took at the gates of the city of York, meaning one thing inwardly and promising an other in express words outwardly, as forthwith appeared: and for that afterwards, by reason of his brother the duke of Clarence's death, he had charged himself and his posterity before God with due desert of grievous punishment" (*Three Books of Polydore Vergil's English History*, from an early translation, ed. Henry Ellis, Camden Society, XXIX [London, 1844], 189–90).

24. *Union*, section on Edward V, fol. i.

25. *Chronicles*, III, 477.

26. This episode was noted from the start as the conclusive demonstration of Richard's tyranny. Vergil outdoes himself: "James Tyrrel, who, being forced to do the king's commandment, rode sorrowfully to London, and, to the worst example that hath been almost ever heard of, murdered those babes of the issue royal. . . . [Men] subduing all fear, . . . wept everywhere, and when they could weep no more, they cried out, 'Is there truly any man living so far at enmity with God, with all that holy is and religious, so utter enemy to man, who would not have abhorred the mischief of so foul a murder?' But especially the queen's friends and the childrens' exclaimed against him, 'What will this man do to others who thus cruelly, without any their desert hath killed his own kinsfolk?' assuring themselves that a marvellous tyranny had now invaded the commonwealth" (pp. 188–89). Vergil must have realized that the crucial issue in the Tudor claims to legitimacy hinged on the right to destroy and replace Richard and not the myth of direct descent from King Arthur. Vergil serves his conscience as a historian by rejecting the Arthurian myth, but if he disappointed his royal patron on this detail, he came through handsomely on the main question. In view of the horror expressed by the sixteenth-century historians and, especially, of the way in which Shakespeare deals with the episode of their murder, I find it difficult to take the following seriously: "Prince Edward is, we suspect, far more than half Woodville; his saucy brother is all Woodville. . . . The little boys killed by their wicked uncle here seem to be very bad little boys indeed, making the murderous intentions of their uncle a ruthless but perhaps preferable alternative to their survival" (John Bromley, *The Shakespearean Kings* [Boulder, Colo., 1971], p. 37).

27. This generally agreed on view of Richmond's role in the play is summed up by Bevington, *Tudor Drama and Politics*, pp. 242–43: "The justifying of this particular overthrow was for obvious reasons universally allowed under the Tudor myth, and Shakespeare's arguments are conventional. Richard is the scourge of God punishing a nation for its rebelliousness, and his destruction is a sign of God's appeasement. The people themselves do not rise against Richard, and even Henry Tudor's role is tactfully discreet. The event is God's alone, and cannot sanction a challenge of established rule in the 1590's."

28. See below, ch. 15.

Chapter VIII

1. See John Figgis, *The Divine Right of Kings* (Cambridge, 1922), pp. 81–106, 137–40; and J. W. Allen, *A History of Political Thought in England in the Sixteenth Century* (London, 1928), pp. 269–70.

2. (1528), fol. xxxii.

3. Quoted in Ernest Kantorowicz, *The King's Two Bodies* (Princeton, N.J., 1957), p. 318.

4. *Mirror*, pp. 64–65.

5. *Obedience of a Christian Man*, fols. xxxi verso–xxxii.

6. The play has also been seen as a paean to kingship: " 'Richard II' ist das Hohe Lied des Königstums und eine des groszartigsten Hymnen auf die königliche Würde" (Joseph Kohler, "Die Staatsidee Shakespeares in *Richard II*," *Jahr.*, LIII [1917], 4). Representative examples of various approaches to the political meaning of the play are presented in the New Variorum edition of *Richard II*, ed. Matthew Black (Philadelphia and London, 1955), pp. 524–33.

7. *Shakespeare and the Homilies* (Melbourne, 1934), pp. 27, 37. Hart suggests that the number of assassinations on the Continent and plots at home inclined Shakespeare to adopt a strongly royalist position: "Perhaps in his insistence on the doctrine of divine right, with its corollary, the sacro-sanctity of the queen, Shakespeare was trying to do the state some service" (p. 76). To stress the uniqueness of Shakespeare's emphasis on divine right, Hart notes that "not one allusion to divine right is to be found in *Edward II* which in this respect contrasts strongly with Shakespeare's *Richard II*" (p. 25). No inferences can be drawn from this comparison, except that in spite

of the general view that Marlowe's play exerted an influence on *Richard II* the two plays are quite different and Marlowe's is not political in essence. It is Hart's thesis that the kings in Shakespeare's plays did not as a matter of historical fact claim divine right, that his historical sources contain no reference to divine right, and that therefore the source of the idea and its corollaries must have been the homilies on disobedience, especially that of 1571. I think it would be difficult to maintain the various portions of this argument without serious qualifications. Of the historical Richard, John Figgis in *Divine Right of Kings*, p. 74, writes: "He certainly believed in the sacredness and in the 'liberty' of his crown more strongly than any of his predecessors, and devoted all his energies to the establishment of a despotism." Holinshed provides support for this view (*Chronicles*, II, 840): "Sir John Bushy . . . did not attribute to him titles of honor due and accustomed, but invented unusual terms and such strange names, as were rather agreeable to the divine majesty of God than to any earthly potentate."

8. Hart (*Shakespeare and the Homilies*, p. 37), quotes the first two of these lines as further evidence that Shakespeare is pushing the divine right of kings. Actually, Carlisle, while protecting the king's feelings, is recommending forceful and prudent action and the use of the royal resources to check rebellion.

9. The phrases are Peter Ure's in his Introduction to the Arden edition of *Richard II*, pp. lxiii–lxiv. My disagreement on this point does not represent a general critical attitude toward this admirable edition. Among other good features, the Introduction deserves mention because of its forthright criticism of the popular notion that Richard is a poet.

10. The impression of ruthless exercise of royal power which Richard's act was expected to make is suggested by a specific provision in the Act of Proclamations under Henry VII that the act did not allow that the king's subjects "should have any of . . . their inheritance, lawful possessions, offices, liberties, privileges, franchises, goods or cattle taken from them." See Franklin Baumer, *The Early Tudor Theory of Kingship* (New Haven, Conn., 1940), pp. 167–68.

11. Compare the philosophic approach to this issue in Shakespeare with Machiavelli's more pragmatic warning in his chapter on cruelty and pity: "If as sometimes happens, he finds he must inflict the penalty of death, he should do it when he has proper justification and evident reason. But above all he must refrain from taking the property of his citizens, for men forget the death of a father more quickly than the loss of their patrimony" (*The Prince*, trans. Allan Gilbert [Chicago, 1941], ch. 17).

12. It is to completely disregard these carefully worked-out sequences to insist that "Gaunt and York make it equally plain that tyranny can never justify rebellion" (Michael Quinn, "The King Is Not Himself," *SP*, LVI [1959], 171). Quinn's essay is, nevertheless, an interesting analysis of the tensions of the play centering in the concepts of divine right, loyalty, and patience.

13. In a detailed analysis of this scene in his *Political Characters of Shakespeare* (London, 1945), pp. 162–67, plentifully illustrated with extensive quotations, Palmer omits any reference or allusion to these lines. Ian Kott, though in a somewhat tendentious political context, stresses this aspect of the abdication: "*Richard II* is a tragedy of dethronement. . . . Dethronement, in fact, of the idea of regal power." "In *Richard II* Shakespeare deposed not only the king but the idea of kingly power" (*Shakespeare Our Contemporary* [New York, 1964], pp. 34, 41).

14. No divinity doth hedge a president of the United States, yet there has been a deep historic reluctance to take advantage of the constitutional provisions for getting rid of him if he is guilty of serious misrule and thus reduce the term of office of the deputy elected by the people. Only one Congress has been rash enough to bring impeachment proceedings against a president and the effort did not succeed.

15. Compare Hooker, *Ecclesiastical Polity*, bk. 8, ch. 9: "Kings therefore no man can have lawfully power and authority to judge. If private men offend, there is the magistrate over them which judgeth. If magistrates, they have their prince. If princes, there is Heaven, a tribunal, before which they shall appear: on earth they are not accountable to any."

16. There are some instructive historical parallels. In the same vein as Carlisle's defense of Richard, Mary Stuart protested at her trial that only God could try queens; and Elizabeth hinted that she might be spared the awful necessity of signing Mary's death warrant if it could be arranged to have Mary conveniently die in her bed.

17. Recent comments indicate a drift away from the idea of *Richard II* as a play embodying a conventional royalist view. For example, Christopher Morris, *Political Thought in England* (London, 1953), p. 100: "*Richard II* may not have seemed to the Elizabethans so obviously royalist a play"; David Bevington, *Tudor Drama and Politics* (Cambridge, Mass., 1968), p. 242: "Increasingly Shakespeare reveals a fascination with the limits of divine right, and explores the unattractive but necessary aspects of compromise in the art of kingship at its best." Ernest Talbert, *The Problem of Order* (Chapel Hill, N.C., 1962), p. 200, compares the art of the histories

with that of Guicciardini and Comines, and remarks, "Unless the critic or reader can be satisfied with dichotomies, we should be thankful that the process of thought here considered contributed to such a result and that *Richard II* is as much a problem play as any of the later 'problem comedies.'" A. P. Rossiter, in the Introduction to his edition of the anonymous *Woodstock*, discusses the sympathetic presentation of revolt in that play, in contrast to the orthodox view. The relation of *Woodstock* to *Richard II* is uncertain. Its main interest in the present connection is that a play for the theatre need not always have followed the rigid conventional line, as is so often assumed. *Woodstock*, though lively, is crude in comparison with Shakespeare's skillful and exhaustive unfolding of the main issue.

Chapter IX

1. H. B. Charlton puts the matter in reverse order: "Somehow [Richard III] frustrates the realization of a satisfying idea of tragedy. . . . So for his next tragedy, Shakespeare looked for a different kind of character in the traditional repositories of tragic heroes. The chroniclers offered him Richard II" (*Shakespearian Tragedy* [Cambridge, 1954], p. xi). Robert Ornstein has a better appreciation of Shakespeare's artistic accomplishment and progress in the histories: "Lacking the artistic precedents and models which the plays of Plautus, Gascoigne, Peele, and Greene provided in comedy, he had not only to create a suitable dramatic form for the History Play but he had also to recreate that form again and again as his vision of politics and history deepened. He was also, I think, more ambitious and adventurous, more willing to experiment and innovate in his History Plays than in his comedies" (*A Kingdom for a Stage* [Cambridge, Mass., 1972], pp. 1–2).

2. "As a godless and bloodthirsty tyrant, he was admirably fitted to be the protagonist of a Senecan tragedy, at that date the only form of tragedy approved by the literary dictators" (J. Dover Wilson, Introduction, *Richard II* [Cambridge, 1954], p. xi).

3. Thomas Starkey, *England in the Reign of Henry the Eighth*, Early English Text Society, ex. ser. XII, 65.

4. *The Boke Named the Governour*, bk. 1, ch. 4.

5. *The Prince*, trans. Allan Gilbert (Chicago, 1941), p. 175.

6. *Mirror*, pp. 64–66. Campbell sums up the attitude and method of this work as follows: "Nor did its ghosts merely bewail the deeds of fortune 'that with unwar strook overturneth the realm of great

nobleye'; rather, they used their lives as examples to expound the current political philosophy, and substituted an analysis of divine justice for the older philosophizing of the uncertainty of fortune" (pp. 55–56). The most extensive treatment of the relationship of *A Mirror* to medieval tragedy is that of Willard Farnham, *The Medieval Heritage of Elizabethan Tragedy* (Berkeley, Calif., 1936). For minor reservations about the emphasis in this work see William Perry, "Tragic Retribution in the 1559 *Mirror for Magistrates*," SP, XLVI (1949), 113–30.

7. *Mirror*, p. 198.

8. J. Dover Wilson is doubtful about its influence in the Introduction to his edition of *Richard II*, p. xxvii, but he seems to accept it in the Introduction to his edition of *Richard III* (Cambridge, 1961), p. xviii. According to Geoffrey Bullough, *Narrative and Dramatic Sources of Shakespeare* (London and New York, 1966), III, 367: "That Shakespeare knew the *Mirror* well is certain. Whether he took much of it for this play is less sure."

9. *Appreciations* (London, 1927), p. 199.

10. Introduction to *Richard II*, p. xx. See also Raymond Chapman, "The Wheel of Fortune in Shakespeare's Historical Plays," *RES*, n.s. I (1950), 1–7, and Arthur Suzman, "Imagery and Symbolism in *Richard II*," SQ, VII (1956), 355–70.

11. Shakespeare sems to have deliberately rejected the wheel image in this play. There are, in fact, only two specific references to fortune's wheel in the histories. One occurs in *3 Henry VI* (4.3.46–47) in which Edward defies fortune ("Though fortune's malice overthrow my state, / My mind exceeds the compass of her wheel"); the other occurs in a ludicrous conversation between Pistol and Fluellen in *Henry V* (3.6.25–39), in which the two list the conventional features of the figure of fortune with comic pedantry.

12. Michael Quinn comments on the relation of Richard's fall to the medieval tradition: "From Skelton's *Magnyfycence* to Marlowe's *Edward II*, dramatists, and others, used the *contemptus mundi* as an excuse or evasion for the fallen man, claiming from their audience or readers a sympathy that forgot its victim's crimes. Shakespeare, however, goes out of his way to stress that the fall of Richard is not the work of an irrational and fickle goddess, though it may seem so to the victim himself" ("The King Is Not Himself," SP, LVI [1959], 180–81). I agree, except for the final clause. It seems so to the victim only initially.

13. For a general discussion of the Phaeton emblem see De Witt Starnes and Ernest Talbert, *Classical Myth and Legend in Renais-*

sance Dictionaries (Chapel Hill, N.C., 1955), pp. 119–20. See also Talbert, *The Problem of Order* (Chapel Hill, N.C., 1962), pp. 169–73. His interpretation of Richard's application of the myth to himself differs from mine. For a brief review of the sun image in relation to the general imagery of the play and references to studies of the sun image see Peter Ure, Introduction to *Richard II*, Arden ed., p. lxii and n. 6.

14. Howard Patch, *The Goddess Fortuna in Medieval Literature* (Cambridge, Mass., 1927), pp. 53–54.

15. According to Holinshed, a representative group attended Richard in the Tower and presented him with a statement of resignation, which Richard read. The statement contains the following: "For well I wote and knowledge, and deem myself to be and have been insufficient and unable, and also unprofitable, and for my open deserts not unworthy to be put down" (*Chronicles*, II, 863). Shakespeare omits any suggestion that Richard submitted under pressure to the reading of a public declaration of wrongdoing and failure imposed on him for political reasons. Richard's declarations of failure in the play appear only as personal admissions and self-accusations arising out of an inner need to express them.

16. For a brief discussion of the mirror episode and references to significant studies of the mirror emblem see Ure, Introduction to *Richard II*, pp. lxxxii–lxxxiii and note. Samuel Chew, *The Virtues Reconciled* (Toronto, 1947), pp. 14–15, concludes on the basis of traditional symbolic associations with the mirror that the spectators would have thought of Richard as "the embodiment of Pride and Vainglory, and also a travesty of Wisdom and Prudence, as indeed he is." This interpretation takes no account of what Richard says.

17. Compare Richard II's " 'tis a sign of love" with Richard III's "There is no creature loves me; / And if I die, no soul will pity me" (5.3.201–2).

18. I recognize the persistence of a widespread inclination to dismiss the Pomfret soliloquy as perhaps decorative but functionally unimportant. Travis Bogard, "Shakespeare's Second Richard," *PMLA*, LXX (1955), 192–209, places particular emphasis on the mirror scene, as the point at which "Shakespeare begins fully to suggest the reality of the suffering of his hero," and contends that what follows act 4 "is not of especial importance" (pp. 207, 208). Of the soliloquy in Pomfret Castle, he says it "seems to be trying without conspicuous success to find a way of imaging the frenzied boredom of imprisonment" (p. 209). R. F. Hill treats it as a rhetorical exercise in which the speaker evades reality: "As a piece of consciously beautiful writing to mark a climax of feeling this soliloquy is in accord

with the manner of rhetorical tragedy. Functionally it is successful to the extent that it furthers the characterization of a man who is prone to self-dramatization, one who endeavours to elude the immediate experience by enclosing it in a cage of words. It fails, however, in tragic impact. It has the content of a tragic meditation, for Richard speaks of his past folly and present misery. But he does not make us feel them. The necessary urgency of language is smoothed away in the controlled patterns of the statement. . . . Further, the surface control is such that Richard appears detached and with his detachment comes ours" ("Dramatic Technique and Interpretation in *Richard II*," *Early Shakespeare* [London, 1961], p. 117). I must dissociate myself from the inclusive "us" above. Both in reading and in performance, the soliloquy impresses me as a moment when Richard is not "detached"—unless we are to assume that the style in general, which is often "consciously beautiful" and often marked by "controlled patterns," is by its nature a barrier to the normal expectations of dramatic communication, in which case there is not much that Richard utters which does not come under Hill's indictment. The attitude toward this work as an elegant apprentice piece in tragedy in which surface meanings are handsomely elaborated leads to misleading oversimplifications; for instance, "The gist of Richard's soliloquies is that man is the sport of Fortune and between conduct and fate there is no link" (F. P. Wilson, "The English History Play," *Shakespearian and Other Studies*, ed. Helen Gardner [Oxford, 1969], p. 33).

19. An article by Donald Reiman, "Appearance, Reality, and Moral Order in *Richard II*," MLQ, XXV (1964), 34–45, can be recommended because it takes *Richard II* seriously as a tragedy and views Richard as one who "faces his own human limitations." Reiman also calls attention to analogies with *King Lear*. So also does Ian Kott, *Shakespeare Our Contemporary* (New York, 1964), p. 35; "*Richard II* is a tragedy of knowledge gained through experience. Just before being hurled into the abyss, the deposed King reaches the greatness of Lear." I suggest that there are also some tantalizing hints of *Hamlet*. Richard finds his world unexpectedly shattered, he gropes for understanding, and he unpacks his heart with words and indulges in witty paradoxes charged with animus. I am not, certainly, saying that Richard is anything like Hamlet, but merely that *Richard II* is connected with the later tragedies in a number of subtle ways.

Chapter X

1. On this incident Robert Ornstein comments, "How astonishing that a politician as astute and cautious as Worcester, one who thinks first and always of his own safety, should bait the King in this way—

unless he had been goaded to the point of defiance by Henry's words and acts" (*A Kingdom for a Stage* [Cambridge, Mass., 1972], p. 129). I would put the matter the other way. It is difficult to imagine a politician as astute as Henry IV treating Worcester in this way unless he had been pushed to the limit and realized that he must either challenge the threats of Worcester and Northumberland or cease to be a king except in name.

2. However, Paul Jorgensen, *Shakespeare's Military World* (Berkeley and Los Angeles, 1956), p. 245, writes, "To what extent Hotspur's scene with the courtier is the result of his own imagination, it is difficult to say." The popinjay Hotspur describes seems, indeed, a most unlikely emissary to the battlefield from the likes of Henry IV.

3. Ornstein comments, "One does not have to be as politic as Worcester to doubt that Henry, who could not ransom Mortimer, would not honor the fair terms of peace he offers the rebels. The judicious Daniel, for example, was convinced that Henry could not possibly have kept his word" (*Kingdom for a Stage*, p. 146). The ransoming of Mortimer posed a very different kind of threat to Henry from that of granting amnesty, and Daniel differs from Shakespeare on a number of significant matters. I must add, however, in spite of some reservations, that Ornstein's two chapters on the two parts of *Henry IV* strike me as one of the best over-all discussions of these plays to have appeared in recent years.

4. Comparison with Daniel's treatment of this episode in *The Civil Wars* places in sharp relief Shakespeare's version of Henry's political aims and character. Of the differences between the two, A. R. Humphreys in his Introduction to the Arden edition of *2 Henry IV*, p. xxxiv, writes: "In Daniel the King strives, fleetingly, to salve his conscience by giving the crown 'up to whom it seem'd to appertain'—presumably to Lord Mortimer. In the play, Henry's concern is just the contrary—it is the thought that the crown so dearly won, may be forfeited through Hal's wildness. . . . Shakespeare will not have Daniel's impulse of resignation. He sacrifices thereby an element of remorseful emotion. But he preserves the King's unwavering tenacity of power." I myself would prefer to substitute the word "purpose" for "power," as representing more accurately the effect of Henry's actions and attitude in the closing episodes of the play.

Chapter XI

1. Hiram Haydn in "The Traditions of Love and Honor," *The Counter-Renaissance* (New York, 1950), ch. 9, discusses the rationalistic and antirationalistic conceptions of honor. *Henry IV* is dealt with on pp. 600–605.

2. L. C. Knights's conclusions on this theme are narrow and pejorative: "Honour, then, is simply military glory—a prerogative of the noblemen who can afford to forget the humbler realities of warfare" *(Some Shakespearean Themes* [London, 1964], p. 41). For somewhat different approaches to this much debated issue see J. Dover Wilson, *The Fortunes of Falstaff* (Cambridge, 1964), pp. 70–73, and Derek Traversi, *Shakespeare from Richard II to Henry V* (Stanford, Calif., 1957), pp. 52–62, 101–3.

3. The sentence comes at the conclusion of an interesting discussion of such parallels by A. R. Humphreys, Introduction to *1 Henry IV*, Arden ed., p. 1. It should be said that Humphreys does not generally allow himself such open-ended analogies, and that his view of the political position of Henry in his introductions to Parts 1 and 2 is balanced and sensible.

4. *Angel with Horns* (London, 1961), p. 52. James Winny, *The Player King* (London, 1968), pp. 65–105, discusses Falstaff as "a satirical parody of Bolingbroke." The effectiveness of some of his comparisons, however, is diminished because of the consistency with which he holds to the conventional idea of Henry IV as an unscrupulous, underhanded, morally bankrupt usurper.

5. L. C. Knights, *Determinations* (London, 1934), pp. 122, 124.

6. *Ibid.,* pp. 126–28. Falstaff's opposition to bloodshed does not extend to the blood of his recruits, whom he leads to the thick of battle knowing that most of them will be killed, to his own profit. C. L. Barber's rebuttal to Knights deserves to be quoted in full: "L. C. Knights, noticing the relation and the burlesque, elsewhere in Falstaff's part, of the attitudes of chivalry, concluded with nineteenth-century critics like Ulrici and Victor Hugo that the comedy should be taken as a devastating satire on war and government. But this is obviously an impossible, anachronistic view, based on the assumption of the age of individualism that politics and war are unnatural activities that can be done without. . . . This interpretation makes a shambles of the heroic moments of the play—makes them clearly impossible to act" *(Shakespeare's Festive Comedies* [New York, 1967], p. 205).

7. Robert Ornstein in *A Kingdom for a Stage* (Cambridge, Mass., 1972) avoids the usual excesses in dealing with the parallelisms and comparisons among characters (see especially pp. 131–36). He is particularly discerning throughout his discussions of the two parts of *Henry IV* in exposing the features of the prince's conduct that undermine our respect for his abilities and personal attractiveness.

8. Not done so much now as it once was, but see "The Elizabethan Audience and the Plays of Shakespeare," *MP*, XLIX (1951), 101–23.

9. William Empson, "Falstaff and Mr. Dover Wilson," *Kenyon Review*, XV (1953), 213–62.

10. *Shakespeare from Richard II to Henry V,* p. 57.

11. Useful general historical background for this chapter is Arthur Ferguson, *The Indian Summer of English Chivalry* (Durham, N.C., 1960).

Chapter XII

1. The primacy of Machiavelli's exposition of the idea of *raison d'état* is maintained in two highly interesting historical and analytical studies of the morality of the power state: Friedrich Meinecke, *Machiavellism: The Doctrine of Raison d'Etat and Its Place in Modern History,* trans. Douglas Scott (London, 1957); and Ernst Cassirer, *The Myth of the State* (New Haven, Conn., 1946). Both books bear an illuminating relationship to the history of this century. Meinecke's work, first published in 1927, represents the rethinking of his earlier works by a distinguished philosophical historian who began with an optimistic view of state power under the influence of Hegel and Ranke, and then went through the shattering experience of the First World War and its aftermath in Germany. Cassirer's book was written in the United States in the shadow of the even more shattering triumph of *Realpolitik* in the years preceding and during the Second World War.

2. Trans. Allan Gilbert (Chicago, 1941), p. 141.

3. *Myth of the State,* p. 115; see the entire section, pp. 106–15; and also Meinecke, *Machiavellism,* pp. 27 ff.

4. *Advancement of Learning, Works,* ed. Ellis, Spedding, and Heath (Boston, 1860–64), VI, 97.

5. See Garrett Mattingly, *Renaissance Diplomacy* (Boston, 1955), pp. 56–57.

6. Quoted from Antonia Fraser, *Mary Queen of Scots* (London, 1968), p. 529.

7. Mattingly is very informative on such matters. Following his account of an episode in which Wolsey, with the connivance of More, arrested the Spanish ambassador after seizing his dispatches and discovering improper conduct, he continues: "In the next hundred years a good many other ambassadors exceeded their mission through zeal for a dynasty, a country, or a cause. But the legal and political questions they raised were less difficult than those . . . cases in which

ambassadors undertook crimes, with the approval or even the orders of their governments. In such cases the actual purpose of the mission included, either from the outset or from some determinable point, a deliberate violation of the law of nations on which the immunity of the ambassador and the whole system of diplomatic communication depended. Sir Thomas Wyatt, the poet, for instance, when the resident in Spain, undertook as part of his diplomatic duties to have Reginald Pole murdered while the cardinal legate was visiting the emperor. Antoine de Noialles conspired to overthrow Queen Mary, not merely with the knowledge but apparently with the orders of the king of France. If Philip II did not instigate or wholeheartedly support the Ridolfi plot to murder or kidnap Queen Elizabeth and place Mary of Scotland on the throne, he watched it with benevolent interest, and showed no disposition to punish or even scold his ambassador to England for his share in it. And though much remains obscure about the similar enterprise twelve years later, the Throckmorton plot, there is no doubt that another of Philip's ambassadors, Bernardino de Mendoza, was at the heart and centre of it, acting this time in full accordance with his master's wishes. By the 1580s treason and murder had become the normal weapon of ideological warfare" (*Renaissance Diplomacy*, pp. 276–77).

8. "In Shakespeare's plays the struggle for power is always stripped of all mythology, shown in its 'pure state.' It is a struggle for the crown, between people who have a name, a title and power" (Ian Kott, *Shakespeare Our Contemporary* [New York, 1964], p. 5).

9. *The First Part of the Raigne of King Henrie the IIII* (London, 1599), p. 65.

10. The efforts at irony or wit are seldom inspired. "Shakespeare made Henry's father talk with almost comic cynicism about how he would use foreign aggression, or a crusade, or something, to avoid civil war" (William Empson, "Falstaff and Mr. Dover Wilson," *Kenyon Review*, XV [1953], 250). "Of the long line of kings that came under his hand for treatment . . . most if not all come to a violent and stupid end, clamoring about their divine right and their kingly ways, defiant or idiotically remorseful" (Wyndham Lewis, *The Lion and the Fox* [London, 1927], p. 165).

11. *Union*, section on Henry IV, fols. ii–ii verso.

12. *Chronicles*, II, 844.

13. Hall, *Union*, section on Henry IV, fol. iv verso. Holinshed, *Chronicles*, II, 852, repeats this passage with little change.

14. Hall, *Union*, section on Henry V, fol. iv verso.

15. *Ibid.*, fol. iv verso–fol. v.

16. Holinshed, *Chronicles*, II, 855.

17. A. R. Humphreys, Introduction, *2 Henry IV*, Arden ed., p. xlv.

18. Holinshed, *Chronicles*, II, 853.

19. *Ibid.*, III, 13.

20. *Ibid.*, III, 57.

21. Hall, *Union*, section on Henry IV, fol. xxxii verso; Holinshed, *Chronicles*, III, 58.

22. Holinshed, *Chronicles*, III, 58.

23. *Ibid.*

24. To Shakespeare's portrayal of Henry IV may be applied with particular appropriateness Auden's general observation on the differences which distinguish historical political drama from tragedy and comedy: "The study of the human individual involved in political action, and of the moral ambiguities in which history abounds, checks any tendency toward a simple moralizing of characters into good and bad, any equating of success and failure with virtue and vice" (*The Dyer's Hand* [New York, 1968], p. 174). Critics are often too ready to categorize Henry IV; for instance: "Shakespeare's heroes, heroines, villains, clowns, wits, form groups with distinct characteristics. My impulse is to place Bolingbroke with the villains and Richard with the heroes" (R. F. Hill, "Dramatic Technique and Interpretation in *Richard II*," *Early Shakespeare*, ed. J. P. Brockbank [London, 1961], p. 118). Where Shakespeare modifies his sources it is usually to Henry's advantage. On this point see Charles Fish, "Henry IV, Shakespeare and Holinshed," *SP*, LXI (1964), 205–18.

25. Frances Ferguson, *Shakespeare: The Pattern of His Carpet* (New York, 1970), p. 82.

26. On this aspect of Bolingbroke's conduct and Richard's reaction to it, see Brents Stirling, "Bolingbroke's 'Decision,'" *SQ*, II (1951), 27–34. R. F. Hill writes: "We cannot chart Bolingbroke's mind. Its silent workings are never glimpsed in soliloquy and little is revealed in public for Bolingbroke never discusses his affairs with his associates" ("Dramatic Technique," p. 115). This is quite true of Bolingbroke in most of *Richard II*. In the *Henry IV* plays, however, he does discuss his affairs with his associates, he has a soliloquy on the cares of being a king, and he reveals a good deal of himself to his son. This difference would support the notion that Bolingbroke's great

reserve in *Richard II* is part of his strategy in making Richard play the main role in the abdication.

27. Derek Traversi, *Shakespeare from Richard II to Henry V* (Stanford, Calif., 1957), p. 45.

28. Honor Matthews, *Character and Symbol in Shakespeare's Plays* (Cambridge, 1962), pp. 30–31.

29. Paul Jorgensen, "The 'Dastardly Treachery' of Prince John of Lancaster," *PMLA*, LXXVI (1961), 488–92, discusses this episode in relation to military opinion and the state of mind in England during the 1590s. A. R. Humphreys, *2 Henry IV*, pp. 237–40, adds some further considerations.

30. *Johnson on Shakespeare*, ed. Arthur Sherbo, *The Works of Samuel Johnson* (New Haven, Conn., and London, 1958–), VII, 512.

31. *Character and Symbol*, p. 49. Humphreys' approach to the idea of necessity is closer to the spirit of the play: "The plays are not primarily religious parables of God's wrath for sin, or mythopoems of Mutability; they deal with men who elect to do what they deem necessary actions. . . . The mainspring is secular, practical, the ensuring of success; and guilt in a religious sense runs second to guilt against the codes of political order. And to this second guilt Henry can reply that he meant to bring political order, not to destroy it" (Introduction to *2 Henry IV*, pp. xlv–xlvi).

32. Marion Parker, *The Slave of Life* (London, 1955), p. 47.

33. *Renaissance Diplomacy*, p. 134. On Henry VIII's appreciation of the merits of this policy see Lacey Smith, *Henry VIII* (Boston, 1971), pp. 174–77. Meinecke (*Machiavellism*, pp. 55–56) points out that even Gentillet, who opposed Machiavelli on moral as well as political grounds, conceded that foreign wars had some justification as a way of keeping experienced armies in a state of readiness. The notion of foreign wars as a safety valve to prevent civil dissension was not confined to the sixteenth century. A striking modern instance is Seward's reply to Lincoln's request for opinions from his cabinet about Fort Sumter. Seward's memorandum begins by decrying civil war "as the most disastrous of national calamities," and recommends that the national issue should be framed not as a party dispute but as "one of patriotism or union." And his advice was, precisely, to busy giddy minds with foreign quarrels. He would demand explanations from European countries, arouse a spirit of independence against European intervention, and if "satisfactory explanations are not received from Spain and France, would convene Congress and declare war against them" (*Complete Works of Abraham Lincoln*, ed. Nicolay and Hay [New York, 1894], II, 12 ff.).

34. Michael Manheim argues that the change in sympathy such as occurs in *Richard II* from Bolingbroke to Richard, is a common feature of plays dealing with weak kings, and reflects the anxiety caused by the situation through the lack of sympathy for a king whose ineptness produces rebellion and a simultaneous feeling of revulsion over the crimes of usurpation and regicide ("The Weak King History Plays of the Early 1590's," *Renaissance Drama*, n.s. II [1969], 71–80).

35. In *De augmentis* Bacon expresses approval of Machiavelli for describing "what men do, and not what they ought to do"; but when he raises the question, "whether injustice may be committed in order to save one's country, or for some great future advantage of that kind," he parts company with Machiavelli. He balances arguments on both sides, and then decides that "men must pursue things which are good and just at present, leaving the future to Divine Providence" (bk. 7, ch. 3).

36. *Machiavellism*, pp. 6–7.

37. *Ibid.*, p. 40.

38. In recent years the tragic aspect of Henry IV's reign has come to be recognized: "The complexities of right and wrong in his usurpation continue in his exercise of power, and the responsibilities of rule, rendered harsh by his own acts, and his capacity for melancholy analysis, ally him with the flawed heroes of the tragedies" (Humphreys, Introduction to *2 Henry IV*, p. xlvii). "The loss in human qualities which appears, in these plays, to be involved in the very fact of political success gives a tragic undertone to its triumphant progress" (Traversi, *Shakespeare from Richard II to Henry V*, p. 9; also p. 82). "For as the plays advance, the paradoxical plight of moral man under the historical and political process grows more disturbing until it reaches something like a tragic solution " (J. P. Brockbank, "The Frame of Disorder: *Henry VI*," *Early Shakespeare* [London, 1961], p. 81). Alvin Kernan, avoiding the conception of tragedy, discovers in both the *Aeneid* and the last four plays of the cycle "a tone of great sadness inextricably mixed with great triumph" ("*The Henriad*: Shakespeare's Major History Plays," *Modern Shakespearean Criticism* [New York, 1970], p. 274). Meinecke, speaking generally and not with direct reference to Shakespeare, contrasts the classical view "which made it possible to view *raison d'état* with a certain calmness . . . the outcome of natural forces not to be subdued," with the influence of Christianity which "has given the problem of *raison d'état* this deeply felt overtone of tragedy, which it never carries in antiquity" (*Machiavellism*, pp. 28–29). The question of the morality of *raison d'état* has become acute in our times. The Nuremberg trials focused the attention of the world on the issue. Rolf Hochhuth's *The Deputy* and *Soldiers* are in essence extensive debates on moral

responsibility of state power. Regardless of their merit as plays, they testify to the intense modern concern over the issue of state morality and its disturbing complexity. It is less easy than it once was to think of Henry IV as a clear and unambiguous case on whom critics can expend their moral indignation.

Chapter XIII

1. In Daniel's *The Civil Wars*, Henry IV expounds a similar view of the prince's position:

> Thou has not that advantage by my reign
> To riot it, as they whom long descent
> Hath purchased love, by custom; but with pain
> Thou must contend to buy the world's content:
> What their birth gave them, thou hast yet to gain
> By thine own virtues, and good government,
> So that unless thy worth confirm the thing,
> Thou never shalt be father to a king.

(Ed. Laurence Michel [New Haven, Conn., 1958], p. 177.)

2. Lester Born, "Erasmus on Political Ethics," *Political Science Quarterly*, XLIII (1928), 520–43, lists in a bibliographical note well over one hundred titles of such works between the twelfth and seventeenth centuries. A good idea of their character may be gained from the following: Lester Born, Introduction to his translation of Erasmus, *Institutio principis christiani* under the title *Education of a Christian Prince* (New York, 1936), pp. 3–130; Allan Gilbert, *Machiavelli's Prince and Its Forerunners* (Durham, N. C., 1938); James Craigie, Introduction to *The Basilicon Doron of James VI*, Scottish Text Society, ser. 3, XVIII (Edinburgh and London, 1950), 63–87; and Franklin Baumer, *The Early Tudor Theory of Kingship* (New Haven, Conn., 1940), pp. 197–210.

3. P. 127.

4. *Union*, section on Edward IV, fol. lx verso.

5. *Education of a Christian Prince*, p. 140.

6. See T. W. Baldwin, *William Shakespeare's Small Latine and Lesse Greeke* (Urbana, Ill., 1944), I, 185–284, and Morris Marples, *Princes in the Making* (London, 1965), pp. 19–65.

7. See a point-by-point comparison of the qualities Shakespeare incorporates in his Henry V with the qualifications set forth by Erasmus and Chelidonius in J. H. Walter's Introduction to the Arden edition of *Henry V*, pp. xvi–xviii.

8. *Education of a Christian Prince*, p. 159.

9. The view that this soliloquy must be read as direct exposition with no implications of character is not convincing. J. Dover Wilson cites as a parallel case the opening soliloquy in *Richard III*, "in which Crookback confidentially informs the spectators that, though there is dissembling to be gone through first, he is 'determined to prove a villain'. In the same way, Prince Hal informs us that he is determined to prove a worthy king, despite all appearances to the contrary" (*The Fortunes of Falstaff* [Cambridge, 1964], p. 41). However, Richard's soliloquy is more than an expository device "to convey information to the audience about the general drift of the play, much as a prologue did" (*ibid.*, p. 41). Richard is letting us in on his motives, revealing plans which he intends to conceal from others, and exulting in his cleverness. In *2 Henry IV* the prince, in his defense to his dying father, refers to "the noble change that I have purposed" (4.5.154). Here at least the reform is calculated.

10. Derek Traversi, *Shakespeare from Richard II to Henry V* (Stanford, Calif., 1957), p. 127. For the opposite view see James Winny, *The Player King* (London, 1968), pp. 132–33.

11. No two critics interpret this aspect of the two plays in quite the same way, but the accomplishment of chivalry in Part 1 and the acceptance of justice in Part 2 are usually noticed. For representative recent comments see Wilson, *Fortunes of Falstaff*, pp. 60–81; Traversi, *Shakespeare from Richard II to Henry V*, pp. 6–7, 108; E. M. W. Tillyard, *Shakespeare's History Plays* (London, 1948), pp. 167–80.

12. Robert Pierce writes, "Like any young man reaching maturity, Hal must emulate his father's role, but at the same time he must escape his father in order to establish his autonomy" (*Shakespeare's History Plays: The Family and the State* [Columbus, Ohio, 1971], p. 172). Pierce's general thesis of "the analogic relationship between family and state" (p. 4) shows up to better advantage in his discussion of the *Henry IV* plays than of the others.

13. *Education of a Christian Prince*, p. 155. Among recent commentators, Traversi (*Shakespeare from Richard II to Henry V*), in his chapters on *Henry IV* and *Henry V*, deals at some length with the problem of the public man and his domination over the private man. At times he leaves the impression, with which I am not in sympathy, that both kings seek popularity and political success merely as ends in themselves, and refers to this as a family trait.

14. It can be objected that the shock is to modern sensibilities only, and that the Elizabethans would have responded altogether differently. The argument is well stated by Wilson, *Fortunes of Fal-*

staff, p. 22: "Shakespeare's audience enjoyed the fascination of Prince Hal's 'white-bearded Satan' for two whole plays, as perhaps no character on the world's stage had ever been enjoyed before. But they knew, from the beginning, that the reign of this marvellous Lord of Misrule must have an end, that Falstaff must be rejected by the Prodigal Prince, when the time for reformation came. And they no more thought of questioning or disapproving of that finale, than their ancestors would have thought of protesting against the Vice being carried off to Hell at the end of the interlude." This not uncommon argument is open to serious objections. It assumes that the response to residual elements of once popular types like the Vice or Prodigal Son or Lord of Misrule is identical to that aroused by such figures in their original appearance as complete individual characters. This takes no account of the mutation which has taken place when these become minor components submerged in a highly original and appealing character. And is it reasonable to suppose that a group of human beings who are supposed to have enjoyed Falstaff "as perhaps no character on the world's stage had ever been enjoyed before" were so unlike us as to observe with indifference their great favorite decline and finally be subjected to a humiliating public rejection without any complexity of response?

Chapter XIV

1. Following a review of conflicting critical views of the later histories, G. K. Hunter comments, with particular reference to *Henry IV* and *Henry V*: "The two attitudes cannot be combined easily: if we are looking for a third possibility should we not look at just this point they agree in rejecting—the self-sufficiency of the separate play?" (Shakespeare's Politics and the Rejection of Falstaff," *Critical Quarterly*, I [1959], 235).

2. *Chronicles*, III, 71.

3. "The first act of the play is taken up with the decision to make war on France, not as a means of busying giddy minds, but on the high moral grounds of righting wrongs and regaining lost rights" (Lily B. Campbell, *Shakespeare's "Histories"* [San Marino, Calif., 1947], pp. 262–63).

4. The act divisions in the folio are confused, but they do not represent a serious editorial problem. The prologue and the four choruses mark off the five logical divisions, and all modern editors follow them in designating the act divisions.

5. Harold Hutchinson, *Henry V: A Biography* (London, 1967), p. 36.

6. This interpretation of the circumstances fits Holinshed rather than Shakespeare: "They determined to assay all ways to put by and overthrow this bill: wherein they thought best to try if they might move the King's mood with some sharp invention, that he should not regard the importunate petitions of the commons. Whereupon on a day in the parliament, Henry Chichelie, archbishop of Canterbury, made a pithy oration, wherein he declared, how not only the duchies of Normandie and Aquitaine, with the counties of Anjou and Maine, and the country of Gascoigne, were by undoubted title appertaining to the King, as to the lawful and only heir of the same; but also the whole realm of France, as heir to his grandfather King Edward the third" (*Chronicles*, III, 65). See also J. H. Walter, Introduction to *Henry V*, Arden ed., pp. xxiii–xxv. On most of the sensitive critical issues of this play Walter provides a useful measure of common sense and relevant learning.

7. H. B. Charlton is confused on this point: "The first scene of *Henry V*—a scene which critics curiously pass by—unmistakably deprives Hal of all personal credit for that decision. He is trapped into declaration of war by the machinations of a group of men whose sole and quite explicit motive is to preserve their own revenues. . . . Hal, in fact, owes his political achievement, not as did his father, to his own insight, but to something so near to intellectual dullness that it permits of his being jockeyed into his opportunities" (*Shakespeare, Politics, and Politicians*, English Association, Pamphlet 72 [1929], p. 16). Aside from the misreading of the sequence of events, there is a further sign of confusion in the persistent use of "Hal," as though we are still back in *1 Henry IV*. Shakespeare differs from Hall, Holinshed, and from Drayton's *Agincourt* in clearly separating Henry's decision to challenge France from the machinations of the clergy.

8. Walter, Introduction to *Henry V*, p. xxv.

9. "In *Henry V* war itself is a theme—its glories, humours, and passions; its dutiful courage and proud cruelty; its brilliant surface and the horrors that lie beneath. Shakespeare presents this theme of war with an impartial but absorbed interest in all its phases" (John Palmer, *Political Characters in Shakespeare* [London, 1945], p. 228).

10. *Shakespeare's Military World* (Berkeley and Los Angeles, 1956), pp. 86–87.

11. See J. R. Waggoner, "An Elizabethan Attitude toward War," *PQ*, XXXIII (1954), 20–23; Jorgensen, *Shakespeare's Military World*, pp. 187–90; and Campbell, *Shakespeare's "Histories,"* pp. 265–72.

12. On the king's responsibility in war and its bearing on this scene see Campbell, *Shakespeare's "Histories,"* pp. 273–79.

Chapter XV

1. *Education of a Christian Prince*, trans. and ed. Lester Born (New York, 1936), p. 163.

2. *Shakespeare's History Plays* (London, 1948), p. 48.

3. The Latin and English texts are available, with an excellent introduction by the editor, Richard Sylvester, in *The Complete Works of St. Thomas More*, Vol. II (New Haven, Conn., and London, 1963). A reader today will be aware that More's lively account is not entirely accurate or free from bias. It is unlikely that a completely fair-minded biography of Richard could have been written during the Tudor period. The first attempt to present a favorable treatment of Richard appeared under the Stuarts—George Buck's *History of the Life and Reign of Richard III*, published in 1646, twenty-three years after the author's death. Since then, there have been numerous attempts to alter the image established by More and Shakespeare, ranging from serious historical studies to hagiography. A critical review of the historical work on Richard up to 1955 (several historical and fictional studies have appeared since) is to be found in the Appendix to Paul Kendall's *Richard III* (New York, 1955), pp. 496–514. A. R. Myers makes a case for a balanced view between the extremes in "The Character of Richard III," *History Today*, IV (1954), 511–21. It seems only natural that the mystery about the princes in the Tower and the partisan spirit of many writers on Richard should have produced a who-done-it, Josephine Tey's *The Daughter of Time* (1951), frequently reprinted.

4. For a systematic account of the growth of the Richard story from the early account of the arrival of Edward IV written in 1471 to Stow's *Annals* in 1580 see George Churchill, *Richard the Third up to Shakespeare* (Berlin, 1900). See also A. F. Pollard, "The Making of Sir Thomas More's *Richard III*," *Historical Essays in Honor of James Tait* (Manchester, 1933), pp. 223–38.

5. Quoted as it appears in Holinshed, *Chronicles*, III, 362; More, *Richard III*, p. 7. The portion in brackets is not in More.

6. Holinshed, *Chronicles*, III, 362; More, Richard III, p. 8.

7. Holinshed, *Chronicles*, III, 362–63; More, *Richard III*, p. 9.

8. Holinshed, *Chronicles*, III, 400. This section not in More.

9. Holinshed, *Chronicles*, III, 406.

10. For Shakespeare's use of his historical and other sources see Churchill, *Richard the Third up to Shakespeare, passim*, and Geoffrey Bullough, *Narrative and Dramatic Sources of Shakespeare* (New

York and London, 1966), III, 221–349. This information is summed up in J. Dover Wilson's Introduction to *Richard III* (Cambridge, 1954), pp. xi–xxxiii, and in his brief summaries of the sources in the notes for each scene.

11. Introduction to *Richard III*, pp. xiv–xv.

12. Sylvester, Introduction to *Complete Works*, II, cii-ciii.

13. For summary accounts of these influences see Irving Ribner, *The English History Play*, rev. ed. (London, 1965), pp. 112–15, and Wolfgang Clemen, "Tradition and Originality in Shakespeare's *Richard III*," *SQ*, V (1954), 248–57. Clemen calls attention to important structural differences between *Tamburlaine* and *Richard III*.

14. Honor Matthews calls attention to the fact that each of the four major mystery cycles which have survived begins with the rebellion and fall of Lucifer, and argues that this episode was symbolically associated with political rebellion and usurpation of the secular throne (*Character and Symbol in Shakespeare's Plays* [Cambridge, 1962], pp. 7–14, 26).

15. Bernard Spivack, *Shakespeare and the Allegory of Evil* (New York, 1958), pp. 393–408.

16. Spivack, speaking of Richard's going after one victim and then another in the early scenes, comments, "through them we shall look in vain for anything in the temper of his performance that corresponds to a passion for sovereignty, or to any other motive that is morally intelligible" (*ibid.*, p. 403). Spivack properly distinguishes a difference in spirit between the early scenes and the later ones, but everything that Richard does from the outset can be shown to form a series of steps toward his great goal.

17. Clemen (*SQ*, V [1954], 250–55) shows how a number of Senecan devices are transformed to new and unconventional uses in *Richard III*. The connections between the Senecan tyrant, its Italian imitators, and the Machiavellian figure in England is traced by Mario Praz, *Machiavelli and the Elizabethans*, Proceedings of the British Academy, XIII (1928), 17–26. One cannot mention Seneca as an influence on sixteenth-century English drama without acknowledging those studies which have demonstrated the serious shortcomings and errors of John Cunliffe's pioneer study, *The Influence of Seneca on Elizabethan Tragedy* (London and New York, 1893). The most important of these are Willard Farnham, *The Medieval Heritage of Elizabethan Tragedy* (Berkeley, Calif., 1936) and Howard Baker, *Induction to Tragedy* (University, La., 1939). These studies reject the influence of Seneca in large part in favor of nonclassical, chiefly medieval, and particularly English materials. G. K. Hunter

returns to this theme with additional evidence in "Seneca and the Elizabethans," *SS*, XX (1967), 17–26. The vigor of his argument and the weight of his learning are such that that the essay is close to being an act of intimidation: "If Seneca's tragedies had not survived," he writes, "some details would have had to be changed—but the overall picture would not have been altered" (p. 24). Well, not quite. Seneca was the most widely known classical writer of tragedy, all of the ten plays attributed to him were translated and published by 1581, and he was greatly admired for his style in an age trained in rhetoric and fond of sententiousness. The writers of the sixteenth century ransacked and absorbed anything that could serve their purposes—look what they did to Plautus and Terence. On the specific point at issue, it is highly unlikely that any dramatist depicting a tyrant would have been unaware of Seneca's several striking examples—tyrants, moreover, who uttered sentiments such as "a Caesar should be feared," which had an up-to-date flavor. The exorcism must be judged less than total, and I am afraid the ghost of Seneca will haunt the bookshelves crying, "Vindicta!"

18. *The Prince*, trans. Allan Gilbert (Chicago, 1941), p. 120.

19. The literature on Machiavelli and Machiavellianism is enormous. I list here items which seem to me of interest to students of Shakespeare, without any pretense that the list is complete even for this limited purpose. The pioneer work, still valuable for the comprehensiveness of its references to drama, is Edward Meyer, *Machiavelli and the Elizabethan Drama* (Weimar, 1897). The impression given by Meyer's study that there was little direct knowledge of Machiavelli in England during the sixteenth century has been corrected; for example, Lily B. Campbell, *Shakespeare's "Histories"* (San Marino, Calif., 1947), pp. 323–26; Gordon Zeeveld, *Foundations of Tudor Policy* (Cambridge, Mass., 1948), especially pp. 186–89; and Felix Raab, *The English Face of Machiavelli* (London and Toronto, 1964). Important supplements to Meyer's book are Mario Praz, *Machiavelli and the Elizabethans*, and Wilbur Sanders, "Machiavelli and the Crisis of Renaissance Political Consciousness," a chapter in *The Dramatist and the Received Idea* (Cambridge, 1968), pp. 61–71. An important recent contribution, which calls attention to the complexity of the English response to Machiavelli and the association of his views with tyranny is N. W. Bawcutt, "Machiavelli and Marlowe's *The Jew of Malta*," *Renaissance Drama*, n.s. III (1970), 3–49. Wyndham Lewis, *The Lion and the Fox* (London, 1927), though directly concerned with Shakespeare, is a wide-ranging work, somewhat diffuse. There are interesting reflections on Shakespeare and Machiavelli in John Danby, *Shakespeare's Doctrine of Nature* (London, 1949); Marion Parker, *The Slave of Life* (London, 1955); and M. M. Reese, *The Cease of Majesty* (London, 1961). I in-

clude a few studies not directed primarily toward the student of literature but useful to him nonetheless. Eric Voeglin, "Machiavelli's Prince: Background and Formation," *Review of Politics*, XIII (1951), 142–68, is a comprehensive review of the general historical context of *The Prince*; Ernst Cassirer, *The Myth of the State* (New Haven, Conn., 1946), pp. 116–62, views Machiavelli's "new science of politics" as a repudiation of the medieval conception; J. H. Hexter, "The Loom of Language," *American Historical Review*, LXIX (1964), 945–68, studies the special function of certain key words in *The Prince* and *Utopia* as a guide to their meaning. Finally, Garrett Mattingly's *Renaissance Diplomacy* (Boston, 1955) gives an illuminating concrete picture of diplomatic activities and the gradual emergence of common practices and ground rules in a difficult and tough game.

20. "It is as the Machiavel—not the merely theatrical Machiavel, but the a-moral political 'realist'—that Shakespeare is primarily interested in him" (L. C. Knights, *Some Shakespearean Themes* [London, 1964], p. 33). See the chapter entitled "Richard III: The Machiavellian Hero," in George Keeton, *Shakespeare's Legal and Political Background* (London, 1967), pp. 312–33.

21. This duplicity separates him from Tamburlaine. Irving Ribner, "Marlowe and Machiavelli," *Comparative Literature*, VI (1954), 348–56, characterizes Tamburlaine as a true Machiavellian hero, in contrast to the Machiavellian of popular lore, Barabas of *The Jew of Malta*, because the former is a man of *virtu* who triumphs in defiance of the gods and fortune, who rules not by the will of God but by merit, who is responsible to no one but himself, and who rules outside the law and with complete authority. Tamburlaine, however, lacks an essential quality of the Machiavellian prince, skill in policy. When, for example, Machiavelli, having listed certain virtues expected of a prince, concludes, "It is not important for a prince to have all these virtues, but it is essential that he appear to have them," he is saying something that Richard would regard as elementary and Tamburlaine would despise.

22. Richard Moulton develops the idea of *Richard III* as a picture of ideal villainy and Richard as "an artist in villainy" without, however, relating him to political villainy (*Shakespeare as a Dramatic Artist* [Oxford, 1906], pp. 90–106). Rossiter derives the histrionic flair from the Machiavellian idea: "What the 'Machiavel' allusion represents is, I believe, Shakespeare's recognition that the programme set before the Prince in *Il Principe* is one that demands exactly those histrionic qualities I have just described: a lifelong, unremitting vigilance in relentless simulation and impenetrable deception" (*Angel with Horns* [London, 1961], p. 17). "Impenetrable" is exaggerated, indeed inaccurate, for Richard.

23. Clarence Boyer notes that "in plays where the villain is the
hero, soliloquies are necessary because without them we should be
deceived in the character of the villain. . . . For the means whereby
he gains his ends is deception, and we should be deceived along with
his dupes but for the soliloquy." Boyer is speaking here of Barabas,
but both for him as well as for Richard it could be said that exposition is not the sole nor perhaps the most important feature of the
soliloquy: for both characters the style gives a lively indication of the
mind and attitude of the speaker. Boyer adds that for such characters the soliloquy, by indicating "the height of his ambition or the
depths of his injuries . . . arouses a certain admiration or sympathy
with which we can accompany him part way, at least, in his career of
crime" (*The Villain as Hero* [New York and London, 1914], p. 53).
Wilbur Sanders describes Richard's soliloquies as "a dramatic representation of the geometric precision and ironic alertness of his mind,
and at the same time, a revelation of the limiting simplicities in
which such a mind deals" (*Dramatist and the Received Idea*, p. 106).

24. Charles Lamb seems to have been the first to call attention to
the importance of the humor. See "G. F. Cooke in *Richard III*,"
Works, ed. E. L. Lucas (London, 1903), I, 38.

25. Danby writes: "This is the ambiguity of his role: to be the
logical outcome of his society, and yet a pariah rejected by that society: a hypocrite, yet more sincere in his self-awareness than those
he ruins and deceives" (*Shakespeare's Doctrine of Nature*, p. 63).

26. This is one reason why confidence men become folk heroes.
The celebrated Yellow Kid Weil of Chicago always maintained that
he was honorable in the practice of his profession: "I have never
cheated an honest man, only rascals. They may have been respectable but they were never any good" (quoted by Saul Bellow, "A Talk
with the Yellow Kid," in *Double Dealers*, ed. Klein [Philadelphia
and New York, 1958], p. 61).

27. *Shakespeare Our Contemporary* (New York, 1964), p. 48. In a
slightly different vein Rossiter writes, "He inhabits a world where
everyone deserves everything he can do to them; and in his murderous practical joking he is *inclusively* the comic exposer of the men-
tal shortcomings (the intellectual and moral deformities) of this world
of beings depraved and sotted" (*Angel with Horns*, p. 16). Yes, but
everyone? Certainly not the princes or Anne. I find, incidentally, the
attempts of some critics to fit Anne into a pattern of justice for past
sins committed or follies undetected somewhat unfeeling and
pedantic.

28. Ian Kott describes the submission of Anne as an act of self-
annihilation: "Lady Anne does not give herself to Richard out of

fear. She will follow him to reach rock-bottom, to prove to herself that all the world's laws have ceased to exist. For when all has been lost, only memory remains, but it, too, must be stifled. One must kill oneself, or kill in oneself the last vestiges of shame. Lady Anne goes into Richard's bed to be destroyed" (*Shakespeare Our Contemporary*, p. 39). Kott applies his idea of the "grand mechanism" with a consistency which makes it reductive, but no one has captured more effectively the undercurrent of political terror that runs through *Richard III*.

29. "Richard, after the death of the princes, is like an artist who has put the finishing touches on a masterpiece. The virtue—an evil virtue—has gone out of him. He will never again be the jocund adventurer in crime" (John Palmer *Political Characters in Shakespeare* [London, 1945], p. 103). The jocund note is already muted in the scene with Buckingham after the coronation, and before the scene ends a new note has emerged.

30. For a further discussion see Sanders, *Dramatist and the Received Idea*, pp. 107–8.

31. *Chronicles*, III, 439.

Chapter XVI

1. "Shakespeare's Politics," *Further Explorations* (London, 1965), p. 14.

2. Two recent collections of essays provide an excellent overview of critical opinions about *Henry V* and help to establish the principal issues: *Twentieth Century Interpretations of Henry V*, ed. Ronald Berman (Englewood Cliffs, N. J., 1968), and *Henry V: A Casebook*, ed. Michael Quinn (London, 1969). Quinn's collection includes brief excerpts from eighteenth- and nineteenth-century opinion.

3. (Cambridge, 1949), p. viii.

4. *Henry V: A Casebook*, p. 20.

5. "The hostile critics," writes M. M. Reese, "have various kinds of objections to the play. They are united only in their dislike of Henry, and then find different ways of rationalizing their prejudice. Purely subjective notions paralyze their judgment, and they write as pacifists, republicans, anti-clericals, little Englanders, moralists, even as arbiters of etiquette, until one is astounded at the prejudice Henry has managed to arouse" (*The Cease of Majesty* [London, 1961], pp. 317–18).

6. *The Meaning of Shakespeare* (Chicago, 1951), p. 218.

7. It is possible to read the choruses in the opposite way; for example: "the Choruses which celebrate his virtues make perfectly plain that this trim watcher rises from his father's vain engrossing of 'canker'd heaps' of gold to genuine magnanimity—the fearless sun king" (R. J. Dorius, "A Little More than a Little," *SQ*, XI [1960], 13–26). It is even possible to cast doubt on the authenticity of the choruses. Warren Smith, "The *Henry V* Choruses in the First Folio," *JEGP*, LIII (1954), 38–57, argues that the choruses were not written for the original production and were probably not by Shakespeare, and that the topical allusion in chorus 5 was not to Essex but to Lord Mountjoy, who was in Ireland during 1600–1603. This view has not received general approval, but the essay raises some interesting questions. Editors have not taken notice of the oddity of a glowing reference to an anticipated triumph for Essex—which in fact turned out to be a disaster—retained and printed some years after his disgrace and execution.

8. *The Tiger's Heart* (New York, 1970], p. 137. This notion has become so well established that it is repeated without question; for instance, by Harry Jaffa, in an essay on *King Lear* in Allan Bloom and Harry Jaffa, *Shakespeare's Politics* (New York and London, 1964), p. 113: "In view of his questionable title to the throne, he [Henry V] is compelled to create a dubious national unity by means of an unjust foreign war." What makes this statement of interest is that the author is a political scientist and the aim of the book is to bring a fresh approach to Shakespeare's political plays. *Henry V* is not one of the plays investigated in detail, and so the author borrows the current view as established dogma.

9. *Meaning of Shakespeare*, p. 224.

10. *Character and Symbol in Shakespeare's Plays* (Cambridge, 1962), p. 32.

11. *Ibid.*, p. 34.

12. *Ibid.*, p. 55.

13. *Shakespeare's Doctrine of Nature* (London, 1949), pp. 89–90.

14. *Political Characters in Shakespeare* (London, 1945), p. 228.

15. *Union*, Section on Henry V, fol. i verso.

16. *Ibid.*, section on Henry V, fol. xlix verso.

17. *Chronicles*, III, 133–34. Eugene Waith calls attention to the influence of heroic chivalric ideals in the first life of Henry V (*Ideas of Greatness* [New York, 1971], pp. 24–26).

18. *Henry V* (Boston, 1919), pp. 191–92. The date is important. Cf. Wilson's views, quoted above, in his edition of the play.

19. *Henry V* (New York and London, 1901), p. 390. Even highly critical historians can understand the basis for the legend: "It is sad that history must also record the cold, priggish, ruthless efficiency of the father of that legend, the barrenness of his glory and the futility of his achievement, yet it cannot forbear tribute to an organizing genius who was a hero to his own day, an upholder of the hard logic of implacable justice, and a heroic myth for generations to come" (Harold Hutchinson, *Henry V* [London, 1967], p. 225).

20. Charles Plummer, Introduction, *The Governance of England* by John Fortescue (London, 1885), p. 8.

21. William Bowling, "The Wild Prince Hal in Legend and Literature," *Washington University Studies*, XIII (1926), 267–334; Mowat, *Henry V*, pp. 60–85, in which he reviews the evidence for the legendary and the real Henry; and C. L. Kingsford, Introduction, *The First English Life of Henry the Fifth* (Oxford, 1921), pp. xxix–xxxii and xxxviii–xliii, for early accounts of the prince's wildness.

22. *Union*, section on Henry V, fol. i.

23. *Chronicles*, III, 6.

24. Geoffrey Bullough, *Narrative and Dramatic Sources of Shakespeare* (New York and London, 1966), IV, 354–55.

25. The allusions and imagery of this speech and its meaning are discussed by J. H. Walter in his Introduction to *Henry V*, Arden ed., pp. xviii–xxii. Of the phrase "new man" which appears in the sources, he comments, "a phrase that had become proverbial even in the sixteenth century and may therefore have lost its original scriptural significance" (p. xxi). It is difficult to believe that an age brought up on the Bible could possibly have failed to associate the phrase with one of the most familiar passages in the Pauline epistles. Much the same could be said for "born again" in *The Famous Victories*. In the copy of the Geneva Bible which I consulted, the verses in which these phrases appear are marked in ink, and while there is no way of dating the markings, they indicate that these passages were regarded as especially notable.

26. *Shakespeare's History Plays* (London, 1948), p. 306. Robert Ornstein, *A Kingdom for a Stage* (Cambridge, Mass., 1972), takes the exactly opposite view, to the extent of regarding the character of the king as the original conception toward which the earlier plays were designed to point: "The consistency of the portrayal of Harry

from his first appearance in *Henry IV Part I* to his last words in *Henry V* refutes the accusation that Shakespeare abandoned his conception of Prince Hal when he came to write *Henry V*. . . . I suspect that Shakespeare arrived first at a conception of Harry as the hero of Agincourt and then deduced from it the personality of the Prince who appears in the *Henry IV* plays" (pp. 182–83; see also p. 139).

27. Pp. xv–xviii.

28. *La Monarchie de France*, ed. Jacques Poujol [Paris, 1961], p. 204. The passage is worth quoting because it shows how fastidiously Henry conforms to approved models: "Et premièrement et avant toutes choses, tous princes et autres qui ont maniement d'États, avant qu'ils fassent telle entreprise y doivent bien penser, et la consulter mûrement, et faire débattre toutes les raisons et querelles qu'ils prétendent aux terres qu'ils veulent recouvrir ou conquérir pour savoir si elles sont justes et soutenables devant Dieu et devant le monde. Car si on le fait autrement, est à croire que Dieu, qui est le Justice et la Vérité infallible, ne sera point à l'aide de ceux qui la font; et si par quelque temps Il permet, pour les péchés de ceux que l'on veut envahir, qu'on les déchasse de leur héritage, toutefois le fin n'en est jamais bonne; et en tout événement, si Dieu ne fait la punition en ce monde de ceux qui contre raison et conscience occupent les biens d'autrui, ne la peuvent échapper en l'autre; et peu leur profite quand ils meurent d'avoir conquis le monde et d'avoir perdu leur âme et acquis perpetuelle damnation." On contemporary views on war and its justification, see especially Lily B. Campbell, *Shakespeare's "Histories"* (San Marino, Calif., 1947), pp. 263–79.

29. On Henry as a model warrior see Paul Jorgensen, *Shakespeare's Military World* (Berkeley and Los Angeles, 1956), pp. 86–100.

30. Pp. xv–xvi. This is quoted from a discussion of *Henry V* in relation to Renaissance conceptions of the epic. Walter's Introduction as a whole is a useful and informative treatment of the important issues relating to the play and encourages a reasonable attitude toward them and the merits of the play.

31. From the Author's Preface, *A Tale of a Tub*.

32. "He is utterly inconsistent with his old self and with any of the pieces of self that make up his patchwork character in the present play" (Tillyard, *Shakespeare's History Plays*, p. 308).

33. Wilson says of it, "One of the most dreadful speeches in Shakespeare, though based on Deuteronomy and no doubt reflecting

contemporary Christian usage, we seem to hear the voice of Tamburlaine himself" (Introduction to *Henry V*, p. xxvi). Wilson goes on to explain the strategy of intimidation, but most critics who call attention to this speech do not and are unforgiving. We must, however, again consider the fact of changing tastes. Writing in the late nineteenth century, Beverley Warner, *English History in Shakespeare's Plays* (New York and London, 1894), p. 51, responded to the speech very differently: "We are now greeted by a noble strain . . . a strain unworn by constant quotation, unhackneyed by trite declamation. Like the splendid harmonies of a master musician it throbs and thrills us as we read, in spite of the declamations of the school-room and the parsing exercises of childhood." The parsing exercises apparently went on for too long.

34. *Chronicles*, III, 73–74.

35. *Ibid.*, III, 81–82.

36. Henry is seen during most of the play in his capacity as a soldier, and it is therefore necessary to guard against turning to his discredit something which originally might have been accepted as a model action. One such incident is the hanging of Bardolph, sometimes adduced as evidence of Henry's shabby treatment of his former friends. Bardolph is condemned for stealing from a church by the duke of Exeter without Henry's knowledge, though Henry approves the action when he learns of it and repeats his orders against theft and coercion of the native population (3.6.111–18). His position on this matter would have been regarded as exemplary in the light of the best military tradition (see Jorgensen, *Shakespeare's Military World*, pp. 88–89). The order to kill the French prisoners has also been cited against Henry. There is some confusion about this incident in the play. The order is first given in order to protect his small army against what appears to be a new attack (4.6.35–38). But in a conversation between Fluellen and Gower it appears that the order was given in retaliation against a group of French raiders who killed the unarmed boys guarding the luggage behind the lines. The king then reappears, angry over the killing of the boys, though this is not specifically mentioned, and sends a herald to command the French to fight or leave the field, and threatens to kill all the prisoners. At that moment Montjoy enters and admits defeat, and the threat is never carried out. Shakespeare seems to have tried to combine two distinct accounts given in Holinshed (*Chronicles*, III, 81–82), and it is not possible to give a consistent reading of this episode in the play. The important consideration is that none of the three possibilities—protection of the troops against a new attack, retaliation for an atrocity against the laws of arms by the enemy, or a threat to prevent the enemy from further action—would have been interpreted to the discredit of Henry as a general. See J. Dover

Wilson's Introduction to *Henry V*, pp. xxxiii–xxxvii (I do not think Wilson has cleared up all the difficulties); Bullough, *Narrative and Dramatic Sources*, IV, 364–67; and James Wylie, *The Reign of Henry the Fifth* (Cambridge, 1919), II, 170–75.

37. *Johnson on Shakespeare*, ed. Arthur Sherbo, *The Works of Samuel Johnson* (New Haven, Conn., and London, 1958–), VIII, 595.

38. Jorgensen, *Shakespeare's Military World*, pp. 248–51, supplies the evidence for this derivation. However, I believe he is clearly wrong in thinking that this scene "restores . . . the genial Hal of *1 Henry IV*" (p. 248).

39. Danby, *Shakespeare's Doctrine of Nature*, p. 88.

40. On the inflated quality of the style see Mark Van Doren's essay on *Henry V* in *Shakespeare* (New York, 1939), pp. 170–79.

41. Frances Ferguson, *Shakespeare: The Pattern of His Carpet* (New York, 1970), pp. 140, 147.

42. M. M. Reese, *Cease of Majesty*, pp. 318, 319. Critics who appeal to the theatre as a way of meeting criticisms of Shakespeare's plays sometimes adopt an intimidating *ad hominem* attitude, not unlike that of certain chronic travelers and adventurers toward their less traveled fellows: "The proof is in the theatre; and critics who dislike the play may fairly be asked to give an honest answer to the question of what their response has been when—if they ever have—they have seen it acted on the stage" (*ibid.*, p. 319).

43. On the stage history see Wilson's Introduction, pp. xlvii–lv, and Arthur Sprague, *Shakespeare's Histories: Plays for the Theatre* (London, 1964), pp. 92–110.

44. Such mythmaking is not unknown in our own times. Writing four years after the assassination of John Kennedy, Walter Lippmann, after reviewing Kennedy's few and for the most part unimpressive accomplishments as president, went on to comment: "I, for one, have learned a new respect for the myth-making process. The popular legend treats him as the new man who, coming to power as the old order of things dissolved, foresaw the shape of things to come. . . . I am glad of the legend and I think it contains that part of the truth which is most worth having. This is the conviction, for which he set the example, that a new age had begun and that men can become the masters of their fate" (*Chicago Sun-Times*, November 22, 1967; the column was widely syndicated). Today, apparently, we build impermanence into our myths as into our other products. Another columnist appearing in the editorial page of the same news-

paper for October 9, 1971, begins: "Recent and forthcoming books, with the Pentagon papers, dispel what glamor was left over from 'Camelot', which is just as well. Working ourselves free of the Kennedy enchantment is, or should be, a matter of high national priority."

45. Warner, *English History in Shakespeare's Plays*, p. 134.

46. For example, "The price of Henry IV's rebellion was paid in full not by himself or his son but by his grandson, and the people of his realm, and this Shakespeare must have remembered when he wrote of the wooing of Katharine. . . . It was a hope to be belied" (Matthews, *Character and Symbol*, p. 34).

47. *De augmentis, Works*, ed. Ellis, Spedding, and Heath (Boston 1860–64), VIII, 441.

48. *Shakespeare's Doctrine of Nature*, p. 101. The phrase appears in connection with *King Lear*, a play in which, according to Danby, "Shakespeare again finds a means of putting the actual society of Power and appetite in a wider frame." Danby's interesting argument cannot be considered here at length; but, briefly, it is not so much that the conflicts in the history plays are false as that they are of a different order. The transfiguring powers of suffering and love are appropriate to tragedy because they are personal and individual; they cannot resolve the conflicts of the history plays because they cannot be institutionalized.

49. The discussion of *Henry V* in Robert Ornstein's *Kingdom for a Stage*, which became available to me after the manuscript of my own study was completed, deserves special mention because it presents with skill and discernment a view of the play which is in important respects different from my own. Ornstein's view of the consistency of the character of the prince and king is quoted in note 26 above. To support this view it is necessary to undercut the pretensions of the king; and in consequence a consistently ironic treatment of Henry throughout, except at Agincourt, becomes unavoidable. The chorus is an unreliable guide: of the conduct of the king and his counselors in act 1 Ornstein comments, "A Falstaff would have had them all at his mercy [true enough] but the Chorus whom Shakespeare provides for the scenes of *Henry V* is not one to examine unexamined enthusiasms" (p. 185). The chorus, however, functions in more than one way: "The Chorus is an interesting figure because in one aspect he is your average patriotic Elizabethan whose eyes moisten at the thought of his nation's triumphs, and in another respect, he is the author's surrogate, a means by which Shakespeare reflects on his art as well as on England's history" (p. 186). Where the heroic and patriotic themes are concerned, the chorus is not to

be trusted: "The Chorus bids us 'gently to hear, kindly to judge the play.' If we have any doubt what kindliness of judgment is we can take our cue from the king" (p. 187; see also p. 177). In a way reminiscent of John Palmer, he asks for a dual response to King Henry and the hero of Agincourt: "Harry's triumph at Agincourt is not a piece of incredible luck. His leadership is inspiring and his men are splendid soldiers, brave and faithful to one another unto the last. . . . Shrewsbury was a personal victory for Hal. . . .Agincourt is a victory in which all England shares, a victory won by men who received from their leader on the dark night before the battle 'a largesse universal' like the sun" (p. 193). Yet a dislike of war, a despair over its inhumanity which is shared by all thinking men today, permeates the whole discussion. "Shall our guide to *Henry V* be medieval and Renaissance treatises on the proprieties of war? Or shall we see war feelingly through Shakespeare's eyes and recognize that, despite the references to justice and mercy and the talk of ancient disciplines and rules, war is an assault on the foundations of civilization? It is a breach in the structure of moral restraints, a hunt in which the pack as well as the quarry are dehumanized, and the most primitive bloodlusts and sexual appetites are unleashed" (p. 191). We cannot, of course, judge Shakespeare by the certainties of any sixteenth-century treatise on any subject; but the choice Ornstein asks us to make here is one from which a critical view of the play becomes difficult since it is somewhat arbitrary and too inflexible. One can readily sympathize with Ornstein's attitude. I share his reservations about the king's lack of appeal, and I respond to Burgundy's description of what war does to a country as I do not to the bravado of the king's speeches at Harfleur. Ornstein makes a good case for an approach to the play which has led some critics to excess, but in method and in over-all judgment of the merits of the play we are in disagreement.

Index

In this index 67 f. means separate references on pp. 67 and 68; 67 ff. means separate references on pp. 67, 68, and 69; 67–69 means a continuous discussion. *Passim*, meaning "here and there," is used for a cluster of references in close but not consecutive sequence (for example, 67, 68, 70, 71, 74 would be written as 67–74 *passim*).

397

Index

Florence, 19 f., 125
Florentine History (Machiavelli), 17, 30
Fluellen (in *Henry V*), 264, 268, 276–77, 279 f., 337, 366, 393
Fortescue, Sir John, 95
Fortune, 21–23; wheel of, 22, 163 f., 370; in medieval tragedy, 157–63, 177, 180; in *Richard II*, 177, 180 f.
France, 29, 84, 292; war with, 263–64, 266–69
French, A. L., 353, 355

Gaultree Forest, betrayal at. *See* John, prince of Lancaster
Gaunt, John of, duke of Lancaster (historical figure), 85, 116
Gaunt, John of, duke of Lancaster (in *Richard II*), 141, 146–50, 166
Gentili, Alberico, 271
Gentillet, Innocent, 378
Germany, 84
Gerson, Jean, 125
Glendower (in *1 Henry IV*), 207
Gloucester, duchess of (in *Richard II*), 146–47
Gloucester, Humphrey, duke of (historical figure), 18, 357
Gloucester, Humphrey, prince of (in *2 Henry IV*), 74; duke of (in *1 Henry VI*), 104; (in *2 Henry VI*), 36–46 *passim*, 74, 110–12, 119, 130, 227, 353
Gloucester, Richard, duke of (in *3 Henry VI*), 116. *See also* Richard III (Shakespearean character)
Gloucester, Thomas of Woodstock, duke of (in *Richard II*), 144–46, 154
God: theories of history and retributive justice of, 14–33

passim, 39, 44–65 *passim*, 71–72, 79–80, 82, 349, 351, 354 f.; and victory in battle, 22–23, 74, 324; and sovereign power, 86–93 *passim*, 96; and tyranny, 93, 123, 363–64. *See also* Divine right of kings; History, ideas of
Goddard, Harold, 313 f.
Gorboduc (Norton), 181, 364
Great place, phenomenon of, 246, 248, 299, 331
Green (in *Richard II*), 151, 155, 236
Greenlaw, Edwin, 10, 347
Grey, Lady (historical figure), 4, 33
Grey, Lady (Shakespearean character). *See* Elizabeth, queen of Edward IV
Grey, Lady Jane (historical figure), 102
Grey, Lord (in *Richard III*), 51, 121
Grindal (tutor of Elizabeth), 252
Guicciardini, Francesco, 30, 369; *History of Italy*, 17–19, 22 f., 25 ff.

Hal, Prince (in *Henry IV* plays), 71–72, 199–210 *passim*, 216–18; education of, 249, 253–62; wildness of, 253, 255, 263, 321, 323, 337, and *Henry V*, 311, 315, 329, 331, 392; mentioned, 227, 247, 381. *See also* Henry V (historical figure)
Hall, Edward, 3–4, 6, 162 f.; as source for Shakespeare, 3–4, 14, 35; and providential history, 14, 16–19, 23–33 *passim*, 348–49; on Henry VI, 39; and Richard III, 44, 48, 56 f., 130, 285 f.; on Henry IV, 79–80, 227–35; on

Index

Index

Index

Index

Warwick, earl of (in *Henry VI* plays), 105, 107, 114–17, 131
Westmoreland, earl of (in *Henry IV* plays), 146, 195; and providential history, 61, 69, 73, 78; and honor, 213, 215; and Prince Hal, 254–55; mentioned, 188, 213, 278
Williams (in *Henry V*), 278, 280–82
Wilson, F. P., 345, 346–47, 372
Wilson, J. Dover, 164, 210, 287, 312, 369 f., 381–82, 392–93
Winchester, Henry Beaufort, bishop of. *See* Beaufort, Henry
Winny, James, 353, 374
Wolsey, Thomas, 375
Woodstock, 369
Woodstock, Thomas of (in *Richard II*): murder of, 16, 65
Worcester, earl of (in *Mirror*), 31–32
Worcester, Thomas Percy, earl of (in *1 Henry IV*), 187–95, 239, 257; and providential history, 60–61, 66–67, 70 f.; and honor, 200, 207, 216
Wyatt, Thomas, 376

Yellow Kid Weil, 388
York, duchess of (in *Richard II*), 34
York, duchess of (in *Richard III*), 303 f.
York, Edmund of Langley, duke of (historical figure), 213
York, Edmund of Langley, duke of (in *Richard II*), 65, 166, 168, 171, 235, 237–38, 260; and divine right, 146–49, 153 f.
York, Richard Plantagenet, duke of (in *1 Henry VI*), 36, 103, 105–7, 131; (in *2 Henry VI*), 38 f., 107–12 *passim*; (in *3 Henry VI*), 113–17, 226
Yorkist claims to throne, 38, 102 ff., 237, 266, 352 f.